Sean Egan is a journalist, auth  culture and sport. He has writt *Collector, Record Collector, Tota* written or edited sixteen books Hendrix, The Rolling Stones United. His novel, *Sick of Bei* collection of short stories, *Don't Mess with the Best, in 2008.*

THE MAMMOTH BOOK OF

Bob Dylan

Edited by Sean Egan

ROBINSON

RUNNING PRESS
PHILADELPHIA · LONDON

Constable & Robinson Ltd
3 The Lanchesters
162 Fulham Palace Road
London W6 9ER
www.constablerobinson.com

First published in the UK by Robinson, an imprint
of Constable & Robinson Ltd, 2011

A copy of the British Library Cataloguing in Publication
Data is available from the British Library

UK ISBN: 978–1–84901–466–3

1 3 5 7 9 10 8 6 4 2

First published in the United States in 2011 by Running Press Book Publishers

9 8 7 6 5 4 3 2 1

Digit on the right indicates the number of this printing

US Library of Congress Control number: 2010941548
US ISBN 978–0–7624-4268-3

Running Press Book Publishers
2300 Chestnut Street
Philadelphia, PA 19103–4371

Visit us on the web!
www.runningpress.com

Printed and bound the UK

CONTENTS

Contents

ACKNOWLEDGMENTS

What if Suze Rotolo had stayed home on July 29 1961? ©Mark Ellen, 2009
Dylan Chronicles ©Mark Ellen, 2004
Useless and Pointless Knowledge ©Mark Ellen, 2009
Reprinted by permission of the author

The Madhouse on Castle Street ©Michael Gray, 2006, 2008
Masked and Anonymous ©Michael Gray, 2006, 2008
Reprinted from The Bob Dylan Encyclopedia *updated and revised edition (ISBN:
978-0-8264-2974-2) by permission of the publishers*

The Crackin' Breakin' Shakin' Sounds ©Nat Hentoff, 1964
Reprinted by permission of the author

The Evolution of 'Mr. Tambourine Man' ©Richie Unterberger, 2010

Bob Dylan: Dont Look Back ©Andy Gill, 2007
A Simple Twist of Fate ©Andy Gill, 2001
Dylan A-Changin' ©Andy Gill, 1995
Reprinted by permission of the author

Eyewitness: Bob Dylan Goes Electric at the Newport Folk Festival ©Johnny Black, 1999
Vinyl Icon – Blonde on Blonde ©Johnny Black, 2010
Dylan in 1966 ©Johnny Black, 1998
Eyewitness: Dylan at the Isle of Wight ©Johnny Black, 1995
Reclaiming The Traveling Wilburys Volume One ©Johnny Black, 1999
Reprinted by permission of the author

Well, What Have We Here? ©Jules Siegel, 1966
Reprinted by permission of the author

Gunfight in Durango: Sam Peckinpah faces Bob Dylan ©Terence Denman, 2010
Rolling Thunder and Renaldo & Clara ©Phil Sutcliffe, 2005
Blackbushe Festival – Nice to See Ya, Bob ©Phil Sutcliffe, 1978
Reprinted by permission of the author

'Tomorrow is Another Day': Two Encounters with Bob Dylan ©Craig McGregor,
1972, 1980
Reprinted by permission of the author

Billy 1

Black Crow Blues

Black Diamond Bay

Blind Willie McTell

Blowin' in the Wind

Bob Dylan's 115th Dream

Brownsville Girl

Call Letter Blues

Can You Please Crawl Out Your Window?

Caribbean Wind

Changing of the Guards

Chimes of Freedom

Clean Cut Kid

Clothes Line Saga

Don't Fall Apart on Me Tonight
Copyright © 1983 by Special Rider Music

Eternal Circle
Copyright © 1963, 1964 by Warner Bros. Inc.; renewed 1991, 1992 by Special Rider Music

Every Grain of Sand
Copyright © 1981 by Special Rider Music

Everything is Broken
Copyright © 1989 by Special Rider Music

Farewell, Angelina
Copyright © 1965, 1966 by Warner Bros. Inc.; renewed 1993, 1994 by Special Rider Music

Floater (Too Much to Ask)
Copyright © 2001 by Special Rider Music

Foot of Pride
Copyright © 1983 by Special Rider Music

Forever Young
Copyright © 1973 by Ram's Horn Music; renewed 2001 by Ram's Horn Music

Gates of Eden
Copyright © 1965 by Warner Bros. Inc.; renewed 1993 by Special Rider Music

God Knows
Copyright © 1990 by Special Rider Music

Goin' to Acapulco
Copyright © 1975 by Dwarf Music; renewed 2003 by Dwarf Music

Going, Going, Gone
Copyright © 1973 by Ram's Horn Music; renewed 2001 by Ram's Horn Music

Gonna Change My Way of Thinking
Copyright © 1979 by Special Rider Music

Got My Mind Made Up
Copyright © 1986 Special Rider Music

Gotta Serve Somebody
Copyright © 1979 by Special Rider Music

Groom's Still Waiting at the Altar, The
Copyright © 1981 Special Rider Music

Handy Dandy
Copyright © 1990 by Special Rider Music

Hazel
Copyright © 1973 by Ram's Horn Music; renewed 2001 by Ram's Horn Music

Highlands
Copyright © 1997 by Special Rider Music

Highway 61 Revisited
Copyright © 1965 by Warner Bros. Inc.; renewed 1993 by Special Rider Music

Hurricane
Copyright © 1975 by Ram's Horn Music; renewed 2003 by Ram's Horn Music

I Am a Lonesome Hobo
Copyright © 1968 by Dwarf Music; renewed 1996 by Dwarf Music

I and I
Copyright © 1983 by Special Rider Music

I Don't Believe You (She Acts Like We Never Have Met)
Copyright © 1964 by Warner Bros. Inc.; renewed 1992 by Special Rider Music

I Dreamed I Saw St. Augustine
Copyright © 1968 by Dwarf Music; renewed 1996 by Dwarf Music

I Pity the Poor Immigrant
Copyright © 1968 by Dwarf Music; renewed 1996 Dwarf Music

I Shall Be Free No. 10
Copyright © 1971 by Special Rider Music; renewed 1999 by Special Rider Music

I Threw It All Away
Copyright © 1969 by Big Sky Music; renewed 1997 by Big Sky Music

Million Dollar Bash
Copyright © 1967 by Dwarf Music; renewed 1995 by Dwarf Music

Mississippi
Copyright © 1997 by Special Rider Music

Most of the Time
Copyright © 1989 by Special Rider Music

Mozambique
Copyright © 1975 by Ram's Horn Music; renewed 2003 by Ram's Horn Music

Mr. Tambourine Man
Copyright © 1964, 1965 by Warner Bros. Inc.; renewed 1992, 1993 by Special Rider Music

My Back Pages
Copyright © 1964 by Warner Bros. Inc.; renewed 1992 by Special Rider Music

My Life in a Stolen Moment
Copyright © 1962, 1973 by Bob Dylan

Need a Woman
Copyright © 1982 by Special Rider Music

Nettie Moore
Copyright © 2006 by Special Rider Music

Never Gonna Be the Same Again
Copyright © 1985 by Special Rider Music

Never Say Goodbye
Copyright © 1973 by Ram's Horn Music; renewed 2001 by Ram's Horn Music

New Pony
Copyright © 1978 by Special Rider Music

No Time to Think
Copyright © 1978 by Special Rider Music

Not Dark Yet
Copyright © 1997 by Special Rider Music

Odds and Ends
Copyright © 1969 by Dwarf Music; renewed 1997 by Dwarf Music

Oh, Sister
Copyright © 1975 by Ram's Horn Music; renewed 2003 by Ram's Horn Music

On a Night Like This
Copyright © 1973 by Ram's Horn Music; renewed 2001 by Ram's Horn Music

On the Road Again
Copyright © 1965 by Warner Bros. Inc.; renewed 1993 by Special Rider Music

One Too Many Mornings
Copyright © 1964, 1966 by Warner Bros. Inc.; renewed 1992, 1994 by Special Rider Music

Only a Hobo
Copyright © 1963, 1968 by Warner Bros. Inc.; renewed 1991, 1996 by Special Rider Music

Only a Pawn in Their Game
Copyright © 1963, 1964 by Warner Bros. Inc.; renewed 1991, 1996 by Special Rider Music

Paths of Victory
Copyright © 1964 by Warner Bros. Inc.; renewed 1992 by Special Rider Music

Peggy Day
Copyright © 1969 by Big Sky Music; renewed 1997 by Big Sky Music

Percy's Song
Copyright © 1964, 1966 by Warner Bros. Inc.; renewed 1992, 1994 by Special Rider Music

Planet Waves sleevenotes
Copyright © 1974, Bob Dylan

Please Mrs. Henry
Copyright © 1967 by Dwarf Music; renewed 1995 by Dwarf Music

Pledging My Time
Copyright © 1966 by Dwarf Music; renewed 1994 by Dwarf Music

Po' Boy
Copyright © 2001 by Special Rider Music

Political World
Copyright © 1989 by Special Rider Music

Positively 4th Street
Copyright © 1965 by Warner Bros. Inc.; renewed 1993 by Special Rider Music

Precious Angel
Copyright © 1979 by Special Rider Music

Pressing On
Copyright © 1980 by Special Rider Music

Property of Jesus
Copyright © 1981 by Special Rider Music

Queen Jane Approximately
Copyright © 1965 by Warner Bros. Inc.; renewed 1993 by Special Rider Music

Quinn the Eskimo (The Mighty Quinn)
Copyright © 1968 by Dwarf Music; renewed 1996 by Dwarf Music

Rainy Day Women #12 and 35
Copyright © 1966 by Dwarf Music; renewed 1994 by Dwarf Music

Red River Shore
Copyright © 1974, by Special Rider Music

Restless Farewell
Copyright © 1964, 1966 by Warner Bros. Inc.; renewed 1992, 1994 by Special Rider Music

Ring Them Bells
Copyright © 1989 by Special Rider Music

Sara
Copyright © 1975, 1976 by Ram's Horn Music; renewed 2003, 2004 by Ram's Horn Music

Saved
Copyright © 1980 by Special Rider Music

Saving Grace
Copyright © 1980 by Special Rider Music

Sean Egan

Subterranean Homesick Blues
Copyright © 1965 by Warner Bros. Inc.; renewed 1993 by Special Rider Music

Sugar Baby
Copyright © 2001 by Special Rider Music

Sweetheart Like You
Copyright © 1983 by Special Rider Music

Talkin' New York
Copyright © 1962, 1965 by Duchess Music Corporation; renewed 1990, 1993 by MCA

Tangled Up in Blue
Copyright © 1974 by Ram's Horn Music; renewed 2002 by Ram's Horn Music

Tears of Rage
Copyright © 1968 by Dwarf Music; renewed 1996 by Dwarf Music

Tell Me
Copyright © 1983 by Special Rider Music

Tell Me, Momma
Copyright © 1971 by Dwarf Music; renewed 1999 by Dwarf Music

Tell Ol' Bill
Copyright © 2005, Special Rider Music

Things Have Changed
Copyright © 1999 by Special Rider Music

This Dream of You
Copyright © 2009 by Special Rider Music

This Wheel's on Fire
Copyright © 1967 by Dwarf Music; renewed 1995 by Dwarf Music

Thunder on the Mountain
Copyright © 2006 by Special Rider Music

Time Passes Slowly
Copyright © 1970 by Big Sky Music; renewed 1998 by Big Sky Music

Times They Are A-Changin', The
Copyright © 1963, 1964 by Warner Bros. Inc.; renewed 1991, 1992 by Special
Rider Music
All rights reserved. International copyright secured. Reprinted by permission.

To Ramona
Copyright © 1964 by Warner Bros. Inc.; renewed 1992 by Special Rider Music
All rights reserved. International copyright secured. Reprinted by permission.

Tonight I'll Be Staying Here with You
Copyright © 1969 by Big Sky Music; renewed 1997 by Big Sky Music
All rights reserved. International copyright secured. Reprinted by permission.

Too Much of Nothing
Copyright © 1967, 1970 by Dwarf Music; renewed 1995, 1998 by Dwarf Music
All rights reserved. International copyright secured. Reprinted by permission.

Tough Mama
Copyright © 1973 by Ram's Horn Music; renewed 2001 by Ram's Horn Music
All rights reserved. International copyright secured. Reprinted by permission.

Trouble
Copyright © 1981 by Special Rider Music
All rights reserved. International copyright secured. Reprinted by permission.

True Love Tends to Forget
Copyright © 1978 by Special Rider Music
All rights reserved. International copyright secured. Reprinted by permission.

Tryin' to Get to Heaven
Copyright © 1997 by Special Rider Music
All rights reserved. International copyright secured. Reprinted by permission.

Tweedle Dee & Tweedle Dum
Copyright © 2001 by Special Rider Music
All rights reserved. International copyright secured. Reprinted by permission.

Under Your Spell
Copyright © 1986 by Special Rider Music and Carol Bayer Sager Music
All rights reserved. International copyright secured. Reprinted by permission.

Union Sundown
Copyright © 1983 by Special Rider Music
All rights reserved. International copyright secured. Reprinted by permission.

Up to Me
Copyright © 1974 by Ram's Horn Music; renewed 2002 by Ram's Horn Music
All rights reserved. International copyright secured. Reprinted by permission.

Visions of Johanna
Copyright © 1966 by Dwarf Music; renewed 1994 by Dwarf Music
All rights reserved. International copyright secured. Reprinted by permission.

Watching the River Flow
Copyright © 1971 by Big Sky Music; renewed 1999 by Big Sky Music
All rights reserved. International copyright secured. Reprinted by permission.

INTRODUCTION

The importance of Bob Dylan to the history of popular music is incalculable.

The man born Robert Allen Zimmerman in 1941 transformed folk music from an anodyne form epitomised by the crooning chart styles of The Weavers and The Kingston Trio into a vehicle for coruscating contemporary social protest. Quickly tiring of both acoustic music and simplistic sloganeering, within a couple of years he turned his hand to rock 'n' roll and in so doing transformed that medium too, bringing the intellectualism of folk lyrics to a genre that was still dominated by Moon-in-June romantic convention. The phenomenal commercial success of his 1965 epic, gritty and streetwise single 'Like a Rolling Stone' effectively gave permission to the entire rock industry to write about anything it liked. Meanwhile, the dazzling lyrical technique on his album of the same year, *Highway 61 Revisited* – particularly the phantasmagoric 'Desolation Row' – established him forever as the poet laureate of rock 'n' roll.

As his career progressed, Dylan's natural genius meant barrier-smashing by default. The back-porch ambience of the 1967 Basement Tapes (not officially released until 1975 but circulating widely on the first rock bootleg) created a fashion for back-to-the-roots music. His heart-breaking but beautiful 1975 album *Blood on the Tracks* was rock's first major divorce record. His late 1970s/early 1980s triumvirate of born-again Christian albums may not have been to the tastes of much of the traditionally agnostic rock audience but they were the work of a brave artist unafraid to haemorrhage sales because of his beliefs. *Time Out of Mind* (1997) was a stunning comeback when many had written him off after a decade of self-loathing, poor product and crippling writer's block. It also saw him breaking even more new ground as the fifty-six-year-old artist gave rock its first heartfelt treatise on mortality.

Of course, all of this pioneering would be irrelevant if Dylan's music was mediocre. Though his celebrated trio of electric albums that changed rock (and folk) forever, *Bringing It All Back Home, Highway 61 Revisited* and *Blonde on Blonde*, appeared in an amazingly prolific period from March 1965 to May 1966, he has produced great music whether he be callow, middle-aged or grizzled veteran. Moreover, he did all of this on his own: unlike the constituent parts of the Lennon & McCartney and Jagger & Richards songwriting teams, he had no composing foil.

It is precisely because Dylan's achievements simply have no equal that his career is the most chronicled in rock history. *The Mammoth Book of Bob Dylan* presents a selection of the best writing on Dylan drawn from across the decades: interviews, essays, features and reviews covering not just his music, but his forays into film, print and other areas. Such selections from the archives are interspersed with new narrative and reviews of every single one of his albums. As well as praise, some dissenting voices are represented.

We hope this collection casts some sort of light on a man who remains an enigmatic figure after almost fifty years in the public eye.

Sean Egan

BOB DYLAN

By Sean Egan

US release: 19 March 1962
Produced by: John Hammond
CHARTS: US# – ; UK#13

SIDE ONE
You're No Good
Talkin' New York
In My Time of Dyin'
Man of Constant Sorrow
Fixin' to Die
Pretty Peggy-O
Highway 51 Blues

SIDE TWO
Gospel Plow
Baby, Let Me Follow You Down
House of the Risin' Sun
Freight Train Blues
Song to Woody
See That My Grave is Kept Clean

Bob Dylan was born Robert Allen Zimmerman on 24 May 1941.

His birthplace was Duluth, but it is more accurate to call Hibbing – also in Minnesota – his hometown, as his family departed the dying ore-mining Duluth when he was around six years old.

Echo Helstrom, Dylan's first serious girlfriend, recalled Dylan's hatred of having to accompany his appliance-store-owning father to repossess furniture on which customers had failed to keep up payments, identifying this as the start of his sympathy for the poor that would later be manifested in his protest songs. However, Dylan probably felt he was a little oppressed himself, despite hailing from a comfortable middle-class background. Dylan's childhood seems to have been somewhat troubled, not so much because of his mother or doting grandmother but because his father never understood his artistic impulses or his disinclination to take over the family business. "I was never going to be anything else, never," Dylan later said. "I was playing when I was twelve years old and all I wanted to do was play my guitar." His difficult relationship with his dad had been hinted at by then in a poem Dylan wrote at school in which he stated, "Though it's hard for him to believe/That I try each day to please him in every little way." Leaving aside what it reveals about the complexity of Dylan's relationship with his dad, it is an astonishing piece of work for a ten-year-old, not just in its language and perception but in its apparently deliberate ambiguity. Dylan has a brother, David, his junior by five years. Despite the precociousness of that poem, and an incredible memory that would be manifested as an adult in his effortless recall of all his often extremely long and complicated lyrics, Dylan was not an outstanding student.

Though Dylan these days cultivates something of an image of an old curmudgeon who only listens to long-dead bluesmen and obscure folk artists, his musical grounding is the flash and (then) modernism of rock 'n' roll. He idolised Elvis Presley (of whom he has said, "When I first heard Elvis's voice I just knew that I wasn't going to work for anybody and nobody was going to be my boss") and Little Richard (he stated "To join Little Richard" as his ambition in a high-school yearbook). He played in bands as a teenager and even got a professional if brief gig as piano player for Bobby Vee just before Vee became a significant recording artist.

Dylan spent much of his childhood and teenage years dreaming of escaping Minnesota's cultural and climactic cold (it's on the border with Canada). Naturally, music was his envisaged escape route. Even before he left Hibbing, he had decided on Dylan as his stage name. Though he has never said it, the perceived necessity for a *nom de guerre* was probably partly to do with the patent Jewishness of his existing surname: not only was it common at the time for showbusiness Jews to seek to shield their backgrounds, but it has been noted that Dylan was very sensitive about being Jewish as a boy. Argument raged for decades over why he chose Dylan, with the former Zimmerman claiming he had an uncle named "Dillon" and insisting, "I've read some of Dylan Thomas's stuff, and it's not the same as mine. We're different." He finally and casually settled it in his 2004 memoir *Chronicles Volume One* when he revealed that he – despite his previous denials – had indeed taken it from Welsh poet Dylan Thomas. The "Bobby" by which he had always been known was abbreviated to "Bob" at the same time because "Bobby Dylan sounded too skittish to me" and he wanted to delineate himself from the pompadoured likes of singers Bobby Vee and Bobby Darin. (He formally changed his name to Dylan in August 1962, between the release of his first and second albums.)

Dylan's conversion to folk seems to have come at about the same time he left home to attend the University of Minnesota in Minneapolis in the autumn of 1959. It was quite shameless. Echo Helstrom later recalled how he had informed her he was now a folkie. She thought it "hillbilly garbage", but Dylan unblushingly replied, "That's the coming thing. That's how I'm going to make it." There again, he might have been playing with her head, something for which he would become known with people. Elsewhere, Dylan has said that becoming a folkie was a matter of practicality, because it meant he could do it on his own with just a guitar and harmonica. He had also claimed that part of the reason he made a name for himself so quickly as a folk artist was, "I played all the folk songs with a rock 'n' roll attitude." Dylan adopted a new idol: folkie and left-wing conscience Woody Guthrie.

Dylan dropped out of university and made his way to New York, where he secured gigs at some of the city's coffeehouses. An effusive piece by Robert Shelton about a Dylan supporting appearance ("A distinctive folk-song stylist") appeared in the *New York Times* on the same day in September 1961 as he entered a recording studio to provide harmonica session work for Carolyn Hester. Shortly afterwards he performed the same service for the mega-selling Harry Belafonte and Victoria Spivey, something which contradicts those who mystifyingly claim that

Dylan cannot play mouth harp to a high standard. By November Dylan was recording his own album after being signed by Columbia Records' John Hammond, a man already legendary for championing the likes of Benny Goodman, Billie Holiday and Count Basie before they were legends.

By March 1962, the twenty-year-old former Robert Zimmerman had released his debut album, *Bob Dylan*, Bob Dylan's eponymous debut album is the joker in the pack of his catalogue. It is an album on which the majority of tracks are covers. There would be later Dylan works mainly or completely comprised of non-original tracks, but they were either Dylan's exercises in playing with the public's perception of himself and a way of drawing attention to a musical hinterland (*Self Portrait*) or a response to writer's block after having already proven his mettle by writing some of the greatest songs of the rock era (his two retro folk albums of the Nineties). *Bob Dylan*, on the other hand, boasted only two original compositions because it was felt that the artist's own numbers were not yet up to the level of the folk standards and outside material they were surrounded by – although by whom this was felt is not clear. That alone gave cause to those who came to Dylan following his second album or later (i.e., the vast majority of his fans) to dismiss the album: Dylan, of all artists, was one defined by his original songwriting vision. Why on earth would a collection of his interpretations of other people's songs – some of them so old as to be public domain – be of interest to those who loved Dylan for his dazzling compositional gift and ultra-modern outlook? The fact that the LP was recorded in his acoustic days only made the prospect of listening to it seem even more unappetizing: with neither poetic songwords nor much instrumentation to brighten things, this one was clearly going to be hard-going.

The cover of the album only added to the impression of this being a dispensable work of a not yet fully formed artist. Dylan's doe eyes, facial puppy fat and guileless expression screamed "ingénue". *Bob Dylan* barely registered on the radar upon its release: not until 1986 did another Dylan album fail to make the *Billboard* charts. It's well known that the disappointing sales of *Bob Dylan* caused Dylan to be dubbed "Hammond's Folly", especially in light of the fact that Dylan was the only artist of

Greenwich Village's vibrant folk scene to be signed by the label. Perhaps not so appreciated is that it continued to sell in very low numbers even when Dylan was renowned across the world. Though the excitement generated by Dylan's 1965 tour of Britain would see it rise to No.13 in the UK album charts, in the 1980s it could be found nestling alongside albums on which anonymous session musicians rendered famous hits in the 99p bargain racks of UK branches of Woolworth.

Yet the album had an impact. though: 'House of the Risin' Sun' was not written by Dylan, it was covered by British R&B outfit The Animals partly because of its presence (and arrangement). John Steel, drummer with The Animals, said, "We loved that first album." Similarly, Rod Stewart – one of the most sensitive of Dylan interpreters in the early Seventies – was clearly nodding to this record's version of traditional song 'Man of Constant Sorrow' when he included it on his own debut album in 1969. Led Zeppelin are said to have placed 'In My Time of Dying' on *Physical Graffiti* because of a first exposure to it on *Bob Dylan*. Meanwhile, in 1979, *The Rolling Stone Record Guide* awarded *Bob Dylan* four stars out of five, a grade higher than the somewhat better known *The Times They Are A-Changin'*.

The album features liner notes by Robert Shelton, in the form of a reproduction of his effusive *New York Times* review and biographical notes under the pseudonym Stacey Williams. Recorded in two afternoons in November 1961, the album is a selection of some of the material Dylan played at the coffeehouses of New York at a point in history when that business description didn't invoke office workers hurriedly grabbing a latte in Starbucks but radicals and bohemians patiently nodding their heads over a cup of mud to the acoustic noodlings of guitar-playing young men who wanted to change the world but strangely saw themselves doing it by delving into America's rich musical history of folk and blues. This scenario partly stemmed from the fact that these people's leftism made them perceive rock 'n' roll and other current forms of popular music as the debased product of a morally bankrupt capitalist system.

Though folk music has always specialized in vistas of despair, it is extraordinary how this record drips with death, doom and fatalism. The songs Dylan has chosen to cover are usually the

narratives of much older men with a lifetime of hardship behind
them and bleak futures in front of them. Who knows what
provided the psychological impetus for this loser posturing,
although we can postulate that the fact that Dylan was at this
point – and would remain through most of the Sixties – a rather
hard and unpleasant person confirms him to be the product of a
childhood that though respectable and materially comfortable
was also unhappy. Surprisingly, the world-weariness is not
absurd in the way one would expect coming from this callow
youth. Such is the roughness of Dylan's voice – and its implication of experience – that it just about works. However, too much
of the album is a downer and embarrassingly the product of a
kid who has something to prove. The album's myth-making and
its apparent origins in grudges about his upbringing reached its
apotheosis in Dylan's public pronouncements shortly afterwards that his very-much-alive parents were dead.

Jesse Fuller's ambiguous love song 'You're No Good' is a spirited opener. Dylan's singing is playful, his guitar is simple but
excitingly strummed and his harmonica plucky if not sophisticated. 'Talkin' New York' was the first Dylan original those people
who'd never seen Dylan live ever heard. It isn't exactly a classic on
any count. The talking blues format is an easy one in which to
write precisely because it is samey-sounding. If Dylan's lyric had
any sparkle, we could easily forgive the one-dimensional melody,
but there is no particular poetry or insight in his generic recounting of a hick's sense of dislocation in the big city.

A gloomy trilogy follows. The doomy and depressing 'In My
Time of Dyin'' is one of several songs on the album old enough
to be out of copyright – or indeed to precede the very notion of
copyright – and therefore fair game for the recording artist's
gambit of inserting "Trad. Arr." followed by his name in the
writing parentheses. The anthem of self-pity 'Man of Constant
Sorrow' is made more palatable by the way Dylan holds notes
in both his voice and on the harmonica for extraordinarily
extended periods. Bukka White's self-explanatory 'Fixin' to
Die' features the riff that would later help make Dylan's own
'It's Alright Ma (I'm Only Bleeding)' hypnotic but here is just
the backbone to another tall tale about what a crushing hand
fate has always dealt him.

The brisk pace and semi-joyous singing on 'Pretty Peggy-O' make it nominally upbeat but a listen to the lyric reveals it to be another grim tableaux of loss and strife. While 'Highway 51 Blues' (written by Curtis Jones and listed on the original sleeve as just 'Highway 51') is a real traditional blues in that the first verse line is immediately repeated, in Dylan's hands it feels much more energetic than the average twelve-bar.

Side two of the original vinyl album started with 'Gospel Plow', which is enjoyable enough but almost comical in the way it shows that even a song of worship can be put through the Dylan rinse cycle of blurred acoustic guitar and harmonica puffing. In 'Baby, Let Me Follow You Down' Dylan namechecks in a spoken introduction Eric Von Schmidt, the man responsible for the modern arrangement of this love song, which is a merciful ray of sunshine in the album's overwhelming gloom and easily the most likeable track. With 'House of the Risin' Sun', another of Dylan's coffeehouse acquaintances Dave Van Ronk gets a "Trad. Arr.", although in his case he was not happy about it, having previously secured an assurance that Dylan would not pre-empt his own recording of his modernisation of the song, another sign of Dylan's calculating and selfish nature at this time. Though the fact that the song was an old prostitute's lament might seem peculiar to rock audiences, the dispassionate distance that was a trademark of the folk-song narrative lent itself to such gender switches. It features some nicely soulful singing.

'Freight Train Blues' is a track that shows that while Dylan's singing might still be rough as a bear's backside, he also knows how to use his limited range, outrageously extending notes and impishly throwing in whoops in this cover of a song whose subject matter sort of fitted in with his contemporaneous and largely fictional claims of having lived the romantic picaresque hobo life by virtue of America's very accessible railway system. The following 'Song to Woody' is a Dylan original about a man who really did live that hobo, train-hopping life. (Surprisingly Dylan only recorded one Guthrie song at the album sessions – 'Ramblin' Blues' – and even more surprisingly left it off the record.) By this time, it feels like we've heard the guitar riff more than once, but the melody is pretty and the devotion sweet ("There's not many men that done the things that you've done").

That one Blind Lemon Jefferson is the author of the closing track 'See That My Grave is Kept Clean' throws into quite comical relief the inchoate sense of persecution that motivated Dylan to plunge so enthusiastically into morbidity on his first outing: though Jews of course have their own problems, did this bourgeoisie whitey really imagine he had experienced the sort of traumas of somebody who was both black and blind?

Bob Dylan, then, is a frequently silly and jejune album, one on which the artist is still working out childhood demons, and doesn't even – it would seem – have the vocabulary or craft to do so via his own songs. Despite this and its sparse, musically one-dimensional nature, it's actually quite enjoyable. *Rolling Stone*'s grade, though, was pushing it for a record that were it not for the artist's name you wouldn't care if you ever heard again.

Yet the album could have been better. 'Hard Times in New York Town' is a far more worthy and funny examination of this Midwesterner's disorientation in his new home than 'Talkin' New York', but didn't make the cut. Dylan expressed regret about the fact at the time to friends, but such omission was to be nothing unusual for him. He was beginning a long, long tradition of leaving great songs in the vaults – sometimes in ways that suggested deliberate self-sabotage – a tradition that makes it all the more amazing that his career has been so illustrious.

Via his protest songs Bob Dylan came to be perceived as the Conscience of a Generation. Some have doubted the sincerity of a man who differed from other guitar-slinging chroniclers of contemporary injustice like Pete Seeger and Phil Ochs in that he almost always opted out of rallies, demonstrations and marches. The following is an intriguing, lateral look at the issue. The Roger McGuinn to whom author Mark Ellen refers was in the period this piece covers known as Jim McGuinn, and would soon be lead singer of The Byrds, who play an important part in the Dylan story. Suze Rotolo lost a battle with lung cancer in February 2011.

WHAT IF SUZE ROTOLO HAD STAYED HOME ON JULY 29 1961?

By Mark Ellen

First published in *The Word*, April 2009

Instead she attends a radio broadcast billed as *An Afternoon of Folk Music* at Manhattan's Riverside Church where she meets the twenty-year-old Bob Dylan. Rotolo's parents are Communists and friends of the Soviet spy Charles Flato, she's already working (aged seventeen) for the Congress of Racial Equality and will travel to Cuba in 1964 to assess the Castro regime when Americans still aren't legally allowed to visit the place. Dylan's interest in political music extends only to performing old songs by heroes like Woody Guthrie but from that night, until March 1964, the pair embark on a turbulent, passionate love affair and he begins writing protest songs of his own. "He did it to impress that girl," Roger McGuinn told me when I interviewed him. "I knew them both at that time around Greenwich Village and Dylan went through that political phase purely because of Suze. She was politically active, she was a leftie, and he was going on that trip with her. The moment that relationship ended he went somewhere else" – and never wrote another overtly political song. "You could see the influence Suze had on him," Sylvia Tyson, a friend of theirs, recently confirmed. "This is a girl who was marching to integrate local schools when she was fifteen." Imagine Dylan never meets Rotolo and, thus, never writes a protest song in his life. Nor do any of his disciples in the Woodstock/anti-Vietnam late-Sixties. There is no tradition of contemporary protest, no Concert for Bangladesh, no Live Aid, no Farm Aid, rap music is solely about shopping and drugs and Billy Bragg's now a colonel in the Queen's Royal Irish Hussars.

The inclusion of Bob Dylan in the BBC television play The
Madhouse on Castle Street *in January 1963 showed great perspi-
cacity on the part of director Philip Saville: the largely unknown
Dylan was still at this point merely Hammond's Folly. As a consequence, British television secured the – in retrospect – amazing coup
of being the first major broadcaster to expose to public ears the soon-
to-be anthem of a generation 'Blowin' in the Wind'. Here, Michael
Gray explains the background behind the programme – and subsequent attempts to track down an extant copy of it following the
Corporation's failure to appreciate the treasure it had on its hands.*

THE MADHOUSE ON CASTLE STREET

By Michael Gray

First published in *The Bob Dylan Encyclopedia* (Continuum)

This was a BBC Television Drama (at the time there was only
one BBC channel), filmed in London on December 30, 1962
and January 4, 1963, and transmitted in the UK that January 13.
It was a consciously modernist play, written by the contemporary white Jamaican playwright Evan Jones, directed by Philip
Saville – a young man of twenty-eight at the time – and starring
the young and relatively unknown ex-RADA (Royal Academy
of Dramatic Arts) and RSC (Royal Shakespeare Company)
actor David Warner, and the still more unknown Bob Dylan.

The plot centres around a man who locks himself in a room
in a boarding house – the "madhouse" of the title – leaving a
note announcing that he has decided to "retire from the world".
His sister and the other residents try to find out why.

Philip Saville had seen Dylan perform in Greenwich Village
and had managed to get the BBC to bring him over, paying a fee
of 500 guineas (at the time a couple of thousand US dollars)
plus expenses; Saville also spent some time with Dylan in
London in this period, Dylan staying as a guest at his home in

affluent Hampstead, entertaining his two Spanish au pair girls late into the night and asking why he wanted to live the family life: why didn't he abandon it for the life of the road?

Saville wanted to incorporate Dylan's striking way with a folksong within the body of a play he much admired, but when it came to it, the play had to be altered at the last minute, separating the singing and acting roles and bringing in David Warner for the latter (as Lennie) because Dylan flunked it when it came to the pre-performance readings. (This solution to the problem was the playwright's idea.)

Dylan (as Bobby) sat on the stairs and sang four songs (though as broadcast they were shown in often fleeting sections, never as whole-song performances): the traditional 'Hang Me Oh Hang Me' (a.k.a. 'I've Been All Around This World') and 'Cuckoo Bird' (a.k.a. 'The Cuckoo is a Pretty Bird'), plus 'Blowin' in the Wind' – which had been recorded but not yet released, which Dylan had been performing in the Village for some time and which Philip Saville particularly wanted to include – and a song written in folksong style by Evan Jones, 'The Ballad of the Gliding Swan', which Dylan amended on the spot and never performed again.

After the broadcast, David Warner rapidly became a star. He was acclaimed for his role in *Morgan, A Suitable Case for Treatment* and for his playing of Hamlet at the RSC, both in 1966, and since then has appeared in almost 150 films including *Straw Dogs, The Omen* and *Titanic*. The tapes and film of *Madhouse on Castle Street* were retained by the BBC until these participants were huge stars, and then, in 1968, they destroyed the footage.

For over forty years this unusual early moment in Dylan's career was thought to have been irretrievably lost – no footage of the play has yet come to light – until in 2005 Anthony Wall, a director of the BBC-TV arts series *Arena*, made an appeal for rare Dylan treasures while planning some extra material to augment the first British TV showing of Martin Scorsese's documentary *No Direction Home* in September 2005.

Pete Read, a schoolboy at the time, had made a recording, and so had Hans Fried, a young music enthusiast who had met Dylan, by chance, in a London jazz-record shop very soon beforehand, and who achieved a reasonably good sound on his tape, using a Baird reel-to-reel machine. For some time, this copy's existence had been known to Ian Woodward, a British Dylan expert and acquaintance of Fried's, and Woodward passed the recording to the BBC. (This was the second time the BBC's *Arena* series had unearthed early Dylan recordings.) Later, and in the nick of time, a third and much superior tape-recording came to light, made by a Ray Jenkins from Esher in Surrey.

Until these tapes were gathered in, the lyrics of 'The Ballad of the Gliding Swan', as improved by Dylan, were lost to posterity. They begin memorably, yet in the style of an ancient ballad: "Tenderly William kissed his wife/Then he opened her head with a butcher's knife/And the swan on the river went gliding by/ The swan on the river went gliding by/Lady Margaret's pillow was wet with tears . . ."

These recordings were supposed to be publicly transmitted at long last in September 2005, within Anthony Wall's *Arena: Dylan in the Madhouse*, part of a short BBC4 'Dylan season'. In the event, not only did the programme spend most of its time on old news footage of Britain going through the exceptionally cold winter of 1962–3 (had the winter been mild, *Arena*'s programme would have lasted about fifteen minutes), and not only did it fail to press David Warner for detail on his recollection of meeting up with Dylan years afterwards (Dylan recalled "You played *me!*" and astonished Warner by remembering the names of all the other actors), but these much-trumpeted recordings were treated in a most dilatory way, with no attempt to play them straightforwardly for all those who had turned their TVs on especially to hear them: and indeed the fragments that *were* played were from the inferior recordings, right until the closing moments of this hopelessly spun-out yet careless programme, when a few seconds of the superior version were played, as if deliberately to taunt the disappointed viewer.

Evan Jones, who had been born in Portland, Jamaica, in 1927, was most highly thought of in exactly the period of *Madhouse on Castle Street*. Film director Joseph Losey, given the chance to direct *The Damned* (1962), threw away the script, used a better one written by Jones, and delivered an uncompromising, bleak thriller. Jones went on to write screenplays for *King and Country, Modesty Blaise, Funeral in Berlin* and many later films. In 1976 his play *The Man with the Power* was commissioned and screened within the BBC's TV-drama series *Playhouse: The Mind Beyond*, which looked at paranormal phenomena. The year before that, he had co-written the BBC's TV-documentary series *The Fight Against Slavery*. In 1999 his memoir 'A Cushion for My Dreams' was collected in *A Tapestry of Jamaica – The Best of Sky Writings*, published by Macmillan Caribbean.

Philip Saville, who had started out his media life as an actor (he played a teenage dinner guest in the would-be surreal 1948 film *A Piece of Cake*), went on to direct, among much else, the film *Stop the World I Want to Get Off* in 1966, the TV series *The Boys from the Blackstuff*, written by Alan Bleasdale (and the critical and commercial success of 1982), *Life and Loves of a She-Devil* in 1985, and the film *Metroland* in 1997.

It should be counted another of his successes that he brought Dylan over to London in 1962 – that he brought him over to Europe for the first time in his life – and thereby introduced him to the English folk scene, to its clubs and prejudices and personnel, to Martin Carthy and so to 'Scarborough Fair' and 'Lord Franklin', and more: not to mention that Philip Saville gave Dylan his first experience of high-production-value broadcasting: network TV that was rife with the sense of its own importance; and all this at the very moment when the 1960s were beginning to dawn.

THE FREEWHEELIN' BOB DYLAN

By Sean Egan

US release: 27 May 1963
Produced by: John Hammond
CHARTS: US#22; UK#1

SIDE ONE
Blowin' in the Wind
Girl from the North Country
Masters of War
Down the Highway
Bob Dylan's Blues
A Hard Rain's A-Gonna Fall

SIDE TWO
Don't Think Twice, It's All Right
Bob Dylan's Dream
Oxford Town
Talkin' World War III Blues
Corrina, Corrina
Honey, Just Allow Me One More Chance
I Shall Be Free

Though Dylan had laid down his eponymous debut in just two afternoons in November 1961, Columbia took four months to release it. By then, Dylan had so outgrown the album he was embarrassed by it. Indeed, he was beginning the recording of his follow-up just a month after the debut had come out. It would be comprised almost entirely of his own compositions.

The early Sixties marked a point where Dylan was growing so rapidly as both person and artist that he often felt distant from a song within weeks of writing it. For example, *The Freewheelin' Bob Dylan* took a cumulative year to complete, with

Dylan abandoning more than one version that was considered to
be near enough finished. His visit to Britain to appear in *The
Madhouse on Castle Street* exposed him to English folk melodies,
some of which he incorporated into new songs for which he
jettisoned older compositions. Moreover, he was prevented by
the record company from including the satiric 'John Birch
Society Paranoid Blues' in case they were sued for libel by that
far-right pressure group. Typical of Dylan's artistic restlessness
and cavalier attitude toward the products of his hard graft, his
sumptuous ballad 'Tomorrow is a Long Time' seems never to
have been seriously considered for inclusion due to complicated
emotional reasons.

Though Hammond gets exclusive production credit, right at
the end of the elongated recording process he was replaced by
Tom Wilson, a cultured, black studio hand not much interested
in folk until he heard Dylan's variant. Sidelining the man who
had signed Dylan was a political manoeuvre by the label after
Albert Grossman – Dylan's manager since May 1962 – had
tried to get Dylan out of his contract on a technicality. This
grubby behaviour by both Grossman and his client – Dylan
complicit in Grossman's mercenaryism and bullying by his
passivity – would be repeated many times in the coming years.

In December 1962, five months before the album's release,
came Dylan's first single. Dylan recorded several tracks for the
album with a band and/or a bassist accompanying him but all
except 'Corrina, Corrina' were discarded because they were not
his compositions. The latter Dylan-rearranged standard
appeared on the B-side of 'Mixed-Up Confusion'. The A-side
was a Dylan original. The single was withdrawn shortly after its
release, presumably because Columbia were embarrassed at the
fact that the raucous rocker on the "title" side made Dylan
sound like he wanted to be Elvis in his Sun period.

In place of the virginal-looking boy on the front cover of the
debut, the cover of *The Freewheelin' Bob Dylan* showed a cock-
sure young man with a woman with whom he was obviously
intimate clinging to his arm. However, that wasn't even the
beginning of the changes that had happened in Dylan's life in
the fourteen months between the two LPs. Some of the songs
herein were already semi-famous because their lyrics had

appeared in folk magazine *Broadside*. (Some of the material Dylan demoed for that magazine later appeared on albums called *Broadside Ballads* under the pseudonym Blind Boy Grunt.) The readership of said Greenwich Village periodical saw the music they loved as entwined with radical politics and the songs Dylan was now writing conformed to that assumption. Discounting the almost meaninglessly abstract The-World's-Unfair subtext of the poverty tableaux of the songs he chose to cover, there was only one whiff of a social conscience on Dylan's first album – a verse in 'Talkin' New York' that refers to people robbing other people with fountain pens and contains a slightly confusing metaphor about hungry people still needing to cut something with their knives and forks. Now, Dylan was suddenly taking a moral stance in his lyrics on all sorts of topics, including war, nuclear-arms proliferation and racism. This might seem unremarkable now, but social protest was not nearly so common in the early Sixties, especially in America where voicing concern seemed somehow unpatriotic and where the overhang of McCarthyism made many severely disinclined to pick up the social stigma of being seen as a "pinko".

The assumption of those who had heard Dylan's covers-heavy first album was that in finding his composing gift on his second, he was giving voice to the feelings and emotions that had been bubbling under his skin but which he had never had the technical wherewithal to articulate hitherto. Such an assumption would be wrong. "I never wanted to write topical songs," Dylan would tell *Long Island Press* in October 1965. "That was my chance. In the Village there was a little publication called *Broadside* and with topical songs you could get in there. I wasn't getting far with the things I was doing . . . . *Broadside* gave me a start." It may be that to some extent Dylan was lying or exaggerating in that quote so as to mischievously further infuriate those who had by then denounced him for abandoning both protest and folk, or even to provide a justification for his switch, but other things bear out the admission of an opportunism as naked as his embracing folk in the first place. None of which should be read to mean that Dylan was a charlatan. Subsequent events and testimony have confirmed that he – at least at that time – shared the liberal beliefs of his circle.

The great irony of Dylan's mercenaryism is the fact that he wrote the greatest protest songs of his era. While the efforts of Pete Seeger, Phil Ochs and Tom Paxton have largely passed from the public consciousness despite them inveighing against injustice in their writing for a far longer period than did Dylan, the latter's protest songs are famous to this day. This was down to Dylan's acute lyrical cleverness, which incorporated a pleasing mixture of the poetic and the conversational.

Dylan's facility with words wasn't yet matched by a knack for a tune. He would in short course become adept at melody, but at this point he was having to resort to appropriation. Tapping into the vast reservoir of folk melody is, it should be noted, distinct from plagiarism. The latter involves lifting an in-copyright melody and passing it off as your own and is theft of intellectual property. What Dylan was doing on *Freewheelin'* was engaging in the ancient folk tradition of taking tunes that have been crafted and modified down the generations and adding his own singular lyrical spin. Album opener 'Blowin' in the Wind', for instance, was recognizable to many folk aficionados as possessing the melody of old anti-slavery anthem 'No More Auction Block'. Dylan added the *coup de grace*, however, in stripping out the by-now redundant lyric and overlaying his own wistful rumination on the futility but possible inevitability of war. "How many seas must the white dove sail before she sleeps in the sands?" he muses. "The answer, my friend, is blowin' in the wind" is his response to this and all the other questions he poses therein about human conflict – an elegant way of saying, "I don't know, maybe never." Despite its ambiguity, 'Blowin' in the Wind' was soon rivalling 'We Shall Overcome' as the adopted anthem of the oppressed.

'Masters of War' is the obverse of 'Blowin' in the Wind'. Refusing to go along with the regretfully shrugged shoulders about war one part of his persona had used in the album opener, it instead tears into "You that build all the guns", "death planes" and "big bombs". The intense litany has a melody appropriately as tight as a coiled spring, which though relentless does not become monotonous. By the final verse, Dylan's anger is such that he is declaring "I hope that you die/And your death'll come soon." Some have dismissed this seething track as naïve, but it accurately sums up the righteous outrage of the young at a time when they were still recovering from the terror induced by the oldies and their ways in October 1962 when the stand-off between the US and the USSR over Cuban missiles led many to believe they were about to experience nuclear annihilation.

Two other songs on the album address the issue of the Bomb from different angles. The seven-minute number 'A Hard Rain's A-Gonna Fall' – Dylan's inaugural epic – that closed the first half of the album in its original vinyl configuration is a conversation between a man and his prodigal son after the latter has traversed an America devastated by a nuclear explosion. (Dylan claims in Nat Hentoff's sleevenotes that he wrote it during the Cuban Missile Crisis but the chronology seems to refute this.) It's an interesting idea that doesn't quite work, partly because Dylan bizarrely doesn't merely adopt the melody of the standard 'Lord Randal' but also its courtly vernacular. Additionally, though lines like "I saw a newborn baby with wild wolves all around it" are fairly unsettling, they don't quite convey the horrors we imagine inherent in a nuclear winter. In 'Talkin' World War III Blues', the aftermath of a nuclear strike is rendered less worrying by a humorous tone and the fact that it is presented as a vision from a dream. It's almost as long as '. . . Hard Rain . . .' but is sufficiently warm and funny that it doesn't feel like it. The other protest song is 'Oxford Town', a sprightly recounting of the travails of James Meredith, the first black student to enrol at the University of Mississippi. Dylan's lyric is not didactic, and makes its point wryly.

Notwithstanding the comments about Dylan's legitimate exploitation of pre-existing melody, 'Girl from the North Country' is pretty close to the source material, Dylan taking advantage of the subject matter of this traditional (the Midwest is also slightly confusingly referred to as the North Country) to pay tribute to one of his own former loves from his homeland with not much in the way of updating. (No one is sure whether it's Echo Helstrom or Bonnie Beecher who is the early girlfriend to whom he is paying tribute, and Dylan rarely helps out on such points.) His guitar picking is pretty, though, his superior technique another thing that rings the changes from the first album. 'Corrina, Corrina', is also, of course, another number whose development is partly down to unknown, long-dead hands. Though this sweet, gentle version is not the full band one from his first single, it notably features drums, the only cut to be so augmented.

Dylan's up-and-down relationship with Suze Rotolo – the attractive young lady on the cover – may have been painful at times but it at least provides him with a worthwhile subject to help replace the hokey fatalism of the first LP. 'Down the Highway' is one of a brace of the album's songs that seems to be about her or informed by their love, although its basic blues structure makes it intrinsically less interesting than the other, despite Dylan's intriguing wiggly guitar lick. His bitter, beautiful, bluffing kiss-off to Rotolo, 'Don't Think Twice, It's All Right', though, is the album's highlight. Said track's finger-picking is almost certainly contributed by session man Bruce Langhorne.

'Bob Dylan's Blues' is a slight song, rambling incoherently from subject to subject, but made a perfectly agreeable way to pass two-and-a-half minutes by the narrator's scuffed vulnerability. 'Bob Dylan's Dream' sees the man who fled the boredom of his hometown pining affectingly for his childhood friends. 'Honey, Just Allow Me One More Chance' is a horny, rip-roaring song adapted from a composition by Henry Thomas. Its chauvinism spills over to the following 'I Shall Be Free' – an impressionistic sequence of images from Dylan's life – although Dylan's admission that he is prone to occasionally "smell like a skunk" is an acknowledgment that he is hardly a prize catch himself.

Not only did *The Freewheelin' Bob Dylan* only just fail to crack the *Billboard* Top 20, it provided a rich source for cover versions by other artists. The album struck a chord. In 1963, it was a huge blast of fresh air: young and vibrant when society and culture was usually middle-aged and staid, irreverent when that was uncommon, informal (right down to the artfully dropped title "g") when that was synonymous with radical/degenerate, risqué when open sexuality was frowned on and unremitting in its condemnation of the faults of society when that society was still presented to itself in chocolate-box terms. If it was occasionally sexist, it was also in places highly tender. The combination of *Freewheelin'* unveiling a major talent and it encapsulating the concerns and vernacular of a new age caused Bob Dylan to enjoy that special moment that happens to a select few songwriters in history when the world perceives them to have their finger on the pulse both aesthetically and sociologically. Dylan was the man of the hour, the darling of the overlapping folk scene and civil-liberties lobby, and it wasn't long before he was being hailed as the Voice of a Generation, spokesman for a young who for the first time in modern history were questioning the wisdom of the people who held the reins of power rather than working out how best to join them in the saddle.

Remarkably, despite several changes of tone, style and approach by him, Dylan's moment would stretch through most of the decade.

THE TIMES THEY ARE A-CHANGIN'

By Sean Egan

US release: 13 January 1964
Produced by: Tom Wilson
CHARTS: US#20; UK#4

SIDE ONE
The Times They Are A-Changin'
Ballad of Hollis Brown
With God on Our Side
One Too Many Mornings
North Country Blues

SIDE TWO
Only a Pawn in Their Game
Boots of Spanish Leather
When the Ship Comes In
The Lonesome Death of Hattie Carroll
Restless Farewell

By the time Dylan's third album appeared, he was the currency.

The accolade of having his lyrics printed in *Broadside* was one thing, but being the composer of Top 10 chart hits was something surely beyond his wildest dreams even when he was making the mercenary switch to folk and subsequently to writing protest. Yes, the Kingston Trio were astoundingly successful, but that contemporaneous folk trio's music was pretty and anodyne in a way that, even were it not beyond his rough-hewn talents, was beneath Dylan's intelligence. It's difficult to imagine that he had foreseen himself sharing in any way the upper echelons of the hit parades of *Billboard* and *Cash Box* (the two competing American charts of the day) with them. But people with more pleasant voices but lesser songwriting gifts than he could propel him up said hit parades by an indirect route. In summer 1963, folk trio Peter, Paul and Mary (a fellow client of Albert Grossman) astoundingly had a *Billboard* No.2 with 'Blowin' in the Wind', and followed it a couple of months later with another Top 10 hit from *Freewheelin'* in the shape of a cover of 'Don't Think Twice, It's All Right'. Dylan was flabbergasted to be told after the first hit that $5,000 in royalties was coming his way.

Though Dylan was not a chart proposition in his own right – his version of 'Blowin' in the Wind', released on 13 August 1963, no more troubled the hit parade compilers than had 'Mixed-Up Confusion' and he would never really be a singles artist – his name and face were becoming increasingly recognized. Journalists were beating a path to this hip young composer's door and nodding solemnly as he responded (if sometimes mockingly) to their probings about how the people who ran the world were getting it wrong. Meanwhile, that brace of Peter, Paul and Mary records heralded what eventually turned into an avalanche of outside covers. Those songs he was disinclined to use because they represented an older, different him did not have to be abandoned to the vaults but, usefully, could be thrown to the slavering dogs that had accumulated around his table in the form of other recording artists who had realised that a Dylan song guaranteed them prestige, a hit or both. Moreover, artists like the New World Singers, Peter, Paul and Mary and Joan Baez clamoured to have Dylan write their album sleevenotes in the knowledge that his words and implicit endorsement gave them greater prestige. Meanwhile, there was a soap-opera dimension to his burgeoning fame. He had struck up a friendship and professional relationship with Baez, another topical folk singer, appearing on stage with her as well as gifting her songs and sleevenotes. When the relationship blossomed into a romance (one which somewhat overlapped with Dylan's relationship with Suze Rotolo), they were inevitably cast as the King and Queen of Protest.

Dylan's reign as the King of both Protest and Folk was actually quite brief. Before his abdication, though, came the apotheosis of that phase in his career: his third album, *The Times They Are A-Changin'*, recorded in six sessions in August and October 1963. Those who claim that Dylan never took seriously his status in the protest movement – that he in effect had his fingers crossed behind his back the whole time – would do well to examine this record, which suggests that whatever reservations he had about what he would soon dismiss as "finger-pointing songs", he was no more immune than any other young man would be to the blandishments of people who worshipped at his altar. On *Times*, he seems temporarily to have succumbed to the whole idea of protest as a force to change the world, his ego causing him to shove aside his misgivings about its naiveté and to just exult in his place on the pedestal. From the stark black-and-white photography of the cover and the proletarian work shirt he is seen wearing on it to the album's complete lack of levity to its sepia-toned vignettes of poverty and oppression, Dylan displays almost – *almost* – no ambivalence about his image of guitar-slinging champion of the dispossessed.

Perhaps we shouldn't be too unfair on the artist. Dylan was no redneck pretending to be a liberal. He may have been of the conviction that none of his songs were going to get the Bomb banned or expedite desegregation in the Deep South, but there's nothing on the album one can point to as incontrovertibly dishonest or insincere. In any case, the record is informed more by simple humanity than didacticism. Additionally, the genesis of 'When the Ship Comes In' indicates that Dylan's fury was far from manufactured: Joan Baez has revealed how Dylan banged out this promise of almost apocalyptical retribution after being turned away from a hotel because he looked scruffy. The worst charge that can be levelled against the album is simply that, artistically, it's not very good.

There are the glorious exceptions. The first is the title track, which remains deservedly one of the most famous of all Dylan songs. In this one number of intoxicating defiance, Dylan encapsulated the generational viewpoint that *Freewheelin'* took thirteen songs to communicate. Dylan demands that people gather round him at the outset, like a modern-day Christ about to issue a proclamation. Despite the old-world language of that first line, the feel of a well-worn phrase about the title line (actually an expression of Dylan's own devising) and the almost biblical smack to imagery like "Admit that the waters around you have grown/And accept it that soon you'll be drenched to the bone", the track was absolutely? Now in its denunciation of a failed social order and the assumption of an unstoppable impetus attached to those who were determined to create a newer, better one. Nowhere does Dylan mention the Atom Bomb, poverty, racial discrimination, political corruption or social authoritarianism but the fact that those are the things he envisages being swept away in the change that he roaringly insists is barrelling down the highway is not in question. His declaration that, "Your sons and your daughters are beyond your command" is a summation of the fact that at no other point in modern history was there such a schism between the generations as existed in the Sixties, whose young – the so-called baby boomers coming of age after a conception surge following the Second World War – had an affluence that made them less dependent on people in power either in government or their own home and therefore better able to question and challenge their mores and edicts. The lyric is simply dazzling, a tornado of imagery with a rhyming scheme that is exhilarating. For all those reasons, it is Dylan's greatest protest song, and is no less brilliant for the fact that it has been overtaken by events. The age group whose values it espoused are now retiring after mixed success when holding the reins of power, but 'The Times They Are A-Changin'' is a snapshot that brilliantly – if vaguely – sums up that generation's unique independence of spirit.

'One Too Many Mornings', the sole other great song on the album, is the polar opposite of the title track's torrential rhetoric, being a lovely, melancholy reflection on either a lover's tiff or a break-up. ("You're right from your side, I'm right from mine.") 'Boots of Spanish Leather' is the album's only other love song. We could forgive the fact that it is another kiss-off to Suze which, though poetically worded, doesn't admit how thoughtlessly Dylan treated his muse in real life were it not so dull.

The paucity of romance on the album is as nothing to the complete dearth of comedy, which both *Freewheelin'* and concert performances had demonstrated Dylan was adept at and which he had proven was not necessarily an inappropriate medium for protest. The topical songs here are heavy indeed.

'Ballad of Hollis Brown', for instance, is a relentless, merciless tale of destitution and desperation portraying a South Dakota farmer who spends his last dollar on seven shotgun shells by which to – as "way out in the wilderness a cold coyote calls" – rescue his large family from this vale of tears. Dylan signs off with the revelation that as the deed is done, elsewhere seven new people are born – an acknowledgment of the endlessness of the cycle of hardship. It's in turn terrifying and tedious, courtesy of Dylan's brilliant tracing of incrementally rising despair and the song's repetitive folk-blues structure respectively. 'North Country Blues' is another poverty tableau, this one from the perspective of an old woman watching her mining town dying around her. Though no doubt many traditional folk songs inform its imagery and story, its verisimilitude is impressive, as is Dylan's understated singing.

The aforementioned 'When the Ship Comes In' can't help but seem a pale imitation of the similarly themed but much better constructed title track. 'With God on Our Side' is a denunciation of the co-opting of the Almighty to justify battle that is well-argued but boring, with the caterwauling short-comings of Dylan's voice painfully to the fore. 'The Lonesome Death of Hattie Carroll' tells the true (if inexactly recorded) story of the paltry punishment meted out to a rich white scion who killed a black maid in a fit of temper. At the close of the song we are finally given permission by Dylan to weep over the injustice after having been admonished at the end of each previous verse and its recounted outrage, "Take the rag away from your face 'cos now ain't the time for your tears." It's persua-sive stuff indeed, if robbed of some power by its monotony and nigh-six-minute length.

'Only a Pawn in Their Game' is nominally protest but leaves the listener frozen in the motion of an upraised fist of solidarity. It sees Dylan commenting on the recent murder of black civil-rights activist Medgar Evers. As Evers had helped enrol James Meredith at the University of Mississippi, already a subject of a Dylan song, a plainly worded denunciation would seem to be on the cards. Instead Dylan portrays the poor white man who supported, or was left unmoved by, the slaying as a victim every bit as much as Evers, enslaved in his bigotry and his poverty by the Southern politician who stirs up racial hatred for his own ends. The closer 'Restless Farewell' is a kiss-off to, well, everything: friends, girlfriends and – in the third verse, some have posited – protest songs. In another sense, it's no departure at all, sharing the morose nature of almost all the rest of the material here.

Dylan's nice turn of phrase was gaining him a reputation as a bit of a people's poet. The back cover of the original album contained '11 Outlined Epitaphs', whose blank verse, unconventional spelling and rebellious tone aligned the artist to another movement: the Beat writers. Interestingly, however, these poems are more self-critical and confessional than the album's songs.

At the time, the mediocrity of *Times* was less obvious. With the media singing his praises, his compositions dotting the charts and his profile growing exponentially, Dylan had momentum behind him. Additionally, in a way it barely mattered that *Times* wasn't a congenial listening experience. Protest, many felt, was more about a state-of-the-union address than pleasure. From today's perspective – where many, though not all, of the issues explored are antiquated and the albums aesthetic worth consequently more germane – what disappoints is how much better the album could have been. The massively prolific Dylan had far superior songs to choose from for inclusion than much of what ended up herein. The stately 'Lay Down Your Weary Tune' and the twirling 'Percy's Song' were better than its worst tracks, while 'Only a Hobo' was better than all but its very best cuts.

The following article was the first major Dylan feature to appear in a national US magazine. Moreover, said magazine – the New Yorker *– was probably the country's most intellectual periodical at the time. Nat Hentoff – who had written the sleevenotes to* Freewheelin' *– was given significant access to Dylan for the piece, observing first-hand the recording of* Another Side of Bob Dylan. *After the interviews for the piece had been conducted, Hentoff recalls Dylan anxiously, repeatedly asking him when the story was going to appear.*

Though the feature saw Dylan continue with the myth-making – repeating the tall tales from his publicity about running away as a child and failing to mention less hip figures like Elvis and Little Richard in his list of musical heroes – in other respects he was remarkably open with Hentoff about such things as why Another Side *– which had appeared two-and-a-half months before the article's publication – contained no protest music, why he felt unable to align himself with any cause and how he knew his fame was a fleeting thing (on which last point he, of course, transpired to be wrong). The unnamed song recorded at the* Another Side *session that Hentoff quotes at length is 'Denise' – essentially an alternate lyric to that of 'Black Crow Blues' – which Dylan has never released. Hentoff was subsequently Dylan's partner-in-crime when Dylan mocked the format of the* Playboy *interview in 1966.*

THE CRACKIN', SHAKIN', BREAKIN' SOUNDS

By Nat Hentoff

First published in *New Yorker*, 24 October 1964

The word "folk" in the term "folk music" used to connote a rural, homogeneous community that carried on a tradition of anonymously created music. No one person composed a piece; it evolved through generations of communal care.

In recent years, however, folk music has increasingly become the quite personal – and copyrighted – product of specific creators. More and more of them, in fact, are neither rural nor representative of centuries-old family and regional traditions. They are often city-bred converts to the folk style; and, after an apprenticeship during which they try to imitate rural models from the older approach to folk music, they write and perform their own songs out of their own concerns and preoccupations. The restless young, who have been the primary support of the rise of this kind of folk music over the past five years, regard two performers as their pre-eminent spokesmen.

One is twenty-three-year-old Joan Baez. She does not write her own material and she includes a considerable proportion of traditional, communally created songs in her programs. But Miss Baez does speak out explicitly against racial prejudice and militarism, and she does sing some of the best of the new topical songs. Moreover, her pure, penetrating voice and her open, honest manner symbolize for her admirers a cool island of integrity in a society that the folk-song writer Malvina Reynolds has characterised in one of her songs as consisting of "little boxes."

The second – and more influential – demiurge of the folk-music microcosm is Bob Dylan, also twenty-three. Dylan's impact has been the greater because he *is* a writer of songs as well as a performer. Such compositions of his as 'Blowin' in the Wind,' 'Masters of War,' 'Don't Think Twice, It's All Right,' and 'Only a Pawn in Their Game' have become part of the repertoire of many other performers, including Miss Baez, who has explained: "Bobby is expressing what I – and many other young people – feel, what we want to say. Most of the 'protest' songs about the bomb and race prejudice and conformity are stupid. They have no beauty. But Bobby's songs are powerful as poetry and powerful as music. And, oh, my God, how that boy can sing!"

Another reason for Dylan's impact is the singular force of his personality. Wiry, tense, and boyish, Dylan looks and acts like a fusion of Huck Finn and a young Woody Guthrie. Both onstage and off, he appears to be just barely able to contain his prodigious energy. Pete Seeger, who, at forty-five, is one of the elders of American folk music, recently observed: "Dylan may well become the country's most creative troubadour – if he doesn't explode."

Dylan is always dressed informally – the possibility that he will ever be seen in a tie is as remote as the possibility that Miss

Baez will perform in an evening gown – and his possessions are few, the weightiest of them being a motorcycle. A wanderer, Dylan is often on the road in search of *more* experience. "You can find out a lot about a small town by hanging around its poolroom," he says. Like Miss Baez, he prefers to keep most of his time for himself. He works only occasionally, and during the rest of the year he travels or briefly stays in a house owned by his manager, Albert Grossman, in Bearsville, New York – a small town adjacent to Woodstock and about a hundred miles north of New York. There Dylan writes songs, works on poetry, plays, and novels, rides his motorcycle, and talks with his friends. From time to time, he comes to New York to record for Columbia Records.

A few weeks ago, Dylan invited me to a recording session that was to begin at seven in the evening in a Columbia studio on Seventh Avenue near Fifty-Second Street. Before he arrived, a tall, lean, relaxed man in his early thirties came in and introduced himself to me as Tom Wilson, Dylan's recording producer. He was joined by two engineers, and we all went into the control room. Wilson took up a post at a long, broad table, between the engineers, from which he looked out into a spacious studio with a tall thicket of microphones to the left and, directly in front, an enclave containing a music stand, two microphones, and an upright piano, and set off by a large screen, which would partly shield Dylan as he sang, for the purpose of improving the quality of the sound. "I have no idea what he's going to record tonight," Wilson told me. "It's all to be stuff he's written in the last couple of months."

I asked if Dylan presented any particular problems to a recording director. "My main difficulty has been pounding mike technique into him," Wilson said. "He used to get excited and move around a lot and then lean in too far, so that the mike popped. Aside from that, my basic problem with him has been to create the kind of setting in which he's relaxed. For instance, if that screen should bother him, I'd take it away, even if we have to lose a little quality in the sound." Wilson looked toward the door. "I'm somewhat concerned about tonight. We're going to do a whole album in one session. Usually, we're not in such a rush, but this album has to be ready for Columbia's fall sales convention. Except for special occasions like this, Bob has no set schedule of recording dates. We think he's important enough to record whenever he wants to come to the studio."

Five minutes after seven, Dylan walked into the studio, carrying a battered guitar case. He had on dark glasses, and his hair, dark-blond and curly, had obviously not been cut for some weeks; he was dressed in blue jeans, a black jersey, and desert boots. With him were half a dozen friends, among them Jack Elliott, a folk singer in the Woody Guthrie tradition, who was also dressed in blue jeans and desert boots, plus a brown corduroy shirt and a jaunty cowboy hat. Elliott had been carrying two bottles of Beaujolais, which he now handed to Dylan, who carefully put them on a table near the screen. Dylan opened the guitar case, took out a looped-wire harmonica holder, hung it around his neck, and then walked over to the piano and began to play in a rolling, honky-tonk style.

"He's got a wider range of talents than he shows," Wilson told me. "He kind of hoards them. You go back to his three albums. Each time there's a big leap from one to the next – in material, in performance, in everything."

Dylan came into the control room, smiling. Although he is fiercely accusatory toward society at large while he is performing, his most marked offstage characteristic is gentleness. He speaks swiftly but softly, and appears persistently anxious to make himself clear. "We're going to make a good one tonight," he said to Wilson, "I promise." He turned to me and continued: "There aren't any finger-pointing songs in here, either. Those records I've made, I'll stand behind them, but some of that was jumping into the scene to be heard and a lot of it was because I didn't see anybody else doing that kind of thing. Now a lot of people are doing finger-pointing songs. You know – pointing to all the things that are wrong. Me, I don't want to write *for* people anymore. You know – be a spokesman. Like I once wrote about Emmett Till in the first person, pretending I was him. From now on, I want to write from inside me, and to do that I'm going to have to get back to writing like I used to when I was ten – having everything come out naturally. The way I like to write is for it to come out the way I walk or talk." Dylan frowned. "Not that I even walk or talk yet like I'd like to. I don't carry myself yet the

way Woody, Big Joe Williams, and Lightnin' Hopkins have
carried themselves. I hope to some day, but they're older. They
got to where music was a tool for them, a way to live more, a way
to make themselves feel better. Sometimes I can make myself
feel better with music, but other times it's still hard to go to sleep
at night."

A friend strolled in, and Dylan began to grumble about an
interview that had been arranged for him later in the week. "I
hate to say no, because, after all, these guys have a job to do," he
said, shaking his head impatiently. "But it bugs me that the first
question usually turns out to be 'Are you going down South to
take part in any of the civil-rights projects?' They try to fit you
into things. Now, I've been down there, but I'm not going down
just to hold a picket sign so they can shoot a picture of me. I
know a lot of the kids in SNCC – you know, the Student
Nonviolent Coordinating Committee. That's the only organisation I feel a part of spiritually. The NAACP is a bunch of old
guys. I found that out by coming directly in contact with some
of the people in it. They didn't understand me. They were looking to use me for something. Man, everybody's hung-up. You
sometimes don't know if somebody wants you to do something
because he's hung-up or because he really digs who you are. It's
awful complicated, and the best thing you can do is admit it."

Returning to the studio, Dylan stood in front of the piano and
pounded out an accompaniment as he sang from one of his own
new songs:

> *Are you for real, baby, or are you just on the shelf?*
> *I'm looking deep into your eyes, but all I can see is myself.*
> *If you're trying to throw me, I've already been tossed.*
> *If you're trying to lose me, I've already been lost. . . .*

Another friend of Dylan's arrived with three children, ranging
in age from four to ten. The children raced around the studio until
Wilson insisted that they be relatively confined to the control
room. By ten minutes to eight, Wilson had checked out the sound
balance to his satisfaction, Dylan's friends had found seats along
the studio walls, and Dylan had expressed his readiness – in fact,
eagerness – to begin. Wilson, in the control room, leaned forward,

a stopwatch in his hand. Dylan took a deep breath, threw his head back, and plunged into a song in which he accompanied himself on guitar and harmonica. The first take was ragged; the second was both more relaxed and more vivid. At that point, Dylan, smiling, clearly appeared to be confident of his ability to do an entire album in one night. As he moved into succeeding numbers, he relied principally on the guitar for support, except for exclamatory punctuations on the harmonica.

Having glanced through a copy of Dylan's new lyrics that he had handed to Wilson, I observed to Wilson that there were indeed hardly any songs of social protest in the collection.

"Those early albums gave people the wrong idea," Wilson said. "Basically, he's in the tradition of all lasting folk music. I mean, he's not a singer of protest so much as he is a singer of *concern* about people. He doesn't have to be talking about Medgar Evers all the time to be effective. He can just tell a simple little story of a guy who ran off from a woman."

After three takes of one number, one of the engineers said to Wilson: "If you want to try another, we can get a better take."

"No." Wilson shook his head. "With Dylan, you have to take what you can get."

Out in the studio, Dylan, his slight form bent forward, was standing just outside the screen and listening to a playback through earphones. He began to take the earphones off during an instrumental passage, but then his voice came on, and he grinned and replaced them.

The engineer muttered again that he might get a better take if Dylan ran through the number once more.

"Forget it," Wilson said. "You don't think in terms of orthodox recording techniques when you're dealing with Dylan. You have to learn to be as free on this side of the glass as he is out there."

Dylan went on to record a song about a man leaving a girl because he was not prepared to be the kind of invincible hero and all-encompassing provider she wanted. "It ain't me you're looking for, babe," he sang, with finality.

During the playback, I joined Dylan in the studio. "The songs so far sound as if there were real people in them," I said.

Dylan seemed surprised that I had considered it necessary to make the comment. "There are. That's what makes them so scary. If I haven't been through what I write about, the songs aren't worth anything." He went on, via one of his songs, to offer a complicated account of a turbulent love affair in Spanish Harlem, and at the end asked a friend: "Did you understand it?" The friend nodded enthusiastically. "Well, I didn't," Dylan said, with a laugh, and then became sombre. "It's hard being free in a song – getting it all in. Songs are so confining. Woody Guthrie told me once that songs don't have to do anything like that. But it's not true. A song has to have some kind of form to fit into the music. You can bend the words and the meter, but it still has to fit somehow. I've been getting freer in the songs I write, but I still feel confined. That's why I write a lot of poetry – if that's the word. Poetry can make its own form."

As Wilson signalled for the start of the next number, Dylan put up his hand. "I just want to light a cigarette, so I can see it there while I'm singing," he said, and grinned. "I'm very neurotic. I need to be secure."

By ten-thirty, seven songs had been recorded.

"This is the fastest Dylan date yet," Wilson said. "He used to be all hung up with the microphones. Now he's a pro."

Several more friends of Dylan's had arrived during the recording of the seven songs, and at this point four of them were seated in the control room behind Wilson and the engineers. The others were scattered around the studio, using the table that held the bottles of Beaujolais as their base. They opened the bottles, and every once in a while poured out a drink in a paper cup. The three children were still irrepressibly present, and once the smallest burst suddenly into the studio, ruining a take. Dylan turned on the youngster in mock anger. "I'm gonna rub you out," he said. "I'll track you down and turn you to dust." The boy giggled and ran back into the control room.

As the evening went on, Dylan's voice became more acrid. The dynamics of his singing grew more pronounced, soft, intimate passages being abruptly followed by fierce surges in volume. The relentless, driving beat of his guitar was more often supplemented by the whooping thrusts of the harmonica.

"Intensity, that's what he's got," Wilson said, apparently to himself. "By now, this kid is out-selling Thelonious Monk and

Miles Davis," he went on, to me. "He's speaking to a whole new generation. And not only here. He's just been in England. He had standing room only in Royal Festival Hall."

Dylan had begun a song called 'Chimes of Freedom.' One of his four friends in the control room – a lean, bearded man – proclaimed: "Bobby's talking for every hung-up person in the whole wide universe." His three companions nodded gravely.

The next composition, 'Motorpsycho Nitemare,' was a mordantly satirical version of the vintage tale of the farmer, his daughter, and the travelling salesman. There were several false starts, apparently because Dylan was having trouble reading the lyrics.

"Man, dim the lights," the bearded friend counselled Wilson. "He'll get more relaxed."

"Atmosphere is not what we need," Wilson answered, without turning around. "Legibility is what we need."

During the playback, Dylan listened intently, his lips moving, and a cigarette cocked in his right hand. A short break followed, during which Dylan shouted: "Hey, we're gonna need some more wine!" Two of his friends in the studio nodded and left.

After the recording session resumed, Dylan continued to work hard and conscientiously. When he was preparing for a take or listening to a playback, he seemed able to cut himself off completely from the eddies of conversation and humorous byplay stirred up by his friends in the studio. Occasionally, when a line particularly pleased him, he burst into laughter, but he swiftly got back to business.

Dylan started a talking blues – a wry narrative in a sardonic recitative style, which had been developed by Woody Guthrie. "Now I'm liberal, but to a degree," Dylan was drawling halfway through the song. "I want everybody to be free. But if you think I'll let Barry Goldwater move in next door and marry my daughter, you must think I'm crazy. I wouldn't let him do it for all the farms in Cuba." He was smiling broadly, and Wilson and the engineers were laughing. It was a long song, and toward the end Dylan faltered. He tried it twice more, and each time he stumbled before the close.

"Let me do another song," he said to Wilson. "I'll come back to this."

"No," Wilson said. "Finish up this one. You'll hang us up on the order, and if I'm not here to edit, the other cat will get mixed up. Just do an insert of the last part."

"Let him start from the beginning, man," said one of the four friends sitting behind Wilson.

Wilson turned around, looking annoyed. "Why, man?"

"You don't start telling a story with Chapter Eight, man," the friend said.

"Oh, man," said Wilson, "what kind of philosophy is that? We're recording, not writing a biography."

As an obbligato of protest continued behind Wilson, Dylan, accepting Wilson's advice, sang the insert. His bearded friend rose silently and drew a square in the air behind Wilson's head.

Other songs, mostly of love lost or misunderstood, followed. Dylan was now tired, but he retained his good humour. "This last one is called 'My Back Pages,'" he announced to Wilson. It appeared to express his current desire to get away from "finger-pointing" and write more acutely personal material. "Oh, but I was so much older then," he sang as a refrain, "I'm younger than that now."

By one-thirty, the session was over. Dylan had recorded fourteen new songs. He agreed to meet me again in a week or so and fill me in on his background. "My background's not all that important, though," he said as we left the studio. "It's what I am now that counts."

Dylan was born in Duluth, on May 24, 1941, and grew up in Hibbing, Minnesota, a mining town near the Canadian border. He does not discuss his parents, preferring to let his songs tell whatever he wants to say about his personal history. "You can stand at one end of Hibbing on the main drag an' see clear past the city limits on the other end," Dylan once noted in a poem, 'My Life in a Stolen Moment,' printed in the program of a 1963 Town Hall concert he gave. Like Dylan's parents, it appears, the town was neither rich nor poor, but it was, Dylan has said, "a dyin' town." He ran away from home seven times – at ten, twelve, thirteen, fifteen, fifteen-and-a-half, seventeen and eighteen. His travels included South Dakota, New Mexico, Kansas and California. In between flights he taught himself the guitar, which he had begun playing at the age of ten. At fifteen he was playing the harmonica and the autoharp and had written his first song, a ballad dedicated to Brigitte Bardot. In the spring of 1960, Dylan entered the University of Minnesota, in Minneapolis, which he attended for something under six months. In 'My Life in a Stolen Moment,' Dylan has summarised his college career dourly: "I sat in science class an' flunked out for refusin' to watch a rabbit die. I got expelled from English class for using four-letter words in a paper describing the English teacher. I also failed out of communication class for callin' up every day and sayin' I couldn't come . . . I was kept around for kicks at a frater-nity house. They let me live there, an' I did until they wanted me to join." Paul Nelson and Jon Pankake, who edit the *Little Sandy Review*, a quarterly magazine published in Minneapolis that is devoted to critical articles on folk music and performers, remem-ber meeting Dylan at the University of Minnesota in the summer of 1960, while he was part of a group of singers who performed at The Scholar, a coffee-house near the university. Nelson and Pankake, who were students at the university then, have since noted in their publication: "We recall Bob as a soft-spoken, rather unprepossessing youngster . . . well-groomed and neat in the standard campus costume of slacks, sweater, white Oxford sneakers, poplin raincoat and dark glasses."

Before Dylan arrived at the university, his singing had been strongly influenced by such Negro folk interpreters as Leadbelly and Big Joe Williams. He had met Williams in Evanston, Illinois, during his break from home at the age of twelve. Dylan had also been attracted to several urban-style rhythm-and-blues perform-ers, notably Bo Diddley and Chuck Berry. Other shaping forces were white country-music figures – particularly Hank Williams, Hank Snow, and Jimmie Rodgers. During his brief stay at the university Dylan became especially absorbed in the recordings of Woody Guthrie, the Oklahoma-born traveller who had created the most distinctive body of American topical folk material to come to light in this century. Since 1954, Guthrie, ill with Huntington's chorea, a progressive disease of the nervous system, had not been able to perform, but he was allowed to receive visitors. In the autumn of 1960, Dylan quit university and decided to visit Guthrie at Greystone Hospital, in New Jersey. Dylan returned briefly to Minnesota the following May, to sing at a university hootenanny, and Nelson and Pankake saw him again on that occasion. "In a mere half year," they have recalled in the *Little Sandy Review*, "he had learned to churn up exciting, bluesy, hard-driving harmonica-and-guitar music, and had absorbed during his visits with Guthrie not only the great Okie musician's unpredictable syntax but his very vocal colour diction, and inflection. Dylan's performance that spring evening of a selection of Guthrie ... songs was hectic and shaky, but it contained all the elements of the now-perfected performing style that has made him the most original newcomer to folk music."

The winter Dylan visited Guthrie was otherwise bleak. He spent most of it in New York, where he found it difficult to get steady work singing. In 'Talkin' New York,' a caustic song describing his first months in the city, Dylan tells of having been turned away by a coffee-house owner, who told him scornfully: "You sound like a hillbilly. We want folk singers here." There were nights when he slept in the subway but eventually he found friends and a place to stay on the lower East Side, and after he had returned from the spring hootenanny he began getting more frequent engagements in New York. John Hammond at Columbia Records, who has discovered a sizable number of important jazz and folk performers during the past thirty years, heard Dylan that summer while attending a rehearsal of another folk singer Hammond was about to record for Columbia Records. Impressed by the young man's raw force and by the vivid lyrics of his songs, Hammond auditioned him and immediately signed him to a recording contract. Then, in September, 1961, while Dylan was appearing at Gerde's Folk City, a casual refuge for "citybillies" (as the young City singers and musicians are now called in the trade) on West Fourth Street in Greenwich Village, he was heard by Robert Shelton, folk-music critic for the *New York Times*, who wrote of him enthusiastically.

Dylan began to prosper. He enlarged his following by appearing at the Newport and Monterey Folk Festivals and giving concerts throughout the country. There have been a few snags, as when he walked off the Ed Sullivan television show in the spring of 1963 because the Columbia Broadcasting System would not permit him to sing a tart appraisal of the John Birch

Society, but on the whole he has experienced accelerating success. His first three Columbia albums – *Bob Dylan, The Freewheelin' Bob Dylan,* and *The Times They Are A-Changin'* – have by now reached a cumulative sales figure of nearly four hundred thousand. In addition, he has received large royalties as the composer of songs that have become hits through recordings by Peter, Paul and Mary, the Kingston Trio, and other performers. At present, Dylan's fees for a concert appearance range from two thousand to three thousand dollars a night. He has sometimes agreed to sing at a nominal fee for new, non-profit folk societies, however, and has often performed without charge at civil-rights rallies.

Musically, Dylan has transcended most of his early influences and developed an incisively personal style. His vocal sound is most often characterised by flaying harshness. Mitch Jayne, a member of the Dillards, a folk group from Missouri, has described Dylan's sound as "very much like a dog with his leg caught in barbed wire." Yet Dylan's admirers come to accept and even delight in the harshness, because of the vitality and wit at its core. And they point out that in intimate ballads he is capable of a fragile lyricism that does not slip into bathos. It is Dylan's work as a composer, however, that has won him a wider audience than his singing alone might have. Whether concerned with cosmic spectres or personal conundrums, Dylan's lyrics are pungently idiomatic. He has a superb ear for speech rhythms, a generally astute sense of selective detail, and a natural storyteller's command of narrative pacing. His songs sound as if they were being created out of oral street history rather than carefully written in tranquillity. On a stage, Dylan performs his songs as if he had an urgent story to tell. In his work there is little of the polished grace of such carefully trained contemporary minstrels as Richard Dyer-Bennet. Nor, on the other hand, do his performances reflect the calculated showmanship of a Harry Belafonte or of Peter, Paul and Mary. Dylan off the stage is very much the same as Dylan the performer – restless, insatiably hungry for experience, idealistic, but sceptical of neatly defined causes.

In the past year, as his renown has increased, Dylan has become more elusive. He felt so strongly threatened by his initial fame that he welcomed the chance to use the Bearsville home of his manager as a refuge between concerts, and he still spends most of his time there when he's not travelling. A week after the recording session, he telephoned me from Bearsville, and we agreed to meet the next evening at the Keneret, a restaurant on lower Seventh Avenue, in the Village. It specialises in Middle Eastern food, one of Dylan's preferences, but does not have a liquor licence. Upon keeping our rendezvous, therefore, we went next door for a few bottles of Beaujolais and then returned to the Keneret. Dylan was as restless as usual, and as he talked, his hands moved constantly and his voice sounded as if he were never quite able to catch his breath.

I asked him what he had meant, exactly, when he spoke at the recording session of abandoning "finger-pointing" songs, and he took a sip of wine, leaned forward, and said: "I looked around and saw all these people pointing fingers at the bomb. But the bomb is getting boring, because what's wrong goes much deeper than the bomb. What's wrong is how few people are free. Most people walking around are tied down to something that doesn't let them really *speak*, so they just add their confusion to the mess. I mean, they have some kind of vested interest in the way things are now. Me, I'm cool." He smiled. "You know, Joanie – Joanie Baez – worries about me. She worries about whether people will get control over me and exploit me. But I'm cool. I'm in control, because I don't care about money, and all that. And I'm cool in myself, because I've gone through enough changes so that I know what's real to me and what isn't. Like this fame. It's done something to me. It's OK in the Village here. People don't pay attention to me. But in other towns it's funny knowing that people you don't know figure they know *you*. I mean, they think they know everything about you. One thing is groovy, though. I got birthday cards this year from people I'd never heard of. It's weird, isn't it? There are people I've really touched whom I'll never know."

He lit a cigarette. "But in other ways being noticed can be a weight. So I disappear a lot. I go to places where I'm not going to be noticed. And I *can*." He laughed. "I have no work to do. I have no job. I'm not committed to anything except making a few records and playing a few concerts. I'm weird that way. Most people, when they get up in the morning, have to do what they *have* to do. I could pretend there were all kinds of things I *had* to do every day. But why? So I do whatever I feel like. I might make movies of my friends around Woodstock one day. I write a lot. I get involved in scenes with people. A lot of scenes are going on with me all the time – here in the Village, in Paris during my trips to Europe, in lots of places."

I asked Dylan how far ahead he planned. "I don't look past right now," he said. "Now there's this fame business. I know it's going to go away. It has to. This so-called mass fame comes from people who get caught up in a thing for a while and buy the records. Then they stop. And when they stop, I won't be famous anymore."

We became aware that a young waitress was standing by diffidently. Dylan turned to her and she asked him for his autograph. He signed his name with gusto and signed again when she asked if he would give her an autograph for a friend. "I'm sorry to have interrupted your dinner," she said, smiling. "But I'm really not."

"I get letters from people – young people – all the time," Dylan continued when she left us. "I wonder if they write letters like those to other people they don't know. They just want to tell me things, and sometimes they go into their personal hang-ups. Some send poetry. I like getting them – read them all and answer some. But I don't mean I give any of the people who write to me any *answers* to their problems." He leaned forward and talked more rapidly. "It's like when somebody wants to tell me what the 'moral' thing is to do, I want them to *show* me. If they have anything to say about morals, I want to know what it is they *do*. Same with me. All I can do is show people who ask me questions how I live. All I can do is be me. I can't tell them how to change things, because there's only one way to change things, and that's to cut yourself off from all the chains. That's hard for most people to do."

I had Dylan's *The Times They Are A-Changin'* album with me, and I pointed out to him a section of his notes on the cover in which he spoke of how he had always been running when he was a boy – running away from Hibbing and from his parents.

Dylan took a sip of wine. "I kept running because I wasn't free," he said. "I was constantly on guard. Somehow, way back then, I already knew that parents do what they do because they're

up tight. They're concerned with their kids in relation to *themselves*.
I mean, they want their kids to please them, not to embarrass them
– so they can be proud of them. They want you to be what *they*
want you to be. So I started running when I was ten. But always I'd
get picked up and sent home. When I was thirteen, I was traveling
with a carnival through upper Minnesota and North and South
Dakota, and I got picked up again. I tried again and again, and
when I was eighteen I cut out for good. I was still running when
I came to New York. Just because you're free to move doesn't
mean you're free. Finally, I got so far out I was cut off from
everybody and everything. It was then I decided there was no
sense in running so far and so fast when there was no longer
anybody there. It was fake. It was running for the sake of running.
So I stopped. I've got no place to run from. I don't have to be
any place I don't want to be. But I am by no means an example
for any kid wanting to strike out. I mean, I wouldn't want a
young kid to leave home because I did it and then have to go
through a lot of the things I went through. Everybody has to find
his own way to be free. There isn't anybody who can help you in
that sense. Nobody was able to help me. Like seeing Woody
Guthrie was one of the main reasons I came east. He was an idol
to me. A couple of years ago, after I'd gotten to know him, I was
going through some very bad changes and I went to see Woody,
like I'd go to somebody to confess to. But I couldn't confess to
him. It was silly. I did go and talk with him – as much as he could
talk – and the talking helped. But basically he wasn't able to help
me at all. I finally realised that. So Woody was my last idol."

There was a pause. "I've learned a lot in these past few years,"
Dylan said softly. "Like about beauty."

I reminded him of what he had said about his changing
criteria of beauty in some notes he did for a Joan Baez album.
There he had written that when he first heard her voice, before
he knew her, his reaction had been:

> *"I hate that kind a sound," said I*
> *"The only beauty's ugly, man*
> *The crackin', shakin', breakin' sounds're*
> *The only beauty I understand."*

Dylan laughed. "Yeah," he said. "I was wrong. My hang-up was that I used to try to *define* beauty. Now I take it as it is, however it is. That's why I like Hemingway. I don't read much. Usually I read what people put in my hands. But I do read Hemingway. He didn't have to use adjectives. He didn't really have to define what he was saying. He just said it. I can't do that yet, but that's what I want to be able to do."

A young actor from Julian Beck's and Judith Malina's Living Theatre troupe stopped by the table and Dylan shook hands with him enthusiastically. "We're leaving for Europe soon," the actor said. "But when we come back we're going out on the street. We're going to put on plays right on the street, for anyone who wants to watch."

"Hey!" said Dylan, bouncing in his seat. "Tell Julian and Judith that I want to be in on that."

The actor said he would and took Dylan's telephone number. Then he said: "Bob, are you doing only your own songs now – none of the old folk songs at all?"

"Have to," Dylan answered. "When I'm up tight and it's raining outside and nobody's around and somebody I want is a long way from me – and with someone else besides – I can't sing 'Ain't Got No Use for Your Red Apple Juice.' I don't care how great an old song it is or what its tradition is. I have to make a new song out of what *I* know and out of what *I'm* feeling."

The conversation turned to civil rights and the actor used the term "the movement" to signify the work of the civil-rights activists. Dylan looked at him quizzically. "I agree with everything that's happening," he said, "but I'm not part of no movement. If I was, I wouldn't be able to do anything else but be in 'the movement.' I just can't have people sit around and make rules for me. I do a lot of things no movement would allow." He took a long drink of Beaujolais. "It's like politics," he went on. "I just can't make it with *any* organisation. I fell into a trap once – last December – when I agreed to accept the Tom Paine Award from the Emergency Civil Liberties Committee. At the Americana Hotel! In the Grand Ballroom! As soon as I got there, I felt up tight. First of all, the people with me couldn't get in. They looked even funkier than I did, I guess. They weren't dressed right, or something. Inside the ballroom, I really got up

44   *Nat Hentoff*

tight. I began to drink. I looked down from the platform and saw
a bunch of people who had nothing to do with my kind of
politics. I looked down and I got scared. They were supposed to
be on my side, but I didn't feel any connection with them. Here
were these people who'd been all involved with the left in the
Thirties, and now they were supporting civil rights drives. That's
groovy, but they also had minks and jewels, and it was like they
were giving the money out of guilt. I got up to leave and they
followed me and caught me. They told me I had to accept the
award. When I got up to make my speech, I couldn't say anything
by that time but what was passing through my mind. They'd
been talking about Kennedy being killed, and Bill Moore and
Medgar Evers and the Buddhist monks in Vietnam being killed.
I had to say something about Lee Oswald. I told them I'd read a
lot of his feelings in the papers and I knew he was up tight. Said
I'd been up tight, too, so I'd got a lot of his feelings. I saw a lot of
myself in Oswald, I said, and I saw in him a lot of the times we're
all living in. And, you know, they started booing. They looked at
me like I was an animal. They actually thought I was saying it
was a good thing Kennedy had been killed. That's how far out
they are. I was talking about Oswald. And then I started talking
about some friends of mine in Harlem – some of them junkies,
all of them poor. And I said they need freedom as much as
anybody else, and what's anybody doing for *them*? The chair-
man was kicking my leg under the table, and I told him: 'Get out
of here.' Now, what I was supposed to be was a nice cat. I was
supposed to say: 'I appreciate your award and I'm a great singer
and I'm a great believer in liberals, and you buy my records and
I'll support your cause.' But I didn't, and so I wasn't accepted
that night. That's the cause of a lot of those chains I was talking
about – people wanting to be accepted, people not wanting to be
alone. But, after all, what is it to be alone? I've been alone sometimes in front of three thousand people. I was alone that night."

The actor nodded sympathetically. Dylan snapped his fingers.
"I almost forgot," he said. "You know, they were talking about
freedom fighters that night. I've been in Mississippi, man. I
know those people on another level besides civil rights campaigns.
I know them as friends. Like Jim Forman, one of the heads of
SNCC. I'll stand on his side any time. But those people that

night were actually getting me to look at coloured people as coloured people. I tell you, I'm never going to have anything to do with any political organisation again in my life. Oh, I might help a friend if he was campaigning for office. But I'm not going to be part of any organisation. Those people at that dinner were the same as everybody else. They're doing their time. They're chained to what they're doing. The only thing is, they're trying to put morals and great deeds on their chains, but basically they don't want to jeopardise their positions. They got their jobs to keep. There's nothing there for me, and there's nothing there for the kind of people I hang around with. The only thing I'm sorry about is that I guess I hurt the collection at the dinner. I didn't know they were going to try to collect money after my speech. I guess I lost them a lot of money. Well, I offered to pay them whatever it was they figured they'd lost because of the way I talked. I told them I didn't care how much it was. I hate debt, especially moral debts. They're worse than money debts."

Exhausted by his monologue, Dylan sank back and poured more Beaujolais. "People talk about trying to change society," he said. "All I know is that so long as people stay so concerned about protecting their status and protecting what they have, ain't nothing going to be done. Oh, there may be some change of levels inside the circle, but nobody's going to learn anything."

The actor left, and it was time for Dylan to head back up-state. "Come up and visit next week," he said to me, "and I'll give you a ride on my motorcycle." He hunched his shoulders and walked off quickly.

ANOTHER SIDE OF BOB DYLAN

By Sean Egan

US release: 8 August 1964
Produced by: Tom Wilson
CHARTS: US#43; UK#8

SIDE ONE
All I Really Want to Do
Black Crow Blues
Spanish Harlem Incident
Chimes of Freedom
I Shall Be Free No. 10
To Ramona

SIDE TWO
Motorpsycho Nitemare
My Back Pages
I Don't Believe You (She Acts Like We Never Have Met)
Ballad in Plain D
It Ain't Me, Babe

The cover of *Another Side of Bob Dylan* features a small black-and-white picture of the artist, arm resting on an upraised knee, gazing thoughtfully into the distance. This time, he's not thinking about the troubles of the world.

The title of the album pretty much said it all: there were no protest songs here. Dylan later claimed that the title was Tom Wilson's and that he "begged and pleaded" with him not to call it that because it sounded like "a negation of the past". This seems a somewhat disingenuous claim. When Dylan wrote of "Lies that life is black and white" in this LP's 'My Back Pages', he was distancing himself from his protest songs far more unequivocally than did the album title, which could have simply meant a collection of compositions that just happened this time round to have no political import. Whether or not Dylan's insistence in the previous album's 'Restless Farewell' that "Every cause that ever I fought/I fought it full without regret or shame" was the apologia for his imminent desertion of protest some have posited it as, on *Another Side* . . . he has clearly moved on, and 'My Back Pages' illustrates that that move is permanent.

The album is frequently guilty of sloppiness and feels insubstantial. Perhaps this is because most of its songs were written within the space of one week (at the end of May/beginning of June 1964) and the album itself was recorded in one evening (on 9 June), with a bunch of sycophantic friends of Dylan in the control booth cheering their friend on and driving Tom Wilson to distraction. Yet it is also a zestful and fun work and includes three of the artist's greatest songs in 'I Don't Believe You', 'My Back Pages' and 'To Ramona'. Additionally, the looseness is a relief after the grim landscapes of *The Times They Are A-Changin'*. As usual, it could have been even better: though the omission of his early stab at 'Mr. Tambourine Man' was for the best, Dylan mystifyingly also left off the exquisite 'Mama, You Been on My Mind'.

On the back sleeve, Dylan offered "Some other kinds of songs", five poems that were expanded to eleven when he released his 1973 book *Writings & Drawings* (a bonus that was one of the few good things about a collection that saw him retrospectively tamper with his song's lyrics, often to their detriment).

'All I Really Want to Do' sees Dylan trying to convince a girl of his honourable intentions. It's a mildly amusing and reasonably well-performed opener, though the average woman would presumably think she has had more romantic overtures than a pledge from the narrator that "I ain't lookin' to compete with you/Beat or cheat or mistreat you." The litany of things that Dylan says he won't do to the girl with whom he simply wishes (he says) to be friends is almost tiresome – the song has made its point after the first two verses. An additional sense of self-indulgence is created by the fact that Dylan struggles not to laugh at something happening "offstage" at one point and audibly sniffs up snot at another.

'Black Crow Blues' is the first released cut on which Dylan plays piano. He would record many more down the years, employing an endearing style that, though it sounds as if he is wearing boxing gloves, is always somehow effective. The song suffers from the same fault of many of the album's tracks, being rather offhand, with its rhyming scheme lazy ("My wrist was empty/But my nerves were kickin'/Tickin' – like a clock"). Though the snaking melody, Dylan's committed vocal perform- ance and his harmonica and piano are all pleasing in their own way, at the end of three-and-a-quarter minutes of existentialist angst we realise we haven't been taken anywhere. 'Spanish Harlem Incident' sees Dylan address the issue of the supposedly hot-blooded, palm-reading nature of "Gypsy gals". The shortest on the album, it's a slightly peculiar song, but it's also choc-full of memorable imagery and great lines like "I got to laugh half- ways off my heels". 'Chimes of Freedom' is the closest thing on the album to protest, although far too generalised and philo- sophical to be mistaken for a denunciation or broadside. Nonetheless, its epic seven-minute length and all-embracing compassion make it a suitable unofficial farewell to that medium. Dylan and a companion duck into a doorway to escape the rain and suddenly feel that the lightning they are gazing on is in fact the flashing of chimes of freedom. It's an awkward metaphor on more than one level – not only does the word flashing have snig- gersome connotations, but the juxtaposition of the audio (chimes) and the visual (flashing) doesn't really make sense. However, the "mad mystic hammering of the wild ripping hail" is just one of several sumptuous phrases peppering the proceed- ings. Meanwhile, one can't help but be moved by Dylan's expansive solidarity for the reluctant soldier, the refugee, the single mother, the disabled, the fugitive from the law, the prosti- tute, ". . . the countless confused, accused, misused, strung-out ones and worse/And for every hung-up person in the whole wide universe".

'I Shall Be Free No.10' is a sequel to the song on *Freewheelin'*. (Nos. 2–9 haven't even turned up on *The Bootleg Series*, so it can be safely assumed the numbering is not serious.) A stream-of- consciousness comedy like its predecessor, it sees Dylan gently mocking liberals the way he had anti-communist hysterics in some of his protest songs, the narrator stating that while he's a liberal he wouldn't allow Barry Goldwater (an anti-desegregation politician of the era) move in next door and marry his daughter, an echo of the mantra uttered (if *sotto voce*) by many ostensibly broad-minded people of the era that while they were pro-civil rights, they didn't want a Negro in the neighbourhood. 'Motorpsycho Nitemare' sees a stranded Dylan having to spend the night in the shack of a reactionary farmer and his lustful daughter. It's mildly amusing but, once more, lazy rhyming and a sloppily wandering melody line makes the listener wonder whether he should invest effort in listening to something Dylan hasn't exactly busted a gut in creating.

'Ballad in Plain D' is a quasi-harrowing tale of the composer's break-up with Suze Rotolo, not the first of Dylan's lovers whom he plainly did not deserve. It's easy to ridicule a song that at over eight minutes is way too long and which is in places cringe-makingly gauche: the simile he picks for Rotolo is, for God alone knows what reason, a mantelpiece. And what exactly is a "scrape-goat"? Yet the song is absorbing, not least because though it is vituperative about Rotolo's supposedly interfering sister, it is also self-lacerating. Additionally, its absolutely confessional nature makes it almost unique in the Dylan canon. And Dylan being Dylan, even in a song of fifth-form linguistic awkward-ness, he comes out with immensely quotable lines, not least the closer wherein friends ask him what it's like to now be free and he enigmatically responds, "Are birds free from the chains of the skyway?" The closer 'It Ain't Me, Babe' might sound chauvinis-tic to modern ears but in an age when men were enchained by assumptions revolving around strength and chivalry, his acidic renunciation of that role gave it a contemporary relevance.

Another Side's trio of classics are worth the price of admission alone. 'My Back Pages' is the album's keynote song, Dylan's *mea culpa* over protest, with the artist admitting that life is not black and white and that in pretending it was he had been as bad as the supposed evil-doers against whom he had issued broadsides. Ironically, its wonderful soaring melody and lyrical refrain "I was so much older then, I'm younger than that now" give it the feel of the type of anthem beloved by civil-rights activists for their utility at rallies. 'I Don't Believe You' finds Dylan bewildered by the sudden coldness of a woman with whom he has just spent the night. A wonderful sprightly melody, incongruously jaunty harmonica, vivid songwords ("Though we kissed through the wild blazing night time . . . Though her skirt it swayed/As a guitar played") and some attractively mewling singing all add up to a sublime song, spoilt only by Dylan clearly showing off once again to his mates in the control box.

Best of all is the beautiful 'To Ramona'. The narrator is telling the titular friend (we presume a lover) to stick to her principles and not cave in to peer pressure. Though during the rest of the album Dylan stumbles jarringly between the poetic and the slapdash, this track has an elegance worthy of Shakespeare: "Ramona, come closer, shut softly your watery eyes/The pangs of your sadness shall pass as your senses will rise/The flowers of the city though breath-like get death-like sometimes/And there's no use in trying/To deal with the dying/Though I cannot explain that in lines." That exquisite opening verse may well be the finest thing Dylan has ever written. There may even be more to the composition. Though Dylan deliberately makes us think it is a love song, he has written many things in the second-person down the years that actually seem on close inspection to be a disguised dialogue with himself. 'To Ramona' may be the first, in which case the track explodes into a completely new dimension – the comfort being offered to someone whose sorrow stems "from fixtures and forces and friends" may well be an articulation of Dylan's internal agony about leaving protest (and by extension several intimates) behind. The final line sees Dylan admit to the person addressed (whomever it may be) that one day s/he might be the one needing comfort – a concept and line so neat that George Harrison appropriated it for The Beatles' 'Old Brown Shoe'.

Though by no means one of Dylan's more famous numbers, the delicate strengths of 'To Ramona' have been recognized both by Dylan (who has featured it in his sets ever since) and by other artists: it has been the recipient of many cover versions, including most unlikely ones by Alan Price and Humble Pie.

Overall, *Another Side of Bob Dylan* is far more enjoyable than *The Times They Are A-Changin'* yet feels far less substantial. The artist makes the obverse of the mistake he made with *Times*;

where he was too earnest on that album, he – with some glorious exceptions – is not taking things seriously enough on this often frivolous LP, either in composition or execution. The album's sales were mediocre in Dylan's home country, but he still had a momentum behind him, a measure of which is the fact that the first and last of the tracks on this slight outing would shortly become substantial hits for other artists.

After Bob Dylan recorded Dave Van Ronk's arrangement of 'House of the Risin' Sun' on his debut, it took two years for a hurt and pre-empted Van Ronk to release a version of the song with which he had become synonymous around the New York folk venues. However, Dylan's act of treachery had momentous consequences for popular music. Not only did British R&B band The Animals become stars via a recording of the song inspired by Dylan's version, but when the inspiration flowed back in the other direction, popular music would never be the same. In these extracts from Animals' biography Animal Tracks, *the band's drummer John Steel and guitarist Hilton Valentine explain a domino effect that was epoch-marking. The "Eric" referred to is Animals vocalist Eric Burdon.*

DYLAN, THE ANIMALS AND GOING ELECTRIC

By Sean Egan

First published in *Animal Tracks* (Helter Skelter)

"We loved that first [Dylan] album," Steel recalls " . . . 'House of the Risin' Sun' was to us the outstanding track from [it]. That's where we ripped 'House of the Rising Sun' from, no matter what you hear about Josh White." That the band were covering a number they'd first heard from that South Carolina bluesman is a fixture of Animals mythology which repeatedly crops up in encyclopedia entries and CD-liner notes. "That was another fairy tale from Eric because we didn't want it to be thought that we were just copying somebody as 'weakened' as Bob Dylan," Steel explains. "It had to come from somebody more obscure as that. Even though Bob Dylan was really fresh and new then, as far as we were concerned it wasn't cool to say that we'd pinched the song from his album. We'd much prefer it to be thought that we were delving into some really obscure stuff."

Valentine agrees. Dylan's rendition of this public-domain song was: "The first version I heard – Eric was aware of the song before that – and basically it was the Bob Dylan version that we took the chord sequence from. He strummed it – it was only him, guitar and harmonica." Valentine decided to use arpeggios rather than strummed figures, arpeggios which gave a hypnotic, winding feel to the arrangement and ones which are now a staple of handbooks for beginners on guitar. "I don't know why," Valentine says of that decision. "I just started doing it and it seemed to work. Nobody was aware in them days that it was going to be such a huge hit and still last and encourage a lot of guitar players to start playing the guitar."

The Animals' transcendent version of what they called 'The House of the Rising Sun' was a number-one hit in the UK in summer 1964. A shortened version of the unusually long (4:27) record subsequently ascended the American charts, following which the group toured the States.

One of the things The Animals most wanted to do in America was to meet another of their heroes, Bob Dylan. Now beginning to realise they possessed the star status that could make such things possible, they made enquires. A meeting was arranged between The Animals and Dylan in the New York [home] of Dylan's manager, Al Grossman. It took place in the room immortalized the next year by being displayed on the front of Dylan's *Bringing It All Back Home* album. The Animals met someone very different from the rough-hewn character they assumed the artist to be from his Voice of the Common Man music.

"It was a bit of a shock just physically to meet him," Steel remembers. "He was a really great-looking guy but he was so fine. It seemed to me his skin was almost transparent. He had this mohair-type jacket and shirt cufflinks – really sharply turned out. This wasn't what we expected. He was very nice."

Even more shocking was the fact that it turned out that the admiration was most certainly mutual. Dylan had been so impressed by The Animals' version of his arrangement of 'The House of the Rising Sun' (which, incidentally, Dylan had stolen from fellow folkie Dave Van Ronk), that it caused a switch in Dylan's musical perspective, one which would have momentous consequences for pop music in bringing the intellectual rigour of folk lyrics into what had hitherto been a musical genre which had mostly addressed trivial, adolescent concerns.

This has long been a source of dispute but Steel insists, "That is from the horse's mouth. That is what he told us. He said he was driving along in his car and ['House . . .'] came on the radio and he pulled the car over and stopped and listened to it and he jumped out of the car and he banged on the bonnet. That gave him the connection – how he *could* go electric. He might have been heading that way already but he said that was a really significant thing for him." Dylan then proceeded to reveal to the band the first fruits of his electrification. Steel: "He said, 'This is what I've just recorded' and he played us 'Subterranean Homesick Blues'. He said, 'What do you think?' and we said, 'You're doing so well with the acoustic folk stuff, you're taking a chance with that, aren't you?' It sounded a little bit like Chuck Berry."

American music journalist Richie Unterberger is the author of an acclaimed two-volume history of folk-rock, Turn! Turn! Turn! *and* Eight Miles High *(Backbeat Books). In this new article drawn from the same sources as those works, he examines the surprisingly halting development of one of Dylan's most famous songs.*

THE EVOLUTION OF 'MR. TAMBORUINE MAN'

By Richie Unterberger

For someone often characterized as impulsive, disdainful of the recording process and uninterested in anything studio-wise bar capturing the moment, 'Mr. Tambourine Man' occupies an anomalous place in the Bob Dylan discography.

Unquestionably one of his major compositions, it underwent an unusually prolonged gestation. It wasn't until almost a year after he started to write it, and about eight months after he started to perform it live, that the official studio version would be recorded. That was preceded by two drastically different unreleased studio versions, as well as one recorded for an unreleased live album and one that was filmed at the world's most prestigious folk festival. For all that, it would take a much abridged cover by another artist both to make the song famous and give it a pivotal role in Dylan's transition from folk singer to rock star.

The genesis of 'Mr. Tambourine Man' can be dated to some time during Dylan's visit to New Orleans from February 10 through February 12 of 1964. The singer was in the midst of a rather crazed three-week cross-country trip by station wagon, a sort of *On the Road* for the just-post-Beat era. Visits to poet Carl Sandburg, Kentucky miners and the plaza where JFK was assassinated mixed haphazardly with concerts and revelry with several friends along for the ride. Perhaps they were having too much fun to have done something as mundane as watch television and missed The Beatles' legendary first appearance on *The Ed Sullivan Show* just a day before they hit New Orleans. If they didn't know about the group then, however, they certainly would by the time they passed through Colorado, where Dylan became a convert to Beatlemania after hearing a station on which no less than eight Beatles songs filled the Top 10.

Pop music was undergoing what may well have been its most seismic change and a song that Dylan had started in New Orleans, 'Mr. Tambourine Man', would be a part of it. This and some others he pecked away at on a typewriter in the back seat of the station wagon signified a sharp shift of direction in his own songwriting. While he had always mixed in personal romantic and humorous songs with his political protest numbers, it was as a topical song-writer that he was primarily known in early 1964. Such compositions were abruptly discontinued as he went in a more poetic direction with lyrics not tied to current events, such as another durable tune he wrote during the same trip: 'Chimes of Freedom'. Yet even by the standards of his just-post-protest efforts, 'Mr. Tambourine Man' was something else again, using imagery so surreal and dream-like that a good number of listeners then and now assume it must have been at least partly drug-inspired.

As with many of Dylan's most popular songs, speculation as to its inspiration has cited several possible sources. In the liner notes to the 1985 box-set *Biograph*, Dylan himself emphatically denied drugs as a spark, charging, "Drugs never played a part in that song . . . drugs were never that big a thing with me. I could take 'm or leave 'm, never hung me up." Scarcely more likely seems the claim by several of his friends, reported in the first credible Dylan biography (Anthony Scaduto's 1971 book *Dylan*), that it was based on a story told to the songwriter by a friend from his pre-fame days in Minneapolis, Ivars Perlsbach. As an infant, Perlsbach had been taken across Europe by a mother escaping from a Russian internment camp, the hardship only broken (so the story went) when children asked local folk musicians to "play a song, mister tambourine man". In the same biography, Dylan vociferously denied that spin as well.

"'Mr. Tambourine Man', I think, was inspired by Bruce Langhorne," Dylan stated in *Biograph*'s liner notes. Recalling a Dylan studio session where said guitarist was asked by producer Tom Wilson to switch to tambourine, Dylan revealed, "He had this gigantic tambourine . . . It was as big as a wagon wheel . . . this vision of him playing this tambourine just stuck in my mind . . . I don't know if I've ever told him that." Langhorne was apparently not the only inspiration: Dylan himself said it had a pinch of Federico Fellini's movie *La Strada*, while his then-girlfriend Suze Rotolo later claimed that it was ". . . a song written about a lonely night Bob had spent wandering the streets after the two of us had quarrelled." Nonetheless, the debt the song owes Langhorne is clearly considerable, so I took the opportunity to ask Langhorne personally, about thirty-five years later: "Are you Mr. Tambourine Man?"

"Yeah," he responded nonchalantly. "I am Mr. Tambourine Man," he laughed. His source, though, is *Biograph*: "He didn't tell me about that. And probably if he did tell anybody, he'd probably deny it." He laughed again. Possibly providing further reinforcement was Richard Fariña's little-noted remark, "He's the tambourine king, lest you doubt!" when he introduced Langhorne from the stage as one of his accompanists during Richard & Mimi Fariña's set at the 1965 Newport Folk Festival.

The song was probably finished a month or two after the New Orleans visit, at the home of Dylan's journalist friend Al Aronowitz. For such an intricate piece he had clearly laboured over and was proud of – playing the song to folk musician friends like Judy Collins, Eric Von Schmidt and Martin Carthy before he'd even performed it – he took an unusually long time to make it available on one of his studio albums. It wasn't a matter of agonising over the finalisation of the tune or lyrics, either. He unveiled it for the first time at London's Royal Festival Hall on 17 May 1964, a recording of which verifies that the song was complete, although he sings of "hidden leaves" instead of "frozen leaves". It seemed destined to be a highlight of his fourth LP when he entered Columbia Studio A in New York on 9 June to cut, in one marathon session, all of the material on *Another Side of Bob Dylan*.

Yet while 'Mr. Tambourine Man' *was* recorded on that date, it was *not* included on the album. Dylan's brief and enigmatic explanation (to Martin Bronstein of the Canadian Broadcasting Company on 20 February 1966) was that "I felt too close to it to put it on," though in the same interview he cited it as one of his key breakthrough songs. The actual recording was so quirky, however, that it almost seemed to verge on self-sabotage. For unfathomable reasons, Dylan – who, though he'd sung duets with Joan Baez and Pete Seeger at the 1963 Newport Folk Festival, had never yet used a singer as a duet partner or back-up harmony vocalist on an official studio release – invited Ramblin' Jack Elliott to sing with him on 'Mr. Tambourine Man'. As it happened, Dylan had dueted with Elliott in concert as well, as a surviving radio broadcast of a 29 July 1961 performance (of a rather unfunny rock 'n' roll parody titled 'Acne') proves.

It was hardly a good omen that Elliott didn't even know the words. He'd only heard the song via a "version" from his wife of the time, Patty, who memorised it after hearing Dylan sing the tune. Maybe it was the modern equivalent of the "oral trad-ition", but it wasn't the best way to ensure a good take, even if Elliott limited himself to singing along with the choruses. "I listened to it once, and I never want to hear it again," Elliott told the *San Francisco Examiner* in 1996. "It was real bad singing. Amazingly bad."

It wasn't *that* bad, but it wasn't as good as it could have been. Lasting near-marathon length for 1964 at almost seven minutes, the recording was mediocre less through bad singing (though the harmonies are a little wayward) than a sluggish pace and perfunc-tory guitar-and-harmonica accompaniment. Such accompaniment was, of course, standard for Dylan recordings of the era, but was something that The Beatles and the British groups that followed them into the US market would soon have him rethinking. It also has an extra line "and if to you he looks blind" (after "ragged clown behind") that throws the rhythm totally off-kilter for a few seconds. It still wouldn't have taken much more work to make an acceptable recording of the song for *Another Side of Bob Dylan*, but for the time being, it was left unissued.

Also curious, and far less reported in Dylan lore than the Elliott duet – at least until its belated 2010 official release on *The Bootleg Series Vol. 9* – is a scratchy demo done for his publisher, M. Witmark & Son, given a date of June 1964 in Clinton Heylin's *Bob Dylan: The Recording Sessions (1960–1994)*. Whether this precedes the Columbia session is unknown, but it's certainly odd to hear a song so identified with guitar backing (in both the official Dylan track and its most famous cover) done with a slightly clumsy piano-only backing whose tempo verges on the jaunty. Perhaps he was thinking it needed something different, or at least slightly more interesting, in the way of an arrangement. Or maybe he or someone thought, for some reason, piano was a more suitable instrument for a recording whose primary purpose might have been to elicit cover versions.

If Dylan really felt too "close" to the song to expose it to the record-buying public, it's strange that he nonetheless continued to feature it prominently in his live performances. He sang it at a workshop at the 1964 Newport Folk Festival on 24 July, introduced by Pete Seeger no less, in a performance now officially available on the DVD *The Other Side of the Mirror: Live at the Newport Folk Festival 1963–1965.* He did it to enthusiastic applause at his Halloween concert at New York's Philharmonic Hall, recorded as a possible live release and finally issued in 2004 as *The Bootleg Series Vol. 6: Bob Dylan Live 1964.* The *New York Times* review of that show (by future Dylan biographer Robert Shelton) even singled out the yet-to-be-released number as "an introspective, symbolist piece that moved in and out of this listener's comprehension but still conveyed a strong mood."

Clearly Dylan couldn't keep it under wraps for too much longer, but even before he re-recorded it for Columbia on 15 January, events were conspiring (perhaps even uncontrollably) to give it far greater exposure than he could have ever envisioned. That rickety take with Jack Elliott turned out to be of some use after all when it made its way to Jim Dickson, co-manager of a fledgling West Coast rock group of ex-folkies, The Byrds. "I heard that Dylan had done a session and was not including 'Tambourine Man', as he had tried it as a duet with Jack Elliott and was not happy with the result," Dickson told me. "The West Coast rep for Witmark, Jack Mass, was able to get me an acetate from that session, and I became a little obsessed with it. I did think everyone should sing Dylan at the time."

"Nobody was really keen on 'Tambourine Man' as I recall when we first heard it," Byrds bassist Chris Hillman told me. "Maybe [Byrds singer-guitarist Jim] McGuinn, but I don't know if anybody else was. But Dickson pounded it into our head, literally, to go for a little more depth in the lyric, and really craft the song, and make something you can be proud of ten-to-fifteen years down the road. He was absolutely right. We were wise-guy little punk kids, and he was our big brother/father figure, but he had a tremendous influence on The Byrds. He pushed for 'Tambourine Man', and put himself out on the line for that one."

The Byrds' version has undergone its share of criticism for being a supposed bowdlerisation of the composition. True, the band did use just one of the original four verses, emphasising the chorus. But they also took it somewhere no one, even Dylan, had imagined. McGuinn's twelve-string electric guitar, John Lennon-meets-Dylan vocal, and the full rock-band arrangement (actually featuring only McGuinn's guitar with session players, though three of The Byrds sang) gave it a pop sheen and rock muscle that sent it to the top of the charts in both the UK and USA following its April 1965 release. In the process, a brand new genre was invented: folk-rock. And the way was paved for Dylan's own electric recordings to invade the Hit Parade; 'Like a Rolling Stone' became a huge hit a few months later.

As a result of The Byrds' success with the song, many listeners, especially young teenagers, wanted to know more about the songwriter, discovering the much-improved – if still acoustic – version of 'Mr. Tambourine Man' on Dylan's March 1965 album *Bringing It All Back Home*, recorded five days before The Byrds' version. Where the mid-1964 arrangements had trudged, this one glowed with grace. Other than a livelier rhythm, the significant change was a lilting, sparkling guitar played by none other than . . . Bruce Langhorne. 'Mr. Tambourine Man' had been brought full circle by its very subject.

"I like it," Langhorne told me. "I think it's a good song. I do. And it's about me," he laughed. "If I had a big ego . . . Well, I do have a big ego. But if I wanted to fuel it, that'd be a way to do it."

BRINGING IT ALL BACK HOME

By Sean Egan

US release: 22 March 1965
Produced by: Tom Wilson
CHARTS: US#6; UK#1

SIDE ONE
Subterranean Homesick Blues
She Belongs to Me
Maggie's Farm
Love Minus Zero/No Limit
Outlaw Blues
On the Road Again
Bob Dylan's 115th Dream

SIDE TWO
Mr. Tambourine Man
Gates of Eden
It's Alright, Ma (I'm Only Bleeding)
It's All Over Now, Baby Blue

Dylan recorded his fifth album from 13–15 January 1965. The quick turnaround doesn't suggest anything too different. In fact, Dylan had changed profoundly as a person and an artist since *Another Side of . . .*

That Dylan was undergoing a metamorphosis that was going to make his shrugging off of protest look like a change of shoes was patently obvious just by glancing at the (rather beautiful) cover: the artist's name in red and the title in blue against a pure white background atop a full colour picture of Dylan sitting before an elegant, red-dressed woman reclining in an opulent living room. Though the covers of his first two albums had been colour, the artist had still been trying to evoke railroads, hard living and solidarity with the working man. Now he was trying to convey something a lot more complicated, even rarefied. This wasn't restricted to Dylan's new foppish penchant for mod suits, high-collared shirts and cufflinks that was also made evident in the picture. In an age where self-referentialism and post-modernism were still rare, Dylan had scattered cultural symbols around the place: a copy of *Time* with current US president Lyndon Johnson on the cover, a fallout shelter sign and albums that, as well as his own last one, included works by The Impressions, Robert Johnson, Ravi Shankar, Lotte Lenya, Eric Von Schmidt and Lord Buckley. The novelty didn't stop there. Though the word "psychedelic" had yet to enter common parlance, the cover was precisely that courtesy of a double exposure that put Dylan and the lady inside a glowing yellow circle. A miracle of happenstance gave the cover an even more surreal air: the woman was actually Albert Grossman's wife Sally but such was her Dylan-like angular facial structure that a rumour soon began circulating that she was Dylan in drag.

The albums on the cover are a bit of a red herring; sleeve photographer Daniel Kramer suggested artefacts and the specific albums were selected by Dylan from Grossman's record collection, not his own. The only extrapolation from them that wouldn't seem too fanciful is that *Another Side of . . .* peeking out from behind a cushion constitutes a message stating "This is what I no longer am." In this new album's music, Dylan is re-embracing his first love. Bobby Zimmerman had always wanted to be a rock 'n' roll star. When he created the persona of Bob Dylan, folk certainly was the "coming thing", as he told Echo Helstrom. But then along came The Beatles, taking America not only by storm but doing so with a new type of rock that made the cheesy chord progressions and twangy primitiv-ism of a lot of early examples of the form seem prehistoric. The Fab Four had revitalised a moribund genre in its indigenous America, leading Dylan to re-embrace it – hence (the suppos-ition goes) the title of the album.

Nobody who had such a huge repertoire of traditional songs as Dylan could possibly be said to hold folk in contempt; however, that it wasn't his first love must have been compounded in Dylan's mind by the fact that he had evidently caught the wrong bus. Now he wanted a piece of the action. And why shouldn't he? Not only had other acts taken his songs into the pop charts, but when Dylan met The Beatles in New York in August 1964, they transpired to be big fans. Accordingly, though side two of *Bringing It All Back Home* was devoted to four epic acoustic classics with socio-political content that none of Dylan's folk fans could possibly be anything other than entranced by, the first side of the LP contained breakneck rock 'n' roll, chugging blues and pretty ballads all augmented by the sounds of a backing band.

The horror this conversion caused is unfathomable to people today. In a society where it is actively uncool to close one's mind to certain types of music and where irony makes every taste permissible on some level, the debates of the 1960s are part of an alien frame of reference. Back then, folkies hated rock and pop because they considered them crass, an attitude wrapped up in the radicalism that went hand-in-hand with the Sixties folk revival: the folkies considered that the people who lapped up the simplistic formulae found on the Hit Parade were partaking of the new opiate of the masses. By going rock 'n' roll, Dylan was – it was felt – selling out. His rock grounding wasn't widely known of at the time, but it would probably have cut no ice if it had been: Dylan seemed to want to be a Beatle, both in his music and his clothing, and the aspiration seemed genuinely pathetic and unbelievably mercenary to many.

There was, though, one fact inconvenient for those determined to despise Dylan for his alleged betrayal of principles: his art was getting better and better. Though his past record means we can't discount ambition and money as his motivation, there is simply no way that the disgusted folkies could pretend to themselves that Dylan's new music was pandering to the teenyboppers. The Beatles, Rolling Stones and Dave Clark Five fans about to buy their first Bob Dylan album were going to be confronted by enough dazzling wordsmithery, scathing wit and intellectual sophistication to blow their adolescent minds.

The album opens with 'Subterranean Homesick Blues', which sees the artist fold a literate, insightful lyric into a close musical cousin of Chuck Berry's 'Too Much Monkey Business' in a way not too dissimilar to how he had previously appropriated folk melodies for his own ends. Though the song ends on a rather feeble, unresolved note (the line "The pumps don't work 'cos the vandals took the handles"), this gritty street vignette is otherwise a superbly worded, breathless and merciless exposure of the fact that for all the effort and ambition in each human life, behind it all lies an identical banality: "Get born/Keep warm/Short pants/Romance/Learn to dance/Get dressed/Get blessed/Try to be a success".

'Maggie's Farm' is an uptempo pop blues song in which Dylan could be genuinely placing himself in the mind of a rebellious farmhand but could also be making a veiled attack on the folkies who wanted to enslave him in their camp. It's pleasantly gnarled but also slightly monotonous, partly because it's a one-note joke, even if the writer does keep it quite interesting with a procession of Maggie's grotesque family members. 'She Belongs to Me' and 'Love Minus Zero/No Limit' are both songs whose titles appear nowhere in their lyrics (a common Dylan trait from hereon). They are also both pretty ballads that idealise a woman to sensitive musical backing. The uptempo 'On the Road Again' sees Dylan amusingly share his gripes about the house of freaks his girlfriend's home constitutes. Not only does he never get fed there, but "Even the butler, he's got something to prove!"

'Bob Dylan's 115th Dream' is a surreal story of discovery ahead of Columbus of an America that is both strangely contemporary and Chaplinesque. It does indeed have that feeling of the fractured and upended reality of a dream. It's packed to the gills with funny scenarios and clever lines ("I ordered some suzette/I said, 'Could you please make that crepe?'"). There is a false start when Dylan collapses into laughter after the musicians miss their cue to come in. One wonders whether Bob should have persevered with the take solo, as the band's generic, featureless instrumentation contributes nothing and demonstrates a fault with Dylan's first major foray into full accompaniment: since his rock 'n' roll teens, Dylan had become unfamiliar with incorporating multiple instruments into his songs. The closest the album comes to demonstrating that Dylan understands that he needs to play with the group instead of simply singing over the top of them is the anthem of existentialist angst (a favourite topic of Dylan at the time) 'Outlaw Blues'. Though it features a bog-standard twelve-bar progression, it's notable that Dylan interacts with the musicians if only on a minor level, leaving gaps for their contributions. Having said that, perhaps Tom Wilson was partly at fault: a close listen to '115th Dream' reveals a percolating keyboard part that is just begging to be mixed higher. Maybe significantly, Wilson was not Dylan's producer for much longer.

Culturally, side one was revolutionary, but aesthetically the acoustic side is far superior. It consists of four lengthy songs, none of which outstay their welcome and all of which have the smack of a grand statement. Proving Dylan's ever-deepening craft, all show off his vastly improved singing and mouth-harp playing and all rise to a climax in the form of a final verse of extra strength with Dylan's voice climbing to a crescendo.

'Mr. Tambourine Man' is a lovely, mellow reverie. Supposedly a paean to the delights of marijuana, like so many Dylan songs it can work on another level completely, in this case as a sort of cousin to Peter, Paul and Mary's children's song 'Puff (The Magic Dragon)'. Whether the titular character is session man Bruce Langhorne, a drug pusher or a pied piper-like figure from a fairy-tale of Dylan's own imagining, it barely matters as we are treated to sublime imagery and introduced to effortlessly unforgettable phrases ("Down the foggy ruins of time"; "My toes too numb to step wait only for my boot heels to be wanderin'"). Though the layering provided by Langhorne's accompanying guitar is agree-able, Dylan's growing confidence as an instrumentalist is illustrated by excellent, lung-busting harmonica work.

'Gates of Eden' has a melody so black and a delivery so intense as to almost be chilling. The opaque lyric positing a utopia where none of the evils and inequities the composer lists are to be found is occasionally awkward (talk of lampposts with folded arms sounds simply silly) but with lines like "Upon the beach where hound dogs bay at ships with tattooed sails", he creates a refined sense of mystery and dread. 'It's Alright, Ma (I'm Only Bleeding)' is even more intense and despairing, and no less hypnotic. In the first verse Dylan tells us that "Darkness at the break of noon/Shadows even the silver spoon". The former seems a reference to Arthur Koestler's anti-communist novel *Darkness at Noon*, and the silver spoon a metaphor for the privileges that capitalism engenders – i.e., no matter how bad the inequities of capitalism, socialism is even worse. This realisation that the utopia he yearns for in 'Gates of Eden' is unattainable makes him conclude, "There is no sense in trying". And that's just the start of a seven-and-a-half-minute extravaganza in which Dylan explores not just inequity but its very definition, as well as the industries and people that thrive on it on both sides of the ideological fence. It's astounding stuff, and far and away above anything ever attempted in popular song before.

'It's All Over Now, Baby Blue' is at 4:10 the shortest side-two song by well over a minute but feels no less substantial than the others courtesy of its gorgeous melody, even more gorgeous harmonica and fervoured singing. Once again, the sound is subtly enriched, this time by William E. Lee's bass. By this point in the album, we have learned that Dylan's new metaphor-heavy writing style means that we may never fully understand these songs, but it's interesting to note that if we assume Dylan is engaged in a dialogue with himself, Baby Blue for whom it is all over might be that man who embraced protest only to tire of the pretence ("Take what you have gathered from coincidence") and was facing the prospect of the wrath of the people he had used/fooled.

It should be pointed out, though, that Dylan still felt like a protest singer to the wider public. He might no longer think in straight lines about social issues (or pretend to) but, whatever the folkies might say, he was perceived by the new pop audience he picked up with this album as cutting-edge, radical, anti-establishment and as much a figurehead for the new informal, liberal society that seemed to be on the horizon as The Beatles and The Rolling Stones. What else was one to make of someone writing, as Dylan did in this album's opener, "Twenty years of schooling and they put you on the day shift"?

As with his previous two albums, Dylan contributes the sleevenotes. For the first time, though, they are surreal narrative rather than verse.

Although the album is artistically a limited success, it had an influence that was greater than its quality. That the use of rock on side one is slightly undermined by its featurelessness wasn't so apparent at the time because there was nothing with which to compare this marriage of the gutsy and the cerebral: the fact that Dylan had smashed the barriers hitherto thought to separate the intellectualism of folk and the earthiness of rock seemed to confer a quality by default. Meanwhile, Dylan was blossoming in ways not dependent on his musical pioneering. Dylan-as-poet begins here. He had always shown an adept turn of phrase, but his previous songs were largely just an elevated version of the colloquial poetry common in folk, his skills undermined slightly by an ungrammatical quality that made sense for his man-of-the-people image but was inelegant. With his embrace of symbolism and allegory and his gravitation toward philosophical statements as opposed to strings of slogans and local colour pieces, his lyrics were suddenly grand and magisterial.

Something else that begins here is Dylan as a truly great singer. Where before he had often seemed callow, if wilfully so, he suddenly sounds authoritative and poised, and in 'She Belongs to Me' his singing is simply divine. Though he would never have a conventionally brilliant voice – and it would continue to be occasionally monotonous and irritating – it would always have a huge presence and soulfulness. There was also an extra quality lent by his Minnesota accent: pronouncing body "baddy", buck "book" and mirror "me'er" and suchlike made for an element of the exotic. Up until around 1978, when his voice began its long, slow deterioration (and with the exception of a period at the turn of the Seventies when his voice got dull), Bob Dylan would be the greatest singer in the world, bar none.

In 1965, Bob Dylan was the coolest thing on two legs, so putting him in the movies was logical, even if it was a documentary rather than an acting role. D. A. Pennebaker's Dont Look Back *(the lack of an apostrophe was deliberate) didn't premiere until May 1967 but preserved for posterity Dylan's persona as it was almost exactly two years previously in April–May 1965 on his final solo tour. The only thing to add to Andy Gill's comprehensive analysis of the film below is that the way Dylan therein cruelly ridicules the self-proclaimed science student sent to interview him was, according to those who knew him, an acerbic trademark of Dylan's at that time.*

BOB DYLAN: *DONT LOOK BACK*

By Andy Gill

First published in the *Independent*, 27 April 2007

D. A. Pennebaker has some unusual notions about musicians. "They're the closest we have in our time to the saints," he told me some years ago, "because they renounce the material world for something else, as a matter of course: they don't see any other way to do it."

He may be right. As the world's leading rock documentarist, director of such ground-breaking films as *Dont Look Back*, *Monterey Pop* and *Ziggy Stardust*, he's perhaps better qualified than you or I to make such statements. After all, he's poked his lens with sometimes embarrassing candour into the lives of stars such as Bob Dylan and David Bowie.

"I think they're quite alike," he believes. "Like Dylan, Bowie lives in a part of his brain that you and I don't know anything about. Both of them have this place in their head they can go into and kind of disappear. I've seen them both do it, disappear on me, right in the middle of a sentence."

Forty years ago, Pennebaker's documentary *Dont Look Back*, a filmed record of Bob Dylan's 1965 UK tour, was first shown to the world, its cinema-verité style and grainy 16mm mono-chrome scenes of grim postwar Britain arriving like a blade of earthy reality stabbed to the heart of 1967's gaudy, multi-coloured psychedelic fantasy-world. Not that anyone – especially in Britain – would have realised that at the time, as for years it proved almost impossible to view, having been rejected by every large distributor as unfit for screening.

"Nobody had ever distributed a film like this before," admits Pennebaker. "In fact, I have a letter from someone at Warner/7 Arts saying, 'This film is ratty, badly focused, it's hard to hear what people are saying – it's a disaster!'." In the event, the 16mm print had its low-key premiere at a former porno theatre in San Francisco, before a 35mm print was shown in New York.

Even Dylan himself was initially uncertain about its viability when he viewed a preliminary screening. "The first time Bob saw it," recalls Pennebaker, "I sat there nervously till he got up at the end and said, 'We're showing it again tomorrow, and I'll make a list of all the changes we have to make'. The next night, he sat there in the front row, with a big yellow pad and pen, all ready – the axe was in his hand, and the hood was on his head! Then at the end, he stood up and showed me the pad: completely blank." Indeed, so enamoured did the singer become with Pennebaker's methods that he made the rarely screened *Eat the Document*, his own little-seen film of his first "electric" UK tour with The Hawks.

Since then, of course, *Dont Look Back* has become universally recognised as one of the great rock movies, its mingling of rivet-ing concert footage and revealing backstage shenanigans offering an unscripted variation on the faux-documentary style of Richard Lester's *A Hard Day's Night*, complete with the scream-ing fans, the limousine escapes, the press conferences, and the hotel-room interludes in which Dylan's guard is most obviously dropped. And so deft is Pennebaker's editing that several running themes – the Donovan wind-ups, the baiting of interviewers – lend the film a narrative drive and completeness that still sets it apart.

This is all the more evident when one gets to see the extra ninety minutes of outtake footage included in the new deluxe DVD edition, a sumptuous two-disc package that also includes the "script" book originally published in 1968 and a lovely little flip-book of the celebrated card-dropping 'Subterranean Homesick Blues' sequence which opens the film, and which has claim on being the first ever pop video (there are also two further takes of the sequence, in different locations). Dylan had seen the Scopitone music-film "jukeboxes" used in France, and wanted to make a film-clip of his own, so he and a roomful of friends sat up all night in his Savoy Hotel room writing the words on cards, and the piece was filmed the following day. Not knowing what to do with it, Pennebaker stuck it in front of his film for reference purposes, and it just remained there, an enigmatic, unannounced opening that served to convey not just what road manager Bob Neuwirth calls Dylan's "industrial-strength charisma", but also his obvious poetic talent and intellectual ambition – who else, in those days, would include a famous beat poet like Allen Ginsberg in their promotional film? Who, come to that, would recognise Ginsberg?

Pennebaker secured the commission to film the tour through the recommendation of Sara Lownds, the pretty young divorcee with whom Dylan had recently become smitten, and would secretly marry later that year. A friend of the wife of Dylan's manager Albert Grossman – whose forbidding presence looms over many of the film's scenes – Sara knew Pennebaker through her work connections at Drew Associates, a film production company, and suggested his name when the idea of a tour film was first mooted.

Pennebaker had originally been attracted to the documentary medium after seeing Flaherty's *Nanook of the North* – "what appealed to me was that he made a film about somebody he liked, and he didn't care if it showed" – and Louis De Rochemont's innovative, Oscar-winning war documentary *Fighting Lady*; although he makes a clear distinction between them and his own work. "I don't think of [my own films] as documentaries because I'm really interested in film as drama, rather than film as information," he explains. "It happens that I use situations that are real, but basically the films are kind of an imagined dream of what happened. They may be quite accurate, but they're still as imagined, as dictated, by me."

These   days,   cinema-verité   film   methods   have become commonplace as technology has become more and more miniaturised: within minutes of a terrorist bombing, footage captured on a cellphone-camera can be broadcast to the world. But back in the Sixties, the medium was literally a labour of love. "Five years earlier, we simply couldn't have filmed it," admits Pennebaker. "The technology simply didn't exist – you needed lighting rigs, and sound equipment that was connected to the camera." Not to mention the sheer weight of the equipment the cameraman had to tote on his shoulder.

To surmount these problems, Pennebaker had taken to adapting his equipment and inventing new devices, including a new sound-synching system that revolutionised the process of documentary filming. "Even the Russians approached me, wanting to know if I'd design a camera for them," he reveals, "but I decided I didn't want to get stuck manufacturing cameras, and declined." For the camera he used to make *Dont Look Back*, Pennebaker installed a new, quieter motor, and replaced the metal gearing with lighter nylon cogs, primarily to minimise the damage they caused to the film. The camera weighed between 10 and 15lbs, but was made heavier by the custom-built 10:150 lens. Pennebaker carried three loaded magazines, each holding ten minutes' worth of film, and using stock that could cope with low light levels, he was able to film relatively unobtrusively, capturing magical moments on the fly, without using lights.

"The advantage of making a film this way," he explains, "with no script and no idea of what's coming next, is that you see things the way you see them in a theatre for the first time, and if they interest you, you follow them, and if they don't, you lag away from them. What comes out is what was interesting to you at that time. You know you're going to miss 90 per cent. But 10 per cent of something nobody had got any of before seemed not bad."

Capturing Dylan on the cusp of his folk and rock periods, the result is a witty, informative and endlessly fascinating portrayal of a star in several kinds of metamorphoses – from folk to rock, from idol to icon – and feeling the constraints of mass adulation whilst gradually realising the kind of power he could come to wield because of it. Other celebrities – Ginsberg, Marianne Faithfull, John Mayall, Dana Gillespie and, in the new scenes, Nico – are glimpsed in passing, sitting in hotel rooms, limousines and dressing-rooms. Joan Baez, with whom Dylan had just finished a ten-date American tour, and was in the process of concluding an affair, hangs around for the first half of the film, clearly unaware that Bob's attentions had moved on, and unsettled by his declining interest in her. There's an amusing running joke about Donovan, Britain's ersatz Dylan clone, climaxing in Dylan's pointed delivery, during an after-hours sing-song, of the lines "The vagabond who's rapping at your door/Is standing in the clothes that you once wore", at which poor Donovan visibly withers; hilarious but poignant shots of a roaring-drunk Alan Price opening a bottle of Newcastle Brown on a backstage piano at the Royal Albert Hall; revealing scenes of Dylan losing his temper with a hotel roomful of hangers-on; berating a hapless journalist from *Time* magazine who doesn't realise he's getting the payback for an earlier *Time* piece that had infuriated the singer; and most revealing of all, perhaps, a lengthy scene involving Albert Grossman and British promoter Tito Burns stretching the definition of business ethics whilst negotiating with TV companies.

"They didn't care that we shot it," says Pennebaker. "It was like, 'We're all on the same side'. Tito really loved his role in this film. I thought he'd want to kill me, but whenever I would see him, he would always laugh, pat me on the back and say, 'You made me a movie star!' They don't see themselves as villains at all, they see themselves as smart, aggressive people."

Likewise with Dylan, "What you see is what you get," claims Pennebaker. "And for everybody I know who says, 'You really savaged that bastard', somebody else says, 'God, he's wonderful'. It's clear that people see what they set out to see. And I'm no different – I guess I tried to make that film as true to my vision of him as I could make it. But as a storyteller, I wanted there to be stories in it."

Pennebaker was aided in this regard by Bob Neuwirth, a singer and painter whom Dylan had met and bonded with at the Indian Neck Folk Festival, and who served as his tour manager. Neuwirth had proved himself Dylan's equal in droll acerbity – he's the one who jokes, "Joan's wearing one of those see-through blouses you don't even want to!" – and he clearly saw part of his job as providing entertaining moments for the camera.

"Bobby Neuwirth understood instantly the theatre of what we were doing," says Pennebaker. "Without saying anything, he would construct 'scenes' that worked." Dylan and Neuwirth were instinctively aware that, despite it being a documentary, the film was just as much a performance as Dylan's nightly steps to the stage – a short journey that Neuwirth likens to a matador preparing to meet the bull. Merely by being in the same room, the camera transformed reality into a performance, which made Pennebaker's job – his rôle, if you like – all the more difficult.

"You didn't try to look bland," he recalls. "You had to take part in their lives, in a way that didn't appear false. So if they told a funny story, you could laugh at it, or tell one of your own. But it had to fit, and if it didn't, they'd call you on it, and throw you out of the room."

Pennebaker's favourite moments in the film are the small, seemingly insignificant details that you probably wouldn't notice unless you too had watched the scenes hundreds of times in the editing room – the way that Dylan provides the perfect full stop to a scene by lighting a cigarette and looking out of a limo window, or the way a protective Bob Neuwirth nonchalantly pushes Dylan back into the safety of his room during a contretemps with management in a hotel corridor. "They catch my eye, like a little jewel sewn into the rough sandals of the poor old beggar," says the film-maker.

As for what he might have revealed about Dylan, Pennebaker regards such matters with equanimity. "If you had gone along instead of me, would you have figured out much about Dylan?" he asks, rhetorically. "It's the process of being there that's interesting. The one sure thing in life is that you never know what's going on in somebody's head. That's what the novel was invented for. You can't point a camera at someone and find out what's in their head. But it does the next best thing: it lets you speculate. People can walk into a room and decide who they're going to like and who they're going to hate, and do it in a second; and I think in a sense that's what the camera's doing with Dylan, and that's probably the best you can hope for." Nowadays, of course, *Dont Look Back* has become the textbook for rock films, its pioneering "rockumentary" approach emulated by dolts like Metallica, and parodied in *This is Spinal Tap*, both of which movies doubtless cost far more than the $10,000 of film stock used by Pennebaker. But it's impossible to imagine another rock documentary having anything like the impact of *Dont Look Back*. For despite the far greater commercial reach of modern showbiz, none of today's stars *matters* in a way that he did back then – when, despite rarely being heard on the radio, Dylan became a global icon simply because his art was so revolutionary, scouring away the trappings of showbiz to reveal something so grippingly authentic it exerted an almost mesmeric hold on a generation, in the process decisively changing the direction of western culture.

"It's impossible to imagine, from this perspective, the impact these songs had," says Bob Neuwirth. "These issues simply weren't dealt with anywhere, outside maybe the union hall. They changed the course of music forever."

Dylan's appearance at the 1964 Newport Folk Festival had occasioned a little controversy in the form of his unveiling of the non-political songs that would appear two weeks later on Another Side of Bob Dylan. *Complained the editor of folk bible* Sing Out!, *"You seem to be in a different kind of bag now, Bob – and I'm worried about it." However, Dylan had at least played unaccompanied that day. When he took to Newport's stage in 1965, he had a Fender Telecaster strapped across his chest, wore a leather jacket and was backed by a full band. What followed marked a turning point. Dylan's effective declaration that the electric side of* Bringing It All Back Home *and his new single 'Like a Rolling Stone' (released five days before the festival) were not aberrations created fury amongst both festival organisers and (despite Al Kooper's denials in Johnny Black's evocative feature below) the crowd. This, though, was only the beginning of the furore.*

EYEWITNESS: BOB DYLAN GOES ELECTRIC AT THE NEWPORT FOLK FESTIVAL

By Johnny Black

First published in *Q*, Dec 1999

FIRST DAY: 24 JULY 1965

Joe Boyd (production manager, Newport Festival): The 1965 Folk Festival came at a time when, on the radio, you were hearing 'I Got You Babe' by Sonny & Cher, which was obviously a Dylan rip-off, The Byrds singing 'Mr. Tambourine Man'. There was something happening. Things were changing ...

Donovan: It was my first big festival ... the audience were in Bermuda shorts and bobbysocks and short hair. I mean, it hadn't happened yet. This was a middle-class folk audience, what I would call "folk purists", who came to hear what they wanted to hear and that's all they wanted to hear.

Joe Boyd: There had been a lot of pressure from Peter Yarrow [of Peter, Paul and Mary] on adding the Paul Butterfield Blues Band to the line-up of the festival. He really put a lot of pressure on the other members of the board to get the invitation, and [board member Alan] Lomax was really against it. Against Butterfield, against white boys doing the blues, really.

Al Kooper (organist): I didn't go to the '65 Newport Folk Festival with Dylan. I went as a regular person who always just bought tickets and went. But Albert Grossman, his manager, saw me walking around and said, "Hey, Bob is looking for you." And so he gave me passes and I sold my tickets. Evidently they'd been calling my house, but I'd already left.

Jonathan Taplin (roadie, Bob Dylan): Grossman, upon hearing that Bob wanted to play electric, hastily put a band together. And the only guys who had electric instruments were Butterfield's band.

Joe Boyd: The performers did what they called workshops during the day, just small performances on the small stages around the grounds. Dylan, of course, was scheduled to sing in the Songwriters' Workshop. This year, the crowd around the Songwriter's Workshop was so immense that it was swamping the other workshops . . . and the officials were starting to get tense . . . Dylan's appearance, his manner, the songs he sang at the workshop, everything added to their disquiet.

Jac Holzman (founder, Elektra Records): The second segment of the workshop was slated to be white urban blues, featuring the Butterfield Band. Due to the amazing sales of 'Born in Chicago' on the Elektra sampler, and the buzz that went with it, I had arranged for them to perform at Newport. Albert Grossman, manager of Dylan and Peter, Paul and Mary, was in full hover over them as future clients.

Michael Bloomfield (guitarist, Butterfield Blues Band): What we played was music that was entirely indigenous to the neighbour-hood, to the city we grew up in. There was no doubt in my mind that this was folk music; this was what I heard on the streets of my city, out the windows, on radio stations and jukeboxes in Chicago and all throughout the South, and it was what people listened to. And that's what folk art meant to me – what people listened to.

Joe Boyd: Lomax was forced to introduce the Butterfield Blues Band at the Blues Workshop, and he gave them an introduction which was very condescending. As the group started to take to the stage, Lomax came off to be confronted by Grossman who, basically, said unkind words about the introduction Lomax had just given. Lomax pushed him aside and said, "Out of my way, Grossman." And the next thing you know is these two men, both rather over-sized, were rolling around in the dirt throwing punches. They had to be pulled apart. Lomax then called an emergency meeting of the board of the festival that night . . . the board actually voted in favour of banning Grossman from the grounds of the festival. George Wein, who was a non-voting advisor to the board, had to step in and say, "Look, I don't have a vote, it's up to you, but I can tell you right now that if you do bar Grossman, you have to prepare yourselves for the walk-out of Bob Dylan, Peter, Paul and Mary, and Buffy Sainte-Marie." So the board dropped the action against Grossman, but there was obviously a tremendous simmering of feeling.

Al Kooper: Me and Bob and the Butterfield Blues Band rehearsed through the night in the living room of some million-aire's mansion in Newport.

Michael Bloomfield: Kooper, me, Barry [Goldberg, organist], and this schwartze Jerome from the Butterfield Band playing bass . . . and he's fucking up on everything . . . and it's sounding horrible and finally, it's time for the gig and Barry and me are throwing up in these outhouses.

Al Kooper: By the time we went to bed at sunrise, we had three songs down.

SECOND DAY: 25 JULY 1965

Jonathan Taplin: We kicked everybody out of the stadium and did a short soundcheck.

Joe Boyd: I said, "How many songs are you going to do?" And they – Butterfield, Bloomfield and Dylan – looked at each other and said, "Well, we only know three, so that's what we're going to do."

Pete Seeger (folk singer): It wasn't a real soundcheck. They were tinkering around with it and all they knew was, "Turn the sound up. Turn the sound up!" They wanted to get volume.

Joe Boyd: Dylan wasn't on at the end of the concert. He was on in the middle. He was on one act before the interval, at around 9:15.

Liam Clancy (folk performer): Dylan came out, and it was obvious that he was stoned, bobbing around the stage, very Chaplinesque actually.

Joe Boyd: . . . and when that first note of 'Maggie's Farm' hit – I mean, by today's standards it wasn't very loud, but by those standards of the day – it was the loudest thing anybody had ever heard. The volume. That was the thing – the volume. It wasn't just the music, it was just the fact that he came out and played with an electric band.

Al Kooper: In 'Maggie's Farm', the beat got turned around so, instead of playing on two and four, [drummer] Sam Lay was playing on one and three. That's an accident that can happen, and it happened, so it was sort of a disaster. I got lost myself.

Joe Boyd: I was lapping it all up. Somebody pulled at my elbow and said, "You'd better go backstage. They want to talk to you."

Jac Holzman: Backstage, an un-civil war had broken out. Alan Lomax was bellowing that this was a folk festival, you didn't have amplified instruments . . .

Paul Rothchild: . . . the old guard, George Wein, Alan Lomax, Pete Seeger. Pete, pacifist Pete, with an axe! "I'm going to cut the cables!"

Joe Boyd: So I went backstage and there I was confronted by Seeger and Lomax and, I think, Theodore Bikel or somebody, saying, "It's too loud. You've got to turn it down. It's far too loud." I said, "Well, I don't control the sound. The sound is out there in the middle of the audience." And so Lomax said, "How do you get there? I'll go out there." I said, "Well, Alan, you walk right to the back – it's only about half a mile – and then you walk around to the centre, show your badge, and just come down the centre aisle." And he said, "There must be a quicker way." So I said, "Well, you can climb over the fence." I was looking at his girth, you know? And he said, "Now, look, you go out there . . . and tell them that the board orders them to turn the sound down." I said, "OK."

Ric Von Schmidt (folk singer): Whoever was controlling the mikes messed it up. You couldn't hear Dylan. It looked like he was singing with the volume off. We were sitting in the press section, maybe thirty yards back, and yelling, "Can't hear ya" and "Cut the band down". Then they went into the next song and no one had changed any dials. It was the same thing, no voice coming through at all.

Al Kooper: They booed. There's no doubt about the fact that they booed . . . What was I thinking at the time? I was thinking we weren't playing too good.

Joe Boyd: There was Grossman and Neuwirth and Yarrow and Rothschild all sitting at the sound desk, grinning, very pleased with themselves and, meanwhile, the audience was going nuts. There were arguments between people sitting next to each other . . . I relayed Lomax's message and Peter Yarrow said, "Tell Alan Lomax . . ." and extended his middle finger. And I said, "Come on, Peter, gimme a break." He said, "Well, just tell Alan that the board of the festival are adequately represented on the sound console and that we have things fully under control and we think that the sound is at the correct level." So I went back . . . and was confronted by Lomax and Bikel again, frothing at the mouth, and I relayed Yarrow's message and they just cursed and gnashed their teeth. By this time, the thing was almost over.

Jonathan Taplin: Bob was getting booed and he walked off.

Bob Dylan: I did this very crazy thing. I didn't know what was going to happen, but they certainly booed. I'll tell you that. You could hear it all over the place.

Al Kooper: A large part of that crowd had come especially to see Dylan. Some had travelled thousands of miles and paid a lot of money for tickets and what did they get? Three songs, and one of those was a mess. They didn't give a shit about us being electric. They just wanted more.

Joe Boyd: Dylan was hiding in a tent. Grossman didn't want to get involved. He wasn't going to bully Dylan about it.

Michael Bloomfield: He looked real shook up.

Jonathan Taplin: I saw Dylan backstage from a little bit of a distance, and he seemed to be crying.

Al Kooper: I was standing right next to Bob backstage, and not only was he not crying, he was feeling good about having played electric. He was happy. That's when Peter Yarrow came up and handed him an acoustic guitar, because the set was so short he just felt there should be more.

Joe Boyd: Anyway, finally, Dylan stumbled back out on stage with an acoustic guitar . . .

Jonathan Taplin: He says, "Does anybody have a D harmonica?" And all these harmonicas were being thrown from the audience.

Liam Clancy: He broke into that 'Tambourine Man' and I found myself standing there with tears streaming down my face, because – I saw the butterfly emerging from the caterpillar . . . I suddenly realised that this kid who had bugged us so often, had emerged into a very major artist.

Jonathan Taplin: The audience thought they'd won. Here was Dylan, no band, back into acoustic folk stuff. And then he sang 'It's All Over Now, Baby Blue' and walked off.

Michael Bloomfield: The next night, he was at this party, and he's sitting next to this girl and her husband and he's got his hand right up her pussy, right next to her husband, and she's letting him do this, and her husband's going crazy, so Dylan seemed quite untouched by it the next day.

Thanks: John Bauldie, Gavan Daws, Jac Holzman.

HIGHWAY 61 REVISITED

By Sean Egan

US release: 30 August 1965
Produced by: Tom Wilson/Bob Johnston
CHARTS: US#3; UK#4

SIDE ONE
Like a Rolling Stone
Tombstone Blues
It Takes a Lot to Laugh, It Takes a Train to Cry
From a Buick 6
Ballad of a Thin Man

SIDE TWO
Queen Jane Approximately
Highway 61 Revisited
Just Like Tom Thumb's Blues
Desolation Row

Newport seems to have crystallised the backlash against Dylan
for deserting folk and "selling-out", serving as a more immediate focal point for ex-fans' anger than the reports that had
filtered back from Britain two months previously that on his
short tour there he was singing stuff like 'The Times They Are
A-Changin' '. Such protest material had been dropped from his
set Stateside, but any qualms Dylan had about it not representing where he was "at" now had apparently been shunted aside so
as to capitalise on the Brits' out-of-date image of him. Both
'Subterranean Homesick Blues' and a belatedly released 'The
Times They Are A-Changin' ' became British UK Top 10 hits
for Dylan on the back of said tour. Dylan seemed to be a man
unashamedly on the make. Hatred and hostility toward Dylan
would be manifested in the ceaseless booing that accompanied

his concerts when he introduced an electric second set in them at Forest Hills in August 1965 and would reach its climax when an audience member shouted "Judas!" at him in Manchester in May 1966. The left who wanted the world changed were deeply conservative when it came to Dylan's music. However, the folkies, the radicals and anyone else who didn't like Dylan – and many pop and rock fans didn't: his voice took some getting used to – were trying to hold back an unstoppable tide. 1965 was Bob Dylan's year. Everywhere you went, there were songs blaring from transistors and televisions that were either performed by Dylan, written by Dylan or inspired by him.

In the autumn, The Turtles had a US Top 10 with a cover of 'It Ain't Me, Babe'. In the UK, Joan Baez just missed the Top 20 with 'It's All Over Now, Baby Blue'. Towards the end of the year, The Four Seasons just missed the US Top 10 with 'Don't Think Twice, It's All Right' under the pseudonym The Wonder Who? Cher made the UK Top 10 and the US Top 20 with 'All I Really Want to Do'. Manfred Mann had a UK No.2 with 'If You Gotta Go, Go Now', starting a tradition of covering Dylan songs published but not released by the artist, one continued in the UK at the end of the year by Baez with 'Farewell, Angelina'. The way 'If You Gotta Go, Go Now' delights in its own daring by mentioning that young men and women have – gasp! – premarital sex has dated it, but at the time its risqué nature was, like Dylan per se, cutting-edge. An artist of a previous generation, Johnny Cash, conferred his seal of approval on Dylan by covering three of his songs on his album *Orange Blossom Special*, including the unreleased 'Mama, You Been on My Mind'. There were many, many other Dylan covers that year, as acts scrambled to shower themselves with the gold dust perceived to reside in his songs, not just in terms of their commercial potential but in the fact that Dylan was the hottest/coolest artist in the world. The biggie was The Byrds' 'Mr. Tambourine Man', a transatlantic No.1 that summer. Unlike the fairly unimaginative Peter, Paul and Mary covers, The Byrds brought something of their own to the party; it remains a classic, transcendent record. That The Byrds were five long-haired, Cuban-heeled, good-looking young men – appearing for all the world like America's equivalent of The Beatles – singing the surrealistic songs of a man

who'd made his name as a folk singer and social radical, helped
create a new concept: folk-rock. This was not a meaningless and
pedantic designation of a sub-genre as happens frequently today
in dance music but an acknowledgment that barriers between
music styles and audiences previously thought immovable were
being torn asunder.

Additionally, that Dylan had created a new vernacular in
popular music was apparent at every turn. An entire generation
of recording artists seemed suddenly to have adopted Dylan's
vocabulary, his expansive lyrical frame of reference, his sneer,
his put-down style, his questioning of tradition and his ambiva-
lent attitude toward romance. These were all novel things at the
time, even his belligerence operating on a higher intellectual
plane than the traditional greaseball snottiness of Elvis and other
classic rockers. The spring saw Simon & Garfunkel secure a US
No.1 with 'The Sounds of Silence', the type of tortured and
poetic rumination unthinkable in pop before Dylan's example.
Sonny & Cher had a transatlantic No.1 in late summer 1965
with 'I Got You Babe', a song you'd swear was written by Dylan,
what with its elongated melody line, groaning vocal and use of
Dylan quasi-trademark "babe", but in fact was merely an example of the sincerest form of flattery. As was 'Eve of Destruction'
by Barry McGuire, written by P. F. Sloan, a pastiche of Dylan's
protest style (though with a rock backing) right down to its
dropped "g"s. Its scattershot denunciation of injustice struck a
chord with a public who sent it to No.3 in the UK and No.1 in
the USA. Britain's Donovan was a Dylan *manqué* (guitar,
harmonica, cap and protest) and his own composition 'Catch
the Wind', UK Top Five in 1965, was a mix of 'Chimes of
Freedom' and 'Blowin' in the Wind'. Donovan had another hit
with a cover of Buffy Saint-Marie's 'Universal Soldier', itself a
blend of 'Masters of War' and 'Blowin' in the Wind'.

The belligerence that Dylan had made fashionable informed
even '(I Can't Get No) Satisfaction' by The Rolling Stones,
whose ambience of dissension was something else unthinkable
without Dylan's example, even if musically it was the Stones'
own brilliant template. Even the mighty Beatles weren't too
grand to doff the cap: their 'You've Got to Hide Your Love Away'
from their august album *Help!* had a colloquialism, harmonica

style, stretched melody and bellyaching tone that fans of Dylan found very familiar. To some extent, the Fab Four extended that sound across an entire album in the shape of December's *Rubber Soul*, albeit refracted through their own undisputed musical genius.

The permission that Dylan's example had given rock/pop as well as folk artists to tackle any subject imaginable was only intensified by the fact that 1965 was the year he released the greatest album ever made. As the rock era was still in its first decade, that achievement was *relatively* easy at the time. Nearly half a century later, though, *Highway 61 Revisited* continues to be the greatest album ever made.

On the (again beautiful) album cover, Dylan looks like a rock star. Sitting on a low step, the wraparound shades he had taken to wearing are clutched in a hand and his once unkempt hair is more stylised and fashionably abundant. Over a motorcycle T-shirt he is wearing something flash and multicoloured that could even be a blouse. His squinting eyes are gazing with a mixture of disinterest and hostility directly at the camera lens. Many a rocker, before and after, adopted such accoutrements and such a pose. But this rocker was not one who simply embraced the clichés, conventions and attitudes of rock 'n' roll, much as he had always loved them. The contents of this record showed that, rather, Dylan was shaping rock to his own devices – giving it a brain to add to the heart, soul and guts it had always possessed.

He had given notice with 'Like a Rolling Stone', the album's first track but already released on 45. It's far more difficult to pronounce a single the greatest ever released than it is an album: because they are individual songs, one's perception of them is far more dependent on one's mood than is the case with an album, the multiple cuts of which provide a greater variety of tone. However, not many people would be prepared to enter into anything more than a half-hearted argument with you if you stated that 'Like a Rolling Stone' sat atop the pile of history's greatest singles.

'Like a Rolling Stone' is a six-minute-long diatribe – a concoction comprised of mostly street vernacular ("You thought they were all kiddin' you") but which doesn't preclude poetic phraseology ("You never turned around/To see the frowns/On the jugglers and the clowns/When they all did tricks for you") – that could be about Dylan's rumoured lover Edie Sedgwick, about his folkie ex-friends, his road manager Bobby Neuwirth or even Dylan himself. More germane to its power is the fact that it features the type of hate never heard on the charts before. Because popular song was preoccupied with romantic love, hurt and disdain were certainly part of its make-up, but never this sort of venom. Dylan is literally jeering at the downfall of a once high-and-mighty person – and the climate of the time made it especially shocking that the person concerned seemed to be identified via his "babe"s as female. This figure – once inclined to laugh at the unfortunate, now not disposed to talk so loud or seem so proud and reduced (it is implied) to prostitution – receives no sympathy from this man who had written so many songs expressing concern for the socially and financially dispossessed. Instead, as the melody rises into a crescendo at the start of each chorus, Dylan howls at her, "How does it *feel*?" It is hair-raising.

It's difficult to judge whether the music behind Dylan – churning, circular instrumentation – is fantastic by design or fluke. The band was comprised of veterans of *Bringing It All Back Home*, except stinging blues guitarist Michael Bloomfield – a direct Dylan recruit – and Al Kooper. Kooper, a guitarist invited to observe the session by friend Tom Wilson, snuck on to the vacant organ, an instrument he had never played before outside of demos of his own songs. Dylan liked the sound he made and demanded it be mixed up, thus giving the song one of its signature sounds. The record opens with a lapel-grabbing crack on the snare drum – famously described by Bruce Springsteen as ". . . like somebody'd kicked open the door to your mind" – but in actuality sticksman Bobby Gregg's edited count-in. Meanwhile, there is an extraordinary moment in the record in the last chorus where everything unexpectedly plunges and halts; the effect it has on the listener is – deliciously – like leaving your stomach behind when going over a hill in a car. What's not a matter of happenstance or unintended consequence is Dylan's singing, which is awe-inspiringly intense.

Columbia refused to release a record that was twice as long as the average chart single. Dylan insisted it not be cut. The stand-off ended when an acetate was given to a New York disco that was a media haunt, prompting radio stations to request the record for broadcast purposes. The label acquiesced to the release, although made sure radio stations had access to a cut-down promotional copy of the single should they wish to play that. Most didn't. The single made No.4 in the UK, and though *Billboard*-centric history records that it was kept off the top of the American charts by The Beatles' 'Help!', it actually made No.1 in *Cash Box*.

It was Tom Wilson's last production for Dylan. A disagreement of some kind between the two caused Dylan to switch to a Nashville-based Columbia staff producer named Bob Johnston, a jolly country boy who may have seemed an incongruous choice for a lacerating, urbanised character like Dylan but whose wide-screen aural imprint clearly pleased his fellow Bob, who would use him for the next five years.

Once recording of the album resumed after the Newport festival, Kooper, Bloomfield and Gregg were the nucleus of the musicians used on the album, with Dylan mixing and matching other musicians according to the songs and/or their availability.

If the folkies were still illogically convinced that Dylan had by definition lost his edge by going rock, they were put right by 'Tombstone Blues'. In the lyric of this relentless, rolling, thunderous creation Dylan depicts John the Baptist vomiting after torturing a thief on the orders of the "commander-in-chief". Even if God and John the Baptist are metaphors for the US president and his military men, it was shockingly blasphemous language for the time, especially in Dylan's homeland. A denunciation of militarism, social inequality and the outrages perpetrated in the name of religion – with references to venereal disease tossed into the brew – it is, yet again, unlike anything ever heard before in rock. Dylan now seemed to fully understand that the band could contribute to the soundscape he was creating instead of being servants of it, meaning that his switch to rock had an aesthetic validity, rather than being merely a cultural statement.

That the lyrical indelicacies and scornful worldview of 'Tombstone Blues' did not preclude sensitivity in the artist's mindset, nor its powerhouse sound rule out subtlety in his music, was immediately proven by 'It Takes a Lot to Laugh, It Takes a Train to Cry'. (Even Dylan's very titles were now pleasing in and of themselves, if incompletely unfathomable.) It's the first and still one of the few Dylan tracks that can be described as impressionistic, its effect dependent more on its ambience than its lyric, even though the latter – a touching, laid-back celebration of the joys of being in love – is plenty good and is delivered with wonderful husky vulnerability by Dylan. Over four leisurely minutes, Dylan and the band enjoy themselves, getting into a groove in which Dylan's harmonica roams in and out at will, and does so magnificently. When Dylan moved over to rock, he could easily have stopped using an instrument that had previously been crucial to add colour and variety to a very basic sound. At this very point in time, contemporaries gifted on the instrument like Lennon, Jagger and Brian Jones were audibly losing interest in it. That Dylan retained it despite now having full bands to help fill in his vision gave him a unique sound in the rock world – he would use it where normally a guitar or keyboard solo would reside on a rock record. Exquisite on every level, this track should be played to silence anyone who claims that Dylan can neither sing nor play harmonica.

'From a Buick 6' is one of the slighter cuts, its generic chugging blues lick making it sound like it belongs more on *Bringing It All Back Home* than here. However, the sweeps of organ and Dylan's harassed lyric – he needs a steam shovel, mama, to keep away the dead, apparently – makes it no less than palatable. 'Ballad of a Thin Man' has bequeathed one of the most famous Dylan lines of all time: "Something is happening here but you don't know what it is, do you Mr. Jones?" Many have assumed that the song is simply Dylan's equivalent of The Kinks' 'Well Respected Man' or The Jam's 'Mr. Clean' – and one journalist named Jeffrey Jones claimed it was written as a put-down of him after he was assigned to write a feature whose central point was Dylan's harmonica work – but people should know better than to assume that a mind like this artist's would stoop to a self-righteous denunciation of a straight/square/conservative. If anything, the lyric sounds like the tale of a straight in a different sense – a heterosexual who stumbles on a gay party, especially in the line, "The sword swallower comes up to you and then he kneels." Similar homosexual references litter Dylan's work, and one Dylanologist – Craig McGregor – has even opined that there is something approaching a conspiracy of silence about this fact. The sultry, oppressive atmosphere created by the music and production perfectly complements the concept of being a stranger in a strange land, with a piano that sounds like the tolling of doom and with Dylan's vocal track sublimely mixed up to make it feel like he is directly in front of the listener's face. Just to make the track perfection, Dylan endearingly almost breaks into laughter on the line "You try so hard but you don't understand . . ."

Proving that his craft continues to deepen, 'Ballad of a Thin Man' is the first Dylan track with a proper bridge, an elongated, suspense-building affair. A similar measure of his development is the fact that trad-spotters were unable to cite any public-domain antecedents to the melodies on this album. Though his magpie tendencies continued to be evident in his lyrics (Kerouac allusions and lifts dot these songs), Dylan was learning to write his own tunes at last.

Side two introduces us to 'Queen Jane Approximately'. One doesn't wish to delve too far into interpreting Dylan's songs for fear of making a fool of oneself by barking up the wrong tree, but surely in verse four the advisers heaving Jane's plastic at her feet to convince her of her pain and convince her that her conclusions should be more drastic are, in fact, the folkies and radicals gesticulating to Dylan's protest records and telling him they were the genuine article and his true wont – therefore making Jane Dylan? There also seems to be a lot of homosexual allusion in the following verse, unless all the stuff about bandits and turning other cheeks is metaphor rather than nudge-nudge. But endlessly absorbing and debatable though the lyric is, these days there is more than just the words to occupy oneself with. When the opening rippling guitar figure is joined by a quick-stepping piano pattern which is then quickly augmented by washes of organ, we are transported places that one-man-and-a-guitar never could have taken us, and when just before the last line of each verse – "Won't you come see me Queen Jane?" – Dylan leaves a gap for a sun-splash guitar arpeggio from Bloomfield, he is unselfishly and ostentatiously acknowledging that fact.

The title track refers to the motorway that goes through Dylan's Minnesota home town but what it has to do with God telling Abraham to kill him a son only to get the response from "Abe", "Man, you must be putting me on", only the artist will ever know. Whether the song's sacrilegious imagery and suggestive content is being employed to put down the setting of his formative years is not quite clear, but what is is the fact that this man has a sublime turn of phrase (has a failing business ever been better described than the venture of Mack the Finger who laments, "I got forty red, white and blue shoestrings/And a thousand telephones that don't ring"?), and brilliant delivery (it would be impossible for him to better convey the urgency and desperation in the line, "Sam said, 'Tell me *quick* man, I got to run" than the desperate way he enunciates it). The song's tempo is galloping and the track punctuated by the strains of a whistle.

Like 'Queen Jane', 'Just Like Tom Thumb's Blues' has a lyric depicting a less-than-blissful scenario floating on delightful, tranquil instrumentation. In this case, the words seem to trace the narrator's descent into a hell that seems related to drug and/or alcohol dependency, and while the precise meaning of lines like "The cops don't need you and, man, they expect the same" remain elusive, the colloquialism and memorable phraseology is once again extraordinary.

The album at this point is already approaching the forty-minute mark, the standard LP length for the era, but Dylan still has a trump card up his sleeve. Most of the album's tracks are in excess of five-and-a-half minutes but with 'Desolation Row' Dylan provides a closer that is well over eleven minutes. Amazingly, it never drags. Dylan tried an electric version of this number but in the end settled for an all-acoustic affair with his rhythm guitar and harmonica accompanied by the decoration of Charlie McCoy on additional guitar and (probably) Russ Savakus on stand-up bass. The inevitable futile attempts have been made to pinpoint a real-life source for the bleak locale, but Dylan is more likely using a notional slummy street as metaphor for the entire world. The song is unbelievably rich. Verse two is about Cinderella, who is accused of being easy but comfortably replies, "It takes one to know one." A character called Romeo comes into her place of work and lays claim to her, only to be told in no uncertain terms by a customer, "You're in the wrong place my friend, you'd better leave." Mayhem, it is implied, ensues: "And the only sound that's left after the ambulances go/ Is Cinderella sweeping up on Desolation Row." The scene-setting, poetry and poignancy are all flawless. It's like a great American short story, only one that rhymes and boasts a great tune and beautiful singing. There are nine other verses just as sublime. The sum is even greater than the constituent parts as Dylan's eyes rove piercingly across freaks, sadists, fortune tellers, has-beens, pious hypocrites, death squads and the heedlessly privileged and his pen summarises their sins pithily and pitilessly. Dylan's singing is world-weary but rises high at the yearning climax of each verse, and as usual he precedes the final verse with an excellent harmonica section. It is a tour de force that is really the only way he could have ended such a magnificent album.

The album's only black mark is the liner note from the artist, which is not merely the gnomic fare usual for his sleevenotes at that time but such gibberish as to barely be worth dragging one's eyes across.

There was one drawback to Dylan moving over to rock: it was a medium that, because he was only beginning to make it grow up, didn't have the means to give him his due. At the time, rock and pop journalism had none of the intellectual rigour to be found in folk-music magazines like *Broadside* and *Sing Out!* Aimed at teenagers and early-twenty-somethings – the only demographic it was assumed would be interested in such music – the pop magazines rarely rose above the banal or idiotic, as proven by the reception of Britain's weekly *Record Mirror* to 'Like a Rolling Stone': "The monotonous melody line and Dylan's expressionless intoning just cannot hold the interest for what seems like the six longest minutes since the invention of time." Today, in the wake of the late-Sixties advent of serious rock critique, the musical and sociological milestone that *Highway 61 Revisited* constituted is widely acknowledged. At the time, it was released into something of a critical vacuum.

Following up Highway 61 Revisited *was a tall order. Though opinions divide amongst Dylan fans as to whether* Highway 61 *or* Blonde on Blonde *is his greatest work, nobody disputes that with the latter album Dylan rose to that tall order quite spectacularly. Johnny Black spoke to some of the album's principals for this examination of a work that was implausibly in the same ballpark as its predecessor.*

VINYL ICON – BLONDE ON BLONDE

By Johnny Black

First published in *Hi Fi News*, January 2010

Nashville, Tennessee, lies 750 miles south-west of Bob Dylan's first stomping ground, New York City. It's just a two-hour plane ride but, when Dylan flew down in February 1966 to record what would become his masterpiece, *Blonde on Blonde*, the two cities were worlds apart.

"Anybody you ask will say that Nashville began when Dylan came down here. That's the way I feel about it, too," states Bob Johnston, who produced not just six Bob Dylan albums but also classics by Simon & Garfunkel, Leonard Cohen, Johnny Cash and too many more to mention. "Nashville was a different place before that. The producers and record people ran the business with an iron fist. They did what *they* wanted to, and the artist was at their beck and call." Dylan and Johnston turned that relationship on its head.

"We didn't know who Bob Dylan was," admits guitarist Wayne Moss, one of the hot Nashville sessioneers whose astonishing instrumental dexterity elevated *Blonde on Blonde* from what everybody was hoping for – Dylan's best album yet – into one of the greatest albums in the entire rock canon. Indeed, many critics now feel that the recordings Dylan and Johnston made together produced the very first albums that could be described with just that one word – rock.

Originally, in the early 1960s, Dylan had been hailed as the saviour of folk music, but then The Byrds gave him his first American No.1 single in June 1965 with their jangling cover of his song 'Mr. Tambourine Man', which turned him on to the potential of the folk-rock blend.

The Dylan/Johnston collaboration meshed perfectly on Dylan's first completely electric album *Highway 61 Revisited*. However, when they re-convened in Columbia Studio A in New York City on November 30, 1965, the magic seemed to have dissipated. Fourteen takes of Dylan's lengthy opus 'Visions of Johanna' were laid down but none were deemed usable.

A successful take of the sardonic 'One of Us Must Know (Sooner or Later)' was recorded on the 25th, but the next four sessions were all either cancelled or unfruitful.

Johnston, however, wasn't ready to throw in the towel. "I had recorded quite a few sessions in Nashville," he points out, "and I knew that the players I used down there would be great for cutting Dylan's songs." Dylan was initially sceptical, but on February 14 the first session began in Columbia's Nashville studio on Music Row.

Dylan's favoured organist, Al Kooper, was then touring with his band The Blues Project, so he flew down from Columbus, Ohio. "Bob had both me and Robbie Robertson [of The Band] on those sessions, to increase his comfort zone," explains Kooper, "because we had both worked with him in New York." Two additional guitarists, Jerry Kennedy and Joe South, converged on Nashville from Miami and Atlanta respectively.

The core of the studio musicians, however, were all local Nashville hotshots. "Bob Johnston had used us on many sessions before Dylan," explains Wayne Moss. "Charlie McCoy played bass and trumpet and was the leader of the band. We had Kenneth Buttrey, the world's greatest drummer, and Hargus Robbins, the blind piano player."

Although Robbie Robertson had worked with Dylan before, he felt a need to prove himself to the Nashville elite. "It was very clique-ish. The musicians that played on sessions there didn't like outsiders coming in . . . it was kind of like, 'What do we need him for?'"

It wasn't until he contributed the impressive bluesy licks on 'Obviously 5 Believers' that he felt he had won them over. "I was doing something that none of them did, so I don't think they felt I was treading on their territory."

Kooper too felt intimidated by just how far ahead of him the Nashville sessioneers were as players. "In 'I Want You', for instance, I had the opening guitar lick in my head and Wayne Moss came up with that amazing sixteenth note run that comes out of it later. I almost fell off the chair when he did that. Nobody in New York could have done that, or even have thought of doing that."

Equally, of course, it's unlikely that anybody in Nashville would ever have come up with the strategy Dylan advanced for the recording of 'Rainy Day Women #12 & 35' – to get the band as drunk as possible before starting.

Henry Strzelecki, appointed to play bass, became so pie-eyed he couldn't stand up. "Or even sit up," notes Moss. It was all he could do to lie on the floor and play the bass pedals on the organ with his hands, while Moss took over on bass guitar.

Unsurprisingly, the playing on 'Rainy Day Women' leaves something to be desired, but Dylan undeniably achieved his aim of creating the atmosphere of a crazed party, with music supplied by a Salvation Army band.

Nor was this the only time Dylan's working methods proved completely alien to the Nashvillians. "We'd never worked with anybody who didn't have all their songs written before they came to the studio," points out Moss, who was stunned when Dylan cut short a session for 'Sad Eyed Lady of the Lowlands' just minutes after they had begun to work on the lyric. "He told us to take a break at about two thirty, and didn't call us back until about 3 a.m. the next morning."

"Everybody else went down, played ping pong, got something to eat, went to sleep," remembers Johnston, "until Dylan came out and said, 'Hey, I got that song finished. Is anybody around?' I went and got everybody up. Dylan says, 'Well, it goes like this . . . G, C, B, dah de dah de dah . . . and he walked away. And all these guys, they didn't know what to do. I said, 'Play. Don't stop. Just keep playin'.'"

Eleven minutes later, it was done. "We played it back and nobody could believe it, because they knew that their lives had changed, Nashville had changed and music had changed."

It's widely agreed that Dylan's wife at the time, Sara Lownds, was his muse for the epic 'Sad Eyed Lady'. The jury remains out, however, on the inspiration for the album's next-longest song, 'Visions of Johanna', although Dylan's mentor, friend and sometime lover, Joan Baez, is the likeliest candidate.

The subject of 'Just Like a Woman' is usually assumed to be former Boston debutante turned Andy Warhol superstar Edie Sedgwick, with whom Dylan had enjoyed a brief friendship.

One song that evidently existed for some while before Dylan went to Nashville was '4th Time Around'. Al Kooper, who knew Dylan had played it to The Beatles, told me that he asked, "if they'd remarked on how similar it sounded to 'Norwegian Wood', and he said, 'When I played it to them, there was no 'Norwegian Wood'.'"

Whether it was Bob Johnston, Nashville, the musicians, or some inexplicable combination of all three, Dylan was spurred into an astonishingly prolific burst of creativity because *Blonde on Blonde* turned out to be not just a great album, but a great double album. As Dylan himself later acknowledged, "At the time of *Blonde on Blonde*, I was going at a tremendous speed."

Rock's first double album hit the streets on 16 May 1966 (believe it or not, the same day as The Beach Boys' *Pet Sounds*) and, although it never rose above nine in America and narrowly missed the top slot over here, the ripples began spreading immediately. Wordsmiths around the world used *Blonde on Blonde* as the spur for their own lyrical flights of fancy; the shift from a market dominated by singles to one dominated by albums was now inevitable, and Dylan's union of rock and country would lead to artists beginning to break down the stylistic divisions that had kept them locked down for so long.

"To me, Dylan was one of that tiny handful of men that you could truly call a prophet," says Bob Johnston all these years later. "He wasn't just changing music, he was changing attitudes, changing our society. And I was able to help him."

BLONDE ON BLONDE

By Sean Egan

US release: 16 May 1966
Produced by: Bob Johnston
CHARTS: US#9; UK#3

SIDE ONE
Rainy Day Women #12 & 35
Pledging My Time
Visions of Johanna
One of Us Must Know (Sooner or Later)

SIDE TWO
I Want You
Stuck Inside of Mobile with the Memphis Blues Again
Leopard-Skin Pill-Box Hat
Just Like a Woman

SIDE THREE
Most Likely You Go Your Way (And I'll Go Mine)
Temporary Like Achilles
Absolutely Sweet Marie
4th Time Around
Obviously 5 Believers

SIDE FOUR
Sad Eyed Lady of the Lowlands

The three most influential rock artists of the Sixties – therefore three of the most influential socio-political figures of that decade – were The Beatles, The Rolling Stones and Bob Dylan. All three represented liberalism, colour and a sceptical attitude towards authority in an age when none of those things were common. Of the three, Dylan had the most influence on the development and widening of the boundaries of the rock medium by virtue of the higher sensibilities he brought to it. Dylan was also directly influential on those two aforementioned fellow recording acts and though it was a two-way street, it wasn't an equal exchange. As Dylan once famously said to Keith Richards, "I could have written 'Satisfaction' but you couldn't have written 'Mr. Tambourine Man'."

However, sales-wise, Dylan wasn't even in the same league as his British musical rivals and friends. Though Dylan's albums sold well enough to chart, they did not have a long retail tail, making their impact quickly and then commercially fading. Meanwhile, though "B. Dylan" in the parenthesis below a title on a record that played at 45rpm was something approaching a guarantor of chart success for several years – in 1966, Stevie Wonder took 'Blowin' in the Wind' into the US Top 10 yet again – Dylan was no hit-merchant himself. He never had a No.1 single off his own bat either side of the Atlantic and after 1966 only ever troubled the singles Top 10 in the UK or USA on two further occasions. If there ever had been an opportunity for Dylan to become a singles artist, it was in the months following the summer 1965 aesthetic and commercial double whammy of 'Like a Rolling Stone'. It was a chance he blew.

In the year after 'Like a Rolling Stone', Dylan released three curious follow-up singles, each of which was patently unsuited to be a 45 and each of which was incrementally less compelling (and in fact less successful): 'Positively 4th Street', 'Can You Please Crawl Out Your Window?' and 'Sooner or Later (One of Us Must Know)'. Some might point to the modest chart success of the first listed (US No.7, UK No.8) and its continued, if low-level, presence on gold radio as vindication of its choice for release. However, 'Positively 4th Street' (September 1965) really bludgeoned its way into the charts by making up for its absence of a catchy tune with bile that was still novel even after 'Like a Rolling Stone'. Recorded during the *Highway 61* sessions and reputed to be written straight after Dylan's hostile reception at Newport 1965, it has been posited as the artist's put-down of all the folkies and radicals who perceived him to have sold out. (Interestingly, Greenwich Village's West 4th Street wasn't the only one in Bob's life: there is also a 4th Street in Minneapolis, where he went to university, and the locals all thought the song was about them.) While straight-talking like "You've got a lot of nerve to say you are my friend" (the opening line) was still thrillingly novel in popular song, and there are a couple of memorable phrases ("I wish that just one time you could stand inside my shoes/You'd know what a drag it is to see you . . . I know you're dissatisfied with your position and your place/But don't you understand that's not my problem?"), the track has no other qualities. The melody is laboured and monotonous and Al Kooper ferociously trying to make his flimsy organ lick interesting only adds to the impression of a poor man's 'Like a Rolling Stone'.

'Can You Please Crawl Out Your Window?' (December 1965) was simply more of the same: a melody that sounded like a bridge between two album tracks providing a backdrop for a barrel-load of abuse, albeit the abuse more literate and the instrumentation possessed of a darker tone. Not exactly a good entrée to his recorded collaborations with The Hawks, soon to be renamed The Band. There are a few good lines ("With his businesslike anger and his bloodhounds that kneel") but, as with its predecessor, the complete lack of rhythm and the meandering melody line made it sound like the work of a folkie who didn't quite understand rock. We know this isn't true from the artistic triumphs of 'Subterranean Homesick Blues' and *Highway 61* – and we know it better now from his subsequent body of work – but one wonders whether some at the time were wondering whether Dylan had hit a dead end with rock. Reputedly, Dylan threw Phil Ochs – a friend and one of the folkies who had supported his move into rock 'n' roll – out of his limousine for telling him it was no smash and this perhaps gives us an insight into why Dylan allowed himself to think it was a suitable choice for single release. Never humble at the best of times, his sky-high reputation had clearly caused him to be now consumed by his ego. (A different version of 'Crawl' recorded at the *Highway 61* sessions was erroneously released with 'Positively 4th Street' on the label before being withdrawn.) Like 'Positively 4th Street', 'Crawl' did not appear on an album, but if this was intended to help recast Dylan as a singles artist, it failed. 'Crawl' made a pathetic No.58 on the *Billboard* charts. Dylan's British fanbase – which at the time was more loyal than his American audience – sent it into the Top 20 in the UK. However, it has failed to enter the public consciousness, almost completely absent from both gold radio playlists and people's memories, whereas the later (and much better) 'I Want You' is lodged in both despite only securing a UK chart-placing one higher.

The regret and self-examination of 'One of Us Must Know (Sooner or Later)' (February 1966) was a merciful relief from the tone of the previous three records – whose uniform viciousness was threatening to turn Dylan into a novelty act specializing in spite – but that didn't make it a good single. Once again, it completely lacks the musical punch requisite for chart material, something compounded by the absence of a bridge and nigh five-minute length. Mordant spiritually and cluttered musically, it's a swirling apologia to (it's theorised) Joan Baez – whom he provoked via his put-downs into walking out on him on the April/May 1965 UK tour – that never hits any highs. It was a complete flop, not even making the Hot 100 in the States. Even his British fans were only able to muster enough enthusiasm to send it to No.33.

By the time this trio of disastrous releases was complete, any possibility of the public perceiving Dylan as a singles artist was wrecked. A fact inconvenient to this hypothesis is the commercial success of his following single, 'Rainy Day Women #12 & 35'. However, that has so much the smack of a novelty record that it would probably have been a hit for anyone. Most people will know it as 'Everybody Must Get Stoned' – the strange title, it is claimed, came from the ages of a mother and daughter who took shelter from a storm in the recording studio – and that vocal refrain blaring out of radio sets was crockery-dropping stuff in April 1966. Dylan's alibi of course was that "stoned" was then still just about more familiar to most as slang for drunk, and in any case the scenarios in the song evoke not inebriation (by whatever means) but the biblical form of punishment. The jaunty ambience punctuated by whooping and Dylan's frequent corpsing didn't *prove* anything. The kids delighted in getting one over on the old and the uncool by sending the record to No.2 in the UK and No.7 Stateside. Approaching half a century later, when the delicious frisson of being in the minority of with-it people who understood what the song really meant has passed into history – even if the song unexpectedly retains a certain validity in a culture where marijuana is actually still frowned on by a generation of authority figures who lit up in their reckless youth – the recording has to rely for its power on its musical virtues. The latter, unfortunately, are slim, unless stomping circus music with bawdy horn parts is your predilection.

'Rainy Day Women #12 & 35', like 'One of Us Must Know (Sooner or Later)', featured on Dylan's album of May 1966, *Blonde on Blonde*. We'll skip over the meaning of the title, with which generations of Dylanologists have wrestled, pausing only to note that it might be intentional that its acronym is "Bob" (or might not) be intended as an acronym of it and that the artist is not employing the common American spelling "blond" (which might mean something or, alternatively, nothing). *Blonde on Blonde* is credited with being the first rock/pop double LP. It probably wasn't: that official 16 May release date cannot be correct, because overdub work was still being done on the album in mid-June, and it didn't make the charts until the end of July. In fact, it seems plausible that a Columbia statistician simply erroneously replaced 16 July with 16 May. However, even if the Mothers of Invention's double *Freak Out!* – released 27 June – beat it to the stores, *Blonde on Blonde* was a landmark on several counts.

It was the first album to have an entire vinyl side occupied by one song (discounting *Freak Out!*'s diptych 'The Return of the Son of Monster Magnet (Unfinished Ballet in Two Tableaux)'). The record was also unprecedented in the handsome and deluxe nature of its packaging, the cover folding out into a colour head-and-torso photograph of the artist that in the days of the twelve-inch vinyl album was big enough to serve as a poster. That the artist was something more than the usual idol to be seen staring down from a teen's bedroom wall was indicated by the fact that Dylan (hair now remarkably bushy) eccentrically chose an out-of-focus shot from the session that produced the cover photograph. As did the fact that the artist's name and the album title were not mentioned on either front or back cover.

"The closest I ever got to the sound I hear in my mind was on individual bands in the *Blonde on Blonde* album. It's that thin, that wild mercury sound. It's metallic and bright gold with whatever that conjures up." It's a comment that Dylan made to Ron Rosenbaum of *Playboy* in 1978 and is frequently quoted even though nobody really understands it. What people do understand, though, is another part of the same quote: "That's my particular sound." Clearly, we shouldn't hold Dylan to something he said when only a third of the way into his career so far. We should also point out that he said that thin wild mercury sound was also to be found on *Bringing It All Back Home* and *Highway 61 Revisited*. However, it's reasonable to assume that *Blonde on Blonde* was special to him then (he only mentioned its predecessors when pressed by his interviewer) and that it probably remains so – although not, significantly, as his definitive artistic statement so far: he told his biographer Anthony Scaduto in 1970 of *Highway 61*, "I'm not gonna be able to make a record better than that one." Others, though, disagree with the latter comment. The consensus now is – and has been for a long time – that it's either *Highway 61 Revisited* or *Blonde on Blonde* that is Dylan's masterpiece, with *Blood on the Tracks* the only other item in his canon entering the equation.

That *Blonde on Blonde* was recorded in Nashville would be an unremarkable fact today, but in 1966 the idea that Dylan – epitome of East Coast cool and socio-political radicalism – would be happy to be backed by the good ol' boys of Music Row Studios, Tennessee, was guffaw-inspiring. Certainly, Dylan, Al Kooper and Robbie Robertson's long hair and outlandish clothes occasioned no little hassle on the streets when they arrived in the city in February 1966. A certain sense of desperation seems to have motivated Dylan to take up Bob Johnston on a suggestion he had made about a year previously regarding recording down south. Sessions for the new album had started in October 1965 but in contrast to the way that the staggering artistic statement of *Highway 61 Revisited* was completed in less than a cumulative week, all Dylan had to show for six days spread across nearly four months in Columbia Studios in New York was 'Crawl' and 'One of Us'. This strange inability of The Hawks/The Band to create in the studio the powerful music they would shortly make with Dylan on stage may be the reason that despite his long association with them, Dylan used them rarely on records, and that only their guitarist Robbie Robertson was invited down to Nashville.

On the first day's recording there, Dylan, Robertson and Kooper laid down with the studio's crack session musicians 'Visions of Johanna', 'Leopard-Skin Pill-Box Hat' and '4th Time Around'. On the second day, they completed the epic 'Sad Eyed Lady of the Lowlands'. The album was finished by the following March after just seven Nashville sessions – and there wasn't a single pedal steel or Hawaiian guitar discernable in any of the (often remarkable) musical landscapes created. These remarkable landscapes were in spite of an approach by which the musicians must have been shocked. Although Kooper had acquainted the band with some of the songs beforehand after Dylan had played them to him in his hotel room, the modus operandi with others was the same as it always was (and mostly has been) with Dylan: few instructions and the musicians left to sink or swim.

Without question, Dylan was on a roll, but that doesn't prove that the album is a masterpiece. 'Rainy Day Women #12 & 35' (the opening track) is the only cut that could plausibly be posited as social commentary. Everything else sees Dylan examining the ups and downs of his own life. While this is legitimate, there is consequently far less of a grand sweep to the lyrics than on its predecessor. Meanwhile, second track 'Pledging My Time' demonstrates much of the problem of conferring classic status on this record. Though, as with any Dylan song, it has the odd great line (he tells his lover, "If it don't work out, you'll be the first to know") and though it is well-played and recorded, it is essentially a slow blues, examples of which dubious genre are scattered across *Blonde on Blonde*. The great blues songwriter Willie Dixon almost always added an imaginative little kink to his compositions that lifted them above the generic, while occasionally artists do something so new and imaginative with the form – e.g., The Jimi Hendrix Experience with 'Red House', Norman Greenbaum with 'Spirit in the Sky', Dylan himself with 'Meet Me in the Morning' – as to surmount its limitations. However, in the vast majority of cases, the blues is boring. Musically rigid (twelve lumbering bars) and lyrically limited (every second line usually repeated), it is too often a lazy recourse, a readymade melodic apparatus for a recording artist suffering from a lack of inspiration. 'Temporary Like Achilles' is similarly well-crafted and even has that rare blues ingredient, a bridge, but is again ultimately sunk by its trappings as well as its tiresomely opaque songwords. The hilarious lyric of 'Leopard-Skin Pill-Box Hat' ("It balances on your head just like a mattress balances on a bottle of wine") is simply wasted on the blues format. Dylan was in no way jumping on the bandwagon following the spike in interest in blues and R&B following the commercial success of the Stones and other lovers of black music – he was steeped in it and had been recording blues from his debut album onwards – but *Highway 61* had shown that he had moved beyond it; playing the blues now was a backward step.

In contrast, 'Visions of Johanna' is the type of creation laughably beyond the average dedicated blues player – and indeed beyond any other recording artists in the world at the time. Right from its classy harmonica fanfare, we realise we are being treated to something special. A seven-and-a-half-minute gossamer opus, it sees the narrator holed up in a soporific room with gently coughing heat pipes. Bland country music washes over him from a radio set but it is too characterless and he (we infer) is too stricken with inertia to switch it off. The narrator is in the company of a girl called Louise, but only because she is readily available and reminds him a little of himself: "But she makes it all too concise and too clear that Johanna's not here." Joan Baez thought the song was about her, but who knows how many ex-lovers Dylan regretted having cavalierly cast off, and in any case none of us need to know the identity of the woman in the song to be utterly enchanted by it. Everything in the recording is exquisite: Dylan's flamenco acoustic-guitar refrain, his quasi-hoarse singing, the middle-distant washes of organ, crisp drumming, the discrete flecks of electric guitar, another electric guitar with a sharp arpeggio motif . . . Johnston's sublime production plays its own part, placing enough echo here and dampening down enough there to add to the atmosphere without being obtrusive. In the context of the album, incidentally, the following 'One of Us Must Know (Sooner or Later)' not only makes more sense musically – sounding like a stepping stone to something else rather than a self-contained thing – but also conceptually, seeming of a piece with 'Johanna'.

Had 'I Want You' been the follow-up to 'Like a Rolling Stone' instead of appearing on 45 in June 1966, Dylan may well have acquired the status of singles artist that his ego at this juncture in his life almost certainly made him wish for. This and the follow-up, 'Just Like a Woman', were absolutely ideal singles: pretty, compact and both boasting chart-worthy bridges, yet their commercialism did not make them anodyne in any way. The tune of 'I Want You' is far too sophisticated to whistle, and the elliptical, mischievous lyric the type that only Dylan was taking into the hit parade then. A lovely little piece of drumming – like a pair of feet shuffling eagerly in the dust before a race gets underway – begins the proceedings. The "time is on his side" line identifies for some the object of Dylan's carnal desire as Anita Pallenberg, the beautiful paramour of The Rolling Stones' Brian Jones, a friend of Dylan's. (A live version of 'Just Like Tom Thumb's Blues' that some consider better than the studio original appeared on the B-side of the 'I Want You' single. It can be found on The Band's box-set *A Musical History*.) 'Just Like a Woman' is even prettier, with an almost parodically dainty melody, but like 'I Want You' there is bite behind the frilly window-dressing. Dylan depicts a female whose ribbons and bows have lately fallen from her curls – but there weren't any references to heroin, amphetamines and love-making in distaff coming-of-age records like 'Happy Birthday Sweet Sixteen'.

'Stuck Inside of Mobile with the Memphis Blues Again' (originally listed as just 'Memphis Blues Again') is one of a trio of tracks on the album in which Dylan says precisely what he wants to say regardless of the running time of the end product. The result sits somewhere between the unmitigated triumph of 'Visions of Johanna' and the tedium of 'Sad Eyed Lady of the Lowlands', the other *Blonde on Blonde* epics. The glossy production and fine musicianship (especially Dylan's warm acoustic guitar and Kenny Buttrey's clipped drumming) certainly make it an easy ride for at least half of its seven minutes. However, it has made its point by then, and Dylan's lyric – a litany of the causes of his frazzled state that includes drugs dispensed by what seems a thinly disguised Grossman – doesn't wear well over the whole course. Not only is it not as shimmeringly poetic or evocative as 'Johanna', but sometimes one is even put in mind by it of John Lennon's comment, "There has been more said about Dylan's wonderful lyrics than was ever in the lyrics at all . . . Dylan got away with murder."

Side three of the original vinyl configuration was as close to conventionality over an extended period that the album got. It boasted five relatively short songs, all either musically uptempo or gritty or both, sort of like The Rolling Stones put through a Dylanesque wash cycle. 'Most Likely You Go Your Way (And I'll Go Mine)' has a blaring harmonica riff and is propelled by a brawny rhythm track in the centre of which incongruously sits Dylan's mellow (if scathing) vocal. One can't quite escape the nagging feeling that the contrasting rough-smooth qualities don't gel but it's enjoyable nonetheless. Following 'Temporary Like Achilles', the perky 'Absolutely Sweet Marie' picks up the tempo again but it never really gets exciting or meaningful – despite the desperate attempts by some Dylan fans to attribute profundity to the line "To live outside the law you must be honest". '4th Time Around' – in which Dylan is again having problems in his love life which he implies once more are of his own making – is funny and attractive. The fact that John Lennon had heard this song before releasing 'Norwegian Wood', his own composition with a very similar tune, suggests that Dylan's title is a sangfroid acknowledgment that he had based his melody on a folk standard himself. On 'Obviously 5 Believers', Dylan – whose harmonica on the previous track is utterly beautiful – selflessly gives way to Charlie McCoy and the latter blasts a fine progression on that instrument in a Dylan song that is unusually gutsy and riff-heavy.

When *Blonde on Blonde* first appeared, there were some complaints about the whole of side four being given over to 'Sad Eyed Lady of the Lowlands'. As it was almost exactly the same length as 'Desolation Row', which had shared a side of an album with three other songs, themselves of above-average length, it hardly seemed value for money. In fact, as *Highway 61 Revisited* had clocked in at fifty-one and a half minutes – ten minutes longer than most albums of the day and twenty minutes longer than many – the facts were closer to being the other way round.

Of course, the massively productive Dylan could have slung on more tracks if he'd had a mind – 'I Wanna Be Your Lover', 'I'll Keep It with Mine' and 'She's Your Lover Now' were just three of the session's worthy songs which did not make the final cut, and he never even bothered recording a studio version of 'Tell Me, Momma', even though he opened his electric sets of the period with it – but that wasn't the point. Dylan was hiving off this song to side four to give an elevated status to a celebration of the virtues of the woman with whom he had fallen in love. Sara Lownds was a transcendently beautiful divorced mother of one who was a friend of Albert Grossman's wife. She became Sara Dylan on 22 November 1965, with the wedding initially a matter of utmost secrecy.

Dylan's marriage to Lownds is now history, as are records with sides: 'Sad Eyed Lady' is now merely – depending on which CD edition you have – track fourteen or track six, disc two of *Blonde on Blonde*. In fact, when the CD medium was new, an astonishingly knuckle-headed decision to cram the whole album onto a single disc resulted in the snipping out of a few seconds of most other tracks and fully forty seconds (mainly harmonica) of 'Sad Eyed Lady'. Not that the latter was an offence against anything but historical fealty: where we never felt bored by 'Visions of Johanna', 'Sad Eyed lady' is beginning to drag by the fifth minute. Dylan's worshipful attitude toward his wife is moving and his heartfelt singing lovely, but so cloaked in metaphor and in-jokes is the lyric that it's largely meaningless to anyone but Mr. and Mrs. Dylan. The instrumentation – a tick-tocking affair with the odd crescendo – is likewise easy on the ear but best dipped in and out of.

As with The Beatles' 1968 'White Album', *Blonde on Blonde* would have been a much more powerful artistic statement had it been trimmed to a single platter. Despite its overrated status, though, it certainly can't be denied that the best of *Blonde on Blonde* is amongst the finest music ever recorded. It's also a stunning achievement on another level: *Bringing It All Back Home*, *Highway 61 Revisited* and *Blonde on Blonde* were released in the space of fourteen months. It's true that The Beatles released a trio of classics – *Help!, Rubber Soul* and *Revolver* – in the space of a year at this juncture in history, but brilliant and innovative in their own ways though those records were, they didn't utterly change the landscape of popular music like Dylan's triumvirate. Furthermore, Dylan didn't have a creative foil the way The Beatles' Lennon and McCartney did (and for that matter the Stones' Jagger and Richards). Nor did The Beatles and the Stones have to put up with the printed hostility of former admirers or the shattering sight of audiences booing every night in protest at a change in direction. Maintaining such brilliance and originality in such quantity against this backdrop is and will forever remain a unique achievement.

It's certainly not one that was secured completely organically. Dylan aficionados refer to the three aforementioned Dylan albums as the "amphetamine rock trilogy". The artist was maintaining his furious productivity and astonishing creativity with the aid not only of "speed" but other stimulants – mostly dispensed by Albert Grossman, who was eager to ensure that the revenue stream of which he was contractually entitled to 25 per cent was maintained – and it was having shattering consequences for his physical health and peace of mind. The harrowing documentary footage shot in Europe in 1966 showing Dylan jabbering to a doctor that he wants to abandon the tour dates stretching ahead of him and go home shows quite vividly that something had to give.

The world tour in which Dylan engaged in 1966, following the recording but prior to the release of Blonde on Blonde, *saw he and The Hawks play stunning music to audiences who booed them to the rafters. There were American, Australian and continental European legs of the tour, but his most vituperative reaction came in Britain, which had hitherto boasted his most adoring fanbase. In this feature, Johnny Black tells, with the aid of first-hand accounts, the story of the most extraordinary tour ever seen.*

DYLAN IN 1966

By Johnny Black

First published in *Mojo*, October 1998

"Well, there's glass in the back of my head," said Bob Dylan. "I'm a very sick person. I can't see too well on Tuesdays. These dark glasses are prescribed. I'm not trying to be a beatnik. I have very mercuryesque eyes. And another thing – my toenails don't fit."

It was 3 May 1966, one day after the spokesman for his generation arrived in England for the first time since plugging in. A year earlier, Dylan had unveiled the first version of his electric group, effectively the Paul Butterfield Blues Band, at the Newport Folk Festival. The partisan folkie crowd had booed and jeered until, according to some reports, Dylan left the stage in tears. The response was even more violent at Forest Hills Tennis Stadium a month later, where cries of "Traitor!" and the mocking "Where's Ringo?" greeted his rock set.

Before too long, he had replaced the Butterfield Blues Band with The Hawks (later to become The Band) with whom he faced hostile audiences all across America, Hawaii, Australia and Scandinavia. In December 1965, Hawks's leader and drummer, Levon Helm, dropped out. "We got up in the morning and Levon was gone," recalls road manager Bill Avis. "It shook us up for a minute, but it was also understood. No one liked the booing. No one liked having stuff thrown at them."

The pressure was intolerable. After midnight, on a plane to Denver during March 1966, Dylan told writer Robert Shelton, "It takes a lot of medicine to keep up this pace. It's very hard man. A concert tour like this has almost killed me."

Replacing Levon Helm for the UK leg was Mickey Jones, former sticksman for Trini Lopez and Johnny Rivers. Jones went on the road with no awareness of the controversy surrounding the electric part of the set. Having already sold over ten million records worldwide, Dylan was not just a popular fellow but a priority act for CBS. As well as record sales, he was generating publishing revenue at an unheard-of rate. In one fortnight at the end of 1965, eighty cover versions of Dylan songs were released as singles. Huge wads of company money were invested in him but, as he arrived in London, doubts about his health were beginning to surface.

Monday, 2 May

The Dylan entourage settles in at the Mayfair Hotel, London, where Bob meets with Paul McCartney, Keith Richards and Brian Jones.

Paul McCartney (Beatle): It was a little bit An Audience With Dylan in those days. You went round to the Mayfair Hotel and waited in an outer room while Bob was, you know, in the other room, in the bedroom, and we were getting ushered in one by one . . . occasionally people would come out and say, you know, Bob's taking a nap or make terrible excuses, and I'd say "It's OK man, I understand, he's out of it", you know?

Mickey Jones (drummer): I have been told that he carried a drug store of prescription medicine with him, but I never saw it.

Tuesday, 3 May

Press Conference, Mayfair Hotel, London; in the evening Dylan takes Dana Gillespie to see John Lee Hooker at Blaises.

Dermot Purgavie (*Daily Sketch* reporter): Publicity men with urgent voices had summoned us for gin and tonic, cocktail onions and, principally, for group analysis of Mr. Bob Dylan . . . He wore a blue suede tunic, blue-and-white butcher-stripe pants and dark glasses. His tangled, woolly hair looked as if it had been pitch-forked onto his head.

Keith Altham (*NME* journalist): For some fifteen minutes, photographers exposed innumerable rolls of film at Dylan looking bored, slumped on a window sill. Finally, he removed his dark glasses as a bonus to the cameramen, but somehow managed to look exactly the same.

   As the reporters filed out of the suite, I took one of Dylan's undercover agents to one side and enquired why a man with Dylan's obvious intelligence bothered to arrange this farce of a meeting. "Man," he extolled, "Dylan just wanted to come along and record a press reception so we could hear how ridiculous and infantile all reporters are."

Keith Richards (guitarist, Rolling Stones): They had to carry him into Blaises, and then I went over to him, and I was pretty frightened of him.

Thursday, 5 May

Adelphi Theatre, Dublin

Norman Barry (reviewer, *Sunday Independent*): The barrage of amplification equipment completely drowned Dylan's nasal voice, which requires the utmost concentration at the best of times. His beat arrangements were monotonous and painful, as folk, useless, and as beat, inferior.

Robbie Robertson: It was the strangest job you could imagine. We were travelling round the world, getting booed every night.

Friday, 6 May

ABC Theatre, Belfast

Un-named reporter, *Cityweek*: The door of the drab dressing room was ajar. A fuzzy golliwog in a tight diamond-pattern suit stood staring at me with wide-open eyes. "What d'ya want?" asked Bob Dylan. His lips hadn't moved. The sound seemed to emit from somewhere in the inner regions of the thick, dark curls ... Eventually, he invited me inside. This wasn't an interview, he emphasised. "We're jest gonna have a l'il talkie."

D. A. Pennebaker (film-maker): We had previously filmed him in England in 1965 for my *Dont Look Back* film and it seemed to me that it had been a drag for him, out on his own like that. In 1966, in the second half of each show he had all these guys with him and from the minute he got out there he was enjoying himself. He was almost dancing with Robbie.

Tuesday, 10 May

Colston Hall, Bristol

Nicholas Williams (*NME* reviewer): Dylan ambled on to the stage and opened the first half by singing 'She Belongs to Me', one of his well-known LP tracks. He continued in the same style, accompanying himself on guitar and harmonica ... For the second half of the show, Dylan changed to an electric guitar, and a five-strong backing group mysteriously appeared.

Jenny Leigh (fan): They buried Bob Dylan, the folksinger, in a grave of electric guitars, enormous loudspeakers and deafening drums. It was a sad end to one of the most phenomenal influences in music.

Robbie Robertson (guitarist): At the time, people were pissed off because they had this purist attitude about Dylan. We did not see what was wrong musically. We were treating the songs with great respect.

Anthea Joseph (music promoter/friend of Dylan): I was the only one that drank. They were all dropping pills and eating acid and generally misbehaving ... Anything that was going to tear my mind to pieces, I had no interest in whatsoever. So I was happy smoking dope in a corner while they ate things.

Wednesday, 11 May

Capitol Theatre, Cardiff, where Johnny Cash arrives backstage.

J. C. Hopkins (fan): Saw Bob Dylan in Cardiff – and though slightly disappointed in him as a person, he's certainly one of the greatest artistes I've seen.

Thursday, 12 May

Odeon Theatre, Birmingham, where The Spencer Davis Group turns out.

Graham Ashton (fan): The show was late starting ... Dylan came on dressed completely in black, and someone even screamed. By the time he reached the mike he was already into 'She Belongs to Me' ... He didn't speak between the songs until just before 'Desolation Row', when he suddenly stopped, looked down and, in slow motion, picked something up, stared at it, and drawled into the mike: "Dirt ... Dirt on the *stage*." Everybody hooted. Dylan grinned.

Muff Winwood (bassist, Spencer Davis Group): While we were backstage after the show, he was telling me and my brother Steve how he was really into ghosts ... and we knew of a very old, massive house in Worcestershire, near Kidderminster, that had been burnt and blackened. And we told him how the guy that had lived in the house had died with his dog and how, if you went there, you could see him walking around with his dog. He was absolutely fascinated and he said "You've got to take me to this place."

Well, we got there – Dylan, the band, girlfriends and hangers-on in four bloody stretch Princess limos – and we started wandering around. The house looked absolutely magnificent – it was a clear night with a great moon and everything ... and of course, somewhere a dog barked! Now, this is likely to happen in the countryside in Worcestershire at gone midnight, but Dylan is convinced he's heard the ghost of the dog. He was like a kid . . . Really child-like enjoyment of the whole thing. It was great fun.

Saturday, 14 May

Odeon Theatre, Liverpool

Barry Feinstein (photographer): We found ourselves in an old abandoned industrial section of the city. These children were running through the streets. I thought it would be great to photograph Bob, a big star name, with them.

Bob had a real soft spot in his heart for kids from lower-income families. He loved them and they loved him, even if they didn't realise who he was.

Vicki Rees (fan): Dylan was at his best. Those people who walked out saying they wanted the real Dylan really meant they wanted the old Dylan.

Mickey Jones: He always seemed to have a lot of energy. On a number of occasions, Bob and I would jump in a limo after the concert and find an all-night hot-dog stand. We would then go back to the hotel and talk about everything under the sun until the sun came up. He would make up for it by sleeping a lot during the day, but no one slept more than Garth Hudson. I said to him once, "Garth, you're sleeping your life away." He just looked straight at me and said, "Don't you know about dreams?"

Sunday, 15 May

De Montfort Hall, Leicester

Christine Kynaston (fan): I was absolutely disgusted at the narrow-mindedness displayed by some of the audience at Bob Dylan's Sunday visit to Leicester. Never before have I seen such an exhibition of childish mentality; they booed and slow-handclapped a man who was merely proving how amazingly versatile he is.

Monday, 16 May

Gaumont Theatre, Sheffield

Mickey Jones: I've been told there was a bomb threat at the Gaumont but, you know, if there was, we were totally unaware of it. It certainly didn't affect us or our performance.

Harry Murray (manager, The Gaumont, Sheffield): We decided to sweat it out. If I had thought for one moment that the audience were in danger I would have cleared the theatre immediately.

Jean-Marc Pascal (journalist, *Salut Les Copains*): Later on, the entire group meets in a suite. Five musicians, four film-makers and sound technicians, one sound man, Tom – the driver of the Rolls who is also acting as Dylan's bodyguard, Henri – who looks after the guitars, Al Grossman, Bob Neuwirth, Fred Perry (from CBS London, the tour manager), Bob Dylan and myself plus a few girls picked up at the end of the show. Twenty people altogether. They have to listen and choose the recordings made of the concert. It's a daily routine . . . Bob is having a film made of the tour for American television and these recordings have to be synchronised later with the pictures . . . At 6 a.m. there are only three or four people left: Bob, myself and a couple of musicians. We talk about John Lennon, Mick Jagger and trends in world cinema.

Tuesday, 17 May

Free Trade Hall, Manchester

Jean-Marc Pascal: At noon the next day, we're off to Manchester . . . When we arrive, Dylan goes to his bedroom to sleep until the concert. The others go to the theatre to set up the sound system Bob has brought with him from America – it's Ampex, the best there is.

Mickey Jones: As I remember, we all walked down to the Free Trade Hall from the hotel for the soundcheck.

Jean-Marc Pascal: Three quarters of an hour before the show is due to begin, Dylan arrives ... while he rehearses briefly with his musicians, two cameramen and soundmen are around him.

Malcolm Metcalf (fan): By the time I got to the Free Trade Hall, it was sold out. I'd long since perfected the art of getting into cinemas via the back door, so I went looking round the side of the theatre and found a door and kicked it in. It led onto a corridor which led right through to the side of the stage. From there, by pushing another door open a crack, we could get a view of the show.

Rick Sanders (fan/usher): Dylan coming to Manchester was the biggest thing of that time. There was more excitement about it than any other gig I've ever been to. I was a student but I used to get evening jobs ushering at the Free Trade Hall for fifteen shillings a time, but the Dylan show was the first proper rock gig I'd worked at.

Mickey Jones: The atmosphere backstage at Manchester just before we went on was no different than at any of the previous shows. We always laughed and had a great time.

Chris Lee (fan): He walked on to the stage in Cuban boots, with a black shirt and this Edwardian-style, yellow-brown tweed jacket and started off with 'She Belongs to Me'. The main thing though, visually, was that great big unruly mop of long curly hair. That came as a shock, because all the publicity shots we'd seen were about two years old.

Paul Kelly (fan): I had decided to take along my camera – a Yashica – to the gig, because there was never any problem about taking pictures at concerts in those days. We'd managed to get seats just four rows from the front and, as soon as the house lights went down, and the spotlight came on, I started taking pictures. I can still remember the moment he came on stage for the acoustic set. I was thinking "God, that's really him. In the flesh."

Kevin Fletcher (fan): During the acoustic set, he seemed very different from the way we'd seen him in 1965. Then, he'd been chatty, joking, very open and fresh, but now the set was more intense. He seemed slower and slurred and he seemed very stoned.

Chris Lee: It was like a church service. People were quiet and attentive but you could feel the tension about whether he would play electric. We'd heard about the booing in Dublin and Liverpool and a lot of people assumed he'd have learned his lesson.

Rick Sanders: During the intermission after the acoustic set, Dylan's manager Albert Grossman, an imposing figure in a cream suit, came round and told me he wanted me to be a body-guard, up on the stage. I was plunked right in front of Richard Manuel. To be honest though, I didn't feel very threatened up there. The band seemed a million times cooler than anyone else in the building.

Chris Lee: When they came on, just before nine o'clock, the Hawks were a rainbow of coloured velvet suits, maroon, purple, green, beige and blue, very Catskills. They had white shirts, and their hair was just starting to grow long. Then Dylan came out with a black Fender and plugged it in.

Rick Sanders: There at my feet was a surging mass of flesh-crazed fans, howling, cheering and screaming, waiting for the spark. I don't think Dylan said anything. Just a glance at the band and suddenly the music started.

Mickey Jones: At the Free Trade Hall show, he would set the rhythm and the tone before we would come in ... He gets the rhythm going, and then Robbie turns it around. He goes "One, two, one, two, three" and it was completely turned around from the rhythm that Bob set.

Rick Sanders: I never heard such an apocalyptic roar. It took your breath away, like a squadron of B-52s in a cathedral. There was wicked crackling guitar over a vortex of sheer noise, with snatches of Captain Nemo organ and mad piano occasionally surfacing.

Chris Lee: They kicked off with 'Tell Me, Momma' and right away people were shocked, stunned, taken aback by the sheer volume. That got polite applause, but by the time they were into 'I Don't Believe You' the audience was divided. It was a sheer affront to the traditionalists. I was just sixteen, and I was used to seeing these people around the folk scene in Manchester, but it was quite bewildering and frightening to see them going apeshit like that. It's hard to convey to people now just how profound the shock was of Dylan going commercial. To those people it seemed he had betrayed all their values, their left-wing principles, the CND movement, their traditionalist sentiments.

Steve Currie (fan): I wasn't too impressed by the velvet suits, but I was even less impressed by the dickhead sat next to me who decided to start booing and shouting along with the others who were scattered around the hall. I told him to fuck off home if he didn't like it. Well, that shut him up and he stayed, but the protest carried on elsewhere.

Stewart Tray (fan, seated behind Dylan on stage): I got the feeling there was something going on. The noise, the booing, the slow-handclapping and all the rest of it. I mean, this was supposed to be like going to a pop concert. People threw jelly babies at pop concerts, they didn't do this kind of stuff. There was fear where I was sat, that Dylan would just walk off.

Chris Lee: At the end of 'Just Like Tom Thumb's Blues', a young, long-haired woman walked up to the front of the stage and passed a note to Dylan. He bowed and blew her a kiss, which brought thunderous applause from the crowd. Then he looked briefly at the note and put it in his pocket. Everyone wondered what the note said, but no one knew until I managed to track the woman down when I was writing my book, *Like the Night*, about the Free Trade Hall gig. Her name was Barbara and her note said "Tell the band to go home" but it was done with the best intentions. They had been embarrassed by the way the crowd was behaving, and worried that he would think they didn't like his music when, in fact, it was just the band they didn't like.

Mickey Jones: Frankly, we didn't care. We were playing our music for us and not for the audience. Bob's attitude was "The first half of the show is for them, the second half is for us" and we truly enjoyed ourselves.

Chris Lee: After 'Leopard-Skin Pill-Box Hat', there was a delay, during which the hecklers started up again. As the slow-handclaps and the booing got louder, Bob went into a routine. It was an old carny sideshow technique, where he mumbled incoherently into the microphone, which had the effect of making people strain to hear what he was saying.

Mickey Jones: He did that on a lot of occasions. He didn't end with the same thing, he'd say something different. But . . . that really got their attention and they'd stop and all of a sudden, they'd pay attention.

Kevin Fletcher: The mumbling completely floored us. We thought it was brilliant and totally effective because as he did it, the crowd just got quieter and quieter.

Chris Lee: Once he knew he had everybody's attention, Dylan delivered one single coherent phrase ". . . if you only wouldn't clap so hard", which had the desired effect of making everybody laugh and briefly winning them over to his side again.

Kevin Fletcher: The famous shout of "Judas!" came from in front of us and a bit more to the centre and, as soon as it happened, there was a kind of hush fell over the crowd. I'd say Dylan was definitely responding to the Judas shout when he said, "I don't believe you." That shout was probably the nastiest knock he ever got.

Chris Lee: The implication of "Judas!", obviously, was that he had sold out the folk movement. Then there was a long gap as he mulled it over before he said, "I don't believe you" in a voice full of scorn and disdain. He turned to the band at that point and said, "Get fucking loud."

Jean-Marc Pascal: Suddenly [during 'Like a Rolling Stone'] a man behind me whispers, "This is really good. It's number one in the States." I turn around to agree and – surprise – realise that he's a policeman. The British police are wonderful.

Rick Sanders: Before anyone realised what was happening, it was suddenly over. I have a memory of Dylan brushing past me and vanishing down a corridor with Grossman.

Malcolm Metcalfe: We'd watched the whole thing through the door from the corridor, terrified all the time that somebody would find us and throw us out. After 'Like a Rolling Stone', we weren't sure if it had ended because there was just this sudden silence, but then the door beside us blasted open and Dylan and some heavies rushed past us and I remember thinking "My God, he's so small." He was sweating profusely and looked exhausted, really wasted. He was practically being carried by his minders with one hand under each arm. They completely ignored us, so we followed them down the corridor and out into the street where they jumped into this big, black limousine and disappeared.

Paul Kelly: By the end, I'd banged off all thirty-six shots and, as it happened, about twenty-six turned out to be useable. During the show, we'd noticed the sound recordist from CBS who had his gear just set up right at the front of the stage. When it was all over we went up and asked him if he would give us the tape. He said "No way man, but it's coming out on an album at the end of this year."

Rick Sanders: People started approaching me, furiously demanding their money back, thinking that somehow I'd be able to give it to them, but the whole thing was finished. As the hall emptied, the band came back on without Dylan, and played some great old rock numbers, Bo Diddley and Little Richard stuff, while the clearers-up moved around them. Dylan by now would be back in the Midland Hotel, I suppose. When it was finally over, we humped the gear back outside for them, collected thirty shillings each for the night's work, and went home. Not one of them had said a word to me, but it was an unforgettable, fabulous night, to have been Bob Dylan's bodyguard.

Mickey Jones: After that show we did talk about the Judas thing, but it didn't seem that it had affected Dylan one bit. We were just convinced that nobody had got it.

Wednesday, 18 May

Travel to Scotland

Mickey Jones: We went everywhere by coach, but Bob had his own car. Now, there were parts of the tour that Bob Dylan was on the coach but, when we went up to Scotland, he went in the car, and we went on the bus.

I've long been a collector of Nazi memorabilia, so that morning I went shopping and bought a large German flag. As we left the Midland Hotel to get on the bus for Glasgow, I unfurled the flag in the middle of the street to show it to the guys on the bus. Man, I was almost run down on the spot by about a dozen drivers. I was still just a kid, and it really hadn't dawned on me how powerful those feelings left over from the war were in England. I guess it was a stupid thing to do.

Thursday, 19 May

Odeon Theatre, Glasgow

Andrew Young (*Scottish Daily Mail* reviewer): Dressed in checked suit, he stood alone on stage and gasped out the protest songs which have made him a millionaire. It was when he came on in the second half, dressed in black and accompanied by a five-man beat group that the trouble started.

There were shouts of "Rubbish" from the purists and "Shut up" from the beat fans . . . To shouts of "We want Dylan" he

replied "Dylan got sick backstage and I'm here to take his place."
Then he walked off stage unperturbed by the boos and cheers
that followed him.

Mickey Jones: There's no doubt in my mind as to why they were
reacting the way they were. They felt that the one person in the
world who would remain true was Bob Dylan. They felt betrayed.
I understand that more today than I did then.

Friday, 20 May

ABC Theatre, Edinburgh. Dylan encounters so many tuning
problems that he throws away his mouth organ.

Andrew Young (fan): You could tell there was something wrong
with Bob's, so I just walked on to the stage and handed him my
own 12/6d mouth organ.

Saturday, 21 May

Odeon Theatre, Newcastle

Mickey Jones: I'll tell you this. The first half of those concerts . . .
he was absolutely bored to tears. And he would come back to the
dressing room and put that acoustic guitar down. Then he would
put that black Telecaster on and you could see the adrenaline
running through his veins.

He was ready to rock. He would jump around in the dressing
room. He could not wait to get on that stage. It's true, sometimes
Bob would hardly face the audience in the electric set. He played
to the band. That was where his focus was, on us. The audience
was only there so we could get paid to do what we loved to do.
We were all in a zone.

Sunday, 22 May

Touring party flies to France, where Dylan spends the night
boozing in Parisian niteries with Johnny Hallyday.

Monday, 23 May

Press conference in Paris.

Q. Are you a happy person, Bob?
A. Oh yes, I'm as happy as an ashtray.

Tuesday, 24 May

Olympia, Paris, with the electric set performed in front of a huge Stars and Stripes on Dylan's twenty-fifth birthday.

Mickey Jones: We were not very happy in France. We thought everyone there had an attitude towards Americans. And they did! I don't remember whose idea it was but we loved the reaction of the audience when the curtain opened and we were dwarfed by the biggest American flag that I had ever seen. It made me and Bob very proud. As you know, Bob and I were the only Americans on the show. The rest of the band was Canadian.

Wednesday, 25 May

Back in London, Dylan is filmed by D. A. Pennebaker during an early morning limo cruise around Hyde Park with John Lennon.

Bob Dylan: Oh, man, you shoulda been around last night, John. Today's a drag.
John Lennon: Oh, really, Bob?

Thursday, 26 May

Royal Albert Hall, London, with Rolling Stones in the audience.

Brian Carroll (IBC sound engineer): I was backstage after helping to set up the recording equipment. Another engineer and I stared in disbelief as we saw Dylan walk up the stairs that led to the stage. This man seemed so out of it that we saw him talking to a fire extinguisher and we both thought that there was going to be a riot when he either failed to appear or stumbled around the stage. Suddenly, a man in a suit led him to the bottom of the stairs and we watched in amazement as he walked up into the lights and gave one of his best performances on the tour.

Mick Farren (rock musician): He was obviously exceedingly stoned and probably taking a lot of pills, that's what we all figured . . . Little did we know – amphetamine and heroin.

Steve Abrams (fan): The most interesting part came in the first half of the concert when Dylan was about to sing 'Visions of Johanna'. He said "Now this next song is what your English newspapers would call a drug song, but I don't write drug songs and anybody who says I do is talking rubbish."

Sue Miles (fan): In the first half he was just earnestly twanging away, groaning away with the old harmonica and the guitar. Out for the intermission, and The Band appeared and I remember thinking, "This is great. This is wonderful. This is proper stuff." Dylan had frizzy, slightly blue hair. He and Robbie Robertson rubbed up against each other all the time. It was great. Half the audience pissed off – all the ones that had rucksacks.

Dana Gillespie (singer/friend of Dylan): After the Royal Albert Hall show, Dylan and I did talk about how he felt though and, although I never heard him say anything derogatory about British fans, I knew he was very surprised by the response because he had felt that England was far ahead of any other country in pop music. When the audience booed and jeered in London, he just rocked more to annoy them.

Johnny Byrne (writer): I happened to be staying in the flat where Dylan came back later. He was visibly vibrating. I should imagine it was the exhaustion and a good deal of substances. He was totally away. There was a yawning chasm between him and any kind of human activity.

Friday, 27 May

Royal Albert Hall, London, with The Beatles in the audience.

Mickey Jones: I do think the best set we did was probably the Albert Hall, the last night. Everybody was lookin' forward to goin' home and we wanted to kinda leave with a bang.

Norman Jopling (*Record Mirror* reviewer): After the interval, he returned with his group and launched into an ear-splitting cacophony ...The hecklers were in full force and just about everything possible was hurled at Bob (verbally – no missiles were seen).

Peter Willis (*Peace News* reviewer): Dylan remained beatifically unaffected by this; during one of the few enfeebled bursts of slow-handclapping he simply made faces, giggled and remarked, "This isn't English music, this is American music."

Norman Jopling: The highlight came when Bob sat down at the piano and did 'Ballad of a Thin Man', which silenced even the folksier elements. He ended up with 'Like a Rolling Stone', jumping and yelling all over the stage and looking (as all the girls said) very sweet.

D. A. Pennebaker: I'm not sure how badly the British audiences affected Dylan. During that tour, we were with him, often filming all night long, and at no point did Bob indicate that he felt these audiences hated him.

George Harrison (Beatle):The thing I remember most about it was all these people who'd never heard of folk until Bob Dylan came around and two years later they're staunch folk fans and they're walking out on him when he was playing the electric songs.Which is so stupid. He actually played rock 'n' roll before. Nobody knew that at the time but Bob had been in Bobby Vee's band as the piano player and he'd played rock 'n' roll. And then he became Bob Dylan The Folk Singer so, for him, it was just returning back.

I felt a bit sad for him because he was a bit wasted at that time. He'd been on a world tour and he looked like he'd been on a world tour. He looked like he needed a rest ...

Mickey Jones: I've heard people say he did it for the money. The reality is he made less money on that tour than any tour he'd ever done. To take that many people and all that equipment and all that air freight cost so much more than if he had done the tour alone. By himself, he would have tripled the money he made so, obviously, he did not do it for the money. He did it because his musical tastes were changin' too.

Robbie Robertson: Dylan had every opportunity to say, "Fellows, this is not working out. I'm going to go back to folk music, or get another band where they won't boo every time." Everybody told him to get rid of these guys, that it wasn't working. But he didn't. That was very commendable.

Saturday, 28 May

Dylan and Sara fly to Spain for a holiday.

Mickey Jones: I don't remember Bob being any more tired and wasted than the rest of us. We were all beat to hell. Garth and I decided to take a ship home instead of flying. It was a way of catching up on some well-earned rest. We sailed from Southampton on the S.S. *New Amsterdam*, the Dutch Line to New York City.

Rick Danko (The Band): We came back from that English tour with Bob pretty fried, man. Then, late in July, Albert Grossman's office called and said Bobby had a motorcycle accident in Woodstock and hurt his neck . . .

Thanks: Pennie Garner, Larry Eden, Jeff Rosen, John Baldwin, Jonathan Green, Barney Hoskyns, Clinton Heylin, Lisa Dewhurst, Sue Langford, Patrick Humphries, Joe Smith, Carl Fish, Aaron "Dr. A." Hurwitz, Ian Woodward, Steve Rothenburg, Darren Henderson, Peter Doggett, Bobby Neuwirth, Stewart Morris, everybody at Helter Skelter, and *Isis* magazine for their kind permission to reprint certain sections of their recent lengthy Mickey Jones interview. Most of all though, the spirit of John Bauldie hovers above (and just ahead of) anyone who, like me, threads a tortuous path through the Dylan maze.

This publication of this lengthy, well-informed article by Jules Siegel was impeccable, if accidentally so: the cover date of the magazine in which it was published was one day after a motorcycle accident which temporarily brought Dylan's career to a juddering halt. After said accident, Dylan would never be quite the same again, thereby giving Siegel's précis of his career thus far – constructed with the help of access to Dylan – the status almost of an elegy for the Bob Dylan the world had known hitherto. Dylan seemed to view it in different terms. "He practically had a heart attack when it came out," Siegel recalls. "He sent a message that he was going to have me 'wasted.' His friends called me up and screamed at me. This confirmed my feeling that I had succeeded."

WELL, WHAT HAVE WE HERE?

By Jules Siegel

Originally published in the *Saturday Evening Post*, 30 July 1966

Quick and little, Bob Dylan scrambled from the safety of a rented gray sedan and ran for his dressing room through a wildness of teenage girls who howled and grabbed for his flesh. A cordon of guards held for a moment against the overwhelming attack. Then it broke and Dylan disappeared beneath yards of bell-bottoms and long hair. After a brief struggle he was rescued by one of his assistants, who methodically tore small and large girls off him, but it was too late. With a pair of enormous shears, a giant blonde girl had snipped a lock of the precious Dylan hair and now was weeping for joy.

"Did you see that?" said Dylan in his dressing room, his pale face somewhat paler than usual. "I mean did you see that?" repeated Dylan, who tends to talk in italics. "I don't care about the hair, but she could have killed me. I mean she could have taken my eyes out with those scissors."

This is Bob Dylan's year to be mobbed. Next year it will

probably be somebody else. But this year Bob Dylan is the king of rock and roll, and he is the least likely king popular music has ever seen. With a bony, nervous face covered with skin the color of sour milk, a fright wig of curly tangles, and dark-circled hazel eyes usually hidden by large prescription sunglasses, Dylan is less Elvis or Frankie and more some crippled saint or resurrected Beethoven.

The songs he writes and sings, unlike the usual young-love pap of the airwaves, are full of dark and, many insist, important meaning; they are peopled with freaks, clowns, tramps, artists and mad scientists, dancing and tumbling in a progression of visionary images mobilized to the massive beat of rock and roll. They often make very little logical sense, but almost always they make very good poetic sense. According to a recent poll, college students call him the most important contemporary poet in America.

He is certainly the only poet who gets his hair snipped off by shrieking teenage girls, but Dylan has always been defied categories. His first fame was as a folk singer and folk-song writer. Last year he modified his style to what has been labeled "folk-rock," a blend of serious, poetic lyrics and rock and roll music, which has brought him his greatest commercial success but has alienated some purists who were his early fans. He is a singer whose voice has been compared to the howl of "a dog with his leg caught in barbed wire"; a performer whose stage presence includes no hip wiggling or even, until recently, any acknowledgment of his audience; a public figure whose press conferences are exercises in a new kind of surrealism in which reporters ask, "Are you planning to do a movie?" and Dylan answers, deadpan, "Yes, I'm going to play my mother."

Yet, Bob Dylan, at the age of twenty-five, has a million dollars in the bank and earns an estimated several hundred thousand dollars a year from concerts, recordings and publishing royalties. He is even more popular in England and Europe than in America. Four hours after tickets went on sale for his recent London concerts at the Albert Hall, the SOLD OUT sign was put up, and at one time five of his LP albums were selling in the Top 20 in London. One paperback book on him has already been published; a hardcover book about him by Robert Shelton, folk critic of the *New York Times*, will be published this winter; a third book of photographs and text by Daniel Kramer is scheduled for winter publication. A two-hour documentary of his English tours will soon be released for theater showing; he is about to begin production of his own movie; ABC-TV has signed him for a television special. A book of his writings, *Tarantula*, is to be published by Macmillan late this summer, with a prepublication excerpt to appear in the *Atlantic Monthly*.

And although he is still not nearly as popular as The Beatles, who have sold nearly 200 million records in four years, his artistic reputation is so great that in the recording business Dylan is ranked as the number one innovator, the most important trendsetter, one of the few people around who can change radically the course of teen music.

"Dylan," says Phil Ochs, a folksinger friend of his, "is the king. He's the one we all look to for approval, the one we're all eating our hearts out about, the one who proved you could make it with the kids without any compromises. If I didn't admire him so much, I would have to hate him. In fact, maybe I do hate him anyway."

Born Robert Zimmerman, May 24, 1941, in Duluth, Minnessota, Bob Dylan is a product of Hibbing, Minnessota, an iron-ore mining town of 18,000 inhabitants about seventy miles from the Canadian border. The Southwestern accent in his singing voice is apparently acquired; he speaks without it. His father is a prosperous, witty, small (five-foot-six), cigar-smoking appliance dealer. His mother, a deeply tanned, attractive woman, is described by acquaintances as extremely intelligent, well informed and very talkative.

Dylan has a brother, David, twenty, who attends St. Olaf College on a musical scholarship, and in the family it was always David who was thought of as "the musical one." Abe Zimmerman remembers buying a piano ("Not an expensive one," he says) when Bob was ten. Bob took one lesson and gave up in disgust because he couldn't play anything right away. David, then five, began taking lessons and has been playing ever since.

Despite his initial impatience, Bob Zimmerman soon taught himself how to play the piano, harmonica, guitar and autoharp. Once he began to play the piano, says Mrs. Zimmerman, he beat the keys out of tune pounding out rock and roll. He also wrote – not only music but also poetry. "My mother has hundreds of poems I wrote when I was twelve years old," says Dylan.

As an adolescent, Dylan helped his father in the store, delivering appliances and sometimes attempting to make collections. "He was strong," Abe Zimmerman recently told an acquaintance. "I mean he could hold up his end of a refrigerator as well as kids twice his size, football players.

"I used to make him go out to the poor sections," Mr. Zimmerman said, "knowing he couldn't collect any money from those people. I just wanted to show him another side of life. He'd come back and say, 'Dad, those people haven't got any money.' And I'd say, 'Some of those people out there make as much money as I do, Bobby. They just don't know how to manage it.'"

In more than one way the lesson was well taken. Dylan today, while professing not to know anything about his wealth, appears to be a very good manager of money, careful sometimes to what might be considered stinginess.

Dan Kramer recalls having to meet him at a hotel. "I called him," he says, "and asked if he wanted me to bring anything up for him. 'A container of tea,' Bobby said. I said, 'Bobby, they have room service in the hotel; you can have it sent up.' He thought about that for a couple of seconds and then said no, room service was too expensive." This was in 1965, the year that Dylan became a millionaire.

But Dylan learned more than frugality in the depressed areas of Hibbing. He learned, as Abe Zimmerman hoped he would, that there were people who knew nothing about middle-class life and middle-class values, people whose American dream had become a nightmare of instalment debt. He seems to have felt a blood tie with them, based on a terrifying sense of his own peculiarity.

"I see things that other people don't see," he says. "I feel things other people don't feel. It's terrible. They laugh. I felt like that my whole life.

"My friends have been the same as me, people who couldn't make it as the high-school football halfback, Junior Chamber of Commerce leader, fraternity leader, truck driver working their way through college. I just had to be with them. I just don't care what anyone looks like, just as long as they didn't think I was strange. I couldn't do any of those things either. All I did was write and sing, paint little pictures on paper, dissolve myself into situations where I was invisible."

In pursuit of invisibility, Bob Zimmerman took to running away from home. "I made my own depression," he says. "Rode freight trains for kicks, got beat up for laughs, cut grass for quarters, met a waitress who picked me up and dropped me off in Washington." He tells of living with carnivals, of some trouble with police in Hibbing, of entertaining in a strip joint.

Be that as it may, he managed to finish high school at the appropriate time and even earned a scholarship to the University of Minnesota. Then the middle-class college boy from Hibbing began to remake his life and his image radically. He moved from his fraternity house to a downtown apartment. He began singing and playing the guitar and harmonica at Minneapolis's Ten O'Clock Scholar for two dollars a night; it is said that when he asked for a raise to five dollars, he was fired. He became Bob Dylan, and has since changed his name legally. This was not in tribute to Dylan Thomas, as the widely circulated legend maintains, but for some reason which he doesn't feel compelled to explain seriously.

"Get that straight," he says. "I didn't change my name in honor of Dylan Thomas. That's just a story. I've done more for Dylan Thomas than he's ever done for me. Look how many kids are probably reading his poetry now because they heard that story."

Dylan also gave up his very conventional college-boy dress – for his first professional appearance in Minneapolis he had worn white buck shoes – and began to develop his own personal style. At first, he was influenced by the uniform of folksingers everywhere – jeans, work shirt, boots, collar-length hair. Now that he's a rock and roll star, the uniform has changed. The boots are still part of it, but the jeans are now tight slacks that make his legs look skinnier than they are. The work shirt has been replaced by floppy polka-dot Carnaby Street English shirts with oversized collars and long, puffed sleeves. Sometimes he wears racetrack-plaid suits in combinations of colors like green and black. His hair seems to get longer and wilder by the month.

In December, 1960, Dylan gave up on Minnesota and took off for New York to try rock and roll, then in an uncertain state and dominated by clean-cut singers like Fabian and Frankie Avalon. It was not an auspicious time for someone who looked and sounded like Bob Dylan.

"I tried to make it in rock and roll when rock and roll was a piece of cream," he says. "Elvis had struck, Buddy Holly was dead, Little Richard was becoming a preacher, and Gene Vincent was leaving the country. I wrote the kind of stuff you write when you have no place to live and you're very wrapped up in the fire pump. I nearly killed myself with pity and agony. I saw the way doors close; the way doors that do not like you close. A door that does not like you needs no one to close it. I had to retreat."

Retreat for Dylan was folk music and Greenwich Village. He was strong medicine for both – nervous, cocky, different from anyone else around.

Arthur Kretchmer, a young magazine editor, remembers meeting Dylan at a party: "There was this crazy, restless little kid sitting on the floor and coming on very strong about how he was going to play Holden Caulfield in a movie of *Catcher in the Rye*, and I thought, 'This kid is really terrible'; but the people whose party it was said, 'Don't let him put you off. He comes on a little strong, but he's very sensitive – writes poetry, goes to visit Woody Guthrie in the hospital,' and I figured right, another one. I forgot all about him until a couple of years later he was famous and I wasn't. You can't always be right about these things, I suppose." Both Kretchmer and his wife are now Dylan fans.

Says Robert Shelton, whose book about Dylan is to be published this winter, "He was so astonishing-looking, so Chaplinesque and cherubic, sitting up on a stool playing the guitar and the harmonica and playing with the audience, making all kinds of wry faces, wearing this Huck Finn hat, that I laughed out loud with pleasure. I called over Pat Clancy [an Irish folk singer, one of the Clancy Brothers] and he looked at this cherub and broke into a broad smile and said, 'Well, what have we here?'"

Not too long after that, Shelton wrote a laudatory review in the *New York Times* of a Dylan performance. About the same time, Columbia Records executive John Hammond met Dylan at the home of folksinger Carolyn Hester, whom Dylan was going to accompany on a new record Hammond was producing. Without hearing him perform, Hammond offered Dylan a two-year contract with Columbia, and immediately hit a snag.

Dylan, a minor of twenty, refused to admit to having any living relatives who could sign for him. "I don't know where my folks are," he told Hammond. "I think I've got an uncle who's a gambler in Nevada, but I wouldn't know how to track him down." Taking another chance, Hammond finally let the boy execute the contract himself.

The young folksinger's first LP was called *Bob Dylan*. It cost $403 to produce and sold, initially, 4,200 copies. By way of comparison, Dylan's most recent record as of this writing, *Highway 61 Revisited*, has sold 360,000 in the United States. All together, it is estimated that ten million Dylan records have been sold throughout the world. His songs have been recorded in more than 150 other versions by performers ranging from Stan Getz to Lawrence Welk, and the royalties, Dylan admits, have made him a millionaire.

In achieving this success, Dylan has had powerful allies. Not the least of these was Billy James, a young Columbia public, relations man who is now the record company's West Coast artist-relations director. It was through James's efforts that Dylan got his first taste of national publicity, but the singer's past was to come between them. In 1963, when Dylan was entering his first flush of fame with 'Blowin' in the Wind', a song which became an unofficial anthem of the civil-rights movement and a major popular hit, *Newsweek* revealed that Bob Dylan was Robert Zimmerman and went on to suggest that not only was Dylan's name a fake but it was rumored another writer had created 'Blowin' in the Wind.' One part of the story was false – Dylan was the author of the song; but the other part, of course, was true: Bob Dylan was Robert Zimmerman.

Dylan was infuriated by the article and blamed Billy James for it. For two years the two did not speak. James won't talk about the incident at all, but people who know both of them say that Dylan attempted to get the public-relations man fired. Two years later, they met at a party and Dylan was all friendship again. When James mentioned the *Newsweek* affair, Dylan put an arm around him and said, "Thousands of people are dying in Vietnam and right at this minute a man is jumping off the Empire State Building and you got that running around in your head?"

One of the great factors in Dylan's early success was his profound ability to articulate the emotions of the civil-rights revolution, which was developing its peak of power in the early Sixties. Recognition of this talent came in dramatic form at the Newport Folk Festival of 1963.

Although he had already appeared once on the program, which is a sort of Hall of Fame of folksinging in action, he was called back to the stage at the end of the final concert. Accompanied by a stageful of folk stars, from Pete Seeger, the gentle "king" of folk music, to Joan Baez, the undisputed queen, Bob Dylan sang 'Blowin' in the Wind' to an audience of 36,000 of the most important folksinging fans, writers, recording executives and critics.

"How many roads must a man walk down before they call him a man?" they sang. "Yes, 'n' how many seas must a white dove sail before she sleeps in the sand? Yes, 'n' how many times must the cannon balls fly before they're forever banned? The answer my friend, is blowin' in the wind, the answer is blowin' in the wind."

Recorded by Peter, Paul and Mary, 'Blowin' in the Wind' was Dylan's first major hit, and very quickly there were fifty-eight different versions of the song, by everyone from the Staple Singers (a screaming gospel version) to Marlene Dietrich. Almost overnight Dylan was established at the top of the folk-music field. Here at last, sighed the folk critics and the civil-rights people, was a songwriter with the true "proletarian" touch, one who could really reach the masses. For two years, Dylan was the musical spokesman for civil rights, turning up in Mississippi, in the march on Washington, at the demonstrations and rallies.

"I feel it," said Joan Baez, whom Dylan had met before Newport, "but Dylan can say it. He's phenomenal."

For a while, Joan and Bobby were to be inseparable, the queen and crown prince of folk music. When Dylan went to England for a concert tour, Joan Baez went with him. As much as anyone's, it was her voice and authority which helped to create the charismatic reputation of Bob Dylan the folksinger.

These days Dylan and Baez are not as close as they used to be. When the rough cut of *Dont Look Back* was screened in Hollywood this spring, Baez was everywhere on the film, in the limousine, at the airport, singing in the hotel room. After the screening, Dylan said to the film editor, "We'll have to take all that stuff of Joan out." He hesitated and then added, "Well, it looks as if she was the whole thing. She was only there a few days. We'll have to cut it down."

Far more important to Dylan, however, was Albert Grossman, who took over Dylan's career and, to a great extent, his life. He is not only Dylan's manager, but also his confidant, healer and friend. Until recently, in fact, Dylan had no home of his own. He lived in Grossman's New York City apartment or the manager's antique-filled country home in Woodstock, N.Y.

He appears to be only vaguely aware of the extent or nature of his wealth, leaving the details to Grossman. "When I want money," Dylan says, "I ask for it. After I spend it, I ask for more."

Dylan has had his effect on Grossman, too, however. "I used to remember Albert as a nice-looking businessman, the kind of middle-aged man you would meet in a decent restaurant in the garment center," says Gloria Stayers, editor of *16*. "Then, a while after he signed Dylan, I met him again. I couldn't believe it. I just couldn't believe what had happened to him. He had long gray hair like Benjamin Franklin and wire-rimmed spectacles, and he was wearing an old sweatshirt or something and Army pants. 'Albert,' I screamed, when I finally recognized him. 'Albert, what has Bobby done to you?'"

A measure of Dylan's relationship with his manager is found in the tone and style he uses in talking to Grossman. Even in the most ordinary conversation, Dylan can be almost impossible to understand. He is often vague, poetic, repetitive, confusing. But his flow of imagery can be startlingly precise and original, and the line of his thought brilliantly adventurous, funny and pene- trating. So, in describing his music he will say, "It's all math, simple math, involved in mathematics. There's a definite number of Colt .45s that make up Marlene Dietrich, and you can find that out if you want to."

This kind of talk is not useful for more than a few situations. Nonetheless, it is the way Dylan speaks to fans, disk jockeys, reporters, acquaintances, and frequently, friends. It is not the way he speaks to Grossman. Then his voice often goes into a kind of piping whine, the voice of a little boy complaining to his father.

Thus, after a concert on the West Coast, at three o'clock in the morning, I told Dylan that his voice was not heard over the blast of the electronically amplified instruments. Grossman lay dozing on the hotel bed, his tinted glasses still on, a slight smile of repose on his heavy face.

"Al-bert," Dylan cried, "Albert, did you hear that? They couldn't hear me. Al-bert, I mean they couldn't hear me. What good is it if they can't hear me? We've got to get that sound man out here to fix it. What do you think, Albert?"

Grossman stirred on the bed and answered soothingly, "I told you in the car that the volume was too high. Just cut the volume by about a third and it'll be all right." Grossman went back to sleep, very much like an occidental Buddha, snoring lightly. Dylan was satisfied.

Grossman's formidable managerial talent is displayed most clearly when Dylan is on concert tour. From Grossman's New York office, the logistics of moving the singer and his crew from concert to concert halfway around the world are worked out with an efficiency that makes the whole operation seem effortless.

On the road the Dylan entourage usually consists of Dylan, his road manager, a pilot and co-pilot for the thirteen-seat two-engine Lodestar in which the group travels over the shorter distances (tourist-class commercial jets are used for overseas and transcontinental travel), two truck drivers who deliver the sound equipment and musicians' instruments from stop to stop, a sound man and five musicians – two guitarists, a drummer, pianist and organist. Grossman flies out from time to time to hear a concert or two and then returns to New York. On foreign tours he usually stays with the group throughout the trip.

Dylan's people are protective and highly attentive to his wants, and Dylan himself, given his status as a star, is neither especially demanding nor temperamental, even when things don't quite go according to schedule.

Last spring, for example, a concert in Vancouver was an acoustical disaster. The arena still smelled strongly of its last

guests – a stock exhibition. It was perfectly round, with a flat
dome that produced seven echoes from a sharp handclap in the
center. Large open gates let sound leak out of the hall as easily as
if the concert were held in the open air. Although Dylan's
$30,000 custom-designed sound system filled eight large crates
with equipment, it could never fill this gigantic echo chamber
with clear sound. Adding to the problem, one of the small monitor speakers placed on stage to enable the musicians to hear
themselves play, was not working.

Dylan's concerts are divided into two halves. During the first, in
which he played his acoustic guitar into a stage microphone, the
sound was patchy; in some spots it was perfect, in others it was very
bad. In the second half, however, in which rock and roll songs were
played on the amplified instruments and electric guitars, the music
was a garble of reverberation, and Dylan's voice was totally scrambled by the echo. The sound man sweated and twirled his knobs,
but it was no use. At one point Grossman ran up to the stage to tell
Dylan he was "eating the mike," that is, getting too close to the
microphone and contributing to the electric jumble. The musicians,
deprived of the monitor, watched each other tensely as they tried to
keep their beat by observation rather than sound.

"Man, that was just terrible," Dylan said when he came
offstage and hurried into the waiting car. "That was just awful. I
mean that was worse than Ottawa, and Ottawa was the worst
asshole in the universe." He turned to each person in the car and
asked them separately, "Wasn't that worse than Ottawa, and
wasn't Ottawa the worst asshole in the universe?" Everyone
agreed that it was worse than Ottawa.

"That was really worse than Ottawa, and Ottawa was the
worst, terrible, miserable asshole in the entire universe," Dylan
repeated, with a certain satisfaction. "Worse than Ottawa," he
mused, and then, laughing, turned around and said, "And
anyone who doesn't think it was worse than Ottawa can get out
of the car right now."

Later he and Grossman discussed the problem again, and it
was agreed that the fault lay in the arena, not in the equipment.
In a better hall or a theater there would have been no trouble.
Dylan's concern now was with the halls in which he was booked
in Australia.

"Albert, it's no good in those arenas," he said. "I just would rather forget about arenas and play theaters. To hell with the money; I mean I would much rather have a good show. Are we going to play any arenas in Australia?"

"We have to," Grossman answered. "We haven't any choice, Bobby. There just aren't enough big concert halls or theaters there. It's not America. The country is still undeveloped."

"Well, all right," said Dylan. "I mean if we have to, but I wish we could play theaters and halls. I mean that place was worse than Ottawa and—" "Ottawa was the worst asshole in the universe," someone chimed in.

"Yeah. The worst in the universe. And this was worse."

At no time, perhaps, was Dylan's closeness with Grossman more important than in 1965, the year Dylan turned from folk music to rock and roll. He had by this time cut three more albums, two of them, *The Times They Are A-Changin'* and *Freewheelin' Bob Dylan*, outstandingly successful, not only in sales but in acclaim from the critics and the civil-rights activists. But he came back from a stunningly successful English tour with a feeling of malaise and a desire for change.

"After I finished the English tour," he says, "I quit because it was too easy. There was nothing happening for me. Every concert was the same: first half, second half, two encores and run out, then having to take care of myself all night.

"I didn't understand; I'd get standing ovations, and it didn't mean anything. The first time I felt no shame. But then I was just following myself after that. It was down to a pattern."

In his next album, *Bringing It All Back Home*, Dylan broke the pattern. Instead of playing either conventional "protest" as it was understood then, or using the traditional folk-music modes, he electrically amplified his guitar and set surrealistic verses to the rock-and-roll beat.

Ironically, it was one of the album's few non-rock songs that brought Dylan his first great success in the pop market. 'Mr. Tambourine Man,' recorded by The Byrds in a hard-rock version complete with falsetto, was a massive hit.

"When 'Mr. Tambourine Man' broke, we didn't know anything about Bob Dylan," says "Cousin Brucie" Morrow, a disk jockey on WABC Radio, New York. "Oh, I remember a few years ago we'd listen to a single of his. It didn't seem to fit the sound then, so we didn't play it. That was all I knew about Bob Dylan until The Byrds hit with 'Tambourine Man.' Then everyone was asking. 'Who's this Bob Dylan?' It's the only time I can remember when a composer got more attention for a hit than the performers did."

Then when Dylan released his new single, 'Like a Rolling Stone,' and his new album, *Highway 61 Revisited*, the folk fans knew Bobby was going to be a teenage idol, and if he was a teenage idol he wasn't theirs anymore. For people who had thought they owned Bob Dylan, it was a bitter disappointment, and Dylan lost a great many people he thought were his friends. "A freak and a parody," shrieked Irwin Silber in the folk-music magazine *Sing Out!* At the Newport Folk Festival of 1965, Dylan was booed off the stage. At his Forest Hills concert in September, the audience listened attentively through the first, folk, half of the program and then began to boo when the musicians came out for the rock portion. This time Dylan did not walk off the stage as he did at Newport, but fought his way through the performance, supported by 80 percent of the crowd. 'Like a Rolling Stone' finally put Dylan across as a rock-and-roll star. He wrote it in its first form when he came back from England. "It was ten pages long," he says. "It wasn't called anything, just a rhythm thing on paper all about my steady hatred directed at some point that was honest. In the end it wasn't hatred, it was telling someone something they didn't know, telling them they were lucky. Revenge, that's a better word.

"I had never thought of it as a song, until one day I was at the piano, and on the paper it was singing, 'How does it feel?' in a slow-motion pace, in the utmost of slow motion following something.

"It was like swimming in lava. In your eyesight, you see your victim swimming in lava. Hanging by their arms from a birch tree. Skipping, kicking the tree, hitting a nail with your foot. Seeing someone in the pain they were bound to meet up with. I wrote it. I didn't fail. It was straight." 'Like a Rolling Stone' climbed rapidly to the top of the charts. It was followed by 'Positively 4th Street' and then by 'Ballad of a Thin Man,' and Dylan's lead was soon followed by other songwriters released from the inane bondage of the "I Love You, Teen Queen" strait-jacket. Soon the airwaves were full of songs about the war in Vietnam, or civil rights, or the general disorder of the world and society in America. It was quickly labeled "folk-rock," and the kids wolfed it down and are still listening to it.

Along with the teenagers, Dylan got a surprising bonus audience – the adult hip intellectuals who had just found out about rock and roll. National magazines began writing favorably about both Dylan and rock, and rock concerts became the social events of the intellectuals' seasons. Allen Ginsberg said, "He writes better poetry than I did at his age . . . I'd say he's a space-age genius minstrel more than an old library poet . . ." One Sunday, the magazine sections of the *New York Times* and the *New York Herald Tribune* simultaneously published long articles on the poetry of Bob Dylan, complete with learned analyses and exegeses of the most fashionable academic-journalist-sociological kind.

Dylan's reaction is predictably thorny. "The songs are not meant to be great," he said. "I'm not meant to be great. I don't think anything I touch is destined for greatness. Genius is a terrible word, a word they think will make me like them. A genius is a very insulting thing to say. Even Einstein wasn't a genius. He was a foreign mathematician who would have stolen cars." Some of his recent songs have brought him new criticism: it has been claimed that the lyrics of 'Mr. Tambourine Man' and his latest hit, 'Rainy Day Women #12 and 35' ("Everybody must get stoned!"), are all about drugs and drug experiences. Grossman denies it. Dylan won't talk about his songs. "Don't interpret me," he says. Talking about drugs, he is typically elusive. "People just don't need drugs," he says. "Keep things out of your body. We all take medicine, as long as you know why you're taking it. If you want to crack down on the drug situation, the criminal drug situation takes place in the suburban housewives' kitchens, the ones who get wiped out on alcohol every afternoon and then make supper. You can't blame them and you can't blame their husbands. They've been working in the mines all day. It's understandable."

During the past year Dylan has got married, fathered a son, Jesse Byron Dylan, and bought a townhouse in Manhattan's fashionable East Thirties. Typically, he has attempted to keep all of this a secret. When his wife, a beautiful, black-haired girl named Sara Lownds, visited him in Vancouver and attended his concert, Dylan was faced with a problem: two disk jockeys were coming up to the dressing room to interview him; how was he to hide his wife from them? "Sara," said Dylan, opening a large closet, "when they arrive I want you to get in here." His wife looked at him quizzically but stepped reluctantly towards the open door. Dylan began to laugh, but it is a mark of the seriousness of his desire for privacy that his wife was ready to get into the closet.

The only thing anyone now will predict for certain is that Dylan will change. "I'll never decay," he says. "Decay is when something has stopped living but hasn't died yet, looking at your leg and seeing it all covered with creeping brown cancer. Decay turns me off. I'll die first before I decay."

JOHN WESLEY HARDING

By Sean Egan

US release: 27 December 1967
Produced by: Bob Johnston
CHARTS: US#2; UK#1

SIDE ONE
John Wesley Harding
As I Went Out One Morning
I Dreamed I Saw St. Augustine
All Along the Watchtower
The Ballad of Frankie Lee and Judas Priest
Drifter's Escape

SIDE TWO
Dear Landlord
I Am a Lonesome Hobo
I Pity the Poor Immigrant
The Wicked Messenger
Down Along the Cove
I'll Be Your Baby Tonight

On 29 July 1966, Bob Dylan had a motorcycle accident on Albert Grossman's Woodstock estate. Following the accident, his upcoming gigs were cancelled and he did not release a follow-up to *Blonde on Blonde* for a year and seven months.

Tales abounded of Dylan being paralysed or a vegetable, the type of ill-informed rumour mill now just about destroyed by the central information-gathering processes of the Internet. In fact, Dylan had sustained cracked vertebrae and was in a neck brace for a couple of months. The enforced idleness must have been merciful to Dylan. The accident may also have been seen by him as a wake-up call. Not only does he seem to have used it as a pretext to extricate himself from the professional obligations Grossman had placed him under, but also to ultimately extricate himself from his manager's clutches completely.

Aside from the brutality of the regime to which the grasping Grossman had subjected him, there was another reason for Dylan to not want to leave his house, which was also in the Woodstock area of upstate New York. Sara Lownds had been very pregnant when she and Dylan married and their first child together was born in January 1966. Dylan adopted Sara's existing daughter, and the couple would have three more children by 1969. The phase of Dylan's life in which he was a media-courting rock god and the epitome of cool was ending as he morphed into an honest-to-goodness family man.

When on 13 October, CBS put out a statement saying that Dylan would not be performing before March 1967, the label must have been terrified. Pop acts released two albums and several singles per year (although expectations were just then changing to one album and several singles per year following the example provided by The Beatles as they leisurely honed what would be *Sgt. Pepper*). The assumption was that if they didn't, their fans would transfer their affections to other artists or even outgrow popular music by the time the absent artist returned. It was actually a reasonable assumption at a point when teenagers constituted the vast majority of the record-buying populace and post-Elvis popular music wasn't yet old enough to have demonstrated an ability to retain its audience across generations. Though Dylan had amassed a certain amount of wealth and was in possession of healthy revenue streams from record royalties and from cover versions – the latter something Grossman would ensure was maintained by hawking around demos of the songs he was writing in his seclusion to other artists – it was a brave decision for him to withdraw from the music industry.

With a long silence by their prized artist lying ahead, Columbia attempted their version of the process by which RCA kept Elvis Presley's name in the limelight after he was drafted. They were at a not inconsiderable disadvantage in the fact that though Elvis's manager Tom Parker had stockpiled new recordings for gradual release throughout The King's absence, Columbia had no such unreleased material to draw upon – or at least none that

Dylan would sanction the issuing of. The only new Dylan product in this period was 'If You Gotta Go, Go Now'. He had tried more than once to capture an acceptable version of the song made a hit by Manfred Mann without success before Tom Wilson had overdubbed musicians onto his acoustic basic track. Wilson had done the same with Dylan's version of 'House of the Risin' Sun', also without permission. Although Dylan vetoed the results of the latter, Wilson's tampering with 'If You Gotta Go' somehow ended up being released on single format in the Benelux countries in January 1967, with – apropos of nothing – 'To Ramona' on the flip.

Otherwise, Columbia could only reshuffle the existing material. Accordingly, in March 1967 (that juncture that it had been implied might see renewed Dylan activity, but didn't) came *Bob Dylan's Greatest Hits*. The title caused Dylan fans to groan. It could only have been dreamt up by a "Mr. Jones". There was a reason for the *Greatest Hits* title being inappropriate other than it being crass and obvious in a way that Dylan's work never was. Bob Dylan hadn't had many hits, or even issued that many singles for a man who had been releasing records as long as he had. 'Rainy Day Women #12 & 35', 'Like a Rolling Stone', 'Subterranean Homesick Blues', 'I Want You', 'Positively 4th Street' and 'Just Like a Woman' were all present, but it would have been pushing it to include his several flop 45s. Of course, that didn't mean that Columbia didn't have enough famous Dylan songs to make up an album: 'Blowin' in the Wind' and 'The Times They Are A-Changin' ' were both well-known from Peter, Paul and Mary versions (and others'), 'It Ain't Me, Babe' through The Turtles and 'Mr. Tambourine Man' via The Byrds. In fact, in a way it was a nice piece of lateral thinking by the label to include Dylan's versions of these songs – after all, the "Greatest Hits" phrase didn't promise specifically that the hits had been achieved by the songs' writer. It certainly must have been an education to kids only familiar with the covers to hear Dylan's superior originals. In fact, the album would have been an education per se for those new to the artist who – like many music consumers do – purchased it because they were attracted by the idea of a best-of. Mammon may have motivated its release and philistinism may have been behind its packaging, but there's no getting round the fact that it is a great collection of music – and surely the most mind-blowing compilation since the whole industry had been kicked off by the release of *Johnny's Greatest Hits* by Johnny Mathis in 1958. (The UK version, incidentally, replaced 'Positively 4th Street' and 'I Want You' with 'She Belongs to Me', 'It's All Over Now, Baby Blue' and 'One of Us Must Know (Sooner or Later)'.) However, nobody can deny the crassness behind Columbia's release the month after *Greatest Hits* of 'Leopard-Skin Pill-Box Hat'. Not only was it no less than the fifth single from *Blonde on Blonde*, but it was butchered by being cut virtually in half.

Despite his withdrawal from the scene, Dylan still had a media presence, and not just because Michael Iachetta of the NewYork *Daily News* tracked him down in May and was able to confirm to his readers that a bearded Dylan was alive, well and not stricken by any of the maladies the rumours were suggesting. May 17 saw the premiere of *Dont Look Back*. (A "companion book" featuring a transcript of the movie and many photos was published in 1968.) The movie documentary of Dylan's 1965 UK tour and the backstage events thereof was already out of date on more than one count. Pennebaker had subsequently covered the far more seismic events of the artist's 1966 tour and Dylan and Pennebaker were trying to finalise the edit of the results – *Eat the Document* – at this moment. However, there had been other developments since then – as demonstrated by the unusual and almost caricatured politeness with which Dylan had greeted Iachetta. Though the journalist didn't analyse this fact, Dylan was clearly undergoing profound changes. As far as the public knew, though, the brilliant but scathing Dylan to be seen humiliating Donovan, Baez and the science student in *Dont Look Back* was the person he still was and the movie only added to his esteem amongst the counter-culture. That cool Dylan persona was spread all across the pages of *Bob Dylan*, a book of photographs by Daniel Kramer published in March and the first "proper" Dylan book, if one discounts the hack-job *Folk-Rock: The Bob Dylan Story* by Sy and Barbara Ribakove (1966). (Robert Shelton's mooted semi-official biography wouldn't appear for another two decades.) Kramer had taken the cover pictures of *Bringing It All Back Home* and *Highway 61* and had, with the artist's permission, followed Dylan around with a camera from August 1964 to August 1965. Dylan tried to obtain an injunction to stop the book's appearance but failed, though this seems to have been a matter of maintaining his peace and quiet; he and Kramer remained friendly. A more up-to-date vision of Dylan was provided by photographs of the man taken by the bizarrely anagram-named Elliott Landy in Woodstock in summer 1968: Dylan is seen wandering around in white shirt, white slacks and sandals, the pictures in which he is not wearing a boxy white hat revealing that his hair is now short. It was the type of outfit in which this guru of cool wouldn't have been seen dead in 1966, and indeed the type of outfit that communicated he no longer cared about clothes and style because he had more important values in his life these days.

Meanwhile, back in 1967, the combination of those teasing glimpses of Dylan and his continued personal absence served to create a mystique even greater than the one he had previously spawned via his poetic songwords and elliptical interview answers. By no design whatsoever, Dylan's mystique was further enhanced when songs he began recording in mid-1967 with his touring group (then still The Hawks and toying with becoming The Crackers but referred to as The Band henceforth in this text) started to leak out to the wider world. Dylan, under pressure from Grossman or his record company or both, had continued writing. He and The Band began informal recording sessions first at his house, then in the basement of a house The Band had rented nearby in West Saugerties nicknamed Big Pink. That thin, wild mercury sound was nowhere in evidence on these new recordings, nor the brutal but beautiful sound Dylan had made onstage with The Band throughout 1966. Partly, this was down to the conditions: the recording equipment was basic, Big Pink's cement-walled basement had its own unique musty acoustics, the personnel couldn't play too loudly because those acoustics hurt their ears, and the recordings of these songs were not meant for public consumption, being designed to be offered to other artists to record. Even when making those allowances, though, there was clearly something very different going on here. While not exactly folk, the music's pastoral feel not only suggested it, but its old-world atmosphere evoked the ancient times when folk music had first been heard. And while the lyrics retained Dylan's twinkle-eyed sense of humour – there were several cartoonish numbers and several others dripping with sex – he was no longer tearing a strip off either other individuals or the world. Themes of spiritual redemption informed several of the songs, and a mordant, unsure tone others. Dylan even *sounded* a different person, that blaring voice now often a mellow croon. Additionally, Dylan and The Band recorded many cover versions and traditional songs at these sessions, especially at the start. Although Dylan has spoken resentfully of the pressure that prompted these recordings, he has also spoken fondly of the relaxed, informal atmosphere that characterized them.

Fourteen of the original songs were copyrighted and put on an acetate. Significantly, Dylan owed Columbia a fourteen-song album as the last instalment of his current contract. The contents were: 'Million Dollar Bash', 'Yea! Heavy and a Bottle of Bread', 'Please Mrs. Henry', 'Down in the Flood', 'Lo and Behold!', 'Tiny Montgomery', 'This Wheel's on Fire', 'You Ain't Goin' Nowhere', 'I Shall Be Released', 'Tears of Rage', 'Too Much of Nothing', 'Quinn the Eskimo (The Mighty Quinn)', 'Open the Door, Homer' and 'Nothing Was Delivered'. Although this collection of demos would indeed have made a fine album, instead, the fourteen songs were circulated amongst recording artists who might be interested in them – Grossman even flying over to London to play them to interested parties – and soon Dylan was on the charts again. Aptly, his first champions Peter, Paul and Mary started the mini-avalanche when their version of 'Too Much of Nothing' was a minor US hit (No. 35) towards the close of 1967. The mini-avalanche of covers would continue into 1968, partly because, though by then Dylan had finally put out a new album, it contained not a single song from what would colloquially become known as the Basement Tapes. In early 1968, Manfred Mann – whom Dylan had publicly named as his favourite interpreters of his songs – made UK No.1 with the song Dylan had copyrighted as 'Quinn the Eskimo (The Mighty Quinn)' but which they retitled 'Mighty Quinn'. (Dylan himself has tampered with the title, reflected in the references to the song in this text.) Though the lyric was opaque, it was also effortlessly anthemic and sounded somehow suffused with wisdom ("Come all without, come all within"). No doubt Manfred Mann, like the public, indulgently viewed the lyric as just more of Dylan's unfathomable poetry. For those inclined to try to discern meaning, the songwords were clearly a veiled resurrection tale ("Everybody's in despair, every girl and boy/ But when Quinn the Eskimo gets here, everybody's gonna jump for joy"). This wouldn't have been such a huge surprise to those who had bought Dylan's belated follow-up to *Blonde on Blonde*. Religious imagery permeated *John Wesley Harding* at every turn.

Although – courtesy of the publishing demos and George Harrison's visits to his friend Dylan in Woodstock – the rock cognoscenti knew of Dylan's sharp change of musical direction, the public didn't. Released two days after Christmas 1967, the style of *John Wesley Harding* was therefore a bolt from the blue to the vast majority of the people who heard it. Even those privy to the extracts of the Basement Tapes Grossman had disseminated would have been more than a little surprised, for this music was not even the Americana produced in Big Pink but had an even older quality than that, feeling like it originated before America had been founded. Of course, electric bass didn't exist back then, but the archaic tone of this parched, unadorned, unflashy music was only heightened by its lyrical frame of reference. Only the final track sounds unequivocally set in the 20th century. The cowboy tableau of the opener seems to identify it as 19th century. A reference to a steamboat whistle in 'Dear Landlord' dates it as set at least after July 1787. The rest depicted scenarios that could have occurred any time after the writing of the Old Testament of the Bible but probably not before the collation of the contents of the New Testament. Biblical characters pepper the songs' lyrics, some named, some simply identifiable as biblical via language and phraseology only familiar to most from King James' syntax. Additionally, the album's themes were contrition and judgment. Combined with Dylan's new smoother, rounder voice it made for an effect that was completely disorienting. Only its uniqueness gave away its origin. This was Bob Dylan music, but not as we knew it.

The album was recorded in three separate Nashville sessions across the course of six weeks in October/November 1967. The songs would seem to have been either kept secret from

The Band or were newly written, as none were played during the Basement Tape sessions. Almost uniquely, there were no outtakes from the *Harding* sessions; Dylan released precisely what he had recorded. The vast bulk of the tracks feature just Dylan on acoustic guitar, harmonica and the occasional piano part, Kenny Buttrey on drums and Charlie McCoy on bass. The only decoration is the steel guitar supplied by Pete Drake on the last two songs on the album. Before the album's completion, Dylan did sound out The Band's Robbie Robertson and possibly Garth Hudson about providing some embellishments, but he/they unselfishly told him the tracks were fine as they were. So it came to pass that Dylan released an album that appeared to cock a snook at the multi-coloured, effects-laden style that characterized popular music in psychedelic 1967.

The title track in one sense sets the tone. It's short, enigmatic and austere as a frontier log cabin. It talks of a western hero who does unspecified acts of goodness and overcomes vaguely defined crises. It's almost as though Dylan is obliquely telling us that his reputation with the public as seer is undeserved.

From hereon in, things get spiritually grim. 'As I Went Out One Morning' is simply terrifying. The narrator goes out to take the air around Tom Paine's and when he does, encounters a fair damsel in chains. When said damsel is offered the narrator's hand but instead takes his arm, the narrator realises she means to do him harm. The narrator asks the girl to leave him, but indicates his ambivalence to the listener by stating he is speaking "with my voice" (i.e., not his heart). The song continues: " 'I beg you sir', she pleaded, from the corners of her mouth/'I will secretly accept you, and together we'll fly south'." Only the hasty intervention of an apologetic Tom Paine saves the man from what we infer would have been a terrible fate. The music accompanying this is just as spooky as the tableau depicted, measured but sinister, and with Dylan heightening the tension by underlining the events of each verse with a doomy harmonica flourish. Like almost every other song here, it ends abruptly, leaving not only an unresolved feeling, but a chill in the air. Few things in rock music are genuinely unsettling, but this is one of a trio of songs on this record to which one is advised not to listen in the dark.

And the meaning? Some have suggested that Dylan is referring to the Bill of Rights dinner he attended in December 1963 where, while receiving the Tom Paine Award, he caused offence by saying he could understand Lee Harvey Oswald. However, the song feels far too troubled and wide in scope to merely be addressing that petty matter. Tom Paine may be Founding Father Thomas Paine (the courtly phraseology employed to tell the tale certainly suggests the eighteenth century) and it seems clear that the south being referred to is not the cotton states but south in a far more frightening sense. The song is just one of many tortured references to temptation that we are to experience.

'I Dreamed I Saw St. Augustine' opens with some superb oscillating harmonica work from Dylan, but idolatry for his craft is not on the artist's mind as he recounts a dream about a man frantically "searching for the very souls whom already have been sold". Exact interpretation of the song seems impossible – although there were two St. Augustines, neither were put to death as the song depicts – but the impressionistic effect is of deep regret at one's actions (the narrator wakes from his dream in anger and terror and sobs). The work of the three-man band is unshowy but brilliant.

With its propulsive rhythm, 'All Along the Watchtower' is the closest the album comes to a conventional rock sound, but retains the ancient-times feel of the surrounding material. A philosophical dialogue between a joker and a thief, it is novelistic and atmospheric and once again ends abruptly and ominously ("Two riders were approaching/The wind begin to howl"). The Jimi Hendrix Experience would have a transatlantic hit with an epic aural expansion of this song in Autumn 1968, but no one should be under any illusion that Hendrix's superb colouring-in of this track is any more brilliant than the pencil original.

Where Dylan had pioneered length in rock songs, now he was favouring brevity: at five-and-a-half minutes, 'The Ballad of Frankie Lee and Judas Priest' is one of the longer tracks. It is also among the scariest. (The title was unsettling to British ears, unused to the American "Judas Priest" epithet; familiarity and the co-opting of part of it by a heavy metal band for their name has dulled its shock factor.) Once more we are presented with a story of temptation, as the two ostensible titular friends have an

edgy conversation which results in Judas Priest, apparently
reluctantly, offering Frankie Lee the loan of some money.
Frankie Lee ends up enraptured by a magnificent house with a
woman's face in every window. He berserkly indulges himself in
the house for sixteen days, but dies on the seventeenth – of thirst.
The final verse sees Dylan tell us that the moral of the story is
"simply that one should never be where one does not belong",
adding that one should help one's neighbour with his burden
and that one should not mistake the house across the road for
paradise. The lyric is alternately sombre and absurd – with the
occasional touch of gallows humour – but the musical performance gives it a layer not to be gleaned from the printed page.
Dylan's singing is even and pseudo-guileless and the combination of that, the weird, dream-like chain of events and the
straight-faced, relentless backing is cumulatively almost as
disturbing as 'As I Went Out One Morning'.

Side one of the original vinyl album ended poorly with
'Drifter's Escape', a tale of a wretched man against whom judgment has just been entered despite him not understanding what
he has done wrong. When a bolt of lightning hits the courthouse,
he escapes in the confusion. It's no more unresolved or opaque
than any of the other songs but is too musically clunky to have
their mysterious power.

'Dear Landlord', a track with a fine piano backbone from
Dylan, sees the narrator imploring the man to whom he is tenant
to show mercy and understanding to him. We'll never know
whether Dylan is addressing Albert Grossman, God or even his
own body but it is immediately clear that this song is sure as hell
not about a rent dispute. It ends with the narrator telling the
addressee, "If you don't underestimate me, then I won't underestimate you." This language of compromise and meekness
– especially phrased so formally – is still rare in rock and was
almost unknown then.

'I Am a Lonesome Hobo' depicts a man as wretched as the
previously mentioned drifter. He has no friends, family or
possessions ("Where another man's life might begin, that's
exactly where mine ends") and can only take pride in the fact
that he has never begged. 'I Pity the Poor Immigrant' sees a
third-person exploration of the same theme that 'I Am a

Lonesome Hobo' tackles from a first-person perspective. "Immigrant" here is clearly meant in a wider sense – somebody who has made a journey from the psychologically familiar rather than a physical journey. The narrator pities a man who "with his fingers cheats and who lies with every breath" but whose empires built on others' suffering will ultimately – as all empires do – crumble. We are once more reminded that Dylan could be talking about his own hitherto merciless and exploitative persona.

'The Wicked Messenger' is the third terrifying track on the album – and the final one suffused with religious imagery and the dread of judgment. It tells the story of a messenger despatched by Eli who is unable to speak without flattery or exaggeration and who one day appears with a note reading, "The soles of my feet, I swear they're burning!" These words are scary enough but the combination of those, the fast pace, a sinister, descending bass lick and the almost hysterical tone to Dylan's voice is blood-curdling. The messenger seems to bring pestilence with him and is ultimately told by angry people, "If you cannot bring good news, then don't bring any!" Once again, the song ends abruptly and begging questions.

With the final two songs, it is strongly implied to us that that wicked messenger had in fact been Dylan, for the latter seems to take the advice given to the messenger by devoting the remainder of the album to no message more profound than the joys of romance. 'Down Along the Cove' is a gently swinging country blues in which the narrator's heart lifts as he sees his true love coming his way and who swells with pride as the people the couple pass realize they are in love. Piano and Drake's steel guitar decorate a slight but sweet song. 'I'll Be Your Baby Tonight' explores the same territory but does so with much more élan. One of the truly classic Dylan songs, it features a superb harmonica riff and great country-pop tune. Dylan proves he's no mere cornball C&W sentimentalist by including a bridge where he mocks the very Tin Pan Alley traditions in which he is indulging by rhyming "moon" and "spoon", only omitting "June" from the trilogy of hackneyed rhymes that people use to disparage such method-correct composition. It's a lovely end to the album in more senses than one, not only leaving a sweet taste in the mouth but reassuring us that the demons that Dylan had been battling on the first ten songs have been vanquished.

John Wesley Harding was a quite extraordinary artistic statement, especially for the times. On a musical level, it was an absolute *non sequitur* to the "far-out" fashions that had raged all year and almost a statement that Dylan was above the rules and trends to which all other pop artists were slave. Not only was the bareness of the album in stark contrast to the multi-coloured soundscapes of the season, but the foreboding of most of it was a dash of cold water for a generation drenched in flower-power optimism. Lyrically, it was simply unprecedented. That description applies to most of Dylan's work so far, of course, but here he was taking a detour that made his renunciation of protest and his abandonment of folk mere blips. Although some of Dylan's long-time fans might have been pleased that the album effectively saw him returning to folk, there was an element that would have horrified them. Many must have been the Dylan freaks at the time who thought – or tried to convince themselves – that the whole album was a spoof of religion, which then was still indelibly associated with social authoritarianism and censoriousness. Having said that, one wonders whether those who cite the album as proof of Dylan's unquestioning acceptance of the verity of the contents of the Bible more than a decade before he is generally recognized as having gone religious are wide of the mark. Dylan used religious imagery to work through his problems on the bulk of the album, but the salvation he details (or implies) within the last two songs is not religion but marriage and family, even if his relentlessly questioning mind leads him to inject a note of ambivalence about that salvation via the mocking of Moon-in-June romantic song sentiment.

Perhaps in a sense Dylan was adhering to at least one of the fashions of the season: the album as story. Whatever that salvation, and however ambiguous Dylan is about it, it can be posited as the end of a journey traced across the record's tracks. *John Wesley Harding* is a concept album more than the preceding, non-narrative *Sgt. Pepper* and no less so than The Pretty Things' *S.F. Sorrow* and The Who's *Tommy*, both yet to be released.

The cover of the album was – like the music it contained – sepia-toned. Dylan seemed to be wearing the same coat he sported on the sleeve of *Blonde on Blonde* as he posed before a tree in the company of Bengali houseguests of Grossman and a local craftsman who appeared to have been chosen because they looked like Native Americans and an old Wild West character respectively, while Dylan's Stetson gave him a cowboy mien. If the consumer for some reason best known to himself turned the cover upside down and looked at the bark of the tree, he would be able to see the four tiny faces of the *Sgt. Pepper*-era Beatles. This detail has now been lost to history: they are invisible in the CD medium. Purchasers of the first edition of the album swear that there were many more faces than those of the Fab Four. The back cover carried sleevenotes from the artist which provided something of a key to the songs, more than one of which made reference to "the glass" – the "plate-glass window" mentioned in said notes.

John Wesley Hardin (without the "g") was an Old West outlaw and indeed a direct ancestor of great songwriter Tim Hardin, who happened to be resident in Woodstock when this album was being written and whose style had much in common with *John Wesley Harding*'s roots music. However, those details go to form just one of several theories surrounding the album's title. What can be said for sure is that *John Wesley Harding* was a unique, strange, fascinating and beautiful work of art which proved that nobody could ever predict what Bob Dylan was going to do.

The album was released, at Dylan's insistence, without fanfare, with no accompanying singles. ('Drifter's Escape' and 'Watchtower' were belatedly issued on 45 in April and November the following year, the latter after Hendrix had had his hit with it.) Despite this, and the curious scheduling (two days after Christmas is a real sales dead spot), it still became Dylan's biggest seller to date.

As for his recording future, in August it had been announced that Dylan had signed a new contract with CBS/Columbia. He had changed his mind about switching to the MGM label, who in any case didn't seem that interested in him, their delay in counter-signing his contract enabling him to withdraw his signature. He made a strange decision to go for a record-breaking royalty rate with CBS rather than an advance. Any recording artist will tell you that creative accounting by record companies makes royalties elusive, whereas an advance is non-returnable cash in one's hand. However, Dylan had other considerations in mind: crucially, the contract allowed him to deliver product as and when he wanted to. This artist was not going to be hurried any more.

NASHVILLE SKYLINE

By Sean Egan

US release: 9 April 1969
Produced by: Bob Johnston
CHARTS: US#3; UK#1

SIDE ONE
Girl from the North Country
Nashville Skyline Rag
To Be Alone with You
I Threw It All Away
Peggy Day

SIDE TWO
Lay Lady Lay
One More Night
Tell Me That It Isn't True
Country Pie
Tonight I'll Be Staying Here with You

In October 1967, folk legend Woody Guthrie died after a long, painful illness.

A concert tribute to the man without whose inspiration he might never have become a star was probably the only thing at this point that could have prised Bob Dylan away from his domestic bliss. On 20 January 1968, Dylan appeared with The Band at the Woody Guthrie Memorial Concert at Carnegie Hall, playing a trio of Guthrie songs that were released on the album *Tribute to Woody Guthrie Part One*, as well as joining in some ensemble performances. Those who imagined that Dylan's first live performance for twenty months heralded his return to being an active recording and touring artist were to be disappointed. He remained off the road, and there would be no Dylan product in 1968 – at least not officially.

The mini-avalanche of covers of Basement Tape Dylan songs continued. The Byrds surprised many by going country with their August 1968 album *Sweetheart of the Rodeo*. Though a group containing great composers, they'd always shown a penchant for Dylan covers and they continued the pattern on *Sweetheart*, which featured 'You Ain't Goin' Nowhere' and 'Nothing Was Delivered'. In the first quarter of the year, 'This Wheel's on Fire' was taken into the British Top Five by the awkwardly named but sumptuously talented Julie Driscoll, Brian Auger and the Trinity. The Band now had their own record deal and in July 1968 released their debut album *Music from Big Pink*. Although they were extremely accomplished in their own right, they cannily exploited the Dylan connection to kick-start their career: the (atrocious) cover painting was by Dylan and the album contained three songs either written or co-written by him, 'This Wheel's on Fire', 'I Shall Be Released' and 'Tears of Rage'. In early 1969, Manfred Mann repeated their UK hit success with 'Mighty Quinn' across the Atlantic. (This was the same year that Fairport Convention proved that even Dylan in French had a magic touch: 'Si Tu Dois Partir', their Gallic version of 'If You Gotta Go, Go Now', stalled only just outside the UK Top 20.)

Dylan's own versions of these songs continued to do the non-commercial rounds, the music-publishing demos coming into the hands of record-industry people and those on the peripheries. In the former camp were the rock stars of the day, who were clearly entranced by the Basement Tapes and even possibly felt liberated by the permission their back-to-basics, lo-fi qualities gave them to end the studio arms race of ever more far-out instrumentation and production. They could probably relate to the Basement Tape material better than the similarly stripped-back *John Wesley Harding* because of the ribald humour absent in the latter work. Several tracks on the Rolling Stones' 1968 album *Beggars Banquet* had an acoustic, back-porch feel. Eric Clapton disbanded Cream to play music less reliant on virtuosity, but before he did he made sure to pointedly title one of their albums *Wheels of Fire*. The rustic *Sweetheart of the Rodeo* seemed to owe more than a little to the Basement Tapes. By 1969, The Beatles were making a virtue of no overdubs with their *Get Back* project (even if it was botched and ended up as the very-much-overdubbed *Let It Be* album). Dylan was influencing the direction of popular music even when he wasn't releasing product. He could even claim the dubious accolade of having caused a great band to splinter. 1969 saw the release of the (actually rather good) album *The Hollies Sing Dylan*. Graham Nash was so disgusted by this retrograde step of an entire album devoted to another person's songs when the group had their own formidable songwriting axis that it was one of the reasons for his departure from The Hollies.

In June 1968, the wider public had their minds focused on the fact that the cache of unreleased Dylan recordings doing the rounds of publishers' offices and artists' managers might actually have an artistic worth in their own right. Jann Wenner – publisher of *Rolling Stone* magazine, the rock bible founded in November 1967 and partly named after 'Like a Rolling Stone' – wrote a front-page article titled "Dylan's Basement Tape Should Be Released". "If this were ever to be released it would be a classic," he opined. Dylan, though, was in no hurry to oblige. This may have had something to do with the fact that though Grossman would cease to be Dylan's manager in August 1969, he would go on receiving publishing royalties from his songs until 1973. By July 1969, two people whose identities are shrouded in mystery realised that there was money to be made from Dylan's dilatory approach to these recordings and put out popular music's first bootleg, originally unnamed but later titled *The Great White Wonder*. This double LP actually only contained seven Basement Tape tracks, the remainder being comprised of miscellaneous material that went as far back as a December 1961 home recording made in the apartment of his girlfriend Bonnie Beecher and came up to as recently as a June 1969 appearance on Johnny Cash's TV show. The common factor with the tracks was that none had yet been officially sanctioned for release. Trust Dylan to change the world yet again without even trying. It was the start of an entire industry, created by the public's unceasing thirst for anything and everything recorded by their idols and fuelled by the astonishing ability of bootleggers to obtain material no matter how well-guarded or obscure. This black market was one Dylan sat very uncomfortably astride: he has always been the most bootlegged rock artist, partly because he – more than any other – left so many worth-while tracks inexplicably in the can, partly because of the fanaticism of his devotees. Dylan could only watch helplessly as people obtained material he had (rightly or wrongly) never intended for public consumption and furthermore made money out of it while he received nothing.

The album Wenner – and the world – got when Dylan did put out new official product bore no relation, invention-wise, to that fourteen-song Basement Tape demo. *Nashville Skyline* was released in April 1969, a gap since Dylan's last official album that was considerably shorter than that between *Blonde on Blonde* and *John Wesley Harding* but was a still unusually long one of fourteen months. However, whereas that previous hiatus brought at its end a work of high quality whose enigmatic nature added to the aura of mystery the long silence had engendered, now he delivered an album that was often lyrically and musically banal. Additionally, it had a feeling of flimsiness over and above its aesthetic demerits: its playing time was a paltry twenty-seven minutes at a time when the rock audience was just learning to feel short-changed if they weren't given forrty minutes for their money. Furthermore, one of the Dylan songs here wasn't even new, while another was an instrumental. More than one of the others sounded like a glorified doodle and/or a jam with a lyric half-interestedly plastered over the top.

For many, *Nashville Skyline* demonstrated that Dylan had nothing to say anymore. The traditional Dylan lyrical style of fierce intelligence and glittering poetry had given way to cliché. Even worse was the backdrop against which these empty lyrics was set. Although people weren't necessarily expecting him to return to the primal energy of the amphetamine rock trilogy, they were more than a little dismayed that for the first time since he had begun recording in Nashville, a Dylan record had the twangy, pedal-steel-heavy sound associated with that city, the style hated by the rock audience because: a) it was whiny, slow and all sounded the same, and b) it reminded them of country's redneck audience, the good ol' boys who despised radical tub-thumpers, peaceniks, draft dodgers and all the other people the rock crowd either were or felt an affinity with. Though the International Submarine Band and The Byrds were examples of rockers who had decided to explore and enjoy their country heritage, theirs was a gritty and street-savvy variant that did its best to keep its distance from the glossy clichés and interchangeable melodies for which the medium was infamous. There was no such ambiguity at work here. While there might have been a mischievous twinkle in Dylan's eye when singing lines like "Love is all there is, it makes the world go around" ('I Threw It All Away'), to attribute every trite sentiment and corny couplet here to post-modernism would be desperate indeed. The almost complete absence of Dylan's trademark harmonica added to the generic feel. As if to underline that Dylan had lost his edge, his singing voice had changed yet again. He really did sound like that gormless bumpkin he appeared to be in the hat-tipping, guitar brandishing cover photograph.

Ironically, despite the album's insubstantiality, more work had gone into its recording (if not its writing) than any Dylan album hitherto. The musicians included old Dylan associates Kenny Buttrey, Charlie McCoy and Pete Drake. Although the three days' worth of sessions in February 1969 was about standard, or even less than, for a Dylan album, the three days' worth of overdubs that followed was unprecedented for a man who took pride in recording everything at the same time.

'Girl from the North Country' starts the proceedings, a duet with country music legend and Dylan friend Johnny Cash, who wrote the record's sycophantic liner note. If fans could get over Dylan being happy to sing alongside a man who had publicly taken the government's side in the Vietnam War debate that was tearing America in two (and some couldn't), it was a pleasant, widescreen expansion of the familiar *Freewheelin'* song, if sloppily harmonised. Incredibly, this track – the only one of many Dylan duets with Cash recorded for the album to make the cut – was a late addition and before its incorporation Dylan was seriously considering releasing an album whose length would have made it a glorified EP.

Following that exhumed oldie, when it then becomes apparent that 'Nashville Skyline Rag' does not have a lyric, the reality sinks in that this is not going to be a heavyweight entry in the Dylan canon. Subsequent Dylan biographers have uncovered the fact that this bluegrass instrumental was nothing more than a studio warm-up until Dylan decided to stick it on the album. It's quite fun – and those slick Nashville sessioners certainly know how to make an improvised track sound well-drilled – but since when had Dylan songs merely been a pleasant alternative to silence for three minutes? Additionally, the fact that the writing is credited to Dylan alone is not just logically unsound but morally suspect: it's a tradition in the music industry that the publishing on instrumentals is shared out amongst all the participants on the recording.

'To Be Alone with You' immortalized the phrase "Is it rolling, Bob?" when Dylan asked his trusty producer at the beginning if he was getting down this take. That is the only thing remotely immortal about this trite, if smoothly done, love song. Dylan's craftsmanship is impressive, but one notes that – unlike with 'I'll Be Your Baby Tonight' – he is nowhere undercutting or mocking the Tin Pan Alley conventions he is following. 'I Threw It All Away' is another country-pop creation. Dylan's regret over his previous spurning of love is touching and Johnston uses a little echo to give it something approaching a grandeur. 'Peggy Day', however, comes close to insulting the listener. Can Dylan's lyrical genius really come up with nothing more clever in this uptempo number than switching around the observation "Love to spend the night with Peggy Day" to (the nonsensical) "Love to spend the day with Peggy Night"? Meanwhile, one gets the feeling that Dylan wrote the line "By golly, what more can I say?" because "I can barely be arsed to finish this fiasco" doesn't rhyme with "Day".

'Lay Lady Lay' and 'Tonight I'll Be Staying Here with You' opened and closed side two. If the rest of the album had been as good as these two beauties, absolutely nobody would have had a problem with it (although admittedly might have had an issue with the idea of Dylan continuing to record such material ad infinitum). 'Lay Lady Lay' is a surprisingly sensual song for the day in which Dylan implores his lover to accompany him on his big brass bed. Treated guitar riffs, a deep bottom end, call-and-response between Dylan and one of the guitars, big, rolling drums, widescreen production techniques and a build to a clean end that provides a satisfying climax, all add up to a Dylan classic. The track was a surprise transatlantic top-tenner after the album's first single 'I Threw It All Away' had gone nowhere. 'Tonight I'll Be Staying Here with You' (the LP's third US single) feels like a bookend to 'I'll Be Your Baby Tonight', that previous, winning album-closing promise of provision of night-time company. The narrator tells his beloved that the people expecting him can go hang and that he will be cancelling his travel plans to remain in her company. Once again, slick popcraft is on display. There is also a great couplet about the transportation ticket he has thrown out the window: "If there's a poor boy on the street/Let him have my seat."

However, sandwiched between those two quality tracks is more songwriting-by-numbers and one track that verges on the idiotic. 'One More Night' is sort of Hank Williams-lite in its lonesomeness and pre-Nashville Sound rawness. 'Tell Me That It Isn't True', a song of suspected betrayal, embraces that Nashville Sound. Both are agreeable, if worryingly dependent on little flourishes from the musicians for a lot of their appeal. But what are we to make of 'Country Pie', a celebration of country and western in which Dylan is once again trying to convince us he really is the shit-kicker gurning on the sleeve? We aren't even given the opportunity to contemplate accepting it on its own terms, for at just past the minute-and-a-half stage, it unexpectedly fades out.

Even if we take the point from the last album that with this record Dylan is continuing to renounce his previous role as the Wicked Messenger, does his determination to bring no news if he can't bring good news actually mean that he has to abandon his greatest gift? Nobody listening to this LP previously unfamiliar with Dylan's work would know that this was an above-average writer let alone the supreme lyric-writing talent of all time. While the point can be made that Dylan's new subject matter – mainly, how wonderful love is – is no less profound than what he was writing about in, say, 'Gates of Eden', why can't he analyse domesticity with the same sharp eye he previously had society's ills? Or write with the same lyrical acuteness as he did in the first verse of 'Ballad of Easy Rider' for that year's smash movie *Easy Rider*? (Roger McGuinn completed the latter song, with Dylan declining to take any formal credit.)

Yet, it can't be denied that *Nashville Skyline* is a reasonably agreeable listen. It's also a highly impressive act of impersonation,

Dylan losing himself completely in the role of unsophisticated, "Aw shucks" country boy. And in any case, who said there was a rule that a Dylan song had to engage your brain rather than set your foot tapping? The way to enjoy this album is to take what one might call the Wings option: just as Paul McCartney's post-Beatles oeuvre becomes far more enjoyable if you don't burden it with comparisons to the work of a certain fabulous foursome, so the qualities *Nashville Skyline* possesses are far easier to appreciate if one pretends one knows nothing about the artist's previous work. Then, you can perceive *Nashville Skyline* as, simply, a sweet little album.

This album's chocolate-box depiction of love infuriated parts of the counter-culture, who saw bourgeois family units as typifying the conformity that held society back. Their fury was only intensified by Dylan's guileless new on-record persona. That they knew it was not the real Dylan – he might be a family man but he couldn't have changed so profoundly from the person who had displayed such insight and venom on records so recently – made that persona seem like a repudiation of his previous values. The suggestion that Dylan was playing a role was completed by a bizarre interview in *Rolling Stone* published two months after the album's release. In a stuttering, stumbling exchange with Jann Wenner, he came across as halfway between innocent and stupid, and did it so well that one would have been taken in by it if one wasn't familiar with his persona from all his previous interviews. He repeatedly pretended he didn't understand questions he found discomforting; used Wenner's first name frequently in the sort of ostentatious friendliness he had always been too cool to show anyone hitherto; employed euphemisms like "passed away" that the old Bob Dylan would have laughed at; bizarrely claimed that when he had once named Smokey Robinson as one of his favourite poets (although not America's Greatest Living Poet as has been spun by Motown), he had been mixing him up with Jean Arthur Rimbaud; and more than once said he had no aim other than "staying out of people's hair". In retrospect, it can be seen as a surreal exercise in throwing people off the scent by a man who didn't want to be bothered by those who still perceived him as leader of the world's youth.

The revelation that Bob Dylan was going to headline the second Isle of Wight festival in August 1969 was big news: his last paid gig had been so long ago – at the Royal Albert Hall in May 1966 – that some assumed he had gone the same route as The Beatles in unofficially retiring from public performance. The gig was advertised using imagery of Dylan in 1966 – clean-shaven, fuzzy-haired, shaded – but when he took to the stage, it was obvious that much had changed. In this retrospective, Johnny Black details the memories of the observers.

EYEWITNESS: DYLAN AT THE ISLE OF WIGHT

By Johnny Black

First published in *Q*, October 1995

17 JULY 1969: DYLAN AGREES TO PLAY AT THE ISLE OF WIGHT

Ray Foulk (festival organiser): We came up with the idea of making it a holiday for him and his family, in a farmhouse at Bembridge with a swimming pool and a recently converted barn, suitable for rehearsing in. We were offering Dylan a fortnight stay there, no expense spared, car with driver. Also we would have him come over on the *QE2*. The fee offered was $50,000 (£20,000).

13 AUGUST 1969: DYLAN'S SON JESSE IS INJURED ABOARD THE *QE2* IMMEDIATELY BEFORE DEPARTURE FROM NEW YORK

Ray Foulk: It was dreadful news. I was, at this stage, in daily contact with [Dylan's agent, Bert] Block. He telephoned me with the news that Dylan had left the ship to go to the hospital and was still in New York. Block said that Dylan would obviously have to fly over at a later date. The accident brought home to us the vulnerability of our position. What if the boy had been killed? Dylan would obviously have cancelled. The event all hinged upon this one human being. It shook us up a bit.

25 AUGUST 1969: WITH JESSE RECOVERED, DYLAN ARRIVES AT HEATHROW

Ray Foulk: He arrived on a regular flight at about 10 p.m. Sara was with him as well as Al Aronowitz. Block and myself were there to meet them. We drove down to Portsmouth in two cars, which took about two hours. It was nearly 1 a.m. when we arrived at Portsmouth seafront, and very cold.

There was hardly anybody around and those who were passed Dylan by without a glance. Because of the cold, we were all drinking tea, waiting for our hired hovercraft to arrive. I still have this image of Dylan wandering around with his plastic cup of tea from the vending machine, in the dark.

I was in the firing line, dealing with Dylan and Block. I wanted to keep Dylan happy [but] I was getting word back from our office that ticket sales were slow and we had to get more publicity out of Dylan. I thought that if we could arrange one main press conference, rather than set up individual interviews, Dylan may well agree to do it.

26 AUGUST 1969: GEORGE HARRISON DRIVES TO FORELANDS FARM, BEMBRIDGE, ISLE OF WIGHT

Judy Lewis (housekeeper): One of the first things Bob asked me to get him was some honey. He was quiet and came over as a very well-mannered person. Most of his time he spent playing guitar with George Harrison.

Ray Foulk: I remember walking through the living room one day and Dylan and Harrison were sitting on a sofa singing the Everly Brothers' 'All I Have to Do is Dream' together. It sounded incredible . . . just like the Everly Brothers. There was a lot less rehearsal going on there than one may have imagined.

Judy Lewis: He took a liking for blackberry and apple pies and fruit cakes. Sara was constantly going on at him about his diet. I was forever supplying endless cups of tea to him and Harrison. After supper some evenings he would ask if I would like him to sing something. I would demote George Harrison to fetch things from the kitchen and help me do the washing up so I would not miss anything.

Bob continually ate my porridge and pies with relish. I think Harrison was in awe of him. They got on very well, but I got the impression Dylan felt Harrison was a bit pushy . . . wanting to play all the time.

27 AUGUST 1969: PRESS CONFERENCE AT HALLAND HOTEL, SEAVIEW, ISLE OF WIGHT

Press: Why did you come to the Isle of Wight?
Dylan: I wanted to see the home of Alfred, Lord Tennyson.
Press: Why?
Dylan: Just curious.

28 AUGUST 1969: JOHN LENNON FLIES IN . . .

Ray Foulk: Lots of helicopters were landing by and using a field next to the farmhouse, and then the visitors would make their way across the field into the grounds of Forelands. The grounds were well kept by a gardener and were immaculate. Then this helicopter appeared and flew over. However, it didn't put down in the field like the rest but landed right down on the lawn, blowing all the flowers away, much to the rage of the gardener. Out of the helicopter strolled John Lennon.

30 AUGUST 1969: DYLAN AND THE BAND REHEARSE IN THE BARN AT FORELANDS

31 AUGUST 1969: DYLAN TOPS THE BILL AT THE ISLE OF WIGHT

Tony Bramwell (Beatles aide): I was up in London, hanging out with Eric Clapton and some others. Early in the afternoon, Eric said, "Let's go to the Isle of Wight to see Bob Dylan." He organised a coach and we met outside Robert Stigwood's office and trundled down with all of Cream and Jackie Lomax, singing and drinking all the way.

Rikki Farr (co-promoter): One moment I shall treasure for the rest of my life was at the 1969 Isle of Wight Festival. We had been trying to convince The Beatles to get back together and play, but it never quite came together. What did happen, though, was a kind of spontaneous superstar jam session in the afternoon at a mock Tudor house where Bob Dylan was staying.

The Beatles came down to watch the show, but in the afternoon they all got together in the house and I saw on stage the most incredible supergroup you could imagine: Dylan, The Beatles, Eric Clapton, Jackie Lomax, all just jamming. Ginger Baker would get off the drum stool and Ringo would step in. Eric Clapton would take a solo, and then George Harrison would take the next one. It was amazing.

Al Aronowitz (journalist in Dylan entourage): Dylan then invited The Beatles to a game of tennis on the Forelands Farm courts. "I'll play on condition that nobody really knows how," quipped John and, as Bob and John teamed up against Ringo and George, Pattie Harrison giggled, "This is the most exclusive game of doubles in the world." The game ended at 5:30 and Dylan piled into a white van along with Sara, Ringo, Maureen and me for the five-mile drive to the festival site. We joked all the way.

Tom Paxton (singer-songwriter): I was having a very good afternoon at the Isle of Wight. I was brought back on three times for encores and, when I came off, Bob invited me into his private enclosure where he introduced me to John Lennon, who delighted me by knowing the name of one of my songs! I hung out with them for the rest of the day.

Julie Felix (folk singer): He looked like a happily married man and father but he was very nervous because he hadn't sung for some years . . . I talked to him for a long time because The Band had gone on, and they were going down really well, it was the first big gig they had done on their own. And so they just stayed out there for an extra hour or something, meanwhile poor Bob Dylan was getting more and more nervous about going on.

Ron Smith (site manager): I remember giving up my seat to a couple of The Beatles, and also seeing Dylan at the back of the stage, in his enclosed area which he wouldn't have anyone else in, with his boozing partner, our security chief. There was a fantastic feeling there.

Jeff Dexter (co-MC): Bob was supposed to go on right after The Band. It was the end of the weekend and I really wanted to get out from behind my decks, get high, and watch Dylan, but there was such a delay. So I kept putting on more records. Eventually I ran back to the main production caravan to see what was happening, and there's Bob, the spokesman for our generation, plus his manager, Albert Grossman, waiting to be sure they've got their percentage of the gate money before he'll go on.

Then our festival doctor, Sam Hutt, supplied me with a little bottle of tincture of cannabis, which I swigged back immediately. Powerful stuff. I was also smoking some incredibly wacky grass by Richie Havens so, by the time I got back to my deck and put on Hare Krishna . . . because George Harrison was out there . . . I could hardly see. I fell face down on the deck halfway through the track and ended up watching Dylan from Richie's knee, with Richie operating me like a glove puppet whenever it came time to clap.

Tony Bramwell: We watched Dylan's set from six feet in front of stage, just along from The Beatles and Terence Stamp . . .

Eric Clapton: He was fantastic. He changed everything. He used to have a blues voice but he changed voices, and then suddenly he was a country and western singer with a white suit on. He was Hank Williams. They [the audience] couldn't understand it. You had to be a musician to understand it.

Rikki Farr: The PA system was 2000 watts, huge for the time, so as well as being heard by the audience, the music was clearly audible to the inmates of Parkhurst jail and the monks in Quarr monastery, who hadn't heard live music since the Second World War.

Jonathan Taplin: The sound at the Isle of Wight was terrific. I remember we liked the WEM system so much that we got one ourselves. The sound just punched through, out of these huge stacks, and my sound guy Ed Anderson was blown away.

Tom Paxton: One thing Dylan sang that I never saw mentioned anywhere was 'Wild Mountain Thyme', which I thought was a nice gesture, to sing a British folk song, like a recognition of the roots of the music.

George Harrison: The concert was marvellous . . . he gave a brilliant performance.

John Lennon: He gave a reasonable, albeit slightly flat, performance but everyone was expecting Godot, or Jesus, to appear.

Levon Helm (The Band): Bob had an extra list of songs with eight or ten different titles, with question marks by them, that we would've went ahead and done, had it seemed like the thing to do. But it seemed like everybody was a bit tired and the festival was three days old by then and so, if everybody else is ready to go home, let's go.

Richard Brown (fan): Dylan was rubbish and, after he finished, everyone wanted to go home at the same time. We jogged to the ferry as the buses couldn't move. Police used hoses to knock people off the terminal roof. Hundreds of us slept overnight in the railway station and got a ferry the next day.

Tom Paxton: What astonished me was the negative reaction in the British press, including downright fabrications, like saying he had run off the stage halfway through the set. It was a magical performance and, afterwards, I went with him and The Beatles to the farmhouse where he was clearly in a merry mood, because he felt it had gone so well. The Beatles had brought a test pressing of their next album, *Abbey Road*, and we listened to that and had quite a party.

SELF PORTRAIT

By Sean Egan

US release: 8 June 1970
Produced by: Bob Johnston
CHARTS: US#4; UK#1

SIDE ONE
All the Tired Horses
Alberta #1
I Forgot More Than You'll Ever Know
Days of '49
Early Mornin' Rain
In Search of Little Sadie

SIDE TWO
Let It Be Me
Little Sadie
Woogie Boogie
Belle Isle
Living the Blues
Like a Rolling Stone

SIDE THREE
Copper Kettle
Gotta Travel On
Blue Moon
The Boxer
The Mighty Quinn (Quinn the Eskimo)
Take Me as I Am (Or Let Me Go)

SIDE FOUR
Take a Message to Mary
It Hurts Me Too

Minstrel Boy
She Belongs to Me
Wigwam
Alberta #2

Dylan wrote in his memoir *Chronicles Volume One*, "having children changed my life . . . Outside of my family, nothing held any
real interest for me . . ."

   Bob Dylan had clearly hoped he had conveyed with *Nashville
Skyline* and the "Staying out of people's hair" interview that he
was no longer (if he ever had been) the conscience of a generation or a counter-culture icon. Certainly, anyone halfway
sentient should have assumed such from the tame, domestic
landscapes of that album and his evasive response to Jann
Wenner's question about whether he had voted in the last,
extremely fractious presidential election ("We got down to the
polls too late"). However, many of his fans merely seemed to take
this as a sign that Dylan was stricken with an illness of which it
was their duty to cure him, and if he was determined to stay out
of people's hair, people were not reciprocating. Since his bearded,
post-motorcycle accident comeback, Dylan's fame had transformed into a curious kind that allowed him to somehow become
invisible in crowds. He was able to walk down the street unac-
costed in a way that peers like Paul McCartney and Mick Jagger
were not. However, the fact that he was more legendary than
famous and the fact that his striking good looks could be transformed into something utterly nondescript by dressing down and
bearding up saved him only from passers-by, not from fanatics.
For the latter, he was a sitting duck. Fans broke into his house in
his absence and had sex in his bed, clumped across his roof in his
presence and frighteningly followed his car in the dark up isolated
mountain roads. When in September 1969 Dylan moved back
into New York City, it wasn't long before his Greenwich Village
house was being visited by one A. J. Weberman, a semi-unhinged
fan who rifled through his garbage and set up the Dylan
Liberation Front. The harassment of isolated freaks and hippies
determined to tempt him out of his semi-retirement was replicated on a grand scale by the organisers of the August 1969
Woodstock festival which was allegedly situated in that area

precisely because Dylan lived there: festival organisers thought that the abdicated king might climb back on his throne and perform a set if this mass gathering took place near his home. Dylan was so horrified by the prospect of hordes of the kind of people who had been making his life hell descending on his neighbourhood that he contrived to put the width of the Atlantic Ocean between him and them by accepting the invitation to headline the second Isle of Wight festival at the end of August. The latter was the only gig he played all year apart from a guest spot with The Band at the Mississippi River Festival in July.

Dylan had already started on his follow-up to *Nashville Skyline* by the time of the Woodstock festival (and, in fact, only two weeks after *Nashville Skyline* had come out) and the fact that some of the tracks he originally recorded were quality numbers that would end up on the fairly worthy next-but-one LP *New Morning* seems to indicate that initially the mixture of covers and originals he was laying down was going to form what might be termed a proper album. However, if that was the case, before the album's release, Dylan changed strategy (as well as studio, relocating from Nashville to New York). He decided to so disgust the denizens of the Woodstock Nation (a new term for the youth/counter-culture that emerged after the legendary festival) that they would finally get the message that he wasn't one of them and leave him alone. Or to quote Dylan, "I said, 'Well fuck it. I wish these people would just forget about me. I wanna do something they can't possibly like . . .'" Looking at the chronology, it could even be the case that Weberman is single-handedly responsible for Dylan making that decision. Accordingly, what might have been an enjoyable mixture of intriguing covers and solid, if not classic, new songs transformed into a colossal "Screw You", a double LP housed in a grotesque Dylan-painted jacket of his own face, it seemed determined to turn back time to not only before Dylan brought brainpower into popular music but before Elvis brought sex into it. The covers – not only of oldies and traditional songs but also of contemporaries' material – were bizarrely chosen. There was also, for the first time on any Dylan LP, significant overdubbing, which was used to add brass, classical strings and female backing singing – all sounds never heard in Dylan's music hitherto and all

rendered here as cheesily as imaginable. Dylan's participation in
the overdubbing was minimal, possibly non-existent. Dylan also
included live versions of some of his own classic songs that were
so bad that he seemed to be questioning their original worth. As
one final apparent hedge against the unlikely possibility that the
public still might not understand the message being communicated, Dylan called the album *Self Portrait*.

If Dylan wanted disgust, he got it. *Rolling Stone* critic Greil
Marcus wrote a review of the album with an opening line that
perfectly summed up the general consensus: "What is this shit?"
Once removed from the burning issues surrounding the release
of the album – the world's youth who wanted Dylan to return to
his supposed former position of their leader are now pensiona-
ble age or approaching it – it is now discernible that the album is
not as bad as people had assumed. That, though, isn't saying
much.

Dylan's own voice doesn't appear on what is one of his few
compositions on the album: female voices enunciate two lines all
the way through opener 'All the Tired Horses'. "All the tired
horses in the sun" is the first. It's difficult to tell whether in the
second line they are singing, "How'm I s'posed to get any riding
done?" or "writing done?". Like all the other originals on *Self
Portrait* but unlike many of his unreleased songs, the words to
this track did not appear in the original edition of Dylan's officially sanctioned collection of lyrics, a re-writing of history that
probably tells us all we need to know about his perception of the
album. The lyric now appears on his official website and claims
that the relevant word is "riding" – but what do they know?

'Alberta #1' is the first of two versions herein of this traditional country blues and is perfectly pleasant, even if like so
many tracks on the album you wonder what is the point of the
consummate songwriter of his generation rendering it. Cecil A.
Null's 'I Forgot More Than You'll Ever Know' was a 1953 Davis
Sisters country hit. Like almost all the rest of the material here,
Dylan sings it straight and the heartfelt and well-played track is
easy on the ear.

'Days of '49' (a sea shanty whose dubious publishing credit
tells us it was written by Alan Lomax, John Lomax and Frank
Warner but was in reality only brought to wider attention by

those folk historians) is an album highlight – a rich, dark, lengthy treat. 'Early Mornin' Rain' is a cover of a ballad by Gordon Lightfoot. It's an intriguing choice: this album could be viewed as an exploration of what makes up identity, and Lightfoot is one of many, many people down the years briefly cited as the "new Bob Dylan". The latter betrays no contempt for the composition by a Dylan manqué, his delicate harmonica a highlight of a respectful rendition. 'In Search of Little Sadie' is another traditional song. This version is not too dissimilar to The Beatles' 'Happiness is a Warm Gun' in the way it lurches from tempo to tempo and genre to genre, though it's difficult to know whether it's intended as a comedy number.

Side two opened with smooth love song 'Let It Be Me' by Gilbert Bécaud, Mann Curtis and Pierre Delanoë, first made famous Stateside by the Everly Brothers. 'Little Sadie' is traditional, given an agreeably percussive and staccato new arrangement by Dylan with an unusual amount of showboating guitar for a Dylan track. 'Woogie Boogie' is a piano-led instrumental with a nice sax climax whose sole writing credit to Dylan is cheeky on more than level, the central progression being hardly more than generic. 'Belle Isle' is a traditional in a courtly vein, with a man pledging his devotion to a "young maiden". The counterpoint provided that courtliness and the decorative strings by Dylan's modernistic voice is rather peculiar. Dylan original 'Living the Blues' is as generic as its title suggests, but is loving pastiche rather than cliché, Dylan lamenting the loss of his baby while female backing singers coo sympathetically and someone (probably Charlie Daniels) peels off some tough guitar work.

So far, then, a mixture of OK and pretty good. The album's first truly bad track, though, comes with the version of 'Like a Rolling Stone' that closed vinyl side two, the one performed at the Isle of Wight festival the previous year. It's a leisurely stroll through the song, with Dylan currently incapable of injecting any of the venom of the original into his vocal and The Band seeming to think a jaunty tone is required. It's sub-pub-band quality.

Side three opened with 'Copper Kettle'. Written by Pete Seeger-discovery Alfred Frank Beddoe, it's a celebration of backwoods life whose lushness – sentimental singing, female backing vocals and strings – would make it sickly in any case, but by now a certain weariness is setting in. Despite the high professionalism and the occasional unequivocally good track, we are asking ourselves why we are listening to Bob Dylan singing other people's songs when not only had that never been all that Dylan was about but almost exactly what he hadn't been about. Moreover, it dawns that he is singing these songs with little nuance or cleverness.

'Gotta Travel On' (written by Paul Clayton, Larry Ehrlich, David Lazar and Tom Six) was a 1959 crossover country hit for Billy Grammer. It's well-played but by this point the feeling that fact provokes is, "So what?" However, there is a difference between the ennui that comes with the feeling that Dylan has made his point with the concept and dismay at being subjected to garbage. We are just about to enter the album's real wastelands. Hart and Rodgers' 'Blue Moon' dates from the golden age of Tin Pan Alley songwriting but probably first became known to Dylan through Elvis's 1956 single. Dylan's rendition is soporific, cocktail lounge stuff. 'The Boxer' was a track on Simon & Garfunkel's mega-selling 1970 swansong *Bridge Over Troubled Water*. The duo were pleasant enough, and issued many classic records, but were Dylan Lite, making their 1966 Dylan piss-take 'A Simple Desultory Philippic' a bit of a cheek. Some have posited Dylan was thinking precisely this when setting about recording his version of 'The Boxer' for *Self Portrait*. Whether or not it's revenge, the cut is certainly atrocious, with Dylan's two vocal tracks out of time with each other and the song taken at an almost contemptuously hurried pace. 'The Mighty Quinn (Quinn the Eskimo)' is another Isle of Wight performance. The first legally released version of the song by Dylan is a ramshackle affair that briefly flares into excitement when Dylan cues Robertson to take a solo. Boudleaux Bryant's 'Take Me as I Am (Or Let Me Go)' closed side three in syrupy style.

Another Boudleaux Bryant creation, in collaboration with Felice Bryant, opened side four in the shape of the prisoner's lament 'Take a Message to Mary'. It's a decent song, well executed, but by now – weary with music with no personality – you don't really care. That the tender traditional 'It Hurts Me

Too' is Dylan solo with guitar only underlines that the artist seems to have regressed, for any of the tracks on his similarly stark, jejune debut would have been preferable to this dull recording. A pair of Isle of Wight performances follow: 'Minstrel Boy' is the only released version to date of this Dylan original dating from the Basement Tapes period. It's a glorified jingle. 'She Belongs to Me' is stripped of the sensitivity and darkness of the studio original and given a totally inappropriate diddley-om-pom-pom finale.

'Wigwam' is another instrumental supposedly written by Dylan. Dylan la-las against a big brass arrangement in a not disagreeable way – but is "not disagreeable" supposed to be what a Dylan track amounts to? 'Alberta #2' – this version faster – brings proceedings to an underwhelming close.

In a sense, there's not much point critiquing a record of which the artist himself said, ". . . if you're gonna put a lot of crap on it, you might as well load it up." However, in the interests of professionalism, and also taking into account the fact that an artist is not always in control of a record's effect on a listener (whether that effect be good or bad) *Self Portrait* is not, objectively, an unequivocally bad album. 'The Boxer' and Dylan's own oldies excepted, Dylan at no point seems to approach this music disrespectfully and he by now has the craft – and the talented colleagues – to make everything at least listenable. Rather than bad, it is a nonsensical album in Dylan's career: the pre-eminent songwriter of his generation did not need to cover the material of other (invariably lesser) writers. The argument made by some (and even semi-implied by the title) that this album is a statement insofar as this is the music that moulded Dylan into the artist we love holds up only so far but, in any case, he chose the very worst time to do a covers album. When an artist is recording other people's songs, he is not putting his personal insight on display but his performance, and though Dylan has almost always been a great if unconventional singer, the period in and around *Self Portrait* marked the one time in Dylan's career when his vocals were boring.

For all those reasons, *Self Portrait* is just as bewildering, exhausting, patience-wearing and insulting (to the audience and Dylan himself) as Dylan wanted it to be.

NEW MORNING

By Sean Egan

US release: 21 October 1970
Produced by: Bob Johnston
CHARTS: US#7; UK#1

SIDE ONE
If Not for You
Day of the Locusts
Time Passes Slowly
Went to See the Gypsy
Winterlude
If Dogs Run Free

SIDE TWO
New Morning
Sign on the Window
One More Weekend
The Man in Me
Three Angels
Father of Night

Nashville Skyline, *Self Portrait* and *New Morning* are, like the amphetamine rock trilogy, of a piece, spiritually and artistically. Also like the amphetamine rock trilogy, they were issued in a truncated timespace, and were followed by a long period of artistic silence. There the similarities end.

New Morning appeared just four-and-a-half months after *Self Portrait*. At a point in history when the standard release gap between albums was a year, people made the assumption that Dylan had been shaken by the tidal wave of derision that greeted *Self Portrait* and had rush-released a follow-up to prove that he wasn't, as some were assuming, past it. That Dylan would in the succeeding years deny that this was the case was dismissed. He would, wouldn't he?

However, the facts to some extent bear Dylan out. Even discounting the songs that ended up on *New Morning* that were first recorded during the *Self Portrait* sessions like 'Went to See the Gypsy' and 'Time Passes Slowly', formal sessions for a new album took place on the first five days of June 1970 (– in other words, after the completion of *Self Portrait* but a few days before its release. However, that doesn't rule out what seems the likeliest possibility: that Dylan lost his nerve about the deliberate awfulness of *Self Portrait* after having delivered it to the record company. The cover of *New Morning* – a moody photograph of Dylan whose border could be interpreted as a frame – even seemed to be asserting that this was the *real* self-portrait. (Two notes on the jacket: he seems to be adopting a mirror reflection pose of the picture of him on the back cover from the early Sixties with blues singer and early champion Victoria Spivey. For the third Dylan album in a row, there is no name or title on the cover.)

Dylan claimed in *Chronicles Volume One* that he was not really trying when he made this record, throwing together a few scraps and slight songs to keep his hand in while simultaneously keeping at bay the people who wanted him to lead them to the promised land. This seems to be contradicted by the recollection of Al Kooper, the album's unofficial co-producer (he gets a "special thanks"), who has recalled that Dylan exasperated him by repeatedly changing his mind about arrangements – hardly the sign of somebody who didn't care.

In some senses, this was a slight album by definition, for it's the artist's first foray into pop – by which is meant not an abbreviation for popular music per se but a generic subsection thereof characterized by sweet, formal melodies, short song lengths and lyrics that are usually sunny, life-affirming and non-intellectual. There have been many classic albums made up of such material – but this isn't one of them.

The gentle, mellow opening notes of 'If Not for You' would have dismayed anyone hoping that this was a return to Dylan's caustic peak, as would its celebration of Dylan's domestic contentment, indeed by implication the salvation his wife

offered him from that caustic personality. The home-loving
family man of *Nashville Skyline* hadn't miraculously disappeared. For those who could get over Dylan's abandonment
of them and their causes, it's quite an affecting song. Yet even
for those who were uninterested in asking Dylan "Which side
are you on?", a feeling of "Is that it?" sets in as the fade starts.
The same unfulfilled sensation attends the album's title track,
which has a similar structure and theme, if a little more
passion and energy. One can't help but notice that there is a
slight gap between Dylan's ambitions and his achievements:
the bridges of both songs fail to soar the way that pop bridges
should.

'Day of the Locusts' deals with the occasion that Dylan
attended Princeton University the day after the release of *Self
Portrait* to pick up an honorary doctorate in music. Many celebrities are surprisingly genuinely chuffed to accept such
meaningless awards but in *Chronicles Volume One* Dylan implies
that he acquiesced to receive this degree to add to the aura of
squareness and conventionality he was deliberately cultivating.
Fair enough, but it's difficult to believe that the ersatz feel of the
song was also a calculated shattering of expectations. When
Dylan sings, "The man standin' next to me/His head was
exploding!/I was hoping the pieces wouldn't fall on me", it feels
like a self-conscious return to the surreal metaphors of his work
in the previous decade. It's also completely undermined by a
boring tune and soporific lyrics.

Even the modest amount of interest people found they could
muster in 'Went to See the Gypsy' has evaporated in recent
years. It was for a long time thought to be a parable about Dylan
meeting Elvis Presley, his childhood hero. (Dylan had evinced a
child-like joy in the "staying out of people's hair" interview
about The King's cover of his 'Tomorrow is a Long Time', which
song Dylan recorded a so-far unreleased version of at the *New
Morning* sessions.) However, Dylan later indicated everyone had
been following the wrong trail when he stated he had never met
Presley, leaving us with a far less intriguing creation, one whose
melodic aimlessness makes us disinclined to attack the lyrical
metaphors anew.

An offbeat pair of songs closed the original vinyl side one.

'Winterlude' is a number in waltz time with a knowingly generic melody, a deliberately clichéd Christmassy feel and a lyric redolent of the Bing Crosby era of pop. The pastiche is clever – and certainly not the kind of thing Dylan had revealed an aptitude for or interest in previously – but admiration for its mimicry is about all such a wisp of a track can induce. 'If Dogs Run Free' is a jazz number with Dylan virtually talking a people-got-to-be-free sentiment over some female scat vocals and impressive ivory tickling by Al Kooper. Again, though, the song's playfulness and warmth can't disguise that it's only mildly interesting, even actually slightly dull.

It's somewhat unwise for Dylan to include a slow blues – 'One More Weekend' – on *New Morning*, as the formulaic nature of that genre only adds to the overall feeling of insubstantiality. 'The Man in Me' is the closest thing to an unequivocal triumph. It sees Dylan once more paying homage to the bliss brought him by his wife. Dylan this time gets the pop formula wonderfully right, courtesy of a divine tune and – for once – a bridge that really takes off.

The album closes with two songs that some interpreted as banal religiosity, although 'Three Angels' and 'Father of Night' started life as songs Dylan wrote for Archibald MacLeish's play *Scratch*, before realising that his views on the project were incompatible with the author's. These compositions may only have been job-of-work but they bolster the album's quality significantly. They also evince a care in arrangement and production so much greater than the rest of the material that they would seem to be closer to Dylan's heart – for whatever reason – than the other cuts. 'Three Angels' is an aural equivalent of a Christmas card, right down to saccharine sentiment. In his spoken-word vocal, Dylan presents us with three horn-playing angels that are part of a Yuletide decoration, sitting unnoticed as people of various types pass by underneath, none of whom – tragically, we are invited to infer – stop to ponder their significance. Celestial organ and a female choir provide suitable accompaniment. It could have been cringe-worthy, but Dylan pulls it off. 'Father of Night' is slightly darker in tone but along the same lines, Dylan celebrating the Almighty and His achievements. This time the female choir coos over a sultry piano part. One wishes the song lasted longer than its brief minute-and-a-half.

In 1978, Dylan seemed to hint to *Rolling Stone*'s Jonathan Cott that his late-Sixties/early-Seventies marital bliss wasn't all it seemed. Speaking of *Nashville Skyline*, he said, ". . . you had to read between the lines. I was trying to grasp something that would lead me on to where I thought I should be, and it didn't go nowhere . . . I couldn't be anybody but myself and at that point I didn't know it or want to know it." In point of fact, a brace of the *New Morning* songs could be interpreted as providing clues in this direction. 'Time Passes Slowly' is a lovely little song, but perhaps only if one doesn't listen too closely to the lyric of this declaration that the narrator is so content with his lot that there "ain't no reason to go anywhere". The nostalgic notes in the words, the pretty tune and Dylan's endearingly homely piano are so distracting that one almost doesn't pick up on the fact that when one is enjoying oneself, time actually doesn't pass slowly. Though we could dismiss this as even a great wordsmith like Dylan groping to express that sensation of drifting on the wind that happiness engenders, one also realises that there might be equivocation intended in his observation that he is "lost in a dream". 'Sign on the Window' is even more peculiar in the way it seems to undercut the message it ostensibly conveys. The narrator talks of a picture-book ideal of a life in which he is married, catching rainbow trout and has a bunch of kids who call him "Pa". Yet when he sings, "That must be what it's all about", it sounds more like a question than a statement – especially when he then repeats the line. Moreover, lovely though 'The Man in Me' is, one can't help but notice how uncomfortable Dylan sounds singing its joyous la-la-las.

Ralph J. Gleason wrote of this album in *Rolling Stone*, the magazine he had co-founded and named partly after Dylan's song, "We've got Dylan back again". It was self-deception even leaving aside the quality of the material. Dylan – that acidic hero of the counter-culture – never would be back again, because, as this album proved beyond any remaining doubts, that person did not exist anymore. Although Dylan may have been a more knowing and layered individual than these mostly "Aw shucks" creations suggested, he was without question now domesticated beyond intellectual curiosity. In time, his intellectual curiosity would reawaken, but it would take a different form.

The only reason many Dylan fans didn't give up on him at this juncture is because he gave them nothing to give up on. Having made his point with *New Morning*, if perhaps somewhat less forcefully than he planned or imagined, Dylan seemed to then decide that he could stand or fall on his recorded catalogue to date. For the next three years, he did something that he had been trying to for the last four years, only to be prevented from doing so by either ego, contractual requirements, outside pressure, his own assumption that he couldn't or a combination thereof. He got off the treadmill. There would not be another bona fide Bob Dylan studio album until January 1974.

An alternative new career as a prose writer didn't seem likely though. The month after the release of *New Morning* saw the publication of *Tarantula*, the novel Dylan had begun in 1965. He had started writing it when still an egotistical young man and, judging by his public comments on it since, had delayed publishing it because as his ego had abated he had realised that it wasn't very good. Whereas John Lennon had been able to produce two worthy and funny books of surrealism despite the fact that at the time his Beatles songwriting was mainly still Moon-in-June stuff, Dylan's superior lyrics did not translate well to printed narrative. *Tarantula*, despite significant revisions by the author was even more impenetrable than his post-*Bringing It All Back Home* album-liner notes. While isolated passages – such as the one about the gentleman who washes himself in the morning with scrambled eggs – are hysterical, it's generally very hard-going. It was greeted with ridicule. Ironically, the interview Dylan concocted with Nat Hentoff for *Playboy* in 1966 – Dylan inserted surreal, rambling, convoluted answers to Hentoff's formal questions in the transcript – was a work of fiction far more adroit and funny than *Tarantula*.

Before the long period of silence, Dylan's fans were given false hope that he would: a) resume live work, b) return not just to music, but to very good music and c) return to music with a political message. It was an impression that must have been strengthened by the release of Dylan's movie *Eat the Document* in February '71, even if this mixture of a documentary of the 1966 UK tour and surrealist buffoonery only had a limited run before disappearing into the vaults. June 1971 saw the release of a cracking new single, 'Watching the River Flow' backed with 'Spanish is the Loving Tongue'. The Charles Badger Clark Jr.-written decades-old cowboy story on the B-side (an outtake from *New Morning* on which Dylan accompanies himself at the piano) is above average. The A-side, though, is something else altogether. 'Watching the River Flow' has been dismissed as vacuity-squared on the grounds that not only is Dylan offering no profound thoughts but that he admits it ("What's the matter with me?/I don't have much to say"). However, Dylan is actually saying quite a lot here – which is not necessarily the same as setting the world to rights. On this track he reinvigorates the blues in a way he signally failed to with *New Morning*'s 'One More Weekend'. Partly this is down to a crack band featuring Leon Russell on piano, Jesse Ed Davis on guitar and Jim Keltner on drums, partly because he opts for speed, partly because he throws in a bridge to alleviate the one-dimensionality of the genre, but mostly because it's just so damn likeable. In this one number about the joys of chewing the cud, Dylan sums up everything about and behind his domesticated years, but does so with great craft and an energy that – though it may be conceptually contradictory – one wishes his work of that period possessed more of.

The month after the release of that single, Dylan stunned and delighted the audience at the two Concerts for Bangladesh at Madison Square Garden by appearing on stage to help with the efforts to raise money for that flood-stricken country. A tidal wave of affection swept over the venue at this rare sighting. Dylan even wheeled out 'Blowin' in the Wind' for the occasion, a song he hadn't played live since 1964. It was the suggestion of George Harrison, whose persuasive abilities and close friendship had secured the coup of his appearance, and despite the fact that Dylan had at first caustically responded by suggesting Harrison play 'I Want to Hold Your Hand' (some reports say 'She Loves You'). Curiously, Dylan had laid down fifteen takes of 'Blowin' in the Wind' in a studio two months previously. Dylan performances occupied an entire side of the triple charity album of the event (which decided to render the country as "Bangla Desh") released in December 1971.

Those who inferred from Dylan's appearances at those concerts that he might be inclined to get political again seemed naïve: helping flood victims was surely simply a humanitarian gesture, even if the complexities of a civil war underlay and worsened the Bangladeshis' suffering. However, three months later those naïfs seemed to be proven right when Dylan absolutely amazed the rock world by returning to protest music. His November 1971 single 'George Jackson' was a composition about an incarcerated villain turned Black Panther who was killed in disputed circumstances by San Quentin guards in August 1971, prompting the infamous blood-drenched riot at Attica Correctional Facility. Dylan wrote, recorded and released the song in lightning-quick time after reading Jackson's book *Soledad Brother*, so it is worthy rather than a classic (and many have questioned whether it is worthy, pointing out that, morally, Jackson hardly walked it like he talked it). However, the single suggested that Dylan was once more a person to whom his disillusioned former fans could relate, as though the man who had written 'The Lonesome Death of Hattie Carroll' had reappeared, shoving out of his path the impostor responsible for everything from *Nashville Skyline* (or even *Another Side of* . . .) onwards as he did so. It even *sounded* like protest-era Dylan: one man and a guitar – at least on the promotional version of the US single; the commercial release had the "big band" version of the song on the A-side. Dylan's absolute commitment seemed demonstrated in the fact that he abandoned plans to put his unreleased song 'Wallflower' on the B-side for the acoustic version: he didn't want to give radio stations the chance to dodge the message.

By now it had been so long established that Dylan wasn't a singles artist that the fact that the record climbed no higher than No.33 in the States and got nowhere in the UK was not a huge shock. It was the principle that counted. Although some mocked Dylan for being a rich man trying to garner some radical chic, the return to a form of activism impressed A. J. Weberman enough for him to announce that he was now going to leave Dylan alone. However, the first sign that Dylan had not completely re-embraced counter-culture values (if indeed he ever had completely shared them) came just five days after the release of 'George Jackson' in the form of the double LP *Bob Dylan's Greatest Hits Vol.II*. Though it came in a classy jacket design with an iconic, onstage, closely cropped picture of Dylan – back to camera, turned head revealing his harmonica – the record company were of course compounding the sin of the crass title of the first Dylan anthology. Those inclined to tut at the title must have been equally enraged by the fact that the album contained five previously unreleased recordings, a traditional ploy to make fans feel compelled to buy material they already had. (The album also gathered up 'Watching the River Flow', shortly making it the only place to easily locate that single track.) The record company could not be blamed this time: the unreleased tracks were Dylan's idea.

The tracklisting was reputedly also Dylan's. As his hits tally since the first volume was even more meagre than it had been then, he had to think as laterally as the compilers of the first compilation. As well as defining hits as songs of his made famous by other people ('Don't Think Twice, It's All Right', 'All I Really Want to Do', 'All Along the Watchtower', 'The Mighty Quinn (Quinn, the Eskimo)'), he sometimes simply ignored the *Greatest Hits* part of the title and pretended it said "My Faves", giving him the leeway for idiosyncratic choices such as 'Stuck Inside of Mobile with the Memphis Blues Again', 'Just Like Tom Thumb's Blues' and 'A Hard Rain's A-Gonna Fall'.

Of the five previously unreleased tracks – all clustered together at the end of the original vinyl side four – 'Tomorrow is a Long Time' is a live recording dating from 1963 and either another expression of the artist's delight at Elvis having recorded it or a nod toward the version Rod Stewart had included on his megasuccessful album *Every Picture Tells a Story* that very year, 'When I Paint My Masterpiece' (previously released by The Band) was recorded at the same sessions as 'Watching the River Flow', and the remainder are re-recorded Basement Tapes songs, Columbia having decided that the genuine Big Pink recordings Dylan offered them for the collection were aurally substandard. 'Tomorrow is a Long Time' suffers from the sonic deficiencies that any solo acoustic live recording of the era does, although a lot of slack should be granted it for its sensitivity and poetic flourishes. Even so, it's not a patch on Rod Stewart's take. The first half of the Seventies was a period when the latter specialized in beautifully rendered versions of lesser-known Dylan tracks: he recorded exquisite versions of this, 'Only a Hobo' and 'Mama, You Been on My Mind'. (This is in addition to his 1979 recording of 'Man of Constant Sorrow', which traditional he had clearly heard on *Bob Dylan*.) Stewart poured even more into Dylan's coffers in 1988 by "writing" a song called 'Forever Young', which he and Dylan came to an out-of-court settlement about. 'When I Paint My Masterpiece' is a curious song, especially considering the fact of it being recorded at the same sessions – possibly the same day – as the track that had declared "I don't have much to say". The artist is imploring a companion to be there with him when he comes up with his greatest work of art. Many must have been the listener who felt that the notion that Dylan's greatest work might be in front of him was rather desperate self-deception, not just because of his recent mediocre form but because if that feat was going to be achieved, it would take melodies profoundly less boring than this one.

Although Columbia's sniffiness about the original Basement Tapes would be disproved, the trio of re-recordings here are wonderful. The three – all already covered by other artists – were recorded in September 1971 with Dylan's friend Happy Traum. Traum's harmony singing lifts the already wonderful 'I Shall Be Released' (a track on The Band's debut) into the stratosphere. The Tom Robinson Band did a version in 1977 which added a bridge that turned the number into an anthem for the unjustly imprisoned, but the imagery about the light coming down from the west unto the east places this in the bracket of Dylan's spiritual songs: such imagery litters his canon, whether it be the narrator of 'Isis' saying, "I came in from the East with the sun in my eyes" or the narrator of 'No Time to Think' stating, "Starlight in the East/You're finally released." Not that you have to be a believer in anything other than great songcraft to find it truly uplifting. In 'You Ain't Goin' Nowhere', Dylan alters the lyric to have a dig at Roger (formerly Jim) McGuinn for mangling the words in The Byrds' rendition that had been included on *Sweetheart of the Rodeo*. Not only does Traum again layer the recording nicely with his harmony, but he plucks a fine banjo accompaniment. Dylan is no slouch on harmonica either. Though Traum is restricted to second guitar on 'Down in the Flood' – a version of which had been released by Sandy Denny a couple of months before the compilation's release – it is almost as high-quality as the previous two tracks. One can't help but wish Dylan and his friend had laid down an entire album of Basement Tape tracks like this; whisper it lightly but these versions are better than the legend-draped originals. At the very least, Dylan could have recorded a version of the compilation's other Basement Tape song 'The Mighty Quinn (Quinn the Eskimo)', represented here via that *Self Portrait* Isle of Wight travesty.

On the UK version of the album, 'Positively 4th Street' displaced 'She Belongs to Me' and 'It's All Over Now, Baby Blue' displaced 'New Morning'. In either configuration, the tracklisting – because there are no out-and-out rockers – made Dylan seem almost like a middle-of-the-road artist (even 'Stuck Inside of Memphis . . .' sounds laid-back in this context), one right in the mellow vein of the singer-songwriters like Carole King, James Taylor, Joni Mitchell and Gordon Lightfoot then in the ascendancy in the music business. However, this compilation – a magnificent collection of music whatever the avarice behind it – demonstrated that none of those people were in Dylan's league when it came to not just lyrical genius but melodic invention and breadth of vision. It was a fitting adieu to the world as Dylan prepared to – rather than continue his musical career let alone re-engage in protest – absent himself from it.

Terence Denman has published books on the First World War and English grammar. He is no Bob Dylan fan. However, he is an expert on Westerns: his next projected work is a study of the spaghetti variety. In this original article, he explores Dylan's twin roles – actor and score writer – in Sam Peckinpah's 1973 Western Pat Garrett and Billy the Kid.

GUNFIGHT IN DURANGO: SAM PECKINPAH FACES BOB DYLAN

By Terence Denman

Sam Peckinpah's *Pat Garrett and Billy the Kid* wasn't the first western to have rock stars strap on a six gun. Howard Hawks employed a baby-faced Rick ('Hello Mary Lou') Nelson as the coolest of John Wayne's posse in *Rio Bravo* (1959). Western fans who love Presley are always delighted that one of The King's best films (from a not too distinguished oeuvre) was Don Siegel's *Flaming Star*, a worthy genre entry from 1960. The Brits fared less well: Mick Jagger was pathetic in *Ned Kelly* (an "Australian western") in 1970, and Ringo Starr was not much better as a very hairy bandit in 1971 spaghetti-western *Blindman*. But with Kris Kristofferson (and members of his backing band), Rita Coolidge (Mrs. Kristofferson on her library ticket), and most famously, or infamously, Mr. Robert Zimmerman all saddling up, *Pat Garrett and Billy the Kid* sometimes seems like a rock festival out west.

Raised in rural California among many families of original pioneer stock, Peckinpah was obsessed with the Old West. After first scripting and directing television westerns, he made four films in the 1960s of real stature and often startling originality: *Ride the High Country; Major Dundee; The Wild Bunch* and *The Ballad of Cable Hogue*. At the heart of all of them was an elegiac but sometimes unprecedentedly violent depiction of the decline of the West. Loners, outcasts, nonconformists and men living by an ancient code beyond its time have to come to terms with, or be destroyed by, industrial technology, social conformity and the triumph of ruthless big business. When he was given the chance to direct a film on Billy the Kid in 1972, it looked like a gift from the gods. Peckinpah had already worked on a film adaptation of *The Authentic Death of Hendry Jones*, a novel about Billy, which became the basis of Marlon Brando's *One Eyed Jacks*. Perhaps the gift was a poisoned chalice. Making *Pat Garrett and Billy the Kid* nearly killed Peckinpah and it remains controversial. To its detractors, it's a slow-paced disaster, undermined by weak scenes, a compromised script and Peckinpah's erratic direction (increasingly alcohol-fuelled). To its supporters, it's a master-piece, brutally butchered by insensitive studio bosses. Acolytes search for the holy grail of the definitive "director's cut". Devotees fight over the respective merits of the extant versions with an almost theological intensity. Bob Dylan's soundtrack is just one controversial facet of the film.

There are some wonderful stories about Dylan's involvement. It's said that Peckinpah would have preferred Roger "England Swings" Miller to write the score and had never heard of Dylan. Even Sam can't have been that drunk. Another beguiling account has Dylan singing 'Billy' (the film's theme tune) to a lachrymose Peckinpah, who then cried out, "Goddammit, who is that boy? Sign him up." A less poetic story has Dylan arriving on the set in Durango to find Peckinpah urinating on film footage he was clearly unhappy with. You'd like all the stories to be true. The coming together of Peckinpah and Dylan is not, perhaps, so strange. By the early 1970s, Peckinpah was a counter-culture hero, with regular write-ups in *Rolling Stone* and the *Los Angeles Free Press* (the former assiduously followed the making of the film). In the United States of the Vietnam War (which Peckinpah had spoken against), Attica and Kent State, his vision of an America drenched in blood and offering nothing but persecu-tion for its outsiders and rebels spoke to many young people.

Rudy Wurlitzer, the film's first scriptwriter, approached Dylan to write the music. Impressed by the script, Dylan asked if there might be a role for him. Wurlitzer wasn't keen, but the film's producer, Gordon Carroll, was. Peckinpah claimed that Dylan was allowed to take over the scoring alone (instead of working with Jerry Fielding, Peckinpah's regular composer) because Carroll "wants to sell a lot of Bobby [sic] Dylan albums". Probably unfair, but Carroll was certainly obsessed with the similarities between Billy the Kid's short, legendary career and those of contemporary rock stars: "the idea that someone could have his life and have it all between the ages of nineteen and twenty-five". Fielding was politically liberal but musically conservative: Dylan's music was "a lot of nonsense which is strictly for teenyboppers". Carroll backed Dylan (he produced the soundtrack album) and Peckinpah got caught in the crossfire. Beset by technical and personal problems, and with a visceral loyalty to Fielding, Peckinpah largely ignored the score until it was too late. When he calmed down later, Peckinpah claimed that he objected not to Dylan's music but to the way that the studio used it in the film. Nonetheless, he and Dylan were a mismatch as personalities. In *Sam Peckinpah Interviews*, edited by Kevin J. Hayes, Peckinpah is said to have recalled in 1974 that he liked Kristofferson and "could identify" with him, but that Dylan was a "giant pain in the ass" and the "most convoluted personality" he had ever met. Peckinpah says he accused Dylan of lifting the first four bars of 'Help Me Make It Through the Night' for part of the soundtrack, "and after that he never talked to me again".

Versions of the film use Dylan's score in different ways. In some releases, his music is a barely audible tinkle, in others the volume setting approaches eleven. Dylan's most famous composition for the film was 'Knockin' on Heaven's Door', dismissed by Fielding as "shit", but covered by everyone from "Slow Hand" Clapton to Guns N' Roses, and several other rockers who fear that the grim reaper is near. In one of the film's edits, the song's haunting lyric provides the background to a classic scene: Sheriff Baker's (Slim Pickens) lingering death after being gut-shot. Peckinpah used the tune but dropped the lyric in his preferred edit. He judged (some believe that Fielding did the judging) that the lyric made the scene too literal and rhetorical. He was probably right, but most versions now usually include both music and lyric as Slim bleeds over the screen. Dylan recorded vocal and instrumental versions at Burbank in February 1973 while the relevant scene was projected above him, with the backing band in tears. An earlier recording session in January, at

Columbia's Mexico City studios, was just as emotional, but for the wrong reasons: Dylan couldn't stand the recording engineer or some of Kristofferson's backing band.

Only 'Knockin' on Heaven's Door' and 'Billy' have lyrics. Apart from the flute-dominated 'Final Theme', the rest of the score is guitar-based instrumentals (with some humming), ranging from the plaintive, languid 'River Song' to the frenetic quasi-bluegrass of 'Turkey Shoot'. Four versions of 'Billy', vocal and instrumental, are heard and the tune is overworked, giving a sense of thinness to the score. Fielding claimed that 'Billy' had "a limitless number of verses that Dylan would sing in random order". In fact, it seems that Fielding decided to spread the versions of 'Billy' through the film. Dylan did plan other material for the film: Clinton Heylin, in *Revolution in the Air*, the first volume of his study of Dylan's songs, mentions 'Billy Surrenders' and 'And He Killed Me Too', and a bootleg recording exists of 'Goodbye Holly' (Holly being one of Garrett's victims).

Opinion differs about how well Dylan's score works. Notably critical is Paul Seydor: in his *Peckinpah: The Western Films*, he says that "Dylan didn't know how to write music that exists to serve some other end than itself". He cites Dylan's "soporifically repetitive guitar-strumming, which ambles monotonously along for over six minutes" at the beginning of the film, and makes "an already long sequence feel much longer". But given the ruminative, elegiac pace of the film, Dylan's slow-burn approach enhances, not detracts, from its unique feel. It's difficult to imagine the film working as well with the traditional orchestral western film music that features, for instance, in Peckinpah's early masterpiece, *Ride the High Country* (Dylan's favourite). The understated quality of Dylan's score makes the explosions of casual violence more powerful.

However, there are issues with Dylan's music. Peckinpah saw the Kid as "no hero" but "a gunfighter, a real killer" and the film often shows Billy in an unheroic light. When he's not shooting fellow miscreants (sometimes in the back), Billy is whoring, boozing or blasting the heads off innocent chickens. Kristofferson's casting as the man known to his mother as William H. Bonney was strange: not only was Kristofferson thirty-six at the time, but his pretty-boy looks and hippy-esque mannerisms don't seem physically right for such low-down meanness (photographs of the Kid show a scrawny, white-trash, buck-toothed psychopath). Similarly inappropriately, Dylan's lyric romantically portrays Billy as a harassed wanderer "playing all alone" while pursued by wicked "businessmen" trying to destroy "your spirit and your soul" because "they don't like you to be so free". Through Dylan's eyes, the Kid seems less a violent outlaw, and more a freewheeling rural anarchist and misunderstood folk hero. Dylan is certainly making a point about the establishment's persecution of the contemporary counter-culture. Peckinpah was clearly fascinated by Billy and does romanticise him at times, but he clearly had a less dewy-eyed conception of his place in history.

Dylan plays the enigmatic-to-the-point-of-catatonic Alias. Though Alias appeared in Wurlitzer's original script and was based on an historical figure, Peckinpah admitted that a rather mannered western on Billy directed by Arthur Penn, *The Left-Handed Gun* (originally scripted by Gore Vidal), provided the main impetus for the character. That film has Hurd Hatfield as a reporter obsessed with chronicling Billy's exploits. Peckinpah claimed that he saw Alias as a "troubadour guitar player", wielding pen instead of plectrum, limning Billy's advance to iconic status, but Dylan often looks incongruous and anachronistic. Peckinpah may have sensed this because Dylan later complained that his role was cut back continually. However, some critics have found Alias a "captivating little figure" and Dylan "Chaplinesque". Seydor, dismissive of Dylan's soundtrack, sees Alias as a clever move by Peckinpah to bring together Dylan's persona as a folk singer and chronicler of frontier outlawry ('John Wesley Harding') with Alias's desire to render Billy into legend. Perhaps, but Peckinpah's strength in casting westerns had been to make perfect use of grizzled veterans, not baby-faced rock stars. The wrinklies in *PGBTK* – Pickens, James Coburn (Pat Garrett), Chill Wills (Lemuel), Jack Elam (Alamosa Bill), Katy Jurado (Sheriff Baker's wife), Barry Sullivan (Chisum) – hold their own magnificently, but Kristofferson and Dylan look at times like little boys lost.

Despite employing musicians such as Roger McGuinn and Byron Berline, the album got mostly bad reviews. Jon Landau in *Rolling Stone* was particularly dismissive: "inept, amateurish and embarrassing". Cut from the context of the film, the music does appear samey and insubstantial, apart from the ever glorious 'Knockin' on Heaven's Door'. However, Dylan's score is now an integral part of the film and of the chequered story of its making.

Dylan clearly saw the episode as worthwhile: in January 1974 he declared that he was "not a movie star but I've got a vision to put up on the screen . . . the Peckinpah experience was valuable in terms of getting near the big action". For various reasons – Peckinpah's distracted mind; Jerry Fielding's unremitting hostility; the brutal editing by the men in suits – we don't have the soundtrack that Dylan intended. Dylan thought the film had been "chopped to pieces" and that his "music seemed scattered and used in every other place but the scenes in which we did it". However, he did not blame the director: he dedicated the album to Peckinpah.

PAT GARRETT & BILLY THE KID/PLANET WAVES/BEFORE THE FLOOD

By Sean Egan

PAT GARRETT & BILLY THE KID
US release: 13 July 1973
Produced by: Gordon Carroll
CHARTS: US#16; UK#29

SIDE ONE
Main Title Theme (Billy)
Cantina Theme (Workin' for the Law)
Billy 1
Bunkhouse Theme
River Theme

SIDE TWO
Turkey Chase
Knockin' on Heaven's Door
Final Theme
Billy 4
Billy 7

On New Year's Day 1972, Dylan appeared as a guest performer at a New York concert by The Band. He also guested at a small John Prine gig in September. These were his only appearances that year and the next. Although he engaged in low-level activity like playing on Doug Sahm's new album, he exhibited no interest in returning to anything like a conventionally defined career as a recording artist. This was despite Joan Baez's kind decision to release a song called 'To Bobby', imploring Dylan to return to recording political songs in which she claimed that voices in the night were crying for him and children in the morning light were dying for him. This followed a year after David Bowie's 'Song

for Bob Dylan', which covered similar territory with less melodrama. All Baez, Bowie and the world were going to get, though,
was Anthony Scaduto's early – 1972 myth-busting biography of
Dylan and – from Dylan – the soundtrack to a cowboy movie.

The commercial release of movie soundtracks on album was
a long established tradition, and often rather lucrative (e.g., *West
Side Story*, which spent more than a year atop the US album
charts). It was little surprise, then, that Dylan's *Pat Garrett &
Billy the Kid* (as the cover rendered it; movie posters favoured
"and" over an ampersand) score hit the stores on 13 July 1973,
although one assumes that as a consequence of his name on the
sleeve it sold a whole lot more than most soundtrack albums, not
least because it was the first album with Dylan's name on the
sleeve for three years. Said sleeve was a highly effective minimalist affair with no picture but just distressed lettering spelling out
the artist name and title.

In *Chronicles Volume One*, Dylan complains that he is more
than a great lyricist – why else, for instance, would Duane Eddy
have recorded a whole LP of instrumental versions of his tunes?
Leaving aside that 1965's *Duane Eddy Does Bob Dylan*(!) was
comprised of only about 60 per cent Dylan songs, he's absolutely right: he has written melodies that are up there with the
best of his contemporaries. However, a soundtrack album from
rock's master wordsmith still seemed a little strange. As with
most soundtrack music, most of it lacks words, while its music is
not really designed to be listened to on its own. Divorced from
the action it underscored, it is of profoundly reduced intrinsic
worth. The fact that the titles of almost half the tracks on this
record (which doesn't always contain the same recordings of
themes/songs as heard in the movie) are variations of the word
'Billy' ('Billy 4', 'Billy 7', etc.) only underlines the functionalism
of screen music. With 'Knockin' on Heaven's Door', though, we
get an addition to the canon of great Dylan songs that, considering the context, is rather unexpected. The sultry first-person
death anthem sees Dylan unexpectedly and skilfully plucking
from his remit something so catchy, intriguing and concise (just
two-and-a-half minutes) as to provide him with a rare hit single.
The US No.12 and UK No.14 it achieved must have provided
an unbelievable boon to the picture's promotion. Though the

idea that Dylan's records had never had the manipulative production techniques of other artists is a bit of a myth, it's noticeable how the budgets and high production values of the movie world provide 'Knockin'' ' a richness we are not used to from Dylan's music, with a huge cinematic soundscape and a sublime mix – Dylan's voice is treated to sound like he's God.

The soundtrack was released reluctantly by Columbia, who had decided that they weren't going to renew Dylan's contract but were nudged into acquiescing to putting it out because it was too late for the artist to take it to another label before the picture premiered. Once the chart success of 'Knockin' on Heaven's Door' had demonstrated that Dylan wasn't the has-been they had concluded, the label wanted to sign him up again, but Dylan – angry about their treatment of the company's ousted president Clive Davis, and possibly a little peeved that Columbia had messed him around after the completion of contract nego- tiations – refused. He went instead to Asylum, an artist-friendly label founded in 1971 and which had merged with Elektra, another artist-friendly label, the following year. However, he did a handshake deal rather than put his signature on a contract.

Columbia retaliated by releasing, on 16 November 1973, *Dylan* – a collection of warm-ups and outtakes from the *Self Portrait* and *New Morning* sessions – only two months before his first Asylum album. It was a remarkable act of corporate spite. The *Bootleg Series* releases have subsequently proved that the label had oodles of unreleased Dylan gems in the vaults and it would have made commercial sense for them to put such high- quality material on this album. That they instead chose to fill *Dylan* with songs which in some cases hadn't even been considered good enough to reside on Dylan's artistic nadir suggests that paying the departed artist back overrode even their money-making instincts. The knife was twisted further by the sarcastically definitive title given the LP. For the record, the contents were 'Lily of the West', 'Can't Help Falling in Love', 'Sarah Jane', 'The Ballad of Ira Hayes', 'Mr. Bojangles', 'Mary Ann', 'Big Yellow Taxi', 'A Fool Such as I' and 'Spanish is the Loving Tongue' (a different version to that on the B-side of 'Watching the River Flow'). It actually did reasonably well in the States (No.17) although Dylan's usually loyal British fans this

time stayed away – perhaps displaying the discretion of greater
insight – and it didn't chart in the UK. Disapproval registered by
Dylan when he subsequently re-signed with Columbia presumably accounts for the fact that *Dylan* was never released on CD
in North America and for the fact that its European compact
disc (given the sub-title *A Fool Such as I*) has been deleted. It can
now only be bought legally second-hand, though there was a
window of three-and-a-half years up until the end of 2009 when
it was available exclusively via the iTunes digital compilation
Bob Dylan: The Collection – the sort of thing that turns the very
concept of "bonus tracks" on its head.

PLANET WAVES
US release: 17 January 1974
Produced by: Rob Fraboni
CHARTS: US#1; UK#7

SIDE ONE
On a Night Like This
Going, Going, Gone
Tough Mama
Hazel
Something There is About You
Forever Young

SIDE TWO
Forever Young
Dirge
You Angel You
Never Say Goodbye
Wedding Song

It's difficult to convey the sense of excitement that greeted the
advertisements in the press in late 1973 stating simply "Bob
Dylan/The Band" and giving details of how to obtain tickets for
those artists' forthcoming joint tour.

Bob Dylan's dual decision at some point in 1973 to make
fully fledged returns to both music-making and live performance seems to have been prompted by two things. One was The

Rolling Stones' colossally successful 1972 tour of America to promote their album *Exile on Main St.*, the other was an impressive large-scale concert by The Band he witnessed in upstate New York in summer 1973.

The live circuit to which Dylan was returning was now very different. Since Dylan had last been on the road in 1966, the mewling young fans who had considered him Judas for abandoning folk were now adults, very few of whom would think in those terms anymore, in part because rock had (in large part because of Dylan) long grown into a respectable form of artistic expression that had fully encompassed the intellectualism and politicisation of folk. The gap between 1966 and 1974 had seen modern popular music's audience grow up with it: apart from his sporadic stage appearances since 1966, this was going to be the first time Dylan had played in front of large audiences primarily over student age. Meanwhile, rock was not the poor relation of the entertainment business anymore in another way. It no longer relied on venues intended for other forms of entertainment like cinemas and ballrooms but had its own circuit of either dedicated venues (many of them able to hold massive crowds) or else venues that, though they weren't specifically intended for rock concerts, hosted them as a genuinely valued supplement to their main business.

Planet Waves, Dylan's comeback album, made commercial and publicity waves by being his first ever No.1 US album. It was to some extent an artificial achievement: though the tour was an astonishing success, the album's sales dropped off quickly. It was suggested in later years that Dylan was underwhelmed by Asylum's distribution of *Planet Waves*, but Dylan did his own damage to the sales by causing the release of the LP to be put back until two weeks into the six-week tour – which began on 3 January 1974 – because he decided to add a liner note. Said note – a rather near-the-knuckle affair in which he wrote of "bar stools that stank from sweating pussy" – was so belated it was originally a loose sheet under the shrinkwrap but, though it graduated to the jacket proper, eventually disappeared and has not been reinstated in the CD's booklet. Meanwhile, though Dylan started out playing a sprinkling of *Planet Waves* songs in concert, by the end of the tour he had given it over to a

nostalgia-fest and 'Forever Young' was the only track from the
new album left in his set (which he sometimes started with a
1963 song of his that he'd never even released called 'Hero
Blues'). (In Britain, *Planet Waves* was released by Chris
Blackwell's Island, another label that insisted commerce followed
art rather than the other way around. Although Dylan had
topped the UK LP charts plenty of times, including with *Self
Portrait*, it only made No.7.)

The album was Dylan's first (non-soundtrack) LP since
Highway 61 Revisited not produced by Bob Johnston. Though
this was presumably because of Johnston's ties with Columbia,
Dylan would never use him again. Nor, indeed, would he ever
employ *Planet Waves*' producer Rob Fraboni in the studio subsequently. The album's working title *Ceremonies of the Horseman*
will be recognizable to all Dylan fans who recall the lyric of
'Love Minus Zero/No Limit', although is no more fathomable
than is the title that replaced it, nor the two sub-titles Dylan put
on the cover: *Moonglow* and *Cast-Iron Songs and Torch Ballads*.
Dylan drew the album cover himself and it is ghastly. Additionally,
the scrawled credits and tracklisting give it a shoddy air.
Fortunately, the contents are a lot better.

Planet Waves is Dylan's only album-length formal studio
collaboration with The Band (which description excludes the
very informal Basement Tapes). One wonders how much better
it would have been had they spent more than the three days
they did recording it in Los Angeles – Dylan noticeably stumbles over his own lyrics sometimes – but this is a far cry from
those disastrous abandoned early sessions for *Blonde on Blonde*.
Those expecting something as immediately catchy and sumptuously crafted as 'Knockin' on Heaven's Door' (which people
no doubt included Asylum) were to be disappointed, but *Planet
Waves* is a very respectable effort. It's evident right from the
opening bars – which feature a galloping drum beat and vigor-
ous accordion – that there is profoundly more energy, musical
and mental, in these grooves than in the sleepy soundscapes of
his last few albums.

'On a Night Like This' sees Dylan telling a companion visiting his log cabin that, "We've got much to talk about and much
to reminisce". Although he implies this person is female and the

occasion romantic, considering what follows – an album drenched in reflection and nostalgia like no previous Dylan record – it may be the case that it is his audience whom he is really addressing. Nonetheless, that the opener is on the surface at least exploring the same domestic concerns as his last few efforts must have dismayed his audience – even though much of it had itself now settled down and discovered the ideology-sapping joys of married bliss. However, we are on a whole different plane to the intellectual aimlessness of *New Morning*.

The latter is further demonstrated by 'Going, Going, Gone'. The album's second track is something that many former fans must have thought they would never see: a new bona fide Bob Dylan classic. A melancholy song of farewell – though whether it's to a person, lifestyle or philosophy is not quite clear – it features some snaking Robertson guitar and a delightful soaring bridge in which Dylan recalls the wisdom imparted to him ("All that's gold doesn't shine") by his grandmother, whom he has mentioned in interviews as a very important feature of his childhood.

As well as nostalgia (Dylan refers to his father at a point before his death but after he had retired), 'Tough Mama' – like several of the songs – is dripping with sex, not the leering, shallow kind of singledom, but the fond, intimate horniness of coupledom. As The Band produce muscular, punchy instrumentation, Dylan's muse is variously celebrated in a nicely syncopated lyric as – among other things – a "sweet goddess" and a "dark beauty", as well as the title phrase. It is clear that she is the person responsible for the lack of ambition Dylan enunciates in his declarations "I ain't haulin' any of my lambs to the marketplace anymore" and "I gained some recognition but I lost my appetite".

'Hazel' seems to be about a Dylan lover predating the tough mama, almost certainly teenage Hibbing sweetheart Echo Helstrom. Dylan's statement that "I wouldn't be ashamed to be seen with you anywhere" arouses memories of Helstrom's public comments that Dylan was from a respectable family and she the wrong side of the tracks. The narrator exults in their matching dreams of escape ("Stardust in your eye/You're going somewhere, and so am I") but in the mournful bridge he is upset that a gulf is being created by the fact that while his ambitions are being realised, hers are not ("I am up on the hill, and still you're not there"). It's a snapshot of a point in Dylan's formative years that is honest and extremely likeable.

In 'Something There is About You', Dylan again harks back to his youth, which word handily rhymes with the city of his birth and younger childhood, although the old girlfriend whose name he invokes and which also rhymes with Duluth – one Ruth – would seem to be poetic licence. Dylan signs off by stating to his current partner that he can't say he will be faithful. Some have suggested that by this Dylan means he is telling Sara that after eight years of relative inactivity he has to go back on the road. Unfortunately, from what we know of Dylan's conduct in his marriage, the literal interpretation seems the more plausible. It's not just this that makes the song less likeable than the others, though, but also the fact that it drags somewhat.

Vinyl side one closed with the album's slow version of 'Forever Young'. It's a touching tribute to the innocence of a child, presumed to be Dylan's oldest, Jesse, with some lovely pulsing organ and the exquisite line, "May you build a ladder to the stars and climb on every rung". Unfortunately, a lot of the goodwill generated by the song is squandered by the fact that it is immediately followed by a second version. Though the faster rendition that opened vinyl side two is two minutes shorter, it offends for its entire duration because its jaunty tone spoils the sensitivity of the lyric and because there is a hubris in thinking a song is good enough to be heard twice. Some attributed the repeat to a lack of inspiration but Dylan had at least one other high-quality new song he could have included ('Nobody 'Cept You').

Fortunately, after that second 'Forever Young' – a repeat about as welcome as a burp – things immediately get back on track with 'Dirge'. This cut's attractions aren't restricted to a remarkably attention-grabbing opening line ("I hate myself for loving you"). An intense creation featuring just Dylan (playing an insistent, dark piano motif) and Robertson (complementing him excellently on classical guitar), it sees Dylan apparently regretful of his previous embracement of fame, although he cleverly couches his words in such a way that the listener can often mistake it for the embarrassment and regret of half of a split couple ("I hate that foolish game we played and the need that was expressed"). It constitutes the second of this album's brace of new Dylan classics.

'You Angel You' is a perky close cousin to 'The Man in Me'. It's not quite as euphoria-inducing as it's meant to be, but pleasing nevertheless. 'Never Say Goodbye' is a less-giddy but also easy-on-the-ear exploration of the same worshipful territory. In 'You Angel You', Dylan in presumably sarcastic reference to the supposed shortcomings of his voice says, "I feel I could almost sing." That he can sing is proven in the opening line of 'Never Say Goodbye', even if the gorgeous, atmospheric huskiness in his voice as he enunciates "Twilight on the frozen lake/A north wind about to break" seems a matter of accident rather than design. Once again, Dylan celebrates his current bliss. He also plays with his audience's analysis of his art, closing the song by mischievously intoning, "Baby, baby blue/You've changed your last name too."

The closing number was a hurried addition, Dylan bringing in 'Wedding Song' when the album was at the mixing stage. Despite the foreboding melody and occasional lyrical hints of friction, it's a fairly straightforward statement of thanks to Sara for rescuing him from a personal pit ("I love you more than life itself, you mean that much to me"). The change in aural tone provided by this solo acoustic performance (recorded in one take) is something of a mercy: over the preceding ten tracks The Band's backing has cumulatively become suffocating. However, though the song is touching, and there are the odd good couplets, it seems to go in circles and long before the end of its 4:39 playing time Dylan seems to be simply reiterating the same points.

Although *Planet Waves* is slender – like *Nashville Skyline* and *New Morning* it feels like a padded-out double EP – what is good on it is far better than the best of those albums. Moreover, though Dylan is nothing like the lyric genius he was in the Sixties, nor proffering a seer's expansive viewpoint any longer, he tackles his narrow subject of domesticity and personal growth with exactly the perceptiveness and cleverness he had failed to on *Nashville Skyline* and *New Morning*.

As with other Dylan albums recorded at the end of artistic slumps, *Planet Waves*' reputation has fluctuated, its stock falling when initial euphoria gradually gave way to a dismayed realization that comparisons to the quality of the music that had first made people love him was self-delusion, and then rising a little again when it was apprehended that this didn't mean it was actually a stinker. It's now clear that *Planet Waves* is a good but minor Dylan album artistically. Historically, it's interesting as a stepping stone to his imminent artistic renaissance.

BEFORE THE FLOOD
(Bob Dylan/The Band)
US release: 20 June 1974
Produced by: –
CHARTS: US#3; UK#8

SIDE ONE
Most Likely You Go Your Way (And I'll Go Mine)
Lay Lady Lay
Rainy Day Women #12 & 35
Knockin' on Heaven's Door
It Ain't Me, Babe
Ballad of a Thin Man

SIDE TWO
Up on Cripple Creek
I Shall Be Released
Endless Highway
The Night They Drove Old Dixie Down
Stage Fright

SIDE THREE
Don't Think Twice, It's All Right
Just Like a Woman
It's Alright, Ma (I'm Only Bleeding)
The Shape I'm In
When You Awake
The Weight

SIDE FOUR
All Along the Watchtower
Highway 61 Revisited
Like a Rolling Stone
Blowin' in the Wind

It's vaguely astonishing that before 1974, Bob Dylan had never released a live album. Several gigs had been officially recorded in the Sixties with a view to commercial release, including major dates at Carnegie Hall and New York Town Hall in 1963, a 1964 gig at the Philharmonic Hall, concerts on his earth-shattering 1966 "Judas!" tour and his somewhat less earth-shattering Isle of Wight performance in 1969. Apart from the latter, aesthetic considerations don't seem to have been the reason for the recordings being withheld from the public.

Although he had allowed in-concert tracks to appear on Various Artists tribute and charity albums, for a variety of reasons, the only live performances Dylan had ever sanctioned for release on any of his own output were the version of 'Just Like Tom Thumb's Blues' on the flip of 'I Want You', the Isle of Wight tracks on *Self Portrait* and the version of 'Tomorrow is a Long Time' on *Greatest Hits Vol. II*. In fact, it's rumoured that the only reason he allowed the release of *Before the Flood* – an aural document of the 1974 tour – was because it was a sop to Asylum, whom he had decided to leave after just one studio album. (Dylan's return to Columbia saw a new contract involving the ownership of his masters after a period of seven years, giving him a degree of control over his own work almost unknown in the rock industry.)

Of *Before the Flood*'s original four vinyl sides, The Band got one-and-a-half sides (which, this being a book about Dylan, will not be examined here), Dylan's solo acoustic part of the live sets is represented by three songs, and the rest of the material is Dylan and The Band together. No producer is listed for the album but Rob Fraboni and Phil Ramone did the mixing of the selections of performances, which, with one exception, came from the last two nights of the tour.

On 'Most Likely You Go Your Way (And I'll Go Mine)', what could be a galvanising opener is spoiled by Dylan's absurd singing, him virtually shouting the last word of lines, and drawing the word out as he does so. Similar histrionics – one wonders if they were a sign of anxiety – also detract from a version of 'Lay Lady Lay' more muscular and busy than the 1969 hit. The absence of the forced hilarity and the parping circus instrumentation of the studio original is a boon to 'Rainy Day Women #12 & 35', as is the faster clip, although one doubts whether it needs Robertson's ostentatious Catherine Wheel of a solo. 'Knockin' on Heaven's Door' marks one of the few songs where both Dylan and The Band calm down and let the song breathe and, significantly, the result is rather good. 'It Ain't Me, Babe', done to a marching beat, is OK, but you do wish Robertson would quit with that snaking guitar. 'Ballad of a Thin Man' is given an interestingly uptempo but still remarkably faithful reading.

While one learns to live with, even like, the variations Dylan brings to his songs here, the virtually yodelled 'Don't Think Twice, It's All Right' is very disappointing, not least because it's a lost opportunity to inject some sensitivity into what is a rather bombastic collection. Dylan's solo 'Just Like a Woman' sees him picking out interesting new melody lines from the song and performing an excellent harmonica solo but he ruins it with his overwrought vocal – the sycophantic applause for which from the audience is plain embarrassing. The audience does, though, provide an iconic crowd participation moment when the line "Even the President of the United States sometimes must have to stand naked" in 'It's Alright, Ma (I'm Only Bleeding)' is greeted by a roar of approval, a spontaneous reaction generated by the apparently impending impeachment of Richard Nixon. (Another sign of the times was the album's front cover depicting an auditorium crowd holding up lit matches and lighters, a newly minted fashion during slowies at concerts.)

'All Along the Watchtower' had never been played in concert by Dylan before the 1974 tour, although of course that's mainly because of his inactivity following its initial release. Here – like almost all his many, many live versions since – his arrangement is less his own than that of The Jimi Hendrix Experience, the author's mark of respect to the man who had thrown light on areas of his creation that he never knew existed. On 'Highway 61 Revisited', Dylan moves in the opposite direction to 'Ballad of a

Thin Man', easing back on the throttle a little, as well as funking it up. The spontaneous moments of the original 'Like a Rolling Stone' (like the leaving-the-stomach-behind bit) could never be replicated so it's meaningless to complain that the version herein is not as good. What's amazing is how good it is, the sheer venom of the familiar one replaced by a more measured, steady rolling meanness.

By the end of the tour, Dylan had started performing 'Blowin' in the Wind' as an encore and it is used as a quite effective closer on *Before the Flood*, apparently no longer considered by its author to be a piece of juvenilia.

Live albums are a shaky medium at the best of times. They are almost always remixed, resequenced and overdubbed to remove bum notes, thus making a nonsense of the supposed raison d'etre of presenting the music as heard by the audience on the day. They also feature only approximations of familiar song arrangements, lacking the sonic layering possible in a studio. Taking into account all those shortcomings of the genre, *Before the Flood* is a respectable example of it. It also, in places, gives an idea of the excitement that existed amongst the audiences in the (mostly Los Angeles) venues in which these particular performances took place over the fact that a living legend had roused himself to place himself in their presence.

In 1975, Bob Dylan released Blood on the Tracks. *It was that thing that many had come to feel he would never produce again: a classic album. In this feature (which he subsequently expanded into the book* A Simple Twist of Fate*), Andy Gill spoke to several of the principals in the making of a record that introduced Dylan to a new generation.*

A SIMPLE TWIST OF FATE

By Andy Gill

First published as "Blood on the Tracks" in *Mojo*, June 2001

You might think that, after his extraordinary achievements of the Sixties, there would be no doubt about Bob Dylan's position in the rock firmament – after all, he did virtually single-handedly drag pop music through its troubled adolescence to a new maturity. But his reputation suffered badly as that turbulent decade slipped uncertainly into the shameless Seventies, with many fans left baffled and angry by the more conservative direction the former spokesman of a generation seemed to be taking on *Nashville Skyline* and the feeble *Self Portrait*. Greil Marcus's appalled reaction to the latter in his *Rolling Stone* magazine review (first line: "What is this shit?") crystallised the response of many who felt their faith had somehow been betrayed. Subsequent releases did little to dispel this impression: *New Morning*, though an undoubted improvement, seemed somewhat undercooked, and the *Pat Garrett & Billy the Kid* soundtrack – 'Knockin' on Heaven's Door' aside – was incidental music with precious little incident to speak of.

When Dylan then defected to rising mogul David Geffen's Asylum Records, his old label Columbia stuck the knife further into his tottering reputation with the indefensible release of *Dylan*, a collection of rags-and-tatters outtakes from *Self Portrait* and *New Morning*, many just rehearsal run-throughs. As they surveyed his dwindling career, a few voiced disappointment that

Dylan hadn't actually died in the motorbike crash and secured his place in the rock firmament alongside Hendrix, Joplin, Morrison and Jones. Perhaps, some glumly mused, the torch had been passed on to the next wave of singer-songwriters that followed in Dylan's wake – to Loudon Wainwright, Jackson Browne or Don McLean, or maybe that wordy young chap whom John Hammond had just signed to Columbia, Bruce Springsteen?

It was generally agreed that if Dylan was ever going to claw his way back to something like his former respectability, he would have to come up with something extra special. That special something would turn out to be *Blood on the Tracks*, the album which transmuted the desire and despair of his crumbling personal situation into a dozen of his finest songs, thereby cementing Dylan's position as the pre-eminent songwriter of his generation. Overnight, he was restored to the pantheon of greats. Michael Gray, whose *Song and Dance Man: The Art of Bob Dylan* had been the first serious full-length critical assessment of Dylan's work, hailed the album in *Let It Rock* magazine as ". . . the most strikingly intelligent album of the Seventies, [one which] legitimised [Dylan's] claim to a creative prowess as vital now as [in] the decade he so much affected", while in America, *Rolling Stone* acknowledged its status by running individual reviews of the album from no fewer than thirteen of the era's top rock critics.

The first inklings of a comeback had come with *Planet Waves*, the first fruit of his new deal with Asylum Records, and the best album he had made in years. In retrospect, it was a flawed work, but at the time it was enough just to hear Bob back with The Band again, and apparently enjoying himself. Apart from the anthemic 'Forever Young', the songs were mostly simple, effusive celebrations of love, though the bitter 'Dirge', with its opening line "I hate myself for lovin' you and the weakness that it showed", sat somewhat uneasily amongst all the hearts and flowers. Still, it couldn't be about his own situation, could it? After all, the same album's 'Wedding Song', with its references to "babies one, two, three" and "you were born to be my bride", clearly referred to his wife Sara, and it was the most fulsome of romantic tributes, with lines guaranteed to melt the hardest of hearts, such as "And if there is eternity I'd love you there again" and "I love you more than life itself, you mean that much to me". What an old softy!

As it turned out, the most significant line in the song was the one admitting "What's lost is lost, we can't regain what went down in the flood", which threw an entirely different light on all the song's other expressions of devotion. Things, it transpired, were far from stable in the Dylans' marriage, and 'Wedding Song' can be viewed in retrospect as the singer's desperate attempt to salvage a relationship heading fast towards the rocks – as if mere words might make up for more destructive shortcomings.

Dylan's life, though, was in the process of changing gear again. His 1974 shows with The Band proved to be the most over-subscribed tour in history, with over 12 million applicants (more than 7 per cent of the entire American populace) vying for the 658,000 available tickets. It was Dylan's first sustained roadwork since 1966, undertaken in a transformed social climate of laissez-faire libertinism, and alongside musicians whose drug and drink habits had grown more extreme in the intervening years. To Sara, it undoubtedly posed a threat to their domestic stability, by re-acquainting her husband with the dangerous rock 'n' roll lifestyle from which she had rescued him once before. To Dylan, it may have been undertaken in an attempt to recapture something of the spirit of his youthful endeavours, though in the event he hated the experience. In the seven years since his last stretch on the road, touring had been transformed into a huge, impersonal business enterprise, with most of the fun replaced by an increased workload of promotional duties. It was, he later claimed, "the hardest thing I had ever done".

When the tour ground to its conclusion, Dylan headed for New York while Sara stayed at their West Coast home on the Point Dume peninsula near Zuma Beach, north of Los Angeles. Designed by architect David Towbin in consultation with the couple, the house was an elaborate, fantastic structure topped by a copper onion-dome, with all the fittings, tiles, glasswork and woodcarvings handcrafted by an army of fifty-six artisans who, according to Howard Sounes's Dylan biography *Down the Highway*, spent two years camped in tents and caravans on the property as they worked. As costs spiralled out of control, the house apparently became a source of friction between Sara, who relished the opportunity to indulge her artistic side, and Bob, who just wanted a bit of privacy again.

Upon his return to New York at the end of April 1974, Dylan started hanging out at his old haunts in Greenwich Village, catching up with old chums like Dave Van Ronk and Phil Ochs, and even, at the latter's behest, giving a somewhat sozzled performance at a Friends of Chile benefit concert Ochs had organised at the Felt Forum. With Sara remaining on the West Coast, rumours soon began to circulate about the state of their marriage, particularly when he started spending a lot of time with Ellen Bernstein, a young A&R executive at Columbia Records, who was later widely believed to be the subject of the most emotionally upbeat of the *Blood on the Tracks* songs, 'You're Gonna Make Me Lonesome When You Go'. He also started taking a course of classes given by art teacher Norman Raeben, which would have a (literally) dramatic effect on his songwriting.

The son of the Yiddish writer Sholem Aleichem, Raeben was a Russian immigrant whose own artistic ambitions had been somewhat sidelined by his success as an art teacher. When Dylan started attending his classes on the eleventh floor of Carnegie Hall, he was a seventy-three-year-old with an exotic past, which Dylan further embroidered with characteristic verve: he was, the singer told friends, a former boxer who had roomed in Paris with the seminal modernist painter Chaim Soutine, and had known the likes of Picasso and Modigliani intimately – claims subsequently denied by Raeben's widow Victoria. He did, however, appear to have achieved a kind of guru status amongst his pupils, wielding his formidable rhetorical gifts with a kill-or-cure indifference to their personal feelings. As each student worked at their own easel, Raeben would move from one to another, critiquing each in turn, loudly enough for all to hear.

"He would tell me about myself when I was drawing something," Dylan later told journalist Pete Oppel. "I couldn't paint. I thought I could. I couldn't draw. I don't even remember 90 per cent of the stuff he drove into me . . . and it wasn't art or painting. It was a course in something else. I had met magicians, but this guy is more powerful than any magician I've ever met. He looked into you and told you what you were. And he didn't play games about it."

According to one former classmate, Raeben was particularly fond of berating his students, including Dylan, as "idiots" for their inability to understand forms in terms of shadow and light, a principle he tested by requiring them to draw an object after viewing it for only a minute or so: real perception, he believed, was a matter not just of looking but seeing.

Whether or not Raeben improved Dylan's painterly prowess is a matter of opinion, but he certainly had a radical effect on the singer's songwriting, with which he had been struggling since around the time of his motorbike accident, finding it now took him "a long time to get to do consciously what I used to do unconsciously". This was all too evident from his recent albums, which, with the exception of *John Wesley Harding*, had been meagre affairs lyrically, lacking the biting wit and inventive imagery of his mid-1960s work. Raeben, he told journalist Jonathan Cott, had taught him how to "see" again: "He put my mind and my hand and my eye together in a way that allowed me to do consciously what I unconsciously felt."

In particular, Raeben had brought Dylan to a more fruitful understanding of time, enabling him to view narrative not in such strictly linear terms, but to telescope past, present and future together to attain a more powerful, unified focus on the matter in hand. The immediate effect of this can be heard on *Blood on the Tracks*, most notably in a song like 'Tangled Up in Blue', where temporality, location and viewpoint shift back and forth from verse to verse, rather in the manner of montaged jump-cuts in a movie, or the fictions of Thomas Pynchon and Don DeLillo, allowing him to reveal underlying truths about the song's characters whilst letting them remain shadowy, secretive figures. (The jump-cut style would be further developed in the artful, dramatic songs Dylan later co-wrote with theatre director Jacques Levy for his *Desire* album, such as 'Hurricane' and 'Black Diamond Bay', though time would be much more strictly controlled in them than in the fluid pieces of *Blood on the Tracks*.)

Armed with his new-found techniques, Dylan retired for a few weeks that summer to his recently purchased Minnesota farm, where he wrote the songs which would make up *Blood on the Tracks*. By July, he was excitedly playing them for friends like Crosby, Stills & Nash, Tim Drummond and Mike Bloomfield, whilst behind the scenes his representatives hammered out the details of his imminent return to Columbia Records. Less happily, the transformative influence of Raeben seems to have driven another wedge between Bob and Sara, as Dylan explained to Pete Oppel: "Needless to say, it changed me. I went home after that and my wife never did understand me ever since that day. That's when our marriage started breaking up. She never knew what I was talking about, what I was thinking about, and I couldn't possibly explain it."

On August 2, 1974, much to David Geffen's disgruntlement, Bob Dylan officially re-signed with Columbia Records at a considerably more advantageous royalty rate than he had previously enjoyed with the company. On September 13, Phil Ramone took a call from Columbia A&R chief John Hammond. "Dylan's in town," said Hammond, "and we need to capture something magical about him."

Phil Ramone is one of the music industry's top producer/ engineers, who since starting his career in 1963 with Lesley Gore's No.1 hit 'It's My Party', has worked with an impressive roster of artists including Frank Sinatra, Barbra Streisand, Billy Joel, Elton John and Quincy Jones. He had been sound engineer on Dylan's 1974 tour, and had spent the summer with producer Rob Fraboni, editing the concert tapes and assembling the performances that would become the *Before the Flood* live album. But it was Ramone's work on Paul Simon's highly acclaimed solo album *There Goes Rhymin' Simon* which had marked him out as a producer with a particular sensitivity to the needs of singer-songwriters, and a shrewd choice to work on Dylan's next sessions.

"John said that Bob was going to be in town and was insisting on using the old Columbia A studio on 54th Street, which then was called A&R Recording," says Ramone. "I think there was a feeling of coming back to Columbia, and to his friendship with John."

If Ramone was lined up at short notice, the musicians had even less time to prepare. Even as Dylan entered the studio three days later, his office was still trying to locate Eric Weissberg, the guitarist and banjo-player who recorded the hit 'Duelling Banjos' for the *Deliverance* soundtrack. Weissberg eventually arrived around six that evening with his band (also called Deliverance), though they ultimately appeared on only one track of the finished album. Indeed, he and his band found working with Dylan a difficult, unrewarding experience, as the singer was playing in an unusual open tuning and was reluctant to explain which key the songs were in, making it almost impossible for the musicians to follow him.

"It was weird," Eric Weissberg later admitted. "You couldn't really watch his fingers, 'cause he was playing in a tuning arrangement I had never seen before. If it was anybody else I would have walked out. He put us at a real disadvantage. If it hadn't been that we liked the songs and it was Bob, it would have been a drag." The writing was on the wall, he understood, when right in the middle of the playback of the session's first song, 'Simple Twist of Fate', Dylan started running through the next song for the musicians. "He couldn't have cared less about the sound of what we had just done," Weissberg realised. "And we were totally confused, because he was trying to teach us a new song with another one playing in the background. I was thinking to myself, 'Just remember, Eric, this guy's a genius – maybe this is the way geniuses operate'." Ultimately, only bassist Tony Brown was called back for further sessions, and it appears to have been Dylan's intention all along to make a pared-down, acoustic album after the fuller sound of *Planet Waves* and the 1974 Tour.

"When I got the call, he said, 'Maybe you need a bass player, but I don't think you'll need drums – we'll just have the bass player figure out the parts'," recalls Phil Ramone. "Well, Bob doesn't rehearse, Bob just starts creating, and these songs start pouring out of him, and the bass player's looking at me like, 'What's wrong with you? Excuse me, but can I write these charts down?' I said, he won't do it the same way twice, he might throw a 2/4 bar in there, or suddenly go to the next part of the verse without the normal turnaround song form. Most songs have some kind of shape, but his shapes were so unpredictable and wonderful that the musicians had to learn a lot on the date."

There was no prior consultation about arrangements with either Ramone or the musicians, something which was easier for the engineer to handle than the players.

"My job," explains Ramone, "was to make sure he was comfortable at the mic, make sure his earphones were working, and just start recording. I've been a part of some momentous occasions where you prepare your studio and yourself and then wait and watch, and sometimes what I thought was the rundown turned out to be the performance; so I just let the tape run. I sat the bass player where he could see Dylan's hands, but if Dylan moved his hands to another chord suddenly, the bass part would be wrong at that point, so we would punch it in later. I never stopped a take. That's the kind of thing you don't do."

The vital thing, according to Ramone, was to let things flow in as comfortable an atmosphere as he could sustain, and not bother the artist unnecessarily. "A lot of artists work from a free-form attitude, and the discipline is to know where the bassline might be," he explains. "Then the parts get created, then later that day, or the day after, you start to add and subtract them. But I think what's incredibly unusual about Bob is the fact that it flows in a most natural way. He's mysterious and very private, and I understood from the people I'd worked with before, like Sinatra, that their privacy is probably the most important thing you get to deal with. Critical to anybody's relationship is how you manage to stay out of the way as the music is coming in – it's not fun to be chatty and silly all over the place. Bob's a serious guy."

Over the next three days, Dylan and Tony Brown recorded the rest of the songs, with organist Paul Griffin (whom Dylan had used on *Bringing It All Back Home* and *Highway 61 Revisited*) and pedal-steel guitarist Buddy Cage overdubbing atmospheric tints to 'Idiot Wind' and 'You're a Big Girl Now', the most emotionally moving pieces resulting from the New York sessions. It was obvious to those involved that these were Dylan's best songs in years. It was also obvious that, in contrast to the song-writer's more oblique works, they were woven from the threads of his fraying personal situation.

"*Blood on the Tracks* was an outpouring of the man's life, in a very troubled time for him, and this was almost cathartic for him in the studio," recalls Ramone. "It was incredible: nobody stopped, nobody said anything, nobody talked very much. It certainly wasn't a social gathering, it was more of a soul being revealed directly to tape. Did I ever think it would become historic? No. I just thought it was a phase in a man's career: it's like running into a painting Picasso did in 1940, as opposed to one he did in 1950 – the essence is what you feel, and when you're in the room engineering it and being part of the production, you definitely come up with feelings that are, you know . . . they were tremendously sensitive areas."

The album came together quickly. Dylan appears to have had a track sequence in mind from the start, and the dozen songs recorded were soon whittled down to ten. 'Call Letter Blues' was discarded in favour of 'Meet Me in the Morning', which was effectively the same arrangement with new lyrics, and the reassuringly jaunty 'Buckets of Rain' – a sing-song number with a melody reminiscent of Tom Paxton's 'Bottle of Wine' – was preferred as album closer to the more involved 'Up to Me', which was perhaps considered too close melodically to both 'Tangled Up in Blue' and 'Lily, Rosemary and the Jack of Hearts'. Both Dylan and Columbia wanted to get the album out within a few weeks, so a cover featuring a sleevenote by New York journalist Pete Hamill (no relation to the Van Der Graaf Generator singer) was quickly assembled, and half a million printed up; but after listening to a test pressing, Dylan postponed its release. Something wasn't quite right.

Three months later, Dylan returned to Minnesota to spend Christmas with his brother David's family. Although a revised January 3 release date was looming, he was still dissatisfied with several of the *Blood on the Tracks* songs and, as was his way, had continued to revise their lyrics, most notably toning down the more obviously autobiographical parts of 'Idiot Wind'.

David Zimmerman, who was himself active in the Minneapolis-St. Paul music scene, both as producer of radio and TV jingles and manager of local singer-songwriting talent, suggested re-recording the troublesome songs at a local studio, Sound 80, with some Twin Cities musicians he knew. The only problem was that Bob required a specific, quite rare, Martin guitar for the songs, and had left his back in New York. David called up a local singer he managed, Kevin Odegard, and asked him to try and find one. Secrecy was of paramount importance to Dylan, and Odegard, whose own debut album had just been released, had proved his discretion earlier when he had accompanied Bob on some publishing demos (including an early version of the *Planet Waves* outtake 'Nobody 'Cept You', which Dylan apparently intended for Tex-Mex country star Johnny Rodriguez to record).

"He called me the day after Christmas 1974," recalls Odegard, who was working as a brakeman on the Chicago North-Western Railroad at the time. "He was asking for a 1937 0042 Martin guitar, which was a very rare thing. I believe he had 'Lily, Rosemary and the Jack of Hearts' in mind, which is what he eventually used it on. It's a small-bodied instrument, known in elite Martin circles as the 'Joan Baez model' guitar, being the same model she often used on stage, and which she introduced Dylan to during his tour of Britain in the Sixties.

"I had no idea where I might find it, but I checked around and located one at a little store in [Minneapolis bohemian enclave] Dinkytown – where Dylan actually spent a lot of his early years – called The Podium. A friend of mine, Chris Weber, owned the shop, and he had it on his wall. This began a long dialogue along the lines of, 'What do you need the guitar for?', and though I knew what the guitar was wanted for, I couldn't tell Chris anything. David Zimmerman then contacted the rhythm section, [bassist] Billy Peterson and [drummer] Bill Berg; together we found [organist] Greg Inhofer, and Chris Weber came along to babysit his very valuable guitar, and wound up playing on the sessions!"

The musicians were all experienced players, particularly Peterson and Berg, who were renowned as the best rhythm section in town, able to turn their hands to anything from jingles to jazz. Peterson, who subsequently became Steve Miller's bassist, was up for anything, but Berg had to be persuaded to play, having been literally on the point of moving out west to pursue his dream of becoming a film animator.

"He had plans to move to Venice, California," says Odegard. "He had rented an apartment, and had his U-Haul trailer packed and ready to go, and was not inclined to take the session! But when told it was Dylan he was going to be working with, he saw the wisdom in that, and took the session. I would say he and Peterson were Dylan's primary creative foils on the project – they were the synergy that made that record great." As it happens, Berg did eventually realise his dream, becoming the lead or "hero" animator for such Disney movies as *The Little Mermaid*, *Beauty and the Beast* and *Hercules*.

Situated at 2709 East 25th Street in the Seward section of Minneapolis, just across the Mississippi River from the bohemian Dinkytown area, Sound 80 Studios was the "best room in town", with two recording studios, a finishing room, and in-house disc-mastering facilities. "We recorded everything from classical music, all the way through pop and rock, down to local polka bands and school choirs and bands," says engineer Paul Martinson, a skilled craftsman who had previously worked with artists as disparate as the St. Paul Chamber Orchestra and Leo Kottke.

Like Phil Ramone in New York, Martinson had only a few days' notice to prepare for the Dylan sessions. "They came up very quickly," he remembers, "so there was virtually no chance for any publicity; David had asked us not to say anything, anyway. They were booked at a time of day when there was not very much activity in the studio – late in the afternoon, evening really – and I believe the first date was on a Friday evening. At the beginning of the first session, Dylan settled in slowly, sitting by himself reading a newspaper as we finished setting up. David talked to him a little bit, as did Chris and Kevin, who knew him a little; but once we started doing the music, he seemed to settle down, and talked to the other musicians. I think he was basically just very shy at the beginning. Then once he got the sense that it was gonna work, and that the session was going well, he relaxed."

Kevin Odegard concurs about the relaxed nature of the session. "Dylan was kind and chatty, comfortable to be with, friendly, engaging," he recalls. "All the things you don't associate with Bob Dylan! He schmoozed with Chris over the guitar when we first got there, they talked about guitars and songwriting for a while. He asked Chris if he wrote, and when Chris said he did, Bob asked him to play something he'd written. So Chris played him a little something he'd written, then Bob said, 'Here's one of mine!': he started off with a C minor chord, then went rather dissonant – it sounded all wrong at first, then gradually, as he went through it, you understood there was a pattern to it, and that it did work."

The song was 'Idiot Wind', which Chris Weber then taught to Peterson, Berg and Inhofer. After four or five takes, a more urgent, accusatory reading of the song, quite different in tone to the melancholy fatalism of the New York version, was in the can. "It has a very different feel to the New York session version," agrees Odegard. "It bears a closer resemblance to, say, the Sixties work than to anything he's done since, particularly with the organ. He overdubbed that organ himself, in fact: he knew what he was going for, how he wanted it to sound – he turned on the Leslie speaker and overdubbed it."

For his part, Martinson was relieved when Dylan expressed satisfaction with his work. "At an early playback, Bob – who was in a separate booth – came into the control room to listen, and commented, 'You have a nice way of picking things up here'. Which of course made me relax right away." After Dylan had punched in a few vocals on 'Idiot Wind', a new, fuller-sounding but less pained version of 'You're a Big Girl Now' was polished off in a couple of takes; Dylan was so happy with what happened that the musicians were called back for another session the following Monday, December 30.

When the musicians gathered again on the Monday, Dylan ran them through 'Tangled Up in Blue', which was still not sounding quite right.

"We were playing it in G, and it was just kind of laying there, not doing much, a little tame," remembers Kevin Odegard. "He said, 'How is it? What do you think?', and I said, 'Well, it's passable', and he gave me that look that he gives Donovan in *Dont Look Back*, twisted his head a little bit: '*Passable?*' he said. Well, I just turned beet-red and sweated right through my clothes – I could feel myself being skewered on the spot! I knew my career was over, then . . . for at least ten or fifteen seconds. But then he scrunched out an imaginary cigarette on the floor, turned his head and looked up, and said, 'Well, OK, let's have it your way, then' – because I had suggested moving it up to A. So we tried it, and the thing had new life: it made Dylan reach for the notes, and gave it a new energy and urgency. After half a run-through, we stopped and did a take, and that first take is the one that you hear on the record." Odegard was also responsible for the little guitar "fanfares" which introduce each verse, which had been inspired by a riff he'd heard on a Joy of Cooking song called 'Midnight Blues'.

Heartened by the success with 'Tangled Up in Blue', Dylan elected to try a take of 'Lily, Rosemary and the Jack of Hearts'. David Zimmerman came out of the control booth to warn the musicians they were about to embark on a lengthier than usual take: "Don't think it's over when you think it's over," he instructed them, "because it's not over. Just keep playing!" In the event, they nailed it in one take. "It was a lot of fun," recalls Odegard, "like going to the movies for everyone." After Billy Peterson had left early to play a gig at a jazz club, a further version of 'If You See Her, Say Hello' completed the session. Peter Ostroushko, a local mandolin player, was called over from a pinball game at the nearby 400 Bar in order to realise Dylan's desire for a high-register counterpoint to the song's melody line, but in the event Bob surprised everybody by playing it himself.

"You can hear a lot of Dylan overdubbing," claims Kevin Odegard, rejecting the accepted view of the sessions as being free of such amendments. "He overdubbed on every single song – he even overdubbed the mandolin, borrowed it from Peter Ostroushko to play what's called a 'butterfly' part, in a higher register; Peter played his part, but Dylan played it as well. And Dylan also overdubbed the flamenco guitar parts on 'You're a Big Girl Now' and 'If You See Her, Say Hello'."

The sessions were over. Paul Martinson made a tape copy of the five tracks for Bob and David, and the players dispersed back to their day-jobs. It was obvious to all the musicians that they had been part of something special, and equally clear that these were Dylan's best, and most personal, songs in years.

"It was obvious what was going on in his private life, that there was some inner turmoil," affirms Odegard. "If you look at the five songs we did, apart from 'Lily, Rosemary and the Jack of Hearts' – which is arguably a musical version of *Renaldo & Clara* – everything was marriage-related, it was clearly about a love relationship, and we all knew who he was married to. We were aware of the impact this would have.

"We knew we were part of the best new Dylan album in some time. It was obvious to us at the time how good it was; as we drifted out of the first session, it was quite a feeling: we knew we had witnessed history. There's a guy named Vinnie Fusco in New York, who is pictured in some of the Dylan biographies, just sitting in a chair during the recording of 'Like a Rolling Stone', and he experienced that same feeling that I'm referring to, of being witness to history: it's obvious when you're there, it's an earth-shaking feeling – you know that nothing that you ever do will top this, and it's going to be something you can tell your grandchildren."

For Paul Martinson, though, history was still in the process of being made. Due to the extremely tight deadline, he met up again with Bob and David a few days later, on New Year's Day 1975, to mix the songs. First up was 'Tangled Up in Blue'.

"As engineers do, I started cleaning things up," recalls Martinson, "working the guitars, separating things out and so on. We got so far, and Bob said, 'I really don't like this!' I said, 'Oh my gosh, what do you want to hear?' So he pulled out the copy I had made for him of the rough studio mix we had done the night of the session, and said, 'I want it to sound like this!' Because it was the only machine I had available at that time in the room, I had made the mix to our best two-track recorder at 15ips, so I thought if there was nothing wrong level-wise, we might as well go ahead and release it that way.

"We proceeded to do that with all of them except 'Idiot Wind', which I had surmised from the studio playback would be a little tough for the mastering engineer to put on a disc – it just needed a little more control of some levels, and so on. There's a lot of powerful instrumentation in that track, and a lot of dynamics, some high-flying peaks that needed to be brought under control. Bob said, 'OK, go ahead and do that, but don't change the basic sound of it'. So we really didn't mix, in the sense of doing more EQ or compression or any of that kind of stuff, like you usually do."

"That's the way *Blood on the Tracks* went to the pressing plant, with four of the songs unmixed – literally, live two-track mixes!"

marvels Kevin Odegard. "It says a lot for Paul Martinson's abilities – he has the perfect demeanour and personality, and was very talented in his own right." As too was drummer Bill Berg, with whom Dylan had spent a considerable time in conversation.

"There was a story that Dylan had asked Bill to go out on the road as part of his European touring band, but Bill had declined, saying he wanted to be an animator," says Odegard. "Of course, all the rest of us in the studio, thinking he was being recruited, were sitting there drooling with our tongues hanging out of our mouths – is it our turn next? Is he going to ask the whole bunch of us to go? But that was not to be.

"It was a collaboration of genius, and there's no question in my mind that Bill Berg was a genius. He's especially proud of 'Tangled Up in Blue': the hi-hat flourish that opens the song is a David Zimmerman production touch – David Zimmerman is really the uncredited executive producer of this masterpiece, both for contracting the sessions, and for the many musical contributions he made. I think his contribution made it a completely different record. It would have been another quiet, sleepy little wonderful Bob Dylan album had it not been re-worked; I would have bought it, and would still be playing it today, but David Zimmerman is the man responsible for making it a masterpiece – and I do think it is Dylan's masterpiece. It's the most consistent, in-tune recording Dylan has made, top to bottom."

Back in New York, Phil Ramone was surprised to hear about the re-recorded tracks. "Oh yeah, I was quite shocked," he affirms. "I thought he was quite happy with what he had. I think it was possibly just a time of new confusion, having moved back to Columbia; they didn't release the record in the two weeks that they had promised to do, and I think he had time to sit around with the tapes for three or four months, and once you do that you reflect, and then you worry, and then typically, you add strings, horns, anything – you'll be playing it for friends, and somebody says, wouldn't it be great if there were horns there, or some great electric guitar or pedal steel, or something. Generally, you try those ideas out when you're on the road, and either you improve on your album or you don't. But you could tell from the feelings in the room that this guy was touching you and himself and everyone else that would hear this music – and the simpler the better, for me."

The composite *Blood on the Tracks* featuring tracks from both sessions was released later in January, going on to become Dylan's most widely respected work. Because the album sleeves had already been printed crediting the New York session musicians, none of the Minneapolis musicians received their due credit; even when Pete Hamill's sleevenote was later replaced with a painting by Dylan's artist friend David Oppenheim, the credits were never revised. The Minneapolis musicians soon acquired a semi-legendary status, though, when, within a few weeks of the official album's release, a bootleg called *Joaquin Antique* surfaced, featuring some of the unissued takes. The relative merits of the New York and Minneapolis sessions has been a subject of keen debate ever since, with many regretting the loss of the more nakedly painful original versions of 'You're a Big Girl Now' and 'Idiot Wind', in particular.

The latter was the most drastically altered lyrically, though the most significant changes were of tone and delivery: in place of the original's haunting air of despair and resignation, the new version was ebullient and vindictive, closer in sound and manner to Dylan's "finger-pointing songs" of the 1960s. Despite the retention of the final refrain's crucial switch from second-person singular to first-person plural, it now seemed to be more about blame than regret, the song of someone battling to restore their own self-esteem, rather than lamenting a tragic loss. The original version of 'You're a Big Girl Now', meanwhile, remains one of Dylan's most harrowing and painful performances, truly like a corkscrew to the heart. 'Tangled Up in Blue', however, is clearly superior in its revised version, as too is 'Lily, Rosemary and the Jack of Hearts', while the mandolin-sweetened 'If You See Her, Say Hello' has, to my mind, a more complex emotional flavour than the bare original.

"We heard the [original versions] shortly afterwards," says Kevin Odegard. "They're quite good – they're wetter, with a slicker New York sound, and I don't know why Dylan didn't like them, because they're plenty good! A lot of people prefer them. But the ones chosen did make it a different record to what it was – it had a certain texture, all the New York work followed that same sonic formula, but we broke away from that in Minneapolis, primarily because of the brilliance of Bill Berg and Billy Peterson."

To many, it appeared as if Dylan had suddenly developed cold feet about revealing too much of his private life in public, though if that was the case, the changes did little to dispel the widespread impression that these songs were torn directly from his heart. In March, he all but admitted as much when, in a rare radio interview granted to Mary Travers (of Peter, Paul and Mary), he responded peevishly to her comment about how much she enjoyed the new album. "A lot of people tell me they enjoyed that album," he said curtly. "It's hard for me to relate to that – I mean, people enjoying that type of pain . . ." But he quickly became just as annoyed with the too-literal interpretation afforded the album, fulminating in his annotations to the *Biograph* anthology: "I read that ['You're a Big Girl Now'] was supposed to be about my wife. I wish somebody would ask me first before they go ahead and print stuff like that. I mean, it couldn't be about anybody else but my wife, right? Stupid and misleading jerks sometimes these interpreters are . . . Fools, they limit you to their own unimaginative mentality . . ."

For all his protestations, however, he and Sara were irreversibly set on divergent paths. A reconciliation of sorts was attempted after he recorded the embarrassingly fulsome tribute 'Sara' for his next album, but the couple were finally divorced in 1977, with Sara's attorney Marvin Mitchelson (who originally coined the term "palimony") securing a half-share of the rights to all the songs written or recorded by her husband since their marriage in 1965, worth something of the order of $36 million. Bob responded with a mixture of desperate jollity – indulging freely in wine, women and fun – and rancorous bitterness, on one occasion (according to biographer Howard Sounes) visiting Rolling Thunder alumni Steven Soles and T-Bone Burnett to play them a set of new, "scathing and tough and venomous" songs about his marital break-up. The songs were never recorded.

It's hard to retain such a pitch of spite and anger for very long, however, particularly when parental duty necessarily throws the estranged parties together as often as it must for the Dylans and their five children, and relations have long since settled down to a more equable level. Indeed, despite the numerous girlfriends (and a second wife, Carolyn Dennis, also subsequently divorced) that he has squired since their split, it's interesting to note that at the Golden Globe Awards this year, according to Kevin Odegard, the woman accompanying Dylan to the ceremony was none other than Sara.

BLOOD ON THE TRACKS

By Sean Egan

US release: 17 January 1975
Produced by: –
CHARTS: US#1; UK#4

SIDE ONE
Tangled Up in Blue
Simple Twist of Fate
You're a Big Girl Now
Idiot Wind
You're Gonna Make Me Lonesome When You Go

SIDE TWO
Meet Me in the Morning
Lily, Rosemary and the Jack of Hearts
If You See Her, Say Hello
Shelter from the Storm
Buckets of Rain

When Dylan complained about assumptions that 'You're a Big Girl Now' was about his wife, nobody bought it.

It could conceivably be the case that it so happened that Dylan's marriage began to unravel just at the point when he began writing songs that almost exclusively dealt with the breakdown of relationships but it would be an extraordinary coincidence, and in any case, why did Dylan respond so caustically to Mary Travers in their radio interview when she told him how much she liked his tortured album? Perhaps Dylan is nitpicking linguistically: a cursory listen to the songs on *Blood on the Tracks* proves that Dylan is adopting more the mantle of a novelist than a confessional singer-songwriter in the way he tackles that theme of relationship break-ups. However, the verisimilitude of each composition – whatever the exact circumstances of its protagonist – clearly originates in the painful burn of personal experience.

It's rather a sad reality that the increasing estrangement of Bob and Sara Dylan was almost inevitably going to lead to his creative renaissance. The adage that happy artists do not produce quality work is simplistic, and is often confused by the fact that in many examples married bliss and lessening of artistic ambition are coincidences, with people tending to find their life partner in their late twenties when it so happens (certainly in the case of rock musicians) they have already built a solid body of work and no longer feel the need to prove themselves. In Dylan's case, falling in love with Sara Lownds was an even more intense matter than finding a life partner is for most people: her love seems to have been for him nothing less than salvation, from the rather unpleasant person he was before, from the clamouring crowd and from the horrific rigours of his career as organised by Albert Grossman. Dylan saw his marriage not as something that might complement his career and his art but something that would replace them. Dylan effectively confirmed this in *Chronicles Volume One*, but Jon Landau had spotted as far back as 1973 in his *Rolling Stone* review of the *Pat Garrett* soundtrack that Dylan had voluntarily slowed down his productivity to an extent no rock artist previously had because he just didn't care. Landau identified *Pat Garrett* as, ". . . part of an attempt to free himself from previously imposed obligations derived from his audience . . . the most significant white rock figure of the Sixties has turned himself into one of the least significant of the Seventies. But the most perplexing aspect of it all seems to be the deliberate intent behind the decline." With that marriage beginning to decay, it was almost a matter of course that Dylan's artistic ambitions would be re-awakened. Happily for Dylan (or his art, anyway), those re-awakened artistic ambitions roughly coincided with him re-obtaining – via painting tutor Norman Raeben – the technique to fulfil them.

As Dylan falling in love was a more intense thing than for most people, then losing that love was commensurately more devastating than it usually is. While Dylan was apparently no angel as a husband, the agony caused by the fact that he had given up virtually everything for his marriage – a focused career, touring and most importantly artistic credibility – forms part of the pained mental background to the songs he began to compose in response.

Debate will rage forever as to whether the first version of *Blood on the Tracks* – the pastoral, exclusively Phil Ramone-engineered one – is better than the one the artist ultimately released after some last-minute Minneapolis re-recordings of five of the songs with a full band that he had previously recorded in more intimate arrangements in New York. (It could be argued that Dylan's brother David was the producer of the latter sessions, but neither he, Ramone or indeed Bob Dylan get a production credit.) Said debate will still rage even if Dylan treats us to a deluxe version of the album with a second disc comprised of the LP as he originally envisaged it.

'Tangled Up in Blue' is Dylan's version of a picaresque novel, its narrator moving from place to place and woman to woman in – it gradually emerges – a vain quest to escape the knowledge that one of his previous loves (which one is not clear) is the person he should still be with. The song employs brilliant background colour as the man telling the story lurches between jobs like cook and fisherman and between lovers – all confusingly referred to as simply "she" – ranging from a soon-to-be divorcee in a jam to a topless dancer to a woman with a penchant for poetry. Dylan employs an apparently effortless but surely agonisingly crafted conversational tone ("All the people I used to know, they're an illusion to me now/Some are mathematicians, some are carpenters' wives/Dunno how it all got started/ Dunno what they're doing with their lives"), but this informality and colloquialism doesn't prevent him from finding ingenious – sometimes awe-inspiring – rhymes for the title phrase at the end of every verse. A black mark is the line about dealing in slaves which – whether it be metaphor or literal – sits uneasily with the linguistic and circumstantial naturalism of the rest of the song. The other is the slight anonymity of the backing. One can't help but notice that this afflicts all the album's long songs (this, 'Idiot Wind' and 'Lily, Rosemary and the Jack of Hearts') and that all of these long songs are Minneapolis recordings, suggesting that the Minneapolis sessioners didn't have the skill to stamp their personality on the music in anything other than short bursts. Despite these drawbacks, it was obvious from this opener that there was something special about this album. 'Tangled Up in Blue' sings with more poetry than the world had heard in Dylan's lyrics for almost a decade.

'Simple Twist of Fate', meanwhile, quickly reminds us that Dylan is capable of writing classic songs that don't rely on an epic scale for their power. It's just Dylan plus Tony Brown on bass telling a tale of a man and woman whose lives briefly bisect, with the point of view switching between them. (First- and third-person pronouns also wander, as on much of the rest of the album.) It's utterly lovely from Dylan's opening languid acoustic guitar figure onwards, while the verse in which the man wakes up alone – "The room was bare/He told himself he didn't care" – is heartbreaking. Again, only a jarring, non-naturalistic passage (the narrator suddenly morphs into a dock-haunting, parrot-sporting quasi-Long John Silver figure) spoils things slightly. If we thought things could not possibly get lovelier than that, we are immediately disabused in the form of 'You're a Big Girl Now'. The apparently patronising title is in fact the suppli-cation of a man who is acknowledging his partner's reduced dependence on him and beseeching her to give him a second chance. When the narrator says the pain of their separation is "like a corkscrew to my heart", we can easily believe him. The accompaniment – slowly cascading acoustic guitar, splashes of piano and a heart-wracked harmonica – is perfection.

In 'Idiot Wind', Dylan laments the fact that his partner doesn't understand him, although it's termed in somewhat more sophis-ticated ways than that old cliché ("I can't feel you anymore/I can't even touch the books you've read"). He also laments the loss of the pre-fame life he can never get back (and Lord knows he tried) when he spits, "I haven't known peace and quiet for so long I can't remember what it's like!" Some old fans loved this track because – you get the feeling – the venom, the Al Kooper-like organ washes and the use of the word "babe" (as in, "You're an idiot, babe") evoke the Dylan of the mid-Sixties. That seems no less shallow than the stance of those critics who expressed regret that the track spoils the album's mood of humility (apart from a false-sounding acknowledgment of personal flaw appended to the song's close). Anger is always a part of a ruptured relationship and it would have been dishonest for Dylan not to have included this song, no matter his failings as a husband.

'You're Gonna Make Me Lonesome When You Go' closed the original side one and is simply exquisite in its economy (just Dylan and Brown again), gorgeous switchbacking melody and the rapid-fire vocal delivery of a bitter-sweet acknowledgment of an impending parting of the ways. Both its charm and the fact that it's the only song on the album under three minutes (in fact, one of only two that clocks in at less than 4:16) made it the perfect candidate for the album's single. 'Tangled Up in Blue' was issued instead, and that makes its own kind of sense, but 'Lonesome' was surely a potential No.1 and an opportunity was lost to make this deservedly one of Dylan's most famous songs. Incidentally, Ellen Bernstein, whose life's itinerary is traced by the lyric of 'You're Gonna Make Me Lonesome When You Go', later described Dylan – providing balance to all the criticisms of him in this text – as ". . . a very caring, loving person and lots of fun to be with . . ."

Side two opened with 'Meet Me in the Morning', and it's symptomatic of Dylan's artistic revival that here he imbues freshness in that most hackneyed form, the twelve-bar blues. It's not even one of his hybrid blues where he cheats by not repeating every second line and inserting a bridge, yet despite its purity of structure the track is never boring, partly because of a compelling acoustic guitar riff, partly because of the imaginative backing, but mostly because of Dylan's plaintive vocal.

'Lily, Rosemary and the Jack of Hearts' is nine seconds short of nine minutes in length but that is not why it's boring whereas 'Meet Me in the Morning' is not. Rather it's because whereas the latter track rises above the restrictions of its form, 'Lily' surrenders to them. It's not quite the cowboy ballad some have posited it as but rather the equivalent of an old-fashioned western movie. The lyric is an impressively sustained generic exercise. It's also subtly clever, Dylan seeding events with casually dropped-in names and facts. Unfortunately, however, it's also as dull as ditchwater. Had Dylan based his vision on the style of his recent colleague Sam Peckinpah, the track might have been interesting, but his preference is not for the authentic grunge and depiction of sordid compromise of such post-modern westerns but instead the unlikely clean surfaces and morally unambiguous tableaux of *High Noon, Shane* and the like. Consequently his characters, settings and events – cultured hero, rapacious bad man, tragic good-time gal, hanging judge, throbbing saloon bar and tail-twist bank robbery – are flat, creaking archetypes. Dylan, as everywhere else on the album, does sing well, but the circular melody – vaguely, and presumably deliberately, redolent of the music heard in the saloon bar in cowboy movies – is so relentless and so featureless that it could almost be a loop. It's a track whose dead weight prevents the album assuming an equal place beside *Highway 61 Revisited* as his masterpiece. Dylan left off a far better song – the exquisite 'Up to Me' – but he would have done well to omit 'Lily' even had he not included that: the LP would still have been over forty minutes without it.

'If You See Her, Say Hello' is another of the album's tracks that causes one's heart to melt at its beautiful simpatico opening notes and which – however unlikely – actually gets better from there. Dylan's narrator enquires of the well-being of a woman with whom he has had a falling-out "as lovers often will". His singing here against organ swells and guitar arpeggios verges at times on hysterical but is also movingly impassioned. 'Shelter from the Storm' – another Dylan/Brown track – sees the composer apparently comparing his beleaguered status in the Sixties to that of Christ ("In a little hilltop village, they gambled for my clothes"), the woman who rescues him from this and provides the titular cover presumably Sara. Despite the historic-al analogy, Dylan throws in a couplet of recognizably modern parlance: "Something there's been lost/I took too much for granted, I got my signals crossed." It's rich, warm, absorbing and generous-hearted. (What seems a flash of spite is the result of Dylan getting the words wrong: his official website's lyrics reveal he meant to sing "They gave me a lethal dose" but sang "she" instead of "they").

On 'Buckets of Rain', Dylan noodles impressively on acoustic guitar while Brown again provides the only accompaniment. The catchy melody is almost nursery-rhyme simple but the sentiment deep as the composer reflects on the situations he has been through in his life and the often impermanent nature of relationships. Unlike all the other love songs here, there is less of a sense of loss and yearning and more a melancholy determination not to be defeated by life. It closes the album on a ruminative, wistful and slightly hopeful note.

Although there is a sense of foreboding in the album's title (the "tracks" being presumably the bands of a vinyl album) and even its tense, blurred profile shot of the artist, few could have predicted from it the quality within. Nor from David Oppenheim's meaningless grotesque back cover art, or the original fawning album-liner notes by Pete Hamill that it replaced in which the writer bizarrely suggested that Dylan had "remained true" by continuing to write about such things as how "young men machine-gunned babies in Asian ditches" when in fact, in his art, Dylan had deliberately turned his face away from such things. (The notes were airbrushed from history for a while, although were briefly reinstated when they were inexplicably considered to be worthy of a Grammy. They now feature in some reissues.)

Dylan might have lost his marriage and his dreams of the salvation marriage could offer but at least he was able to regain the artistic plateau he had sacrificed for those things. What is remarkable about Dylan's re-acquiring of his dormant genius is how quick it was. While *Planet Waves* at least saw him no longer trading in banalities, from there to *Blood on the Tracks* just one (exact) year later is a staggering upwards leap. 'Tangled Up in Blue' in itself would make a man's reputation, but there are several songs significantly better than that on the record.

Not that Gleason and company had "got Dylan back again". Dylan wasn't the fiery young rebel he had been in the mid-Sixties any more than his original fans were. His mainly gentle music wasn't fiery either. This mainly gentle album wasn't the sort to mollify the punks who would start railing against the rock establishment the following year for the way they had betrayed the medium's visceral principles: those kids were not going to be able to relate to *Blood on the Tracks* until they themselves had been through the trauma of the break-up of a long-term relationship, nor were its pastoral landscapes going to fulfil their natural desire for an uptempo urban sound. In fact, this album proved that a rock artist could create great music irrelevant young people – hitherto a notion largely considered a contradiction in terms. While the early-Seventies singer-songwriter movement produced records with a patina of maturity, their calm, reflective moods were largely illusory, for those records were usually made by people in their twenties who had not been through the certainty-shattering crises that are engendered by the break-up of a deep and long personal bond. *Blood on the Tracks* was a grown-up's album. If it wasn't rock's first (Carole King's 1971 album *Tapestry* was streaked with the pain of experience), it was certainly its most well-observed and well-crafted so far.

Even after the hugely successful 1974 tour, the public perception of Dylan had remained as that of a relic of the Sixties. While thousands flocked to see him perform his oldies, and to witness a legend in the flesh, he was viewed as a man whose best, or even just merely great, work was behind him. Nobody would have acclaimed him as a great artist if *Planet Waves* had been his first album. With *Blood on the Tracks*, relief shivered through his fanbase at the realisation that the humiliation of him producing records inferior to those of his scores of imitators was over. Dylan had for the first time since *John Wesley Harding* released an album that people didn't have to kid themselves they loved.

THE BASEMENT TAPES

By Sean Egan

(Bob Dylan & The Band)
US release: 26 June 1975
Produced by: Bob Dylan & The Band
CHARTS: US#7; UK#8

SIDE ONE
Odds and Ends
Orange Juice Blues (Blues for Breakfast)
Million Dollar Bash
Yazoo Street Scandal
Goin' to Acapulco
Katie's Been Gone

SIDE TWO
Lo and Behold!
Bessie Smith
Clothes Line Saga
Apple Suckling Tree
Please Mrs. Henry
Tears of Rage

SIDE THREE
Too Much of Nothing
Yea! Heavy and a Bottle of Bread
Ain't No More Cane
Crash on the Levee (Down in the Flood)
Ruben Remus
Tiny Montgomery

SIDE FOUR
You Ain't Goin' Nowhere
Don't Ya Tell Henry
Nothing Was Delivered
Open the Door, Homer
Long Distance Operator
This Wheel's on Fire

Although Dylan was going through terrible travails in his personal life, in one sense 1975 saw him on top of the world, receiving the kind of acclaim for current work he hadn't known since 1967. Perhaps it was this feeling of artistic validation that caused him just five months later to sanction the release of a selection of the archive treasures that were the Basement Tapes, for which his fans and the critical community had been clamouring for almost a decade.

Though it has been suggested that the resolution of a legal dispute between he and Albert Grossman may have freed Dylan to allow the legendary recordings' commercial release, it's difficult to imagine Dylan taking advantage of that freedom if he had not just delivered one of the greatest albums of his career and one of the best albums of the current decade. What would have screamed "has been" more loudly than an artistically floundering artist digging into his past? *Blood on the Tracks* had completely changed the landscape for Dylan.

The fact that the world had been eagerly awaiting the legal release of these mythical recordings for so long is an indication of the esteem in which they were held by those who had heard them. It does rather seem that Dylan himself, however, has never regarded them as highly. This seems manifested not only in the dismissive comments he has made about them down the years but by the fact that he shows no interest in releasing a box-set version of them via the *Bootleg Series* he inaugurated (or at least consented to the inauguration of). It's also manifested in the travesty that was the 1975 *Basement Tapes* album, a travesty that makes such a box-set so necessary.

"The twenty-four songs on these two discs are drawn from sessions that took place between June and October 1967 on home-recording equipment in the basement of Big Pink, a house rented by some members of The Band in West Saugerties, New York." This statement, or variations thereof, has appeared on *The Basement Tapes*' jacket and in its CD booklet, ever since its first appearance. It is simply a mistruth.

The Basement Tapes was compiled not by Dylan but by The Band's Robbie Robertson. Not only did Robertson give over an inordinate proportion of the double album's two dozen tracks to recordings by The Band (six, plus two Dylan songs performed by The Band without the composer's participation), but several of the tracks on which Dylan doesn't play are not from the Basement Tapes at all. It's a known fact that 'Bessie Smith' was simply an outtake from The Band's 1971 album *Cahoots* and there are question marks over more than one other. Robertson has effectively subsequently admitted this semi-fraud with a feeble argument about feeling he had a leeway to draw from a wide variety of sources if he considered the relevant song to possess a homemade feel in keeping with the Basement Tapes' lo-fi ambience. For anyone who knew anything about the Basement Tapes, the fact that Band tracks of dubious provenance displaced crucial Dylan songs of the relevant period like 'I'm Not There', 'I Shall Be Released', 'Quinn the Eskimo (The Mighty Quinn)' and 'Sign on the Cross' was unforgivable. Meanwhile, Robertson decided to "fix" some of the tracks with overdubs that might make them technically better but was a nonsense historically. The final insult was that none of the oldies and traditional songs that Dylan and The Band had fun revisiting together at these sessions were included, but a new version of the public domain 'Ain't No More Cane' by The Band on their own was. Or perhaps the final insult is the way that Robertson tried to cover his tracks: The Band's recordings seem to have been subjected to a dirtying up and a mixing down to mono; the album's second track, for no reason related to its lyric, is called 'Orange Juice Blues' as if to somehow create a link to the first, genuine Basement Tape track 'Odds and Ends', which does mention OJ; The Band's character song 'Ruben Remus' is sequenced adjacent to Dylan's character song 'Tiny Montgomery'. Perhaps significantly, Columbia had recently queried the presence of Band tracks on *Before the Flood* when the ensemble still owed the label an album. Certainly though they are – courtesy of their undeniable talents – easy on the ear, Band tracks like 'Katie's Been Gone' and 'Bessie Smith' are also noticeably generic, both chords- and lyrics-wise – as though written hurriedly to fulfil a commitment.

Almost none of this was known at the time. It would take analysis by Dylanologists across several years, gradually emerging contradictions and leaked admissions and – most importantly – the ferocious data-gathering capacity of the Internet to cause the pieces to fall into place and the fact of the semi-fraud that had been perpetrated on the public to emerge. In 1975, the album was taken at face value by the public and critics – as both a long-standing desire fulfilled and a good listening experience – and was received rapturously. It only added to the goodwill in the air toward Dylan.

Sequencing out the aesthetically quite good but conceptually meaningless Band tracks makes for a much better album, both because they are not sonically of a piece with the Dylan material and because they get in the way of immersion in Bob Dylan's singular mindset of the time, one alternately resentful (of Grossman), humble (trying to be a better person), ribald (he and Sara are clearly enjoying each other's bodies), questioning (religion is entering the equation) and good-humoured (some of the funniest and jolliest songs Dylan has ever written are here).

Although Band tracks written by The Band are not relevant to this text, their versions of two Dylan songs, probably recorded later but written in this period and played during the original sessions, are germane. 'Don't Ya Tell Henry' is a good, punchy version of a fine slab of surrealism. With 'Long Distance Operator' it matters less that we are not being given access to either a genuine Basement Tape or Dylan version, for it is of a lower grade both in its conventionality and its blues structure.

Speedy album opener 'Odds and Ends' is, like the vast majority of Dylan Basement Tape tracks, short and quirky. The narrator complains about the lack of time his partner has for him, manifested by her spitting orange juice over him "like you got some place to go". As with much else here, the lyrical style is a delightful mixture of colloquial and surreal ("You take my file and you bend my head", "I shake my face"). 'Million Dollar Bash' takes that style of ordinary language put through a mangling machine yet further, Dylan telling us stuff that is nonsensical but which somehow we understand: a big dumb blonde has "her wheel gorged", while her friend Turtle has "his cheeks in a chunk, with his cheese in the cash". These and others in a cast of grotesques are turning up at the titular event. It's like a bizarre comic book and the couplet, "I looked at my watch, I looked at my wrist/I punched myself in the face with my fist" is laugh-out-loud funny, not least because of the insane earnestness with which Dylan enunciates it.

'Goin' to Acapulco' is one of the few long songs (5:26) and is a change of both language and tone. The narrator of this mordant, naturalistically worded track is a very unfulfilled man ("It's a wicked life but what the hell, everybody has to eat") on his way to see a female companion (implicitly a prostitute) to provide a rare ray of sunshine in an existence he keeps trying to kid himself is not too bad. The sense of the film of history covering 'Goin' to Acapulco' is even more evident in 'Lo and Behold!', which has a dark, oak-like texture, as well as phraseology ("I pulled out for San Anton'") that could place it at almost any point in American history. It's another surreally light-hearted song ("I found myself a vacant seat, and I put it down my hat") and – in the verse about Molly's mound – not the first to exhibit a complete filthiness. Also evident in this song – which sums up the peculiar ambience of the Basement Tapes – is an Americana by virtue of its slang ("I sure was slick") and its itinerary of US place names that drip with myth for US citizens themselves, let alone denizens of other countries.

'Clothes Line Saga' is a family tableau revolving around a drying wash containing "a couple pairs of pants which nobody really wanted to touch". The house's parents bicker. A day passes. A passing neighbour imparts some gossip. The neighbour then enquires if the clothes are the lugubrious narrator's. He then asks him if he helps out here with the chores. The narrator is noncommittal on both questions. The neighbour blows his nose. The father of the house says the mother wants the clothes brought in. The narrator takes them in and shuts all the doors. In the middle of this domestic minutiae narrated at a snail's pace, Dylan unleashes a sarcastic "Whoo-hoo!" It's a unique song in the rock canon, and truly hilarious.

'Apple Suckling Tree' is a brawny but breezy number that sees Dylan return to the subject of his loins. 'Please Mrs. Henry' is either the ballad of a put-upon lodger or, more likely, one whose inebriation makes him imagine he is put-upon. Dylan for once can't keep a straight face as he executes more of his intriguing dislocation of grammar ("Why don't you look my way and pump me a few?"). 'Tears of Rage' (lyric by Dylan, melody by Richard Manuel) is another abrupt switch to mordancy, Dylan suddenly sounding much older ("What dear daughter 'neath the sun would treat a father so?"; "Life is brief"). God knows what he's on about, but once again it's impressive how un-rock – how un-twentieth century even – the whole thing sounds, even if it doesn't really need its 4:09 playing time to make its point.

'Too Much of Nothing' feels like a precursor to 'I Pity the Poor Immigrant' and parts of 'Dear Landlord' in its denunciation of the emptily gluttonous life, although the tone is more gentle than in those songs. The choruses – in which Dylan gives instruction to send his regards to Valerie and Vivien and to despatch his salary to them "on the waters of oblivion" – gives a relatively mundane subject a dimension of poetic mystery. "Well the comic book and me, just us/We caught the bus" is the utterly charming couplet that opens 'Yea! Heavy and a Bottle of Bread', another enjoyable slice of nonsensical whimsy with a dash of obscenity.

In the absence of 'Sign on the Cross' and 'Quinn the Eskimo (The Mighty Quinn)', the blues-inflected (but melodic) Ark allegory 'Crash on the Levee (Down in the Flood)' (as the song previously called 'Down in the Flood' is billed here) is just about the only clue to Dylan's burgeoning interest in religion in the wake of the motorcycle accident. It was also of course one of the few Basement Tape songs that the public had already heard a Dylan version of. This full-band version nicely complements the two-man *Greatest Hits Vol.II* rendition. 'Tiny Montgomery' is another musty, murky, archaically worded track that sounds like it could have been recorded in 1867 just as easily as 1967, had recording equipment (and electric organ) been invented by then. It's also another track with a peculiar and weirdly named cast of characters. Even as one enjoys it, one really does wonder from what arcane part of Dylan's brain these cultural non-sequiturs have emerged.

'You Ain't Goin' Nowhere' is another nice full band alternative to a Happy Traum duo version we have previously heard, adroit clicking percussion propelling this resignation to (as opposed to embracement of) domesticity. The slow but sprightly 'Nothing Was Delivered' sees the narrator remonstrating with someone who has failed to live up to his obligations but softening his criticism through a sense of powerlessness in the face of that person or a distaste for confrontation, or both. It's difficult to escape the feeling that this is a number addressed to Albert Grossman by a Dylan whose personality was rapidly changing: a couple of years before, he would have relished the spat. 'Open the Door, Homer' is another example of fractured reality and syntax with a chorus that is no less catchy for it requiring us to sing along with something we will never understand. 'This Wheel's on Fire' (melody by Rick Danko, lyric by Dylan) is a dark, rich concoction with a rousing chorus that may be a reference to Dylan's motorbike crash but which is either way impressively doom-laden ("Best notify my next of kin this wheel shall explode").

The eight years in which the Basement Tapes remained unreleased seemed at the time like an eternity and their consequent mythic status was underlined by the rather self-conscious – if rather good – wraparound album cover photography, which depicts Dylan and The Band posing with their instruments in front of a box marked "The Basement Tapes" alongside a cast of some of the characters mentioned in the songs. It is now a third of a century since the *Basement Tapes* album and its legendary status has been diminished, not by it being freely available but by its botched nature. Said botch has subsequently prompted the release of lovingly, knowledgeably compiled and sumptuously packaged bootleg box-sets like *A Tree with Roots* (4 CDs, over 100 tracks) that puts Robertson's version to shame. Though Dylan – who has to keep in mind a listenability factor that bootleggers don't – would probably never countenance a release as massive as *A Tree with Roots* with its multiple takes of songs, there is surely a two- or even three-CD set of the best takes of each song crying out to be released and to thereby finally give the world an authentic, representative version of the Big Pink recordings.

DESIRE

By Sean Egan

US release: 16 January 1976
Produced by: Don DeVito
CHARTS: US#1; UK#3

SIDE ONE
Hurricane
Isis
Mozambique
One More Cup of Coffee (Valley Below)
Oh, Sister

SIDE TWO
Joey
Romance in Durango
Black Diamond Bay
Sara

Clearly energised by recent artistic accomplishments, in 1975 Bob Dylan embarked on both the most ambitious album project of his career and the most ambitious series of live performances: *Desire* and the Rolling Thunder Revue respectively.

Discounting the strings and brass of the eminently discountable album *Self Portrait*, *Desire* saw Dylan go for big soundscapes for the first time. Also for the first time (excepting some Basement Tape material), he had a collaborator on his songs. Jacques Levy, though then primarily a stage director (including the first production of *Oh! Calcutta!*), was known to rock fans for having co-written several songs with Roger McGuinn for The Byrds, most notably their wonderful 1970 'Chestnut Mare'. According to Levy, it was Dylan's suggestion that the two work together. Even if it hadn't been Dylan who made the overture, the decision to collaborate was still rather strange. It might have made sense in the early Seventies when Dylan had lost his mojo (albeit possibly wilfully), but he had just come off the back of *Blood on the Tracks*, which contained some of the greatest lyrics even this genius had ever devised. The only explanation for his decision in the absence of insecurity or lack of inspiration seems a manifestation of the yearning he has expressed more than once in interviews to have been in a set-up like The Beatles or the Stones, where responsibility and pressure was shared.

It would be unfair to expect Levy to have brought about an improvement in Dylan's recent lyric quality level – barely possible – but it would seem reasonable to assume that Levy is responsible for an outward-looking quality to the album unusual in Dylan's post-*Highway 61 Revisited* output. That said, on a selfish note it is rather irritating for the Dylan chronicler that he doesn't know which of the two men to praise or even credit regarding songs' constituent qualities. For reasons of convenience, any track's merits or demerits will be attributed here to Dylan alone, although a small degree of justification for this is provided by the fact that Dylan is the man singing the songs and the artist whose name the album bears. Levy incidentally went on to direct the Rolling Thunder tour, giving it its unusually stagy feel.

Desire marked another personal innovation for Dylan. When he recruited Emmylou Harris to provide exotic accompaniment, it was the first time he had shared lead vocals. It seemed rather copycat behaviour – Dylan simply imitating country-rock star Gram Parsons, who had employed Harris in the same way on his posthumously released *Grievous Angel* LP – but the results were certainly easy on the ear.

The recording of the album got off to a shaky start due to the fact that Dylan had no idea how to set about getting on tape his newly large-scale visions. While his abrupt, no-instructions, sink-or-swim approach had been proven to work with an intimate huddle of sidemen, he was now working with numbers for which it was not practical. At the album's second session on 28 July 1975 (all took place in Columbia's Studio E recording studio in New York during five days that month, excluding a couple of overdub sessions), Dylan had a staggering twenty-one musicians around him. Somewhere in that mob was Eric Clapton. Perfectly understandable that Dylan would want to employ one of the great guitarists of his generation, but for some reason fathomable to only Dylan himself Clapton found himself lining up alongside five other axe-slingers that night. Over the album's following three sessions, the personnel was whittled down to something sane/manageable.

None of the songs are in the same league as the best *Blood on the Tracks* inclusions, but they all exhibit care and craft above and beyond anything on *Nashville Skyline* through *Planet Waves* inclusive. The great, high-gloss production by Don DeVito (miraculously administered despite the difficult circumstances inherent in Dylan's perennial insistence on spontaneity) adds to the feeling of substantiality. But the album is fundamentally weakened by its two self-conscious epics, 'Hurricane' and 'Joey'. The fact that Dylan kicked off the album with 'Hurricane', a song calling for the release of a man allegedly unjustly imprisoned for triple murder, must have sent the A. J. Webermans of this world into paroxysms of pleasure, but the apparent return to protest music looks less admirable when one examines the facts. In shades of Dylan dashing off 'George Jackson' after being moved by *Soledad Brother*, Dylan seems to have composed 'Hurricane' (with Levy) in an emotional state soon after reading Rubin "Hurricane" Carter's autobiography *The Sixteenth Round*. With 'George Jackson' – an impressionistic anthem – this didn't matter so much, but 'Hurricane' is a narrative that purports to be a recounting of the truth. Dylan had to re-record the vocal when it was pointed out that the original lyric's allegations against two people of robbing bodies was libellous, but many of the remaining contentions are dubious, ranging from major issues like Carter's location at the time of the killings to more minor but still credibility-puncturing matters such as how successful a boxer Carter could have been without his incarceration. There were factual errors in 'The Lonesome Death of Hattie Carroll' too, but the subject's behaviour didn't make strict adherence to the facts absolutely necessary to dispel doubts about her: Dylan's lack of any reference to Carter's violent behaviour outside of the ring and his criminal history constitute lying by omission, and this in turn makes the listener wonder why he would feel the need to be so selective with his facts. Dylan first released the song on a double-sided single a la 'George Jackson', then *Desire*. He has never played 'Hurricane' live since January 1976.

Those are the facts – what of the song? Staccato acoustic guitar and sleek violin from Scarlet Rivera propel a recording that never drags despite its eight-and-a-half-minute length. Though the lyric is sometimes clumsy (what does "Pistol shots ring out in the barroom night" mean?), Dylan's creation of a sense of careening injustice and his cinematic scene-setting is adroit. Also impressive is his street vernacular: "The wounded man looks up through his one dyin' eye/Says, 'Wha'd you bring him in here for? He ain't the guy!'" That Carter's innocence is far from unambiguous is quite a shame. The compassion and lyrical and instrumental dexterity of 'Hurricane' deserves a more worthy subject.

Many – including, famously, noted rock-critic Lester Bangs – also had moral problems with 'Joey', the song that opened the original side two of the album. A eulogy to Joey Gallo, a New York mobster gunned down in 1972, it caused some to blanch at its depiction of a "king of the streets, child of clay", who was miraculously devoid of the traditional anti-black sentiment of Italian-Americans and didn't like children to be exposed to guns. Bangs and co were largely wrong-headed: unlike 'Hurricane', this song doesn't purport to show the objective truth but rather adopts, novel-like, a point of view, presenting Gallo from the awed perspective of an unspecified colleague or family member. Unless we're really to believe that lines like, "I heard his best friend Frankie say, 'He ain't dead, he's just asleep'," are genuinely written from a ringside seat. (This is notwithstanding Dylan's very silly comment in an interview, "I never considered him a gangster, I always thought of him as some kind of a hero, in some kind of a way", which – even sillier – seems to have gone unchallenged by the interviewer.) The objection should actually be to the length: over eleven minutes. Though the backing is infinitely richer and more interesting than that of another epic, 'Lily, Rosemary and the Jack of Hearts', and the lyric not only captures a mafiosi's affectionately mythologising self-delusion but does so with some wit ("'What time is it?' said the judge to

Joey when they met/Five to ten', said Joey. The judge says, 'That's exactly what you get'"), none of this can stop the song from outstaying its welcome, which fact isn't helped by its slightly depressing nature. Though Dylan began playing 'Joey' live for the first time in 1987 at the urging of the Grateful Dead's Jerry Garcia, he has slightly distanced himself from it by claiming – in, if not quite contradiction of his "hero" comment, then at least counterpoint – that Levy wrote the lyric. One wonders whether Dylan would have done better to simply leave off 'Hurricane' and 'Joey'. Not only did *Desire* have very long songs (four of the tracks range from just under seven minutes to just over eleven), but it was a very long album for its time (three-and-a-quarter minutes short of an hour, nearly twenty minutes more than the era's standard). Even without those two tracks, the album would have still come in at a respectable thirty-seven minutes-plus. Alternatively, Dylan could have simply replaced them with the album's high-quality outtakes 'Rita May' and 'Golden Loom'.

'Isis' is a tall tale in which the narrator finds he can't hold on to his wife and goes off in search of a treasure that turns out to be a mirage, but not before the perilous journey claims the life of his companion. When the narrator returns to Isis, she accepts him, albeit in an offhand manner. What this parable says about Bob and Sara's marriage will no doubt remain a mystery, but the song is pretty good, albeit probably not quite deserving of nigh on seven minutes.

'Mozambique' is simply delightful. Like 'You're Gonna Make Me Lonesome When You Go', it's a perfect three-minute pop song, albeit on a grander scale. Though many associate the African country of the title with the phrase "trouble-spot", Dylan is showing the other side, explaining how he loves to be there with his lady. The glorious bridge is the epitome of life-affirming: "Lying next to her by the ocean/Reaching out and touching her hand/Whispering a secret emotion/Magic in a magical land".

'One More Cup of Coffee (Valley Below)' is one of only two songs here written by Dylan alone. A slow, sensuous, Latin-esque number, its talk of illiterate beauties, sisters who see the future and a father who presides over a kingdom and teaches his daughter how to throw the blade puts it in Gypsy territory – or a clichéd idea of Gypsy territory – which territory the narrator is shortly to leave for an unspecified but implicitly unpalatable purpose. It has that mysterious, unresolved quality of much of *John Wesley Harding*.

Those who thought Dylan's overt religiosity only started with 1979's *Slow Train Coming* are directed to the bridge in 'Oh, Sister', which states, "We grew up together from the cradle to the grave/We died and were reborn and left mysteriously saved." The man addressing the sister of the title is only her sibling in the sense that their father is (if you buy into this sort of thing) the Father of us all. It's a take on Christianity that is likeable in its honesty, acknowledging the conflicts and temptations of the devout life.

'Romance in Durango' is a cowboy ballad whose South-American setting provides the excuse for a tinge of mariachi brass and a chorus sung partly in Spanish. Unfortunately, it has the sort of elongated melody lines that Dylan has to strain to render, which brings out his voice's worst whining qualities. Meanwhile, the evocation of atmosphere is a little too good, with the oppressive, sun-baked vistas conjured inducing a soporific sensation in the listener. 'Black Diamond Bay' is novelistic, a third-person narrative depicting the actions of a disparate group of people on an island that, unknown to them, is just about to be sent to the ocean floor by an earthquake. The final verse switches to the first person and the point of view of a man who has just seen a report of the catastrophe on the seven o'clock news and – distant from the events – can't muster any emotion stronger than boredom. Unfortunately, we the listener feel a little like that, for, well-drawn though the characters are, and often with an impressive economy of style ("She wears a necktie and a Panama hat/Her passport shows a face/From another time and place/She looks nothin' like that"), none of them are particularly salubrious, meaning that being moved doesn't come into the equation. Also, by now, it's becoming obvious that the combination of Scarlet Rivera's violin and Dylan's voice means that that there is one sound element too many that can switch quickly between pleasing and cringe-making.

Album-closer 'Sara' is (quite logically) the other sole Dylan composition present. That Dylan is throwing away the security of the mask of metaphor to write his first confessional song since 'Ballad in Plain D' probably says much about a desperation in the face of bleak prospects for his marriage. 'Sara' uses almost soap-opera-level imagery to trace the downwards trajectory of his relationship with his wife: scenes of his children playing joyfully on a beach give way to an image of desolate, kelp-strewn dunes. It's effective despite the sudsiness. Against a slow backdrop dominated – as with so much of this album – by mournful violin and heavily echoed drumming, Dylan pleads with Sara not to leave him. He talks of "staying up for days in the Chelsea Hotel writing 'Sad Eyed Lady of the Lowlands' for you" and says, "You must forgive me my unworthiness." All of which was heard by Sara in the studio control booth as Dylan committed it to tape.

Desire's jacket art was unusually plush for a Dylan record, with a full-colour cover picture of Dylan in profile and a back cover littered with exotic imagery and tinted photographs. Long-time friend, poet Allen Ginsberg, provided another fawning liner note Dylan didn't need, while Dylan provided traditionally inchoate notes of his own that the world didn't need. Although *Desire* was a limited aesthetic success – and though stand-alone contemporaneous single 'Rita May' flopped – the combination of good reviews and Dylan's raised public profile due to the Hurricane Carter campaign and the Rolling Thunder tour sent *Desire* to No.1 in the USA and made it Dylan's fastest-selling album thus far.

The first, 1975, leg of the Rolling Thunder Revue was a rock tour like no other and Renaldo & Clara *a movie like no other. The one begat the other, and both sprang from Bob Dylan's singular vision. Phil Sutcliffe tells their intertwined stories.*

ROLLING THUNDER AND *RENALDO & CLARA*

By Phil Sutcliffe

First published as "Bolt from the Blue" in *Dylan: Visions, Portraits and Back Pages*

After the stunning comeback tour with The Band in 1974 and the release of the universally applauded *Blood on the Tracks* the following March, Dylan might have felt entitled to punch the air a time or two. But it seems that fundamental restlessness in his nature allowed triumphalism no elbow room.

Taking a spring break in Europe, he decided that The Band tour had been "nothing but force", a sort of greatest hits steamroller campaign. So he tried to relax into his true instincts. "I was in Corsica just sitting in a field overlooking some vineyards," he told music writer Larry Sloman. "I recall getting a ride into town with a man with a donkey cart and I was . . . bouncing around on the road there when it flashed on me that I was gonna go back to America and get serious and do what it is that I do."

He meant touring: nothing grand, theatres or clubs, places he could drive to. Pick up some kind of band of friends, a "gypsy caravan" thing. "It's in my blood," he concluded.

Thinking about the tour one afternoon back home in Malibu, he watched a thunder storm "boom, boom, boom, boom, rolling from west to east. So I figured that should be the name."

That summer, looking to record an album then put the Rolling Thunder Revue together, Dylan resumed his immersion in hip New York – and, incidentally, his part-time separation from his wife. Conveniently, he found that just hanging out at The Other End in Greenwich Village brought him every connection he needed.

Down there one night in June, he hit it off with Jacques Levy, an off-Broadway theatre director and songwriter. Within a month they had completed much of what became *Desire*: 'Romance in Durango', 'Joey', 'Mozambique', 'Isis', 'Oh, Sister', 'Black Diamond Bay', 'Hurricane'. At once, Dylan started recording. Through his usual trial-and-error period – which saw Eric Clapton and British R&B group Kokomo sidelined – he built a basic band via friends he saw at the club.

Mick Ronson thought he was passing through but didn't. Guitarist Bobby Neuwirth joined. Ramblin' Jack Elliott's Mr. Fix-It bassist Rob Stoner soon became Dylan's de facto MD because of the rapport and concentration that enabled him to instantly deduce changes of chord and rhythm by watching Dylan's fingers and pounding boot heel. Dylan encouraged them to recruit musicians they liked, so Stoner pulled in drummer/pianist Howie Wyeth and Neuwirth called up David Mansfield (mandolin and more), Steven Soles (guitar, from Los Angeles) and T-Bone Burnett (guitar, from Texas). Dylan took a shine to Scarlet Rivera when he saw her walking down the street with a violin case in her hand and asked her over for a try-out.

By August, it emerged that the album was done and tour rehearsals had begun. Lou Kemp, a childhood friend of Dylan's taking a break from his Minnesota fish-canning business, had suddenly popped up talking road-managerial logistics.

The band joked about doing it in a station wagon. But Dylan was serious. He had a cause: to free Rubin "Hurricane" Carter, a black New Jersey middleweight who certainly couldn't have been champion of the world, as Dylan's song claimed – he'd won only six of fourteen fights after clearly losing his title challenge against Joey Giardello in 1964 – but who probably didn't commit the triple murder for which he had been sentenced to life in 1967. Dylan had read his autobiography, visited him in jail, and reckoned "this man's philosophy and my philosophy were running on the same road".

Into October, with the tour opening on the 30th, Dylan sought more big names. Old pals Roger McGuinn and Allen

Ginsberg were delighted to sign up. But Dylan knew it would be really something if his ex-star-crossed lover Joan Baez would appear with him for the first time in ten years. Kemp rang her and she said, "I'm doing my own tour – unless Dylan asks me personally." So he did.

Evidently, Dylan still needed more women and, at The Other End on October 22, he snagged Ronee Blakley, new star of Robert Altman's *Nashville*. The following night, Dylan announced Rolling Thunder at a Gerde's Folk City bash for owner Mike Porco's sixty-first birthday. He was still on the pull for additional talent, but Patti Smith turned him down because she saw "no space" for her talents on the bill and Bette Midler, another strong candidate, disqualified herself by throwing a glass of beer over Smith for reasons unknown.

Two nights later, in the small hours, Dylan slipped behind the wheel of a cumbersome green-and-white Winnebago camper van bearing the logo "Kemp Fisheries Co" and headed north to Falmouth, Massachusetts.

Using one of his favoured aliases – either Keef Laundry or Phil Bender – he checked into the Seacrest Hotel, where rehearsal space had been booked, and was shortly joined by the entire tour party. They arrived in two buses: "Phydeaux", a luxury model borrowed from Frank Zappa by Rolling Thunder promoter Barry Imhoff and appropriated by the band, and the significantly named "Ghetteaux", an old banger carrying assorted extras such as Levy, Ginsberg, his boyfriend Peter Orlovsky and Orlovsky's girlfriend Denise Felieu (they worked as baggage handlers). In addition, there was a fifteen-person crew hired by Dylan to film a fantastical variant on the standard on-tour movie – this to be scripted by the team's latest arrival, hot young American playwright Sam Shepard.

The tour opened with two nights, October 30/31, at the 1,800-seat Plymouth Memorial Auditorium, then zigzagged away through Massachusetts, Rhode Island, New Hampshire, Vermont and Connecticut.

Dylan seemed confident from the outset. In Plymouth, he rather startled a *People* magazine journalist by saying, "I don't care what people expect of me. Doesn't concern me. I'm doin' God's work. That's all I know." Quite why this involved donning white face paint on stage remained enigmatic. In one interview he related it to *commedia dell'arte,* possibly just to make people look it up (a sixteenth–eighteenth-century Italian street theatre movement). Another time he said, "I put it on so you can see my face from far away". When Bruce Springsteen – or "Springfield" as Dylan called him then, not necessarily by accident – visited backstage in New Haven and his girlfriend asked about the slap, Dylan droned, "I saw it once in a movie". At a couple of venues he waved his more wide-eyed disciples in the direction of identity issues by wearing plastic masks on top of the white face – one of President Nixon, the other, eerily, of himself – but he had to cast them aside when it was time to blow his harmonica.

Not surprisingly, at first the band didn't get it. They felt confusion, chaos. The need for more rehearsal. The uselessness of all rehearsals. Ronson, used to Bowie's precision, shook his head over Dylan's flightiness: "He's all over the place some nights . . . being a bit shaky on his timings, key changes and all, he doesn't know what he's doing half the time . . . plus he never plays anything the same way twice." Baez admitted she was struggling to follow Dylan during their duets, though Ginsberg suggested, "He's teaching her how to sing those songs by over and over again looking into each other's eyes . . ."

But outsiders Shepard and Sloman thought the music was great way before the nervous players knew it. Running up to four hours, the shows flowed through a diverse first half as Neuwirth, Burnett, Soles, Ronson, Blakley and Elliot showcased their best material, then climaxed with a few songs from Dylan (among them 'When I Paint My Masterpiece', 'A Hard Rain's A-Gonna Fall' and 'Isis'). After the break, a small *coup de théâtre* saw Dylan and Baez start singing 'The Times They Are A-Changin' ' before the curtain came up. Then they'd reel on through their duets (including 'The Lonesome Death of Hattie Carroll', 'I Shall Be Released'), solo acoustic Baez ('Joe Hill', 'Diamonds and Rust') and Dylan ('Mr. Tambourine Man'), a bit of McGuinn ('Chestnut Mare'), followed by a hoedown rock-out finish with more of the unreleased *Desire* songs ('Hurricane', 'One More Cup of Coffee', 'Sara') rounded off by 'Just Like a Woman' and a singalong closer Pete Seeger himself would have approved, Woody Guthrie's 'This Land is Your Land'.

The music surely was transcendent at times – as confirmed by just about every track on the *Bob Dylan Live 1975* double-CD issued in 2002. The film, though . . . that was more the work of the Jokerman. At least, it left the Revue party with little time for tour ennui to set in. Bizarre events, albeit of utterly artificial contrivance, filled their days.

At Lowell on November 2 a deputation led by Dylan and Ginsberg visited Jack Kerouac's grave to pay their respects arty-Manhattan style. A large crucifix near Kerouac's flat gravestone provoked Dylan into what Ginsberg described as "this funny monologue, asking the man on the cross, How does it feel to be up there? Dylan was almost mocking, like a good Jew might be to someone who insisted on being the Messiah, against the wisdom of the rabbis . . ."

On Rhode Island a couple of days later Shoshone medicine man Rolling Thunder turned up from Nevada (where, a.k.a. John Pope, he worked as a brakeman on the Southern Pacific). A friend of Grateful Dead drummer Mickey Hart who named a 1972 album after him, Rolling Thunder had lately published a book of autobiography and assorted sagacities which Dylan read, hence the invite. The shaman promptly proved his worth by creating his own movie scene; he summoned the band to the beach at dawn to perform a "Tobacco Ceremony" which McGuinn deemed "very cool" when he'd previously considered such things "kinda jive".

To a sensibility of the Peter Kaye kind, the highlight of the whole movie farrago would have been the tale of the Edgar Allan Poe impersonator. When, on November 21, the tour approached Poe's hometown, Boston, someone said it would be a brilliant idea to stage an encounter between him and Dylan. They knew a Lower East Side pool hustler with a sideline in Poe impressions and had him driven up. At the hotel he donned frock-coat, wig and moustache and, by way of audition, delivered a barnstorming performance of "The Raven". But schedules went to hell, they never got to the scene, and, permanently out of shot, the Poe impersonator moped back to New York.

Sam Shepard despaired of the movie, saying it had "fallen into smithereens till it has no shape or sense". But one thing it did do was give the women of the tour the chance of some role play to offset the stress inflicted on them by the confinement of Rolling Thunder and Dylan's eternal ambiguities.

Baez cut loose during a little barroom improv at the Dreamaway Lodge, Becket, Massachusetts, an idiosyncratic watering hole recommended by Arlo Guthrie. More or less inevitably dressed as a whore, she started in on Dylan with "Why did you always lie?" "I never lied. That was the other guy," he said. "What would've happened if we'd got married Bob?" she curveballed. "I married the woman I love," he said, crushingly. She swiped back, "Didn't you used to play the guitar?" "No, that was the other guy." "Oh, you mean that little Jewish brat from Minnesota? His name was Zimmerman." "Yeah."

The trouble was Dylan looked as though he loved it. And that was before Joni Mitchell joined the tour in New Haven (November 13) and Sara Dylan in Boston (November 21 – in his book *Behind the Shades*, Clinton Heylin avers that at this point Dylan had to move a female publicist out of his quarters to make room for his wife). The friction arising from this concatenation of powerful women – Blakley pitched in too – was dubbed The Battle of the Berets.

Heylin reckons that Howard Alk and Ron Howard, two of the movie's directors, actually asked Sara to join the tour because they thought the marital tension would make good cinema and they probably got "the shot" when they persuaded both her and Baez to play whores and "reminisce" about their love lives. It was probably a relief all-round when, on November 26 in Augusta, Maine, Dylan's mother Beattie joined the tour – "The 'mysterious' Dylan had a chicken-soup Yiddish mama," marvelled Ginsberg – and her son had to behave himself somewhat.

Meanwhile, Dylan aside, the men had a rather less intense time of it – immersed in their all-night muso jams, distracted by the ministrations of the man with the duffel bag full of cocaine (deductible from per diem payments at $25 a gramme), getting their rocks off via the usual horseplay and practical jokes.

And still, as the Revue swung up through Canada before the climactic New York show, almost everyone started to talk of their regret that Rolling Thunder was almost over. McGuinn said, "It was a great big rolling party, out there with all your friends . . . amazing". Tough cookie Baez retained her positivity:

"I've never seen such a spirit among people". And T-Bone Burnett took it as terrific (if ambiguous) therapy: "Dylan's given me reason to live. I only want to be shot about ten times a day now."

Until Montreal Forum on December 4 – the twenty-ninth show in thirty-six nights – to the band Rubin Carter was just a song. Then on December 7 suddenly the whole gang came face to face with him – oddly enough, at the Edna Mahan Correctional Institution for Women, Clinton, New Jersey, where "Hurricane" lodged among a hundred separately housed male inmates.

The Revue did the show right there. Roberta Flack, a late special guest substitute for Aretha Franklin, went down a storm. Dylan could hardly miss with 'Hurricane' and the prisoners even took a shine to Ginsberg's recitation of his poem "Kiss Ass": "Whites will have to kissass Blacks for peace and pleasure". Only Joni Mitchell, in ornery mood, failed to get across – according to Stoner, "Two minutes into her set, hoots and catcalls sailed up over the makeshift stage . . . That tomcat face of hers puckered into a wicked sneer. 'We came here to give you love,' she lectured them. 'If you can't handle it, that's your problem.'"

The following night at Madison Square Garden she revealed what was on her mind. Having taken the trouble to talk to Carter on the phone several times, she had decided – quite probably in error – that he was "faking it" to take advantage of "a bunch of white, pasty-faced liberals". So when Baez asked her to introduce Muhammad Ali, who had been campaigning for the ex-boxer long before Dylan got on the case, she said her line would be, "We're here tonight on behalf of one jive-ass nigger who could have been champion of the world and I'd like to introduce you to another one who is". Baez said maybe someone else should do the job.

Still, the show went as well as ever and for four-and-a-half hours. Dylan poured it on inexhaustibly, inspirationally and just plain affably – calling Robbie Robertson on to play guitar on 'It Takes a Lot to Laugh, It Takes a Train to Cry' and duetting 'Knockin' on Heaven's Door' with McGuinn. When he opened the second half with Baez and 'The Times They Are A-Changin'', she was dressed in exact imitation of him down to the flower-bedecked gaucho hat and the white-painted face . . .

Even Ali and Carter couldn't stop talking about Dylan. Ali said, "You know, when they asked me to come here tonight I was wondering who this guy Bob Dylan was. He ain't as purty as me though, you'll have to admit." Then when Ali got Carter on the phone live from Clinton, "Hurricane" started quoting 'It's Alright, Ma (I'm Only Bleeding)': "Walk upside down inside handcuffs/Kick my legs to crash it off/Say okay I've had enough/ What else can you show me?"

By the time the entire Revue rallied round one last time for 'This Land is Your Land', even this notably apolitical big-time rock crowd probably believed they were in on something.

Sam Shepard, redundant scriptwriter, saw Dylan just twice more that night. After the finale, he was in the dressing-room when Dylan raced in "ripping the harmonica brace off his neck, make-up dripping in long streams, red eyes popping out" and hollered "Rubin's been acquitted! He'll be out by Christmas!" (this proved a false rumour). Then at the aftershow reception in the MSG's small neighbouring hall, The Felt Forum, Dylan grabbed Shepard, Ronson and a few others – mostly women – and led them to an underground car park where they boarded his Winnebago and drove off.

"Now we're hitting the streets and Dylan's starting to crank this monster up to around fifty," wrote Shepard in his *Rolling Thunder Logbook*. "I'm losing track of time and space but it seems we're hitting midtown [when] he brakes the sucker and bails out in the middle of the road . . . Dylan's gone again and it's only us. Just like it was before we got on."

The Rolling Thunder Revue of 1975 made waves, though not really for Rubin Carter; he was bailed, retried, found guilty again and not finally released until 1985 when an appeal court found "grave constitutional violations" in that second go-round.

For Dylan, the Revue had led to or presaged big changes. The failure of his marriage (Sara started divorce proceedings on March 1 1977). The less permanently wounding failure of the tour movie *Renaldo & Clara*. His whole-hearted embrace of playing live which eventually became The Never-Ending Tour.

Rolling Thunder had been a grand affair. As *New York Times* critic John Rockwell wrote after the MSG concert, the tour had "kept the flames of artistic involvement in political causes alive for the 1970s ... Mr. Dylan has reinvigorated the flagging New York folk-rock scene ... Most important of all, however, he has reinvigorated himself."

Sources: *Rolling Thunder Logbook*, Sam Shepard (Penguin); *On the Road with Bob Dylan* (Three Rivers); *Bob Dylan Live 1975*, booklet, Larry "Ratso" Sloman; *Bob Dylan: Behind the Shades*, Clinton Heylin (Viking); *No Direction Home: The Life and Music of Bob Dylan*, Robert Shelton (Penguin); *Bob Dylan Performing Artist 1974–1986*, Paul Williams (Omnibus); *Shadows and Light*, Karen O'Brien (Virgin); *Patti Smith*, Victor Bockris (Fourth Estate); *The Mansion on the Hill*, Fred Goodman (Jonathan Cape).

Renowned writer Craig McGregor was one of the few friendly media faces Bob Dylan encountered on his first visit to Australia in 1966. He was rewarded with a personal audience that made him one of the first members of the public to hear the upcoming Blonde on Blonde *album.*

In 1971, McGregor was in New York, a place he had never thought he'd visit (hence his "Like fucking hell" mental response to Dylan's suggestion that he make his way to America), the result of which was Bob Dylan: A Retrospective (1972), *a book which managed to round up just about every important piece of writing published on Dylan up to that point with the one exception of Tom Paxton's denunciatory* Sing Out! *article "Folk Rot" (Paxton refused permission). Once again, it would seem, McGregor was in Dylan's good books: when the artist visited Australia in March 1978, Dylan granted him another exclusive audience. McGregor made the most of his opportunity, drawing out some of the most candid answers Dylan has ever given in interview.*

Dylan makes several noteworthy comments but the most intriguing passage has to be that where he disavows religious dogma: many have assumed that the emotional journey traced in the songs of Street-Legal *(most of which were probably written by this point, seeing at it was recorded a month later) paved the way for Dylan's conversion to Christianity.*

"TOMORROW IS ANOTHER DAY": TWO ENCOUNTERS WITH BOB DYLAN

By Craig McGregor

First published as part of "Introduction" and "Bob Dylan" in *Bob Dylan: A Retrospective* (revised, Australian edition)

PART I

The first time I heard of Bob Dylan was when Pete Seeger was touring Australia. It was back in the early Sixties and I was writing on pop, jazz and folk music for the *Sydney Morning Herald*. At his opening concert in Sydney, Seeger sang mostly traditional songs; but towards the end he began singing some contemporary songs by Tom Paxton, Malvina Reynolds, and one by "a young New York songwriter called Bob Dillon." (I had to check with Seeger later even to get the name right). It was 'Who Killed Davey Moore?' and Seeger sang it superbly. It knocked me out. I still think it is one of the best of Dylan's early songs, with a moral concreteness that in too many of his other "political" songs fades off into melodrama and rhetoric. (A couple of years later, when composer/musicologist Wilfrid Mellers was in Australia, he wound up a lecture on the development of Western pop music by playing Ray Charles, The Beatles, and Seeger's recording of 'Who Killed Davey Moore?' – he liked it too.) I got to know Mellers, who is the most perceptive of the academic commentators on pop music. When I reviewed the concert for the following morning's paper I was lukewarm about Seeger's treatment of traditional songs but excited by Dylan's reworking of the old 'Cock Robin' ballad. Who the hell, I asked, was Dylan?

Who indeed?

A little later Dylan's records began arriving in Australia. The first to be released was *The Times They Are A-Changin'*. By then I was writing a regular column on pop culture, and I spent a rhapsodic half-page on Dylan and his album. The song that impressed me most was 'With God on Our Side,' though it worried me too: there was that lapse in the fifth verse, "fried," which is simply the wrong word, and there was that rather swooning ambivalence of the last verse – Dylan wrestling with the traditional Problem of Evil, and not prepared to give God away. Most critics seem to regard that song as a statement of atheism, but I have never thought so: Dylan has too tangible a concept of God, and that last verse is too supplicatory. It sounds more like someone who still wants to believe in God, but doesn't like what he is finding out about Him. By the time of 'Gates of Eden' Dylan is on the way to a solution: he has turned toward a transcendentalism which derides not God but those who posture in His shadow. Religious symbolism continues as a major motif in Dylan's later work, rising in a crescendo to *John Wesley Harding* and then levelling off into what seems to be a sort of calm acceptance of belief in *New Morning* – but more of that later.

After *The Times They Are A-Changin'* Dylan's two earlier albums were released in Australia. Except for a couple of critics, and the folk fraternity, the reception was hostile. Then the other albums started coming out. By now Dylan was a world figure, and had become as important to young people in Australia as he had in the United States and the rest of the world; but the disc jockeys and mass media still lampooned him as part of their general attack upon youth culture – and its subversive politics. When Dylan went pop some of the older Left intellectuals who had supported him as a radical "folk" poet turned against him too: for a similar regression, chart the course of Irwin Silber, then editor of *Sing Out!* and an early champion of Dylan's. (It is to their credit that Silber and his Australian counterparts later came around to recognising the importance of Dylan's explosion of folk into pop music, but it took them a long time. Some songwriters who were contemporaries of Dylan, notably Tom Paxton, performed the same double somersault: one of the most savage attacks ever made upon Dylan was by Paxton in a column titled "Folk Rot," written at the height of the folk/rock controversy.) Anyhow, I found myself as a sort of lone overground defender of Dylan. Even Richard Neville, co-editor of *OZ* magazine (he and two friends founded it in Sydney) and later a pop proselytiser, had attacked rock as "an asylum for emotional imbeciles." But young Australians were buying Dylan's records, despite the media barrage against him, and in enough numbers for ole Albert Grossman to figure maybe Bob should do something about it. So in April 1966, Dylan, the Band, and Grossman arrived to tour Australia.

Sydney Airport. Early morning. Gulls, bitumen tarmac, hip kids in knee-high boots, camel-hair jeans, Zapata moustaches. Boeing 707, in from Honolulu. Pause. Doors open, the first passengers disgorged, blinking in the unfamiliar sunlight. Another pause. Then Dylan. I assumed it must be he, though he looked smaller and frailer than I'd imagined. Descending the gangplank he was talking to some of The Band, but walking across the tarmac he was by himself: a tiny, lonely figure. Customs. Then, at last, into the main hall, where fans besieged him. He gallantly accepted a fifty-foot pop-art fan letter glued together from magazine and newspaper clippings, signed himself "The Phantom." Black corduroy suit, black suede high-heeled calf-length zipper-sided boots, dark glasses, a halo of long ringleted hair: Dylan, 1966. He held up his hands (look, no stigmata!), turned away and made it across to the press room, where the TV cameras and reporters were waiting. The Band, wearing dark glasses and sombreros, and the greying bulk of Albert Grossman followed. Dylan was smiling, being obliging. He settled himself down on a sofa for the press conference. The arc lights switched on. I sat down beside him, to his left. Downcast eyes, hooked Jewish nose. The crucifixion was about to begin.

It was soon obvious that nearly everyone there had already made up his mind about Dylan. Or their editors had. He was either a Protest Singer, or a Phoney, or preferably both; and they weren't going to be put off by any of that shit about him just being someone who wrote songs. Nobody welcomed him: the first questions were hostile, brutal, stupid. Dylan tried to answer seriously at first, but it was a lost cause. A few mumbles. Nobody listened. A young guy from the *Sun* kept interrupting with a line of questions drilled into him by his paper: get him to admit he's a phoney, that all this protest stuff is bullshit . . .

"Isn't all this protest music a fake?"

"Huh?"

"It's phoney, isn't it?"

"Huh?"

"Are you a protest singer?"

"I haven't heard that word for a long time. Everybody knows there are no protest songs any longer – it's just songs."

"If you aren't a protest singer, why does everybody say you are?"

"Everybody? Who does?"

"*Time* magazine."

"Oh, yeah."

"Why have you started playing rock and roll?"

"Is that what they call it?"

"Why have you gone commercial?"

"I have not gone commercial. I deny it" (with Bible-swearing hand upraised). "Commercial – that's a word that describes old grandmothers that have no place to go."

"Do you always have a troupe of twelve people travel with you?"

"Twelve?"

"Are they all members of your band?"

"Er, yeah, that's right" – with a sideways look at Uncle Albert standing grinning against the wall – "they're all just members of my band."

"Why don't you play by yourself? Why do you need so many? Is this all a stunt? Are you a professional beatnik?"

"Huh?"

"Are you a professional beatnik?"

"Well, I was in the brigade once – you know, we used to get paid money – but they didn't pay me enough, so I became a singer."

"Why do you wear those crazy clothes?"

"I look very normal where I live. I'm conservative by their standards."

"Does it take a lot of trouble to get your hair like that?"

"No, you just have to sleep on it for about twenty years."

"What does your family think of you?"

"I don't see my family any more – they're out in the Midwest."

"Why don't you see them?"

"Well, I would never be able to find them."

"What would you be if you weren't a songwriter?"

"A ditchdigger called Joe."

As the lights burned the pace warmed up. Are you an atheist? Are you an agnostic? Are you a pacifist? Are you against war? Are you for war? What's your message? Are people important to you?

"People are deathly important to me," said Dylan.

"What's your real name?"

"William-double-yew-Kasonavarich."

"Why did you change it?"

"Wouldn't you change yours if you had a name like William-double-yew-Kasonavarich? I couldn't get any girlfriends."

Dylan kept his cool throughout, answering each question in a

mumbled hip patois, and had a gracious word for everyone –
including Pete Seeger ("rumbustacious") and The Beatles'
songs ("side-splitting"). I asked a couple of questions, but they
got swamped in the torrent of hostility. Dylan didn't need any
help. In the end I got up and walked across to the side of the
press room, where Grossman and The Band were standing
watching the circus. "They don't even realise he's putting them
down," I said to Grossman. He grinned.

Dylan made one or two attempts to get across. He wrote
songs, he said, for himself; it was just an accident that other
people liked them. Why didn't he write songs about Negroes?
What? Why didn't he ... ? He didn't write songs about
Negroes because all people were different and you have no
respect for me, sir, if you think I could write about Negroes
as Negroes instead of as people. And he had changed his
name to Dylan not because of the Welsh poet ("I don't care
for Dylan Thomas") but because his mother's name was
Dillon – at this stage he was still peddling that line. And the
best song he'd written, he thought, was 'Like a Rolling Stone,'
because the words and music came together there and usually
they didn't.

At last the reporters gave it away. (In print they all attacked
him. A PHONEY A CHARLATAN! They might as well have
stayed at home). Then Dylan gave a separate interview to a
bland, buttoned-down, sincere-suited TV smoothie. The interviewer started well, but the pauses got longer and longer and the
questions more and more distraught as he ran into Dylan's
rapid-fire, surrealistic responses. Finally he asked whether
Dylan, having written the well-known song 'God's on Our Side'
(sic) was deeply religious?

"Yes, I am deeply religious," said Dylan. "But I don't ask
other people what they're deeply religious about." Pause. "I
believe in numbers."

The interviewer ran a sticky finger around his collar, stumbled to a dead halt. Silence. The cameras whirred, the lights
blazed. Dylan looked thoughtfully at his boots. The interviewer
opened his mouth.

"CUT!" he shouted at the cameraman.

There was another long, agonising silence while the

interviewer tried to think of what to say next. At last he succeeded. The cameras rolled.

"Mr. Dylan, is this your first visit to Australia?"

"Yes."

Silence.

"CUT!" shouted the interviewer.

By this time Grossman and Robbie Robertson were rolling in the aisles. The press disappeared. Dylan was left alone, stretched out on the settee like an Ottoman seductress. "Hey, Bob – why don't you interview yourself?" Grossman yelled at him. Immediately, moving swiftly between settee and interviewer's seat, Dylan improvised an instantaneous parody of everything that had just happened.

Dylan: "How long is it since you saw your mother?"

Dylan: "About three months."

Dylan: "Why don't you see her more often? Doesn't she approve of your music?"

Dylan: "Well, my mother doesn't approve of it but my grandmother does."

Dylan: "I see you've got about twelve people there with you: what's that, a band? Don't you play pure music any longer?"

Dylan: "No, man, that's not a band with me. They're all friends of my grandmother . . ."

It went on and on, a hilarious spoof, but by this time I was laughing too much to take notes. And I had to get home; I'd decided to write something about it all. But it wasn't over yet. On the way out Dylan was mobbed again by the kids who had given him the fifty-foot fan letter, a-jostle in jerkins and Toulouse-Lautrec blazers. One of them, a guy in short-cropped hair and moustache, was called Skull. "Nothing means anything, does it?" said Skull to Dylan. "That's what you're saying, isn't it?" Dylan hesitated. I could see he didn't want to hurt Skull, but he didn't want to be forced into another false corner either – shit, he'd just fought his way out of one. "No, I didn't say that," said Dylan. "You must mean that! Why did you sign yourself The Phantom then?"

demanded Skull. Dylan looked at him. "Because you asked
me to," he said kindly.

Next day the staid *Sydney Morning Herald* ran on the front
page the article I wrote about Dylan. The sub-editors cut it in
half, but they kept the title ('Bob Dylan's Anti-Interview') and
all the stuff about Dylan putting down the press and parodying
the whole performance. They even left the last paragraph intact:
"Like I said to Albert, this boy's got talent. Why don't you put
him on the stage sometime? He could be as big as – well, as big
as Robert Zimmerman né Dylan, who happens to be, quite
simply, the most creative and original songwriter in the world
today." I was still at home when the telephone rang. It was
Dylan's road manager. Was I going to Bob's concert at the
Stadium that night? Hell yes, I was going to review it. Well, Dylan
wanted to meet me.

The stadium. A giant, ramshackle hangover from the turn of the
century, built of timber and rusty galvanised iron. It reeks of lini-
ment, blood, sawdust. Along the dark, subterranean corridors,
ghostly pictures of long-forgotten boxers, champions of their
time: Les Darcy, Vic Patrick, Jack Hassan, Leo Hennessy, Jimmy
Carruthers. The Stadium was built specially for the world title
fight at which Jack Johnson, after years of pursuit, finally caught
up with the reigning white champion, Tommy Burns, and
chopped him to pieces in the ring; there's still a photo of it there,
Johnson with his shaven skull and huge, black body, Burns backing off with both gloves held up in fright, and one of the biggest
crowds in Australia's fight history watching from beneath grim
felt hats. A half-century later, another massive crowd, drawn to
a different ritual: that breathless, uptight tension as you hit the
lines outside, people clotting together, glare on, nightblack down,
something moving, has it started . . . ? As my wife and I walk
inside the main arena, Dylan's road manager, who has been
waiting at the entrance, catches me by the arm. Come backstage
at the interval, OK? OK. Lights down, spots on. The stage is
where the ring usually is, surrounded on all sides by infinite rows
of seats and bleachers which stretch away into the darkness. The
crowd is unusually quiet, expectant. At last Dylan comes on,
alone: a frail puppet with acoustic guitar held uncomfortably

across his chest, a harmonica rack around his neck. Golliwog hair, pale surreal face, wobbly neck, brown check suit. Without a word he launches into one of his old songs, simple strums on the guitar but blowing the mouth harp like a virtuoso, holding and straining the melody lines till you fear they'll snap. As soon as one song is finished he starts the next. The stage revolves jerkily, facing a different quarter of the audience each turn. On the far side some people keep shouting for 'With God on Our Side.' Dylan brushes them aside with his hand, a cool put-down, but at last sings 'The Times They Are A-Changin'.' For his last number before the intermission he sings 'Visions of Johanna.' It seems to go on and on and on. The tension is electric.

Release. People spill into the cool outside. We go up to Dylan's dressing room. He is squatting down on his heels on the floor, electric guitar already around his neck. Grossman and The Band are there. Dylan mumbles hello. Yeah, he dug what I wrote. People don't understand what he's into. He got The Band because the songs needed it; he wanted something to fill in the spaces between the words. (Muddy Waters: "Before that it had just been a harmonica and me or the mandolin and me. But you've got a lot of empty spaces. But when you've got four, five or six pieces working you've always got a full bed of music there for you, waiting on you.") He is jumpy, nervous, unable to keep still. I have to bend down to talk to him, end up squatting alongside like a courtier. What's he doing now? He's into movies, man. But not normal movies, different. Improvised? No, man, that's just a fashion. Different, dig? Dylan is worried about his electric guitar, the sound, is everything right? Robbie Robertson tells him, for the fifth time, where to plug in. Dylan is by turns plaintive, querulous, accusing. I get the clear impression the rest of the band is taking care of him: they treat him like a baby – respectfully, but like a baby. It occurs to me, for the first time, that he is stoned, and not on grass: he isn't anything like the calm, self-possessed guy I saw at the airport. Dylan turns back to me. What am I doing on a newspaper? I try to explain I'm a writer, I write books, but Dylan isn't listening. Editors cut you to pieces, man. You wanna get out. But I dig what you're tryin' to say. How does he find Sydney, playing here? Makes me feel really at home, man; just like Texas. I start

asking him about this religious theme in his work, how it isn't
God but God's acolytes he's attacking, but he cuts me down.
Everyone's got it wrong, man. I am finding it hard to talk to
him. Grossman wants to know about the feedback – is there
any feedback out there? Feedback? There's a popping, hissing
sound in the mike when Bob's up close, I say. No, says
Grossman, grimacing, he's talking about *feedback*. I feel foolish.
Dylan gets up, strides around the dressing room, a tiny white
box. He finishes a cigarette, picks up a copy of the program; it
includes his long "autobiographical" poem, 'My Life in a
Stolen Moment.' "Don't take any notice of that, man," says
Dylan. "It's stuff I had to put out at first, y'know, PR stuff . . ."
He's still edgy, twitchy, hyperactive. Hey, come up to his hotel
room after tomorrow night's show, huh? He's got the acetates
on his next album, he wants me to hear them. OK. It's time for
the second half. Robbie Robertson grabs hold of Dylan, points
him toward the door. Dylan whirls, disappears. The Band
troops out after him. Shouts, a shockwave of applause. We walk
back to our seats. Dylan has plugged in, The Band has plugged
in, the noise is tremendous. You can only just hear Bob's voice,
sawing away above the organ: "How does it fe-ee-e-l? How
does it fe-e-e-l? To be on your own . . . ?"

Next night I hear the show again, and go up to Dylan's hotel
room afterwards. It is in the centre of Kings Cross, Sydney's
entertainment district. Bob appears at the door of his room. "Hi,
Craig. Come in." He is friendly, relaxed-normal. I walk inside.
His bed is unmade and a copy of a paperback Bob has been
reading is lying opened on the sheets, cover upwards. Norman
Mailer's *An American Dream*. There are other paperbacks scattered around, magazines, toilet gear, bits and pieces. It looks like
the room of any college kid: untidy, unpretentious, strewn with
the paraphernalia of learning. I have a sudden rush of understanding for Dylan, because it is so familiar. *Deja vu*. I feel, for
the first time, I am going to get through to him. Hell, I might
even have something to give him. We talk quietly for a few
seconds, and Bob mentions that he is waiting for Albert to get
back. Like a fool, I say I thought he was coming in just as I
caught the elevator. Bob asks me to hold on for a few minutes
and disappears down the hallway to the suite which has been

hired for him and The Band. I wait, and pick up an acoustic Gibson guitar in the corner. It is the one Bob had been playing. The guitar is out of tune, so I tune it and play some slow blues. Then fingerpick some. I am into my fifth number, and wondering what in the hell has happened, when not Bob but Robbie Robertson walks in. "Bob says come down, he wants you to hear those songs."

I walk into the main suite. It is a big room. Grossman is there. And most of The Band. They are lounging back on sofas, untalking. Bob is slumped in an easy chair, motionless. He is wearing shades. Head propped against the back of the chair, staring up towards the ceiling. He doesn't notice me enter. Grossman motions to Robertson. "What're we gonna do?" says Robbie. The others are looking at me. "Bob wants to play 'em to him, so play 'em," says Grossman. Robertson shrugs, gets out an acetate, puts it on the portable record player. 'Most Likely You Go Your Way and I'll Go Mine.' They are the acetates of *Blonde on Blonde*, not yet released. I sit on the floor, propped against a bed. It is a bad scene. I concentrate on the music.

After the first side has finished, Bob stirs. "What do you think of that, Craig?" He is mumbling. I feel stupid. First time through, I haven't been able to catch many of the words; like usual, I just let it wash over me. "I like the piano; I like the whole sound." Robertson makes a gesture of disgust. Bob says, "No, that's all right, it means something." Second side. Third side. Nobody says anything. Robertson obviously doesn't want to go on with it. Albert insists. Fourth side. Bob hasn't moved; he seems to have passed out. I get to my feet, thank Grossman, mumble something about how much I liked the songs. With some reservations. What? demands Grossman. Well, say, 'Just Like a Woman' – too sentimental. Grossman rounds on me, real anger showing through that pudgy bland facade. "Bob has never written anything sentimental in his whole life!"

I walk towards the door, stop, turn backwards towards Dylan. He is still slumped in the chair, head tilted towards the ceiling. Behind the shades, eyeless. I am filled with a strange, shifting mixture of pity and remorse. *Ave atque vale*, Bob.

★   ★   ★

It should end there, really. But everything has its sequel. Except death. And even that sometimes . . .

Just before Dylan left Sydney for the rest of his tour the local folk fraternity – singers, songwriters, musicians – decided to give a party for him. I was asked to invite him. "Will you be there?" he asks me on the phone. "Yes." "OK, I'll come." The party is held in a terrace house in Darlinghurst, a slum of whores, artists and auto-repairs stores. By midnight Dylan still hasn't appeared, and everyone is uptight. I play a few blues, split for home. Dylan arrives shortly afterwards. No one calls me. Later they tell me it is another bad scene: a couple of The Band put on a big act, Dylan puts the hard word on a blonde model, everyone stands around in awe, until finally Jeff St. John, a crippled singer with a rock band called The Id, accosts Dylan and bombards him with weird questions. Exit Dylan.

Melbourne. My brother goes to see the show. "Dylan was stoned out of his mind," he writes me. "Nearly fell off the stage. Spent most of the show making up to his lead guitar player . . ."

Perth. The Far West. Last stop in Australia before the tour of England. Dylan sends a message to me, via another writer. Try and make it to the States, man.

The States? Oh sure. Like fucking hell.

PART II

So, twelve years after, Dylan is back in Australia, sitting curled up in a chair with his long toenails and longer guitarist's thumb-nail, scruffy, unprepossessing, laid-back, apparently together, with a four-hour realer-than-reality film *Renaldo & Clara* out in the States and a tour of worshipful Japan behind him and outside, in the humid police-stricken streets of Brisbane, kids half his age are already lying around the Festival Theatre beneath lights which say BOB DYLAN GEORGE BENSON WRESTLING to see if Bob Dylan is what they think he is, like, you know, idol of millions, spokesman for his generation, genius, trapeze artist . . .

He looks much the same. Shaved most of his beard off; remnants straggle down the sides of his mouth. Soft, gentle voice. Still got his sense of humour, though it's hard to make him smile. Short pants. Romance? Looks like he needs mothering. Like he keeps saying, he's been through a lot of changes.

"Please, Mr Dylan," repeat the two girls who have been waiting outside the Crest International for his autograph, no parlour groupies these but high-school kids, like many in the audience later that night. "Not tonight," says Dylan, and strolls on through the city square. He is dressed, conservatively, in black-and-white floral shirt, pants with coloured kneepatches, waistcoat and gym shoes. His bodyguard is in white pants and shirt, moustache, brown-felt top hat with a Joker stuck in the brim, looking as if he could have strolled off Sam Peckinpah's *Pat Garrett and Billy the Kid*, which had Dylan in a similar role. The sound man is in funereal black.

"Jesus, look at 'em!" says a redneck voice from a cab at the lights. Straight Oz, circa 1950. Jeers from other cars. "They let 'em out once a year." Beery, raspy, undertone of violence. Yesterday the Queensland cops broke up the women's march, threw truckloads into cells.

Dylan strides on. Yeah, Brisbane reminds him of Mobile. "With the Memphis Blues Again." Tonight is the opening of his Australian tour, his first since that tense, spaced-out, disaster-edge tour of 1965. Dylan of *Blonde on Blonde*. A frail, anguished puppet in a brown check suit, chemicals in his blood and visions in his brain, just before the crack-up. He's still frail, but cool.

What would you like to talk about?

I've got nothing on my mind right now. I've no axes to grind with anybody or anything. I'm back workin' again and I'm relatively happy doing that. I was off for two years.

Not the last two years.

Yeah, the *last* two years. I did one tour in between, but I can't go that long without touring.

You mean before you did the Rolling Thunder tour?

We did the Rolling Thunder in 1975, 1976, and then did another one after that to help support this movie we were doing. You didn't see the movie yet?

No. Renaldo & Clara – *it hasn't been released here.*

I think you'll like it. It isn't for everybody, but I think you'll like it. It got a lot of criticism, but that's because people have expectations; they shouldn't really but they do.

I like the idea that it's four hours long.

It isn't too long.

Have you been disappointed in the reaction to it?

Ah . . . the *people* who go and see it, I can feel resistance to it, by people I don't know who are very critical of it. But they miss it. They're not lookin' at it the way it should be seen, I know. At this point it's fading away, just like the last album is fading away.

You mean in your head.

Yeah. After you've done it, you've done it, so I'm not in any position to defend it against people who are critical of it. I don't feel I have to defend it anyway. There's enough people who like it who, if they felt like it, would defend it. Do you know Daryl Poncison?

No.

He's a writer; he writes books, but they turned a couple of them into movies: *Cinderella Liberty*, and *The Last Detail*. They are both movies about sailors, they were playing in the States for a while. He just wrote another one called *The Ring*, it's about the circus. Possibly he'll be working with me on the next movie, which we want to have a script for. I think you'd like his books.

Tell me why you're getting back on the road again: do you really like it?

It's not that I like it or dislike it; it's what I'm destined to do. Muddy Waters is still doing it, and he's sixty-five. In the States there's a lotta old guys that are doing it, and I kinda feel that when I'm that old, as long as I can do it I guess I will do it, because it's all I did ever do, or want to do.

Do you find it still gives you a charge – do you get energy from it or does it take it out of you?

Well, it takes it and gives it. It's a kick to sing these songs that were written in 1961, 1962, and to feel that they're still alive right now, I mean that's an incredible rush, just for that. If I couldn't sing those old songs I don't think I'd be doing it.

What about these new arrangements?

They're not new in the sense that the melodies have changed. I'm still playing three chords, but the *lines* are there whereas the lines were never there before, it would be all melody based upon old folk songs. The lines became clearer to me as time went on, the structure of all those songs, so what's happened is that I've gotten down to play the line on the guitar or piano, the basic structural line of the song which holds it up. That's all it amounts to when they say new arrangements, because they aren't really new arrangements, they're just stronger lines.

When you say line, you don't mean just the melody or the tune . . .

Well, it's the line of the melody which can be broken down and simplified. Some of the lyrics have changed.

You're doing them faster, rockier than before?

No. I don't listen to that kind of music much, you know, I only listen to the old music: the old blues singers and the old country singers. No, they're about the same. I get energy just knowing they are still alive, and that the lines are so strong even after all these years.

But changing them makes it possible for you to keep singing them, and re-singing them?

Every time I sing 'em they are real to me. I've been through so much that some of them are even more real to me now than when I written them – then I could *feel* what they were about, but now I can *understand* what they're about.

But do you ever feel that in changing some of your old songs, you're untrue to the person that you were when you wrote them?

No, I feel I'm pretty true to that person. There was a period of time when I couldn't relate to that person, but now I can. I relate more to the person that wrote those songs than I do to the person I am that's walking around, in most cases.

I don't know whether to believe you when you say that.

Yeah, it's true. I have new songs, too. We aren't going to be playing any of them – maybe we'll play one, we did one in Japan, we
didn't do it in New Zealand, it's a real simple song which we
worked up. We got a couple of them. See, I'm also working with
this band, trying to hold a permanent band together, which I've
never done before.

What are some of the new songs, Bob?

I don't usually have a title until after I've written them. There's
one called 'Changing of the Guard,' another one called 'Her
Version of Jealousy' . . .

HER VERSION of Jealousy?

Yeah. (Laughing) Another one called – I've forgotten it.

Can you tell me more about them?

Man, I really can't, they just have to be sung. They must reflect
on this energy field that is happening now, in the same way that
the old ones reflected on that. I mean, I get criticised for not
writing songs like I used to write . . .

Do people still do that?

All the time! It seems all I see is criticism. I get criticised for not
writing songs like those old ones, but why should I when I'm still
singing them? I couldn't write any song like that old song that
would be *better* than it.

When did you write these new ones?

I wrote a bunch of them in the fall, and before this tour; I had
about seven or eight of them. I think I'll be writing a few more
on this trip. I'll record them when I get back to the States in
April, and that album will be out by spring.

Have you got a title for that yet?

No.

*So these are all songs you've written in the last few months, since you
broke up with Sara?*

Yeah, since that divorce thing happened.

Are they related to that?

Not really; we were breaking up for a long time. So it doesn't reflect too much of that.

How come you seem so at ease at the moment? I mean, I'd like to know the secret . . .

I'm not really, I just appear that way! This is a pretty easy place to be, this town; it's a pretty easygoing place.

I didn't think you liked Australia too much last time you were here.

Well, we had a rough time last time. I think we came before any of the big groups came, before the sound was sophisticated; they put us in boxing arenas and wrestling arenas – in one place we followed, I think, Gorgeous George into an arena where the stage moved . . .

That was Sydney! The stage turned a quarter of a revolution every now and then, if I remember.

Do they still have that building?

No, they've torn it down. It was old Sydney Stadium, where Jack Johnson took the world heavyweight championship from Tommy Burns in the early part of this century and became the first black heavyweight champ . . . there used to be a lovely old photograph in the aisle leading into the Stadium, Johnson and Burns in the ring together, with this great sea of thousands of felt hats watching the black champ beat the white man for the first time.

I saw a photograph of that.

You probably saw it there. Well, things have changed a bit; but have you been here long enough to notice anything?

I think we played here before. I don't see much change in Australia, just in the streets I've walked around, since the last time I was here. Perhaps just a little bit . . . (Laughing) Progress doesn't seem to have touched down in the streets over here. People are still the same in the pubs.

★　　★　　★

Soundcheck. Enormous, unbearable waves of amplified static blast from the speakers. "Good size hall," says Dylan. "It's gonna be hot here tonight." He wanders, lonely as a cloud, past the rows of empty seats, slumps into the back row, and listens while the band warms up: flute, organ, sax, percussion. It develops into a slow blues jam. Dylan strolls up the stage steps, does a couple of lithe kick-ups for his back, picks up his electric guitar, joins in. A quick signal, and the band switches to a faster blues: 'It Hurts Me Too.' Dylan feints at the mike, starts singing: "When things go wrong, go wrong with you . . ." He catches a frog in his throat, stumbles to a halt, coughs, starts again. His voice is harsh, identical to that on his first album. But now he is a small, ageing figure with a lined face in an empty hall. A long way from Hibbing, Minnesota.

Slow hum. Unfinished. 'Hard Workin' Man,' complete with blues falsettos. 'The Man in Me.' Unfinished. Reggae riff. Dylan lights a cigarette, smokes casually while playing. 'If Not for You.' Dylan's dissatisfied with it, cuts it short with an abrupt wave of the hand. I get the feeling, suddenly, that Dylan is singing them for his wife, Sara . . . and doesn't like the way they are coming out.

A couple more numbers, the sound switching from left bank of speakers to right. Finally Dylan lays his guitar down, wanders backstage. There are trestle tables in the corridor for him and the band to eat at. Outside it is getting dark. Clots of people are converging on the Festival Hall. Less than an hour to opening.

What's your next project going to be?

Just more records, and hopefully another movie.

Any priority there? Which are you most interested in?

Just making more songs.

You don't feel yourself changing over to movies?

I want to make more movies. On this last one we did the best with what we had. We have a small crew . . .

What's the next one going to be about?

It's about evil. Good and evil.

Oh yeah – anything else?

That's mainly it. It's a kinda complicated story to spring on you, or give it away. We're gonna try and have most of it scripted and outlined before we even start. It can't cost nearly as much money as this one did, and it can't take nearly as much time to do.

Is that partly because you're disillusioned with the idea of improvised scripts?

No, not really. The people who got down on this movie are intellectual people, not just the people who want to get out of their house and see a movie. Those people seem to find something in it worthwhile. It's that Establishment intelligentsia that got down on it so hard, and I don't know whose fault that was: it was probably our fault in showing it to them. But when people see what they've written, and haven't seen the movie themselves, they decide, what the hell, if they say this about it I guess it can't be any good, and they don't give it a chance. We hurt ourselves in showing it to all those critics, but we were open about it and thought it was good. But it doesn't really affect me, because when I started out singing I just had a small group of people following me, and most people didn't know what I was doing anyway. The same Press that was putting my work down back then is the same Press that's doing it now, nothing's really changed that much.

Have you ever thought of trying to do a really extended musical work?

No, I don't have any of them ideals; but other people do, and they're doing it with songs I've written. There's a group in New York that's doing a play using a lot of songs, and they're a group of clowns – ex-circus clowns who all quit the circus for one reason or another and came to New York and choreographed a whole play using songs I've written. Things like that. I don't have the time to do that.

Have you thought of, not using your old songs, but writing a complete opera, musical, the sort of thing Gershwin did?

I feel too young yet to do that. I still haven't written all the songs I really want to write. It would be a good idea if you were stationary in the one place for a while.

Or is it that you feel you don't have to prove yourself in some substantial form like that?

Not to me, I don't. The idea attracts me. But my mind can't hold something for that long period of time, with songs which are all in a certain vein, like *Porgy and Bess*, or something like that. I would love to be able to do that, but I can't sit down and map it out. I lose track of my thoughts and I get too involved in other things to keep coming back to such a big thing as that. I don't think I could concentrate on that right now. I don't think those things like *Tommy*, or what have you, are what you're talking about.

What about other directions?

That's it, I don't have any direction but one.

Which is that again?

That's this one, straight ahead.

What about writing apart from songwriting?

No. I do once in a while, but you really have to get laid back for that. You got to be finished up with one aspect of things and go lay back and you'll get it, you know. I'd like to do that too. But it isn't the time for me to do that; maybe when I'm eighty or ninety.

What about poetry?

No, I'm not writing too much of anything but songs.

Sounds as though you've refined yourself down.

I was pretty spread out a few years ago, trying to do this and do that, and it didn't make much sense to me, I didn't get anything much out of it, I was too wired up; so I'm back just doin' that one single thing now.

How much of a success do you think you've made of your personal life in the last few years?

My personal life? My personal life is pretty hard to keep track of. I've kind of narrowed it down to what I care about, you know, who I care about, what I care about, and when I care about. I've narrowed it down as fine as I can to that. Being in this kind of situation you meet a lot of people that are attracted to you, and also you become attracted to quite a few people, and you can't really be sure many times whether that's true or not, so you just have to let that situation run its course. But in the recent past I don't even give it a chance to run its course, I just kind of stay with my old friends and my old loves and old mates, you know, and at least that allows me to work. The rest of it don't allow me to work. If I get hung up I could disappear into the jungle for three or four months, I've done that.

Does that mean you feel you're faced with a choice between your music and your private life?

My personal life suffers because of that. I think ultimately man is better off if he can stay in the one place and see the world revolve around him, rather than have to be out there revolving. I try to stay put as much as I can, but I can't all the time, and I guess my personal life has suffered because of that. The privacy thing I don't think about too much any more. I never went after fame or fortune, but I didn't turn it down. That was one of them things I had to learn how to adjust to . . .

And now you've got it you don't want to let it go.

Now I have it, it's not that I don't want to let it go, because I don't believe I'm attached to it, but I *can't* let it go, there's no way I could let it go, because people know me. But a lot of people know me, and then a lot of people know the image; you get a lot of resistance from people who just know the image, who can't see through it.

I still think it fucks you around.

No doubt about it.

What you do about it, I'm not too sure.

It fucks you around in a lot of ways, but you have to be open to ... it's not a burden that's just been placed on someone to drive them down.

Can you channel all that into your songs?

No, I don't write from that, I don't use that; I don't figure anybody cares about that, I personally don't care about it, I don't even care if someone else is into it; I think it's a superficial thing, fame and fortune.

I meant more, you write songs about Sara – I wonder whether you can channel your private emotions into your music, that's one of the reasons you're able to write songs. You suffer, and that comes out in your songs.

(Pause) That particular song, well ... Some songs you figure you're better off not to have written. There's a few of them layin' around.

There's some parts of your life you'd rather not have lived, also.

Yeah.

The hall is packed. Hip, moustached, kurta-topped acolytes in their twenties. Onstage a string octet of ladies in long evening gowns and men in dinner suits is playing its Bach out. Australian content (Muso Union rules). They bow. Everyone claps. The oval stage darkens, the band runs on, plugs in, blasts off on a rhythm-and-blues version of 'Hard Rain.' More claps. Enter Dylan: white blouse, grey waistcoat, Regency curls. Ovation. He picks up his guitar and starts into an uptempo 'Mr. Tambourine Man.'

It's a puzzle. The tune is familiar, but the song isn't. Dylan sings it in a deep, fuzzy voice. Then 'I Threw It All Away.' Rock 'n' roll version, with a three-girl back-up chorus in the wings and the chords crudified into rock raunch. 'Shelter from the Storm.' The puzzle deepens. The melody of this song has never been up to much, but Dylan has flattened it even further so he can sing it fast. In fact he declaims it rather than sings it, and so with half a dozen others: 'Ballad of a Thin Man,' 'I Shall Be Released,' and a frenzied 'Like a Rolling Stone' ("I'm sorry, we played that a little too fast," Dylan apologises into the mike).

The audience claps loyally, but they are obviously taken aback. The old, anguished Dylan (and his songs) has disappeared. In his place is Mr. Bob Dylan the Conjurer, the Magic Man, Ole Mr. Vaudeville with his Box of Roles and Tricks, manipulating the songs and scenarios like a Circus Master: I am reminded of Fellini, and all those clowns and masks and illusions of reality, and the Rolling Thunder Revue ("It was like a carnival," says someone), and *Renaldo & Clara*, top hats and make-up and make-believe . . . "Mankind cannot bear too much reality." T. S. Eliot said that.

Dylan circles around the stage, archly twirling the mike wire, singing some of the slow songs with florid, Italianate phrasing, almost parodying them. The band's music is very white. Hurdy gurdy. Energy without passion. Dylan gets his best reception from the songs he sings straight, like 'Girl from the North Country,' for which he abandons his electric guitar for the first time in favour of violin, flute, harmonica. But there's not a single number in which the old Dylan sings, alone, with acoustic guitar.

We have lost Dylan the troubadour, I am thinking. The man who spun songs out of himself. Instead we've gained Dylan the Music Man, the performer, leader of the troupe, Shakespeare's strolling band of players. The diminution is clear. But the songs . . . the songs are still the finest written this century, anywhere, by anyone. And they keep coming. Dylan's first film: *Dont Look Back*. He's got more sense than to try to photocopy himself.

Dylan ends the first set with a punchy, blues-drenched coda. INTERVAL. Sweet scent of grass in the aisles. People rush the soft-drinks sellers. Couple of young cops standing up back, caps off, long curly hair. People seem excited, expectant. Is it going to work?

Have you got into any religion since I saw you last?

No, no dedicated religion, I have not gotten into that. No dogma. I don't usually do that, I usually play my guitar. I don't know why, I've never gone on any of them guru trips. I've never felt that lost.

I thought for a while there you were moving back to your Jewish background.

No, I don't have much of that background to go back to, so if I was going to a Jewish religion, or Islam, or Moslem, Catholic, or whatever that religion might be, I would have to go *to* it; I don't have that religion to fall back on. What I have to fall back on is just my own isolated existence. I don't really think too much about those things.

But in the interview you did with Jonathon Cott there were a lot of references there . . .

Oh, Jonathon, yeah, he had all these sayings with him; we were just sitting around getting loaded, y'know, and he would bring out these quotations, which sounded really good.

But you responded to them.

Yeah, I'm excited by those kind of principles on life, and moral codes, that are part of any religion. They get to me. But as far as organised religion goes, I don't see myself as partaking too much of that.

But whether you realise it or not, that Jewish thing must have given you a very heavy imprinting; I've assumed that's stayed with you, and that in a way you still draw on it.

Possibly. It's possible. But I don't know how Jewish I am. See, with these blue eyes, which are Russian. Y'know, back in 1700s, 1800s, I know I have some different blood in me.

What sort of blood?

Cossack blood. I don't know how anyone could escape it, anyone of my family that lived back then.

Did you say somewhere you had some gypsy blood in you, is that right?

I'm not sure. From the questions I've asked of my old family, and the answers I've been given, I know there's Russian blood in me.

Where does that come from?

It comes from Odessa.

That's where you get blue eyes from?

Probably, because in Odessa mostly everyone has the colour of my eyes.

Have you been there?

I've never been there. I don't know if I'd like to go there either. (Laughing)

Sounds to me as though you're constructing a very exotic past for yourself.

No, I don't do that! I just . . .

You, Django Reinhardt . . .

No, no, I don't know about the gypsy thing, I might have said that to somebody once, I'm not sure about that, because that's from Rumania.

Do you feel very Jewish, Bob?

I don't know what Jewish people feel like!

That's a nice answer! For Christ's sake, you know what I mean . . . as a New York . . .

As a New York Jew?

Yeah.

(Laughing) I'm not from New York!

Isn't that part of you?

I feel a part of all people, really.

You don't feel proud of that background?

I feel proud of what I am. How proud can you be? I mean, there's so many people walking the earth, like, if everyone among us is gonna feel proud of who they are, mankind would be in a hell of a mess.

Maybe mankind is in a hell of a mess.

I feel proud of my accomplishments.

Sure. But often people try to link themselves to a tradition.

If you check back on my work, it doesn't link itself to a tradition.
Not any one that I've ever heard of.

But your music does.

Well, my music, yeah; but that's all Stateside music.

*That's still a tradition. You mention blues singers, and so on; they're
traditions you've hooked into.*

Musically.

But not personally?

I don't know. I feel life is going by at a tremendous speed. What
I feel one moment I usually don't feel the next moment. I don't
hold on to any period of time for too long. Even all the things
I've ever written, or said, or done, I sometimes think it's all a
joke, really, in certain periods of time.

*Do you ever look at it and think it could have been said or done by
someone else?*

No. I think I was meant to write that.

So you see yourself there still.

Yeah.

*I think the reason a lot of people link themselves to traditions is they
feel they have no importance otherwise . . .*

Well, tradition is great if you've got a community, and a society;
then tradition will hold you up as long as you're living. But if
your society is crumbling, what right do you have to be part of
that tradition?

But that makes you a sort of freewheeling atom, like the Lone Ranger.

Well, most people in the States right now are pretty
freewheeling.

Do you like that, though? Do you think it's good?

No. I don't think that's any good at all.

But that's what you're doing.

I don't have any choice. I would prefer a steady family life.

But that didn't work.

That didn't work. That *really* didn't work. You know, I could be happy pounding metal all day, going home to a big fat wife, and eating a meal, and, y'know, going to bed. That would be my idea of happiness. (Laughing)

You mean, that's your romantic idea of happiness for someone else, but not you.

No, it's my idea for me! (Laughing) I'm still open to that.

You ought to hang that on your motel door.

Otherwise, if I didn't believe in that, I'd be burned out by now; some of the things I've done . . .

It puts you in a hard position; you've got nothing much to prop you up.

But I never did. When I was last here, twelve, thirteen years ago, it was the same thing.

You were propped up pretty much with drugs then.

Yeah, we were taking a lot of chemicals back then, which doctors prescribe for entertainers and athletes . . . But those were different days, things were a lot simpler then, we were all on the way up.

You mean it's harder at the top!

Ah, at the top it's pretty difficult, you could fall at any time. No, it doesn't really worry me. Because morning always comes so quick that I don't have a chance to think about it.

Is that the only reason you don't worry about it?

You don't have much of a chance to think, really, on this level.

The only time you get a chance to think is when you're thinking about your work. It's not a healthy thing, it can't be for everybody. But to make it you really have to cross a lot of things off.

I wouldn't have thought that you, of all people, would have to worry for one instant any longer about proving yourself. You don't still feel any need for that, do you?

Yeah, I'm always trying to . . . it's not proof of yourself, like in the old days. What is it . . . I feel like I've had it, you know; and I'm doing it; I know it; and if the audience is still there, well I'm still here. If not I'll be in the corner bar playing. I don't have that youthful desire to prove I can go out and conquer the masses. A tour like this is just a tour. There is no great meaning to it. I'll be touring a lot, it's just what I do. I'm not sure about the event, and what it means to the people. To us we're just going on playing.

Do you think you can extend yourself much more?

I don't know. I don't really think so. I think I've pushed it as far as I can, and I'll just have to maintain it on this level.

I'm surprised to hear you say that.

Well, I can write new songs, and I can sing 'em, but they're always going to be sung in the same way. I mean, my style is pretty well defined. Everything about what I do is pretty well defined by this time. Sure, you could ask Paul McCartney that same question, and he might say, oh yeah, there's more to do, there's more limits to reach . . . But not really.

Does he say that sort of thing?

I don't know if he does. He could; but it would only be a superficial thing. I don't have that urge to learn any more technique than what I already know. If I was to go on and push farther I'd have to learn more technique, and I've done that. I don't figure I can do any more with that technique.

But you're willing to take on films, which means learning a whole new technique.

Yeah, but the film is an image. I'm not so sure how great a love, or great a need, I have for that. I know I do now, because I figure . . . I'm looking at the film as a painting, and if you can get character into that painting, and make it come alive, that's what my intentions are. I don't know if that's the right way people are making films nowadays; some are, but most I don't think are. I'm trying to get more out of that film. But in reality it isn't as great as standing on stage and singing. For me it's not that much of a kick, but it is a kick to get your vision across.

It's a nice thing to do anyhow: make a film.

It is, if you believe in it.

Do you do much painting these days, like you used to?

I haven't done much painting for a long time. I miss it. I'd like to get to a place eventually like Churchill, you know, just sit around and paint! And write your memoirs.

It sounds as though you're mature, that's what it sounds like.

I don't think so. Maybe I have matured, or mellowed, or whatever them words are, but it isn't like that inside. What I've learnt to do, which I didn't learn in the old days, is just hold it, in order to put it out when the right time is. So when people say he's mellowed, or matured, that's true, and I've gone through a lot of changes so it is true, but I just hold back most of the time, till it's the time to let it out. And if I didn't have that way to let it out I'd probably be just as crazy as everybody else, if not more so.

Whereas as it is you're absolutely sane!

Yeah, right. (Laughing)

To reach a stage where you're pretty confident, and can hold back and let it out when you want to, I'd have thought that must feel pretty good.

I've always been confident, though. I went to New York confident. I didn't know what I was goin' to have, what I was goin' to do, but I was confident I was going to come through. I wasn't going to roll under any wheels. I feel pretty confident now, in what we're doing. I don't know how much pleasure it gives me, but I know I'm doing what I'm supposed to do.

When I said "mature," I suppose I was thinking of artists like Michelangelo and da Vinci, who reached a stage where they had all the technique, and at that stage they did their greatest work. Do you feel that could happen to you?

No, I don't feel I could be a Michelangelo or da Vinci. Those guys had too much isolation back then. They were given the nod; it's hard to find anybody that society will do that for these days, so you're pretty much on your own. Michelangelo and da Vinci weren't really on their own, they were pretty much supported. And encouraged. Their work was respected in its time.

But so are you, and so is your work.

Well, I don't know if it is or it isn't. I never think about it, because I don't want to believe it – in case tables turn, or white goes to black, I don't want to be prepared, I don't want to be unprepared.

Can you give me any idea as to where your work might move?

No. It's in the same old place it's always been, it's not movin' anywhere, it's staying right where it is. It won't get any more complicated or simple than it is. New thoughts come, and, y'know, new ideas, new feelings; and I can't say what they're going to be.

I was thinking that, sometimes, you get some idea of what sort of shape your life is going to take for a while.

Oh, yeah. I've had them ideas.

Did they ever turn out right?

No, they never do. Things change so fast, so quickly. Just turn around, everything's gone.

One of the reasons I bothered to do that book about you was at that stage I thought I could half-understand what you were doing, in relation to myself: you were acting it in one way, I was acting it out in another. But I don't know that I can now.

I bet you can. I'm just doing the same thing. You get to a point where you're just doing it. That's the point I'm at now. I'm just doing it. I don't think about it any more.

Faced with something like the choice that you were faced with, in your life . . . if I understand it at all . . . you know, the family thing . . .

Well, you've got to have that. I expect to have that. I just didn't make it one time. But I mean, I still got my kids. I got five kids. I see them quite a bit of the time. But . . . er, I expect to, have that too. Again.

Sounds like a failure, Bob. By you there, somewhere.

What, in my marriage?

Yeah.

Right at the start . . . It wasn't a failure . . . it was a . . . Maybe it was a failure. Marriage was a failure. Husbandry . . . husband and wife was a failure. But . . .

Not husbandry.

Father and mother wasn't a failure.

How were you at husbandry?

Husbandry, I wasn't a very good husband. I don't know whether I was or wasn't, I don't know what a good husband is. I was good in some ways, as a husband, and not so good in other ways . . . But, I feel my true family relationship is up ahead of me somewhere.

You mean, you'd try it again? You'd get married again?

Oh yeah.

You like that.

Yeah, I like comin' home to the same woman. (Pause) It was a failure. You got to take the bad with the good. It didn't disillusion me at all.

Did it knock you around to have a real failure like that, because I don't think you had a failure up till then . . .

Oh yeah! (Laughing)

What were your other failures?

I failed at school.

That was a long time ago.

Not so long. My life seems to have flashed by in a minute. When you think about it . . . but then again, "there's no success like failure."

That's a nice line!

I believe it, too. It wasn't a failure . . . If you fail at one job, and you pick up another job, which you like more, well then you really can't consider what happened a failure. There aren't really any mistakes in life. They might seem to knock you out of proportion at the time; but if you have the courage and the ability and confidence to go on, well then that failure, you can't look at it as a failure, you just have to look at it as a blessing in a way.

When you say that, you're not saying you believe everything is predestined, are you?

No, I don't believe everything is predestined; but it is in a way. We're sitting here right now in the present, but we could talk about yesterday, and if we want to look at yesterday we could see that it was all predestined, because it was; if we're looking back everything is predestined. And tomorrow we'll be looking back on today, and today will have been predestined: we just won't know it now. So in a way I do believe in predestination; but only when you get to the place you can look back on does it become proof of itself.

Or make sense.

Right. But you can't project into the future, which probably gets conflicted with predestination. Things upset you, which you don't have any understanding or knowledge of at the time.

Does that knock you around?

Yeah, it knocks me around. Usually when you're caught up in the turmoil of some personal event, and you can't seem to work it out, and you're impatient with time doing it, you become impatient, and then you decide to get angry. But if you've been through it enough times to know it does work itself out, well then it just doesn't mean as much. That's what's happened to me, anyway. I still get booted around in my personal life, here and there, but er . . . I just try to understand that . . . *tomorrow is another day.*

How do you handle it?

Well, fortunately I handle it just by working. I just forget it and go back and work, rehearse, make records, or play, and then when I turn around whatever it was was bothering me ain't there anymore. Sometimes that's true, sometimes it's not true, sometimes it is still there . . .

Do you think you become a bit desensitised as time goes on, through that process?

Probably do, yeah.

Does that worry you?

Yeah, it bothers me sometimes. Sometimes I can't even be sensitive to my own needs.

You got a litmus paper test, you can hold up and say, how's my sensitivity rating?

I wish there was some kind of test like that. I don't deny it makes you insensitive to the flow and activity around you. But then again, it makes you more sensitive, because you get more inward.

Maybe you become wiser.

As you go on, you begin to realise, if nothing else at least you're alive. If you've been around enough times you realise what it is *not* to be alive, and to go down, and have that feeling of going down, and if you've had enough of them times they build up – especially in my life, when I got to a point . . . where I just . . . I don't want . . . at least I'm alive!

Jesus, I hope we get wiser, Bob, that's what I'm holding out for.

I don't want to get wiser. (Laughing)

★   ★   ★

The lights go down again. Dylan starts singing while the crowd is still filing back from the soft drinks. It doesn't seem to worry him. He seems looser, more relaxed, and the band sounds funkier. The concert is beginning to warm up. 'One More Cup of Coffee' gets a terrific reception. Then a low-key 'Blowin' in the Wind,' in which Dylan over-emphasises the word "free": it becomes melodramatic, extravagant. He would never have made that mistake once. But 'I Want You,' sung as a slow ballad, builds and builds . . .

The turning point of the whole evening is 'Don't Think Twice, It's Alright.' It's a classic early song of Dylan's, both slow and bitchy. But he has rearranged it as a jaunty reggae number: and it is such a daring, disrespectful thing to do, so damned shocking, so *irreverent*, and it works so well, Dylan standing his own music on its head and making it funny and endearing and mocking at the same time, affectionately satirising the man who wrote it, that suddenly I realise: Jesus, HE'S BROUGHT IT OFF! He's the Virtuoso, Mr Maestro, utterly reworking his old material, making it not better but different, and caring not a damn what he loses in the process, or gains, and what anyone thinks. It's life, and life only . . .

Dylan has been on stage for almost two hours. The audience is stunned, elated: it's like watching a man on a trapeze. Song after song they can't recognise until Dylan's halfway into it. He sings 'All Along the Watchtower' to the arrangement he used on record for 'Hurricane,' complete with electric violin solo by David Mansfield: it is a dazzling, imaginative *tour de force*. 'It's Alright, Ma' is the same: tough, fast, emotional. Mrs. Zimmerman's Son As A Rock 'n' Roll Star.

By the time Dylan closes the concert the audience is ecstatic. They stamp, cheer, whistle, howl, scream, clap and kiss each other. Dylan, who is not given to encores, comes back with 'The Times They Are A-Changin',' disappears for good. So does the band. House lights on. Roadies materialise. The crowd refuses to shift. More classical music. The crowd drowns it out. The promoter appears. It's costing him a thousand dollars. No, they won't budge. Finally, incredibly, Dylan reappears. 'Knockin' on Heaven's Door.' In reggae. IN REGGAE? You heard it . . .

Did you have a motorbike accident at all?

You mean back in 1966? After I left here? Yeah . . .

It wasn't just a cover-up?

No, I was put out of the picture. That was it, for me.

And you nearly did wipe yourself right out?

Well, it wasn't that the crash was so bad. I couldn't handle the fall. I was just too spaced out. So it took me a while to get my senses back. And once I got them back I couldn't remember too much. It was almost as if I had amnesia. I just couldn't connect for a long, long time. And what was happening around me I didn't want to connect with anyway. And what had happened in that period of time was that music had become very big. There was people doin' my songs. When I was working, I was nothin'. Talk about criticism now – there was more criticism back in those days than there is now. We'd get no good reviews; every time I put out an album the only good reviews would come from the musical papers; no one else knew what I was doing, or could care less . . .

After I was knocked off, knocked out, I guess people thought I was gone, wasn't about to come back, so they started elevating me to a level of which no one could come back from. I wasn't out there working; and then acid became very big; and when I got back, I couldn't relate to that world, because what I was doing before that accident wasn't what was happening when I got back on my feet. We didn't have that adulation, that intense worship, I was just another singer really, but I had a loyal and intense following. And when I went back on the road I was more famous than I was when I'd gotten off the road. I was incredibly more famous. And I had a lot of people coming who weren't my true fans, I was just another famous name. These people didn't understand what I had done to get there, they just thought I was a famous name and I'd written songs Jimi Hendrix was singing, that's all they knew.

And so I picked up a lot of new fans, and I made some records, and went on, y'know . . . I was half there and half wasn't. And when I finally did get back up to a place where I could express

myself again, it surprised a lot of people. Because they didn't
know that that's what it was all the time.

When you see me on stage now, I mean, you don't get that
feeling that I might die after the show. Whereas that's what
happened the last time here.

*What was the place that you got back to, where you felt you could
express yourself? Was that a particular album?*

No album. I haven't made one album yet that I figured I
really . . . I haven't made an album since *Blonde on Blonde* that I
felt I was all there for. I have written songs that were worthy of
it; I haven't been able to perform them properly, but the ideas
were there. I haven't been able to get them down right. I could
relate to the idea in an abstract way but I wasn't able to get it
down right, the way I felt I needed and wanted to, to bring it
home.

Which songs were those?

From the *John Wesley Harding* album to the *Desire* album I've
written a lot of songs which I felt real close to; I don't feel I
performed them that well on record, or performed them with the
proper meaning; but it doesn't reflect on the songs at all, it
reflects more on me. And I didn't get back into doing what it
was, with everything blocked out of the way, until like, maybe,
the end of the first Rolling Thunder tour. Or the second Rolling
Thunder tour – at least I was doing the best I could in the environment I was in. And now I'm also doing the best I can within
this environment; and I expect to go on and even do more acoustical things.

Are you doing any acoustical things on this tour?

I'm not doing any acoustical things, but we do some stuff which
you'd think it was acoustical, but there's another level to it, it's
just with guitar, organ, saxophone, but it brings it out in a way
where you think it would be just me playing the guitar.

Why aren't you doing any acoustical things?

I'll tell you one reason, but you wouldn't probably believe me, is
because I haven't found a magic guitar. I think I might have

found one now, but I haven't found one where I could feel completely at one with. In my kind of thing you have to have the proper instrument. I played acoustical songs on that Band tour, in '74, but I pushed too hard. I played acoustical guitar on the Rolling Thunder tours, but I had to push too hard. And for my type of style I can't really afford to push too hard, because I lose the reason behind the song. If you heard me sittin' in a room singing I wouldn't be pushing too hard.

It pressurises you, doesn't it?

Yeah. I never used to push too hard in the old days, and I was playin', y'know, an hour by myself and an hour with the band, and yet I was never pushing myself.

What's the guitar you found?

A guitar passed my way, I think it might be it's just telling me to use it.

Which of the songs you've done in the last few years are the ones you feel are close *to what you've just been talking about?*

There's a bunch of them in *Blood on the Tracks*. And there's half a dozen of them off *Desire*. 'Knockin' on Heaven's Door' is a good song. There's a bunch of good ones on *John Wesley Harding*; and *Nashville Skyline* there's good songs on.

Which are the ones on Blood on the Tracks?

'Idiot Wind,' 'Big Girl Now,' 'Tangled Up in Blue' . . .

I've always thought 'Tangled Up in Blue' was a great song, I really like it.

Yeah, I like that one too.

Without knowing anything about it, I half-assumed that Blue might be Joan Baez.

Joni Mitchell had an album out called *Blue*. And it affected me. I couldn't get it out of my head. And it just stayed in my head and when I wrote that song I wondered, what's that mean? And then I figured that it was just there, and I guess that's what happened, y'know.

It's not the same Blue as in 'It's All Over Now, Baby Blue'?

No, no. That's a different Blue. That's a character right off the haywagon. That Baby Blue is from right upstairs at the barbershop, y'know, off the street . . . a different Baby Blue, I haven't run into her in a long, long time.

You're being serious?

Yeah. I've never looked at Joan Baez as being Baby Blue.

Do you see much of her these days?

(Pause) She was on two tours with me. I haven't seen her since then. She went to Europe.

You involved in her?

No, no . . .

Listening to 'Tangled Up in Blue,' I got the feeling it's like an autobiography; a sort of funny, wry, compressed novel . . .

Yeah, that's the first I ever wrote that I felt free enough to change all the . . . what is it, the tenses around, is that what it is? *The person* . . . The he and the she and the I and the you and the we and the us – I figured it was all the same anyway – I could throw them all in where they floated right – and it works on that level.

It's got those nice lines at the end, about "There was music in the cafes at night and revolution in the air" and "Some are mathematicians, some are carpenters' wives/I don't know how it all got started, I don't know what they do with their lives . . ."

I like that song. Yeah, that poet from the thirteenth century . . .

Who was that?

Plutarch. Is that his name?

Yeah. Are there a lot of Dylanologists around still in the States?

I don't pay much attention to that.

Is Weberman still around, who was going through your garbage? I've lost touch with all that . . .

I've lost touch with it too.

Well, you've changed cities, for a start.

Yeah. Get my own garbage dump. (Laughing)

But are you still hassled by people projecting on to you and your work, at that level?

I get over-enthusiastic fans. But I never did pay much mind to that.

And you've got some good, close friends that you can just spend time with?

Yeah, I still have the same old people I've always known.

Why have you built this great place on the West Coast?

That's been built into a big thing out of nothin'. What had happened was that, somehow, we found ourselves in California in '73, or '74, and we were living on the beach, and I didn't like it, it was too noisy: traffic was on one side of the beach, ocean was on the other side. Couldn't eat in your sleep. So I found an area out there which was a little bit more remote, but very close by, and wasn't so glamorous and attractive to most of the Hollywood set. It was an older area, up on a cliff. I bought a house up on a hill and I figured it was too small, I was going to remodel it. But we soon found out it was pretty impossible to remodel it in any old way, because they have these laws, y'know, you can't build this on such-and-such; it was discouraging. Anyway, I found a man one day who was pretty much like me in a lot of ways, but he was a contractor, and he didn't have hardly anything going, he was doing one house in the Canyon or some place, and he said, well you can do anything! You just draw it up and we can do it. Well, what happened was, we already had plans filed for one part of the house, but then we drew up another room one night, and filed that, and then drew up another room, and we just got carried away with this house! One thing led to another, and it got to be a whole scene – it got to be a big scene up there, we had thirty people livin' in the back buildin' the house, and seein' as we could build it, I figured to go ahead and build it. So we built it, and . . . it's standin' there now. (Laughing)

Are you going back to it? Sounds like a symbol . . .

I don't know. Don't know if I'll go back to it, don't know if I'll sell it.

You don't want to become a prisoner of it, like Randolph Hearst.

Can't afford to become a prisoner of it. The day I start to become a prisoner to it is the day I blow it up, or somethin'.

I know what you mean about being too close to the sea. I lived for a while at Byron Bay, lived and wrote there with my family, right on the beach; it was beautiful, and spectacular, and idyllic, and after a while it really got me down, because I've come to think of the sea as embodying some active principle. It becomes oppressive, a challenge. So now I'm living here in the bush, which is like the passive principle here in Australia . . .

Do you have electricity?

Yeah. That's about all we've got. No hot water, no nothing . . . an old wood stove. But it's really lovely, because there everything is waiting for you to put your own energy into it, you're not having to be challenged all the time. I really feel I'm going to do some good work there.

(Pause) I'm lookin' for a place like that.

After the show Dylan goes back to the Crest, has a shower, joins the rest of the circus in the downstairs bar. He's pleased with his reception, but tired. Sits around. Doesn't talk much. He isn't travelling with anyone.

I leave him at the table with a half-empty can of beer. The night is coming down. So is the concert high. The bar is emptying. Dylan's the one in white.

> *Yeah, it knocks me around. Usually when you're caught up in the turmoil of some personal event, and you can't seem to work it out . . . you become impatient, and then you decide to get angry . . . That's what's happened to me, anyway. I still get booted around in my personal life, here and there, but er . . . I just try to understand that . . . tomorrow is another day.*

He delivered the line with the faintest hint of Scarlett O'Hara/ Vivien Leigh anguish. The self-parody is perfect. Going up in the lift, I notice that on the programme note he's listed himself as BOB DYLAN, Entertainer. Hmmmm. And more . . .

HARD RAIN/STREET-LEGAL

By Sean Egan

HARD RAIN
US release: 10 September 1976
Produced by: Don DeVito and Bob Dylan
CHARTS: US#17; UK#3

SIDE ONE
Maggie's Farm
One Too Many Mornings
Stuck Inside of Mobile with the Memphis Blues Again
Oh, Sister
Lay Lady Lay

SIDE TWO
Shelter from the Storm
You're a Big Girl Now
I Threw It All Away
Idiot Wind

Hard Rain was another Bob Dylan album with a generous running time, over fifty-one minutes. Considering the contents, such generosity turned out to be unwarranted.

The innovation and eclecticism of the Rolling Thunder Revue had captured the public's imagination and many who had witnessed it wanted a souvenir album, while many who had heard about it were intrigued by the prospect of at least a sample. Dylan responded by giving everyone what they least wanted: a Rolling Thunder live album that was totally unrepresentative of the Revue. *Hard Rain* offered no tracks from the first, rapturously received leg of the tour – even though much material had been recorded on it – but instead selections from the second leg, which began in April 1976 and which most considered to have lost the spark evident on the first leg (the public's lack of interest led to several cancelled shows). Judging by the quality of the material, they were also by no means the best selections. The phenomenally talented guitarist Mick Ronson (most famous then as David Bowie's sidekick) doesn't bring much to the party, nor do noted fellow axe-slingers T-Bone Burnett and Steven Soles. Scarlet Rivera's sumptuous skills are also present to no apparent effect.

Those assuming that the album would contain the *Freewheelin'* anthem 'A Hard Rain's A-Gonna Fall' would be mistaken, the title instead seeming to be another of Dylan's in-jokes. Negligible opener 'Maggie's Farm' attempts a funkiness and features female backing vocals. The relation of the melody of 'One Too Many Mornings' to that of the original is even more tenuous than is that of the version of 'Maggie's Farm' we've just heard to its progenitor, and while Dylan has made what we now call re-imaginings of his songs his trademark, one doesn't see why the quiet acoustic jewel from *The Times They Are A-Changin'* actually needs an abrasive, blaring makeover.

'Stuck Inside of Mobile with the Memphis Blues Again', unusually for this album, shaves time off the original instead of adding to it. However, as with several of the tracks here, Dylan adds a tinge of melodrama the absence of which on the perfectly fine studio template proves is unnecessary. 'Oh, Sister' is a merciful respite from the metallic, rattly grunge, with Dylan's soulful vocal to the fore, even if the arrangement is over-busy. 'Lay Lady Lay' is a complete reworking of the old favourite, with a new staccato arrangement and huge backing vocals, as well as melody tweaks that make some of it sound like a Stax record and lyric changes that make it more risqué. It's the kind of thing that can be irritating if you just want to hear something resembling the lovely original – and let's face it, most of even Dylan's audience do – but it's interesting and competently done.

It's back to the overwrought arrangements and purposeless deforming of melody for 'Shelter from the Storm', a Godawful racket with a clichéd big ending that a third-rate heavy metal act would be proud of. Though not acoustic, 'You're a Big Girl Now' is rendered with some sensitivity, especially the lovely rippling piano, but the album's general fault of overkill is

summed up by the stupid blam blam *blam* swells of instrumentation. 'I Threw It All Away' has a hilariously apt title in this
context: Dylan tosses aside the quality of this sweet *Nashville
Skyline* number by jettisoning any resemblance to its original
melody and singing it as though in agonised, grimacing, eyes-
slitted constipation. Unspeakably bad.

'Idiot Wind' is given a quasi-reggae rhythm as well as the now
familiar teasing out of a new melody. The "chestnut mare" of the
lyric is now a "smoking tomb", though whether this tweak was
made so as not to offend Rolling Thunder Revue musician
Roger McGuinn – co-composer of The Byrds' 'Chestnut Mare'
– is unknown. It's difficult to imagine McGuinn or anyone else
straining to hear the lyric over yet another metallic aural
hailstorm.

Hard Rain's cover features a close-up facial shot of a pancaked
and eyelinered Dylan. Its release coincided with the broadcast of
an NBC TV documentary of the same name consisting of one of
the two concerts this album was drawn from.

STREET-LEGAL
US release: 15 June 1978
Produced by: Don DeVito
CHARTS: US#11; UK#2

SIDE ONE
Changing of the Guards
New Pony
No Time to Think
Baby, Stop Crying

SIDE TWO
Is Your Love in Vain?
Señor (Tales of Yankee Power)
True Love Tends to Forget
We Better Talk This Over
Where Are You Tonight? (Journey Through Dark Heat)

When Dylan began recording *Street-Legal* in his own Rundown
Studios in Santa Monica, California in April 1978, it was his

first formal studio work in two-and-a-half years. What he began committing to tape showed a man in profound pain.

The outward-looking nature of *Desire* departed along with Jacques Levy and when Dylan turned his view back onto himself, he saw a wasteland. His experiences between *Desire* and *Street-Legal* marked probably the most traumatic period of his life, for it was the juncture at which it was obvious his marriage had irretrievably broken down. Sara filed for divorce on 1 March 1977. As with many divorces, an incredibly nasty custody battle ensured, one in which – also as with many divorces, particularly American ones – the wife made claims in court documents of domestic violence. Such claims have routinely been aired again every time a journalist has written about the Dylans' split but, for the record, no charges were ever brought against Bob Dylan, no other woman has ever claimed he hit her and it is Sara, not Bob, who has a conviction for violence following an incident where she went to collect their children from school and struck a teacher who asked to see a custody order. Custody of the children was ultimately awarded to Sara and one of the conditions to which Bob Dylan was made to agree so that his children remained in his new home state of California was that he never again see his current girlfriend.

Dylan's movie *Renaldo & Clara* was released on 25 January and got the poor reviews to be expected of a four-hour picture featuring befuddling improvised highbrow scenes in which, for instance, Dylan played Renaldo while musician Ronnie Hawkins played Dylan, even if the inserts of Rolling Thunder Revue performances make it a bit more easy on the backside. Dylan has subsequently withdrawn it.

Understandably, it was a very tortured man who wrote and recorded *Street-Legal*, and it is his tortured state that seems to have made Dylan become a man of God, a process detailed across the album's songs.

Once again, *Street-Legal* is an album of a generous length (over fifty minutes) and once again one wonders whether dropping the weaker tracks would have enhanced its reputation. Probably not, for the album was not only finished by Dylan's own admission in a rush prior to his world tour, but is fatally weakened by an horrendous production. Or perhaps that should be recording technique. Dylan's obsession with recording in what he considers an authentic way reached its *reductio ad absurdum* here, with him concluding for some reason that both earphones and separation were an unnecessary innovation and allowing the instruments of his new gospel- and R&B-inflected band to bleed into each other in the four- or five-day no-cans recording process. The result was a predictable mess, although perhaps the blame can't be placed there when it comes to the atrocious drum sound, which is pounding at the temples and insinuating its unwelcome way into the central nervous system by the second track. *Street-Legal* stands alongside David Bowie's *Let's Dance* as an album by a major artist apparently designed to give the listener a headache.

The above comments apply to the original release of *Street-Legal*, which remained in circulation until 1999, when out of the blue Dylan decided to sanction and issue a remix, one which has now superseded the original version. He was not the first major rock artist to authorise or supervise a new mix of a previously released album: way back in 1972 the Grateful Dead put out a version of their 1968 LP *Anthem of the Sun* with a much cleaned-up sound. Lately, though, belated remixes had become far more prevalent, such as the sonic overhaul given The Stooges' 1973 album *Raw Power* in 1997, Pete Townshend's remixing of Who material and Frank Zappa's obsessive sonic tampering with much of his past. This fashion was subsequent and possibly consequent to the erosion of the notion of the original mix as sacred territory that had gradually taken place once artists started allowing their work to be remastered for CD issue. Two decades too late it might have been, but *Street-Legal*'s remix was also welcome, undoing much of the harm done by the recording process, even if it was never going to make it a great album.

"Sixteen years!" Dylan sighs at the beginning of seven-minute opener 'Changing of the Guards', the amount of time, of course, he had then been a public figure. The implicit world-weariness is representative of the album. Though the lyric rewards concentration, Dylan's songwords are becoming noticeably more obscurely metaphorical than at any time since the mid-Sixties, which rather acts as a barrier to understanding, somewhat unfortunate with an album on which Dylan is clearly trying to communicate something to us. The female singers who echo Dylan on the first line of each verse and the (rather unimaginative) strains of saxophone can't disguise the fact that Dylan's melody is rather pedestrian, another of the record's consistent faults.

'New Pony' is a blues with real power. Dark and menacing, it explores the emptiness of the world of the flesh. Dylan's use of a pony metaphor is hardly startling considering the way "ride" is everyday slang for the sexual act and his publishing company's title "Special Rider" is a blues term for favourite sexual partner. What is startling – and unsettling – is that he follows that metaphor to its logical conclusion: "She broke a leg and needed shooting." This line follows shortly after the almost as disturbing opening gambit, "I had a pony, her name was Lucifer." The girl singers are an important component, their collective, almost maddening repetition of the phrase "How much longer?" after Dylan's recounting of each detail of his sexual escapades a counterpoint perfectly summarising the lack of fulfilment nagging at Dylan's consciousness. Even in the remixed version, the drums are too high on this track, although that is also somehow in keeping with its disturbing ambience – as though we are being deliberately tormented.

'No Time to Think' is intermittently impressive for its ornate phraseology and mischievous Dylanesque humour ("Your conscience betrayed you/When some tyrant waylaid you/Where the lion lies down with the lamb/I'd have paid off the traitor and killed him much later/But that's just the way that I am") but once again we are frustrated in our willingness to travel with Dylan on his self-journey by the obscurity of his references, something that frays our patience well before the end of the 8:19 playing time.

'Baby, Stop Crying' is the first of two songs that seem to allude to one of Dylan's great musical heroes, myth-wrapped bluesman Robert Johnson. This ballad, lyrically similar in parts to Johnson's 'Stop Breaking Down Blues', became a minor hit single in the UK courtesy of its quasi-catchiness, mildly pretty backing vocals and smooth saxophone breaks from Steven Douglas. Although it has a superficial attractiveness, there's also something slightly sinister and patronising in Dylan's manner, which is symptomatic of yet another problem with the album: at no point is the narrator of any of the songs someone to whom we can warm.

'Is Your Love in Vain?', which opened the original side two of the record, might be making a reference to Johnson's 'Love in Vain', although it's a million miles from the blues except in spirit. Dylan's increasingly grizzled voice negotiates this song's rich arrangement and catchy (if not exactly adventurous) melody with some difficulty. The listener, meanwhile, negotiates what feels like Dylan's audition of a prospective partner or wife with similar awkwardness. To be repulsed by the couplet "Can you cook and sew/Make flowers grow?" might be going a little far – different men, women and couples have different tastes and wants – but once again we are aware of a certain condescension from the composer and an uncomfortable feeling that we don't like him too much.

The album's one incontrovertible classic is 'Señor (Tales of Yankee Power)'. The Señor of the title is clearly the Almighty ("Señor, let's overturn these tables/Disconnect these cables/This place don't make sense to me no more"). Smoky saxophone, just discernible backing coos and undulating piano provide a rich, ripe and atmospheric backdrop to Dylan's account of his low ebb, and are even enough to banish for its duration uncharitable conclusions that he has turned to God or spirituality because of the consequences of his own unfaithful behaviour in his marriage (the "unworthiness" to which he referred in 'Sara').

'True Love Tends to Forget' is almost a pop song, both because of its primary-colour melody and its terminology ("I'm getting weary looking in my baby's eyes"), but a bridge in which Dylan recalls "I was lying down in the reeds without any oxygen" and "Saw you drift into infinity and come back again" reminds us we are operating in deeper intellectual waters than the type of material usually heard in what was by 1978 no longer called the Hit Parade. The song's overall whining tone of complaint continues into the so-so 'We Better Talk This Over', on which a half-hearted attempt is made to create a country feel which is undermined by the relentless dank oppressiveness of the album's production.

The closing 'Where Are You Tonight? (Journey Through Dark Heat)' seems to be the album's key song. Once again, Dylan is communicating he is in pain ("Horseplay and disease/ Is killing me by degrees") but this time there is relief from that pain, with the last lines revealing he has found salvation via "a pathway that leads up to the stars", a "sweet paradise". However, that salvation has not come without a heavy price in "the scars" and the absence of the person – we infer Sara – who should be sharing this salvation ("Without you it just doesn't seem right"). All of this made much more sense when it soon emerged that Dylan had become a born-again Christian. Though this lyric is well done, it's probably only interesting if you are a Bob Dylan fan and have therefore a passing interest in his life. The niche appeal of the words is compounded by the fact that the track's music is not particularly appealing, although a blast of electric guitar work at the close is not only attractive but almost startling: this kind of virtuosity is almost never heard on Dylan records. It also makes us realise something else: the guitar work occupies this space because this is the first Dylan album ever without harmonica. Dylan also dispenses with acoustic guitar.

Street-Legal was released into a world in which its type of obsessive navel-gazing and celebrity self-pity was suddenly very unfashionable and derided. Though punk had crested, its legacy was such that this juncture of history was one in which it seemed that never again would artistic self-indulgence by rock stars be tolerated. However, it's probably not that which engendered the negative reviews, but simply that even without that maladroit recording process and original mix, *Street-Legal* is simply not that good. 'Señor' excepted, the most attractive thing about it is its intriguing full-colour cover depicting Dylan in long shot, head bent forward, looking out of a stairwell entrance.

On 15 July 1978, Bob Dylan played his biggest gig since the Isle of Wight when he headlined a festival at the Blackbushe Aerodrome in Surrey, England. That he was the main attraction for the 200,000 assembled when Eric Clapton and the then trendy Graham Parker and the Rumour and Joan Armatrading were among the other acts proved his enduring popularity. However, this was – unbeknownst to the public and Dylan himself – the end of an era. Courtesy of a new, alienating direction in his music starting from the following year, Dylan would never be as big again. This eyewitness view of the event by Phil Sutcliffe freezes in time Dylan on the cusp of profound change, both personal and commercial.

BLACKBUSHE FESTIVAL – NICE TO SEE YA, BOB

By Phil Sutcliffe

First published (in longer form) in *Sounds*, 22 July 1978

In a miserable summer, the weather held good for the second open-air mega-binge to be staged this year. Some 80,000 "pop fans" (who does the *Sunday Times* think it's insulting?) had already decided to risk buying a ticket in advance to the opening of a new rock hypermarket at Blackbushe Aerodrome on the Surrey/Hampshire border and the unexpected arrival of the sun lured untold thousands more out of their laundromats to see Bob Dylan's "Thank You" British concert.

Maybe it was the site – flat, and uncomfortable, especially if you happened to be sitting on the runway – but the Great British "festival" spirit never seemed to permeate the multitude. The atmosphere remained restrained, even among the most committed punters who occupied the first hundred yards or so in front of the stage. Further out to the fringes an air of bemused detachment pervaded. You had to be a good deal closer to the stage than in the natural "bowl" at Knebworth to feel involved.

Disconsolate at not being able to see the bands, many people opted for treating the whole affair like an open-air hi-fi demon-stration – squatting in clusters, paying as much attention to the music as they might to their own records at home. Or they found their own distractions in the form of drink, dope and each others' bodies. They certainly weren't a contemporary festival crowd, and for some the realities didn't match up to memories of the way we were (or thought we were).

In many ways the site let down the music, which deserved a better response. For a start the show ran pretty much to time. The gaps between acts were seldom more than half an hour and even Dylan came on only forty-five minutes or so after Joan Armatrading had departed. The sound system was excellent apart from some points where the delay towers caused echo. And perhaps most important of all, every act on the bill played a good set.

The interminable delays for buses to the site from Fleet Station, the rip-off 50p parking fee for dear old NCP on top of the ticket price, all the minor hassles, were outweighed by the quality of the music on offer. After all, even the police were cool, restricting most of their muscle for ticket forgers and generally leaving those intent on self-abuse/enlightenment to get on with it.

Backstage it was one of the most sumptuous liggers' play-grounds yet constructed outdoors. A series of record-company tents provided almost limitless food and drink for those with the aplomb to collect the various badges, stickers and cards that were needed to gain admission. The *Saturday Night Fever* Tax Loss Award was won by RSO, who managed to hang chande-liers inside their marquee. The Egalitarian/Let's Make This The Big One For Joan Armatrading Award went to A&M who eschewed a tent in favour of trestle tables that didn't require twenty-seven separate passes to approach.

Unfortunately, anyone attending the concert with an official function to perform who wasn't directly employed by Harvey Goldsmith faced something of a lean time. Photographers were harassed to the point of extinction whether they had official passes or not. In fact a photographer's pass didn't actually permit you to photograph the stage at all. Despite the fact that dozens of these passes were handed out by press officer Alan Burry, no one was allowed access to any vantage point that might enable them to take a worthwhile photograph (with the exception of Harvey's own man of course).

They, and any journalist reviewing the event, were restricted to the Press area which permitted a view of approximately one thirtieth of the stage (give or take a thirteenth). Only those performers venturing forward to within imminent danger of toppling off the edge were visible – their backing bands were never seen. Perhaps the best evidence of these privations came when the corrugated iron protecting the "privileged few" in the liggers' area was broken down by the seething populace outside but as soon as the inrushing hordes saw that their view was actually worse than before they turned and fled back, one of them even helping the security guards to replace the barrier.

The fact that these difficulties, and your *Sounds* persona being non grata (obscure politics we won't trouble you with), could be shrugged off in the petty spirit in which they were presumably intended is due entirely to Robert Allen Zimmerman who performed a lengthy and magnificent set which provided adequate compensation for all those who missed him at Earl's Court and a few extra goodies for the people who caught him twice. The changes made to his set during his European travels have added further dimensions to his performance – in particular the addition of 'Gates of Eden', played solo with a harmonica slung round his neck, gave an intriguing flashback to the early Sixties Dylan, outweighing the loss of 'Love Minus Zero/No Limit'.

If he couldn't produce the same electric atmosphere at Blackbushe that he did at Earl's Court, he didn't disappoint anyone who could get close enough to feel enveloped in the sound. In return he seemed genuinely grateful for the response (not to mention the fee) and told us he'd be back before long. With the evident enjoyment he's getting from playing at the moment that may not be too far away.

Like moths to a flame they came from as far away as Camberley and Basingstoke: Bianca Jagger, Ringo Starr, Wilko Johnson, Mick Jones, Billy Connolly, Brian Lane (Yes manager), John Ameson (Penetration manager), Jenny Agutter, John Cooper Clarke, Barbara Dickson, Bob Harris, Rory Gallagher, Terry Wilson Slessor, Jeff Bannister, Denny Laine and a Dulux dog that could have been Paul McCartney's Martha though she refused to comment.

Bianca graced all the backstage hospitality tents with her presence. Our fashion correspondent writes that she was wearing clothes with a matching body. Ringo, grey and worried-looking, complained that he couldn't see the stage from the liggers' enclosure and was plonked (that is, placed) on a chair in the open stage front area for Clapton's set.

Billy Connolly said "Hi!" and gripped a *Sounds* man firmly by the urinal. By the arm, by the urinal. They had never set eyes on each other before but the Big Yin was obviously playing safe. John Cooper Clarke's record company had slapped "Hippie's Graveyard" stickers on all the "Dylan Concert" road signs but the laureate elect was there, browning it out.

Wrong-end-of-the-telescope figure walking through the last bars of his band's testing-testing workout of 'My Back Pages' into the spotlight. A slow roar from the far-flung crowd. He steps into the square foot of stage I can see, which is a relief. That is, I can see his top half at least. Black leather-jacket, black top hat, and . . . is that shades or black eye make-up? Shades. I'm not close enough to see his face as I could at Earl's Court, and I'm going to miss that contact, that closeness which focuses the misty myth (to hell with the divinity crap and listen to the man).

Though maybe that whine of a voice will be immortal. "Baby stop crying/It's tearing me apart." Of course, what he used to write was far more elaborate in its imagery. These words could as easily be hack Tin-Pan-Alley. So everything rests on the performance. And Dylan has the indivisible quality, of saying it and meaning it and being able to project it no matter what the setting.

The distant dwarf leans intently into the mike and 'Baby, Stop Crying' emerges from the stacks as a giant a hundred feet high and almost crying with passion – a great span of emotion behind the quarrelsome words from anger at the womanly wall of grief to guilt at having been the cause of it. The ground is familiar to everyone, the aural cinemascope experience of it something quite new, so big yet so clear. More than he has ever done on record Dylan live delivers his meaning. Sometimes it's quite a discovery after all these years: he makes sense!

He mutters, "Thank you, we're starting to get going" or something like and around me people ask each other urgently "What'd he say?" because they can't make out that Brando drawl and they want to because anything this man says might be, you know . . . IT.

'Shelter from the Storm': "I offered up my innocence and I get repaid with scorn." His new band and his new arrangements are chopping the songs up into edible bites, jerky chunks of stiff riffs, segments of word and sound like a long but well punctuated sentence. Coherence is the key. Sound sense.

He puts aside his guitar, holds the mike to still his hands because he's never had much practice at just standing there singing, finds that tipping his hat like Oliver Hardy is something else he can do. Alan Pasqua at the piano is shaking tail for his leader, curtain of long hair swinging, swaying through 'It's All Over Now, Baby Blue'. With the almost nonchalance of an almost-classy conjurer Dylan produces his harp from the palm of his hand and blasts his first raucous solo for which a mighty whoop rises from the crowd (because it hasn't all changed?). 'Girl from the North Country' touches me more than ever before. A hopeless love and tenderness. The guy who can't think of a message for the woman he's lost and wonders about whether she's got a coat to keep her from the howlin' wind.

The liggers are starting to wilt, skulk back to the Moet Et Chandon champagne tent and the major business of their visit – being seen and getting bombed. They miss scalding versions of 'Maggie's Farm' and 'Like a Rolling Stone'. I had always curled my lip at these songs because these were at the centre of his transition from protester to rocker which I took a while to accept. But these '78 treatments I can't resist. Everybody is bellowing choruses, moaning with pleasure, bopping into each other in the gloom.

The band, which is generally no better than workaday, gets inspired. Pounding brick on brick of thick music. Sod me! Completely different from the best songs earlier in the set because these words could just as well be gibberish. The girl singers are hollering as if they are naked (I can't see them but their voices are stripped bare).

This is an obvious crescendo. And Dylan is precisely a third of the way through his set. No interval here as there was at Earl's

Court so instead he seems to deliberately slacken pace and tension. A couple-more from *Street-Legal* then a slightly bizarre section in which the backing singers and the Alpha Band each do a song of their own choice. Only Carolyn Dennis's black old blues 'A Change is Gonna Come' works at all. When Jo Ann Harris warbles through 'The Long and Winding Road' disbelief and dismay contest supremacy on the faces near me and Steven Soles of the Alphas is appalling, singing "What would we do if nobody's dreams came true?" then advising us with extreme unction "Think about it." Dylan introduced him as "a genius" which I take to be an atypically loose use of language.

But it's all right. A blue spotlight picks out Dylan alone, strumming an acoustic (which we thought we would never see again) and he sings 'Gates of Eden'. The details don't reach me though I used to know them by heart. Just the cool blue concentration spreads.

'True Love Tends to Forget'. Another new love song. I haven't got the flavour of it yet. It's probably quite mediocre. But it occurs to me that, whatever else, he is never sentimental and that's one reason why we still trust him (despite wealth, fame and star paranoia).

'Blowin' in the Wind' has taken on a quiet, musing tone, the questions asked rather than spat out as militant rhetoric. 'I Want You' is slowed almost to a full stop and the imagery remains opaque even though every detail is now audible. What it does is pitch you back relieved on to the totally understandable chorus "I want you so bad" and that is moving enough though the thought seems a bit pretentious on writing it down.

For the last hour I'm conscious that the end must be close and I'm a cup running over but wanting more. 'Masters of War' is menacing, stunning, sung over a rock-solid riff culled from 'Louie, Louie'. 'Just Like a Woman' simplified, calm and friendly. 'To Ramona' magnificent, an eternal song swirling out of the ether with the crisp instrumental phrasing delineating new moods and meanings, my favourite love song, it's lovely ("Your cracked country lips I still long to kiss as to be by the touch of your skin!").

'Don't Think Twice' a vicious cynical joke against white men singing the reggaes, a vicious bitch about women, a vicious self-parody and throwback to the desperate mood of the *Hard Rain* album. Yeah Dylan is still shocking, over-the-top, chilling. Still. I keep saying "still". But who am I reassuring? Did anyone who matters ever doubt him?

'All Along the Watchtower', 'It's Alright, Ma': roaring rock. "Even the President of the United States must sometimes have to stand naked". He finishes the set with 'Forever Young'. Cynicism a burnt-out shell, this is his purest song perhaps, fusing his own innocence (it does survive, another reason we trust him) with the audience's. Hope, if not faith. My girlfriend says, "It's a hymn." Wood for the fire. He encores with 'Changing of the Guard' then 'The Times They Are A-Changin' '. Hope, if not faith. Dylan says, "Thank you" and time and again, "I wanna come back to see you real soon."

I've loved Bob Dylan for half my thirty-one years. Seeing him at last this summer has only deepened that feeling and strengthened it with respect for his care, energy and boundless imagination. He is the only rock artist I know of who could do a live album every year and each one be an original gem. For confirmation have another listen to 'Lay Lady Lay' on *Nashville Skyline, Before the Flood* and *Hard Rain.* That's the sort of radical approach he brought to bear throughout the Blackbushe epic. Physical discomfort and isolation from the stage made it a less magical occasion than Earl's Court. Nevertheless it was richly satisfying.

Despite the high finance and heavy-duty wheeler-dealing surrounding him he stays straight. Showbiz only takes. Dylan gave us everything he'd got.

BOB DYLAN AT BUDOKAN/SLOW TRAIN COMING

By Sean Egan

BOB DYLAN AT BUDOKAN

Japan release: 22 November 1978
US release: 23 April 1979
Produced by: Don DeVito
CHARTS: US#13; UK#4

SIDE ONE

Mr. Tambourine Man
Shelter from the Storm
Love Minus Zero/No Limit
Ballad of a Thin Man
Don't Think Twice, It's All Right

SIDE TWO

Maggie's Farm
One More Cup of Coffee (Valley Below)
Like a Rolling Stone
I Shall Be Released
Is Your Love in Vain?
Going, Going, Gone

SIDE THREE

Blowin' in the Wind
Just Like a Woman
Oh, Sister
Simple Twist of Fate
All Along the Watchtower
I Want You

SIDE FOUR

All I Really Want to Do

Knockin' on Heaven's Door
It's Alright, Ma (I'm Only Bleeding)
Forever Young
The Times They Are A-Changin'

Bob Dylan at Budokan is the bastard of Dylan's catalogue.

In February 1978, he embarked on a tour of Japan, his first visit to that country. It was decided ("They twisted my arm", said Dylan of Columbia) to issue a double album of selections from two of his eight concerts at the titular venue. That it was originally only released in Japan almost suggests that Dylan and his label were slightly ashamed of it: prepared to reap the dividends of the Japanese market (then as now a surprisingly lucrative part of the global record industry) but wary of putting it under the noses of more discriminating occidental consumers. When stories began circulating not only of the inevitable import demand for the album and the creation of bootleg copies but also of Dylan fans who possessed copies making tapes for friends and acquaintances for a couple of pounds, commerce kicked in and a Western release was arranged five months after the Japanese edition. At which point *Bob Dylan at Budokan*'s aura of value evaporated and people began viewing it as simply a mediocre, even atrocious live album.

For those still convinced of its low quality, it was partly pre-ordained. While making *Street-Legal*, Dylan received a fax from his Japanese promoters stating the titles of some songs they expected to form part of his repertoire. Humiliatingly, on his "alimony" tour, Dylan does not seem to have had the option of saying no. Surely, even with the best will in the world, somebody forced to sing a song is not going to give 100 per cent? Meanwhile, Dylan's big band experiment had failed on *Street-Legal* and could hardly be expected to succeed when it was transplanted to the stage. Dylan's donning on the Japanese tour of the type of flashy showbiz outfits he had never worn before – which he had in fact been seen as the antithesis of – also attracted ridicule. It was almost as if Dylan were trying to conjure the spirit of Elvis Presley (in his Las Vegas period anyway), the boyhood idol whose death he has admitted had shocked and shaken him the previous year (although something he hasn't admitted is that

that devastation may have been intertwined with the low ebb the divorce proceedings brought him to). And if the album's fifty-plus minutes on each disc was typical Dylan generosity, some could have done without that generosity extending to a gratis poster, the type of gift that seemed somewhat beneath a man of Dylan's stature.

Then there is the tampering. Every song on *Bob Dylan at Budokan* makes the re-imaginings of *Before the Flood* and *Hard Rain* look like Little League stuff. Opener 'Mr. Tambourine Man' sums up the album: it's slickly played and the smooth-rolling way Dylan sings it – against the background of female backing vocalists – makes us question whether he understands what the song is about anymore. And as for the tweeting flute – is he taking the piss? That the blissful mellow feel of the original recording is nowhere to be found is also representative: *At Budokan* just never quits with its overkill. No stone is left unturned in its determination to do everything differently to how we've ever heard it: Dylan tweaks melody lines and underlines them with backing vocals to make them more stylised and mainstream-sounding and he throws in instruments like a mad chef tossing in ingredients willy-nilly: sax, flute, violin, dobro, flute, even a clicking sound in 'Ballad of a Thin Man' after the line "he clicks his high heels". He seems to feel obliged to get value for money from the musicians he is employing regardless of whether their deployment is appropriate for a particular song. With the exception of the slowed-down, semi-pastoral 'I Want You', respite there is none. Where silence, delicate noodling or subtlety exists on the original recording, here you will find huge vocal swells, emphatic percussion, a guitar break or a brass passage.

While it might be presumptuous for us to imagine that we know better than Dylan what his songs mean and what the appropriate accompaniment is, surely he can't seriously think that 'Ballad of a Thin Man' is something that deserves to be rendered like it's the incidental music of a hammy horror flick? The saxophone solo in 'I Shall Be Released', meanwhile, sounds like it belongs on an anodyne love song by Chicago, and the revamped bridge of 'Going, Going, Gone' (words also changed) is turned into a strutting, wailing soul extravaganza.

Gradually, though, one succumbs. Once the surprise – even

appalled horror – has worn off, the objective mind recognizes
that this is good stuff. We are slowly reassured that Dylan can't
have approached these sets with contempt, both by the fact that
their slickness betrays too much rehearsal and hard work for
that, and by sublime individual passages such as Dylan's lovely
harmonica work on 'Love Minus Zero/No Limit'. Then there is
the fact that some of his experimentations are incredibly intriguing, for instance a reggae version of 'Don't Think Twice, It's
All Right' and a marching, horn-augmented 'Maggie's Farm'.
By the end of the original first vinyl side, only a severe curmudgeon would not be just sitting back and enjoying it.

One of the reasons the album works is that the superb band are
here able to show their chops in a way that *Street-Legal* didn't
allow them. Only 'The Times They Are A-Changin'' doesn't lend
itself in some way to the ornamentation, its stark generational fury
being non-negotiable. Additionally, Don DeVito's production is
inevitably better here than it ever could have been under the
circumstances of that album's recording. Dylan is also a likeable
stage presence. If the professionalism, passion and interaction
with the audience present on this album were exhibited to even
the remotest degree in Dylan's modern stagecraft, he would see a
considerable improvement in his negligible live stock.

Dylan's Far East tour, incidentally, also saw another Dylan
release initially exclusive to foreign shores. *Masterpieces* was a
compilation issued in the Japanese and Australian markets in
March 1978. A triple album, it idiotically represented 'Like a
Rolling Stone' via its *Self Portrait* version. In all other respects,
though, it had clearly been compiled by an expert/fan, for it
featured mouth-watering rarities and even never-previously
released tracks, significantly all clustered together on one side:
an alternate 'Mixed-Up Confusion' (whose official version was
itself by now pretty much untraceable), scarce B-sides in the
shape of 'Just Like Tom Thumb's Blues' (live) and 'Spanish is
the Loving Tongue' and scarce A-sides 'Positively 4th Street',
'Can You Please Crawl Out Your Window?', 'George Jackson'
and 'Rita May'. Like *At Budokan*, it eventually got a Western
release, but unlike the live album it has frustratingly fallen out of
print, which means those aforesaid tracks have become rarities
again. Considering the treats we have been given by Columbia/

Dylan in the form of the *Bootleg Series*, it is strange that nobody seems able or willing to put all his officially released works that are, for whatever reason, hard to come by on one collection.

SLOW TRAIN COMING
US release: 18 August 1979
Produced by: Jerry Wexler/Barry Beckett
CHARTS: US#3; UK#2

SIDE ONE
Gotta Serve Somebody
Precious Angel
I Believe in You
Slow Train

SIDE TWO
Gonna Change My Way of Thinking
Do Right to Me Baby (Do Unto Others)
When You Gonna Wake Up
Man Gave Names to All the Animals
When He Returns

Though claims that *Slow Train Coming* was the first properly produced Dylan record are not accurate – *Blonde on Blonde* and *Desire* were just two previous high-gloss Dylan LPs – it certainly marked the first time Dylan had opted for a famous producer. Jerry Wexler's production credit had appeared on records by, amongst many others, Ray Charles, Wilson Pickett and Aretha Franklin. Sessions took place at the legendary Muscle Shoals studio in Alabama in the first two weeks of May 1979, where Dylan for the first time ever agreed to overdub his vocals rather than record them as the basic tracks were laid down. He also agreed to instrumental overdub sessions. Wexler and his partner Barry Beckett impart a smoothness and a medium-paced groove to each and every track.

The cynical might suggest the smoothness was Dylan's equivalent of a spoonful of sugar to make the bitter medicine go down. For the first time since 1964, Dylan was trying to set the world to rights in his music, but his protest songs now were not about civil rights and the nuclear bomb but the world's godlessness. His new spiritual concerns dominated every song and were signposted in the picture-book-style front-cover artwork in which the pickaxe wielded by a man helping build the railroad for the titular train doubles up as a cross.

The Christianity, though, is not the problem with this record. You don't have to be a believer to enjoy a clearly religious song like 'Oh, Sister' or 'Quinn the Eskimo (The Mighty Quinn)'. Rather, the problem is that Dylan has abandoned rational thought processes in his embrace of evangelicalism, thinking in straight lines and speaking in slogans. This necessarily undermines his lyrical genius. What sort of nuance of viewpoint or honesty about inner conflict is possible when one is publicly stating, as he does in 'Precious Angel', "Ya either got faith or ya got unbelief and there ain't no neutral ground"? The album also provokes a profound feeling of intellectual disgust, for the idea that a man of the fierce intelligence displayed in, say, 'It's Alright, Ma (I'm Only Bleeding)' could consider the story of the Ark or the six-day Creation literal truths is preposterous, as is his failure to find the vengefulness of the Old Testament and the gentleness of the New Testament mutually contradictory. This is surely someone who is kidding himself. Furthermore, one can't escape the contemptuous feeling that this self-delusional fundamentalism is purely and simply a refuge from the traumas of his recent marriage break-up.

As per, the record is a generous length, forty-seven minutes this time. Though the band is completely different to that on *Street-Legal*, for the second album in succession Dylan dispenses with harmonica. The presence of half of soft-rockers Dire Straits – Mark Knopfler on guitar and Pick Withers on drums – may strike some as a joke: Knopfler's Dylanesque vocal on Dire Straits' 'Sultans of Swing' was flat-out, almost gormless imitation. However, his and his Straits colleague's contribution is significant. Barry Beckett on keyboards, Tim Drummond on bass and the Muscle Shoals Horns are a million miles from being slouches too. It's just a pity that one of the best backing bands of Dylan's career and one of his greatest production jobs isn't matched with more palatable material.

Opener 'Gotta Serve Somebody' illustrates the point.

Sheened, smooth and superficially pleasant as it is, there is no cleverness in the lyric, which is little more than a litany stating that however privileged somebody is, he is master to one of two people, God or Satan. Lines like "Might like to wear cotton, might like to wear silk/Might like to drink whiskey, might like to drink milk" are simplistic, unimaginatively phrased juxtapositions that a child could write. The chiding tone is also distasteful. Whereas Dylan once dismissed his protest material as "finger-pointing songs", at least they weren't, as almost all of these compositions are, finger-wagging songs. A conflict is deliberately being created with the audience: the majority of his listeners likely to be non-religious is actively condemned for its non-belief. Is the person singing these songs really the same man who had savagely mocked the unforgiving tone of the Old Testament in 'Tombstone Blues' and 'Highway 61 Revisited'? Or the person who had sung on *John Wesley Harding*, "Hold your judgment for yourself"?

Lucky for Dylan a woman – there is dispute about which one – helped convert him to God, enabling him to write something resembling a traditional love song. Lucky for us too, for the sense of gratitude in the ballad 'Precious Angel' alleviates slightly the album's overall lack of generosity and warmth – if, that is, we can ignore that "no neutral ground" line, and another in which the artist seems to exult in foreseeing "When men will beg God to kill them and they won't be able to die." In 'I Believe in You', Dylan casts himself as a martyr who is losing friends because of his newfound faith. The self-pity (which arouses no sympathy from us – who wouldn't want to rid themselves of this bore?) is unfortunate, because the fine melody, sweetly strummed acoustic guitars, keening electric guitars and subtle drum work make for a pretty concoction.

The track 'Slow Train' is musically brilliant. Though not uptempo – nothing here is – it has a galvanisingly brutal rhythm, some finely peeled electric-guitar work and an impressive snaking tune. But a listen to the lyric reveals Dylan to be babbling self-contradictory nonsense, one moment stating, "Man's ego is inflated/His laws are outdated", the next displaying a somewhat unenlightened obsession with worldly matters with the observation, "All that foreign oil/Controlling American soil". Moreover, when he complains about "sheiks walkin' around like kings/ Wearing fancy jewels and nose rings", the tone and phraseology is ironically reminiscent of much of the world's anti-Semitism.

'Gonna Change My Way of Thinking', which opened the original vinyl side two, is a blues with a syncopated edge courtesy of a cowbell, a staccato guitar riff and a horn section. Dylan says he plans to "stop being influenced by fools", but it's uncomfortably apparent that his definition of fools might not be the same as most of his audience's. 'Do Right to Me Baby (Do Unto Others)' sits oddly with the surrounding material, starting with the lines: "Don't wanna judge nobody/Don't wanna be judged." It has the trappings of a love song and would actually sit easily on a secular album. Here it sounds completely hypocritical. 'When You Gonna Wake Up' features compressed drums, fine brass lines and great warbling electric piano. Unfortunately, it also features a lyric that rants about "men who can't hold their peace and women who can't control their tongues".

'Man Gave Names to All the Animals' is by a long way the album's most interesting song. Not that the reggae backing is any superior to that of the rest of the uniformly musically excellent tracks, nor is it a change in subject matter. It's just that it sees Dylan mercifully approaching his subject/obsession from a lateral angle. He lists various wild beasts and their qualities, each verse ending with the handle devised by (English-speaking) humankind for said living thing. After we have gone through the bear, cow, bull, pig and sheep, we come to "an animal as smooth as glass/Slithering his way through the grass." However, when the expected rhyme for "Saw him disappear by a tree near a lake" doesn't materialise but an ominous sudden ending does, we realise that the naming is taking place in the Garden of Eden. It's not exactly profound – Dylan's description of a bull is "He saw an animal that liked to snort/Horns on his head and they weren't too short" – and one hopes it is what it sounds like – a song for children – rather than a yet further simplifying of Dylan's currently uninspired wordsmithery. It is, though, finally a song we can quite like. It has inspired two different illustrated children's books.

'When He Returns' is a finale featuring just Dylan and piano, almost like a torch song for Jesus. It's a bookend to that previous prediction of resurrection 'Quinn the Eskimo (The Mighty Quinn)', but whereas the earlier song was musically upbeat and promised "when Quinn the Eskimo gets here/everybody's gonna jump for joy", this one is musically mordant and predicts a somewhat less appealing scenario: "The strongest wall will crumble and fall to a mighty God."

Those whose impressionistic memory of Dylan's Christianity is that it immediately caused him to haemorrhage fans are wrong. This album not only did very good business, but it gained Dylan his first Grammy for his vocal on 'Gotta Serve Somebody'. The latter song, in making (with non-album B-side 'Trouble in Mind') a US No.24, was his biggest hit since 'Knockin' on Heaven's Door'. Part of the reason for this was that Born Again Christianity was not unusual in America at that point. Dylan's music had already followed the trajectory of millions of Americans' lives – idealistic youth, disillusion with politics, marital bliss, the trauma of divorce – and like it or not, millions of Dylan's baby-boomer countrymen at this juncture were also belatedly finding God as they entered middle age. Dylan actually picked up some new fans as a consequence of his change of outlook.

None of this, though, can take away from the fact that *Slow Train Coming* is ultimately nothing more than a shameful waste of some outstanding backing tracks.

SAVED

By Sean Egan

US release: 20 June 1980
Produced by: Jerry Wexler & Barry Beckett
CHARTS: US#24; UK#3

SIDE ONE
A Satisfied Mind
Saved
Covenant Woman
What Can I Do for You?
Solid Rock

SIDE TWO
Pressing On
In the Garden
Saving Grace
Are You Ready

In the wake of the release of *Slow Train Coming*, Dylan could examine his new spiritual direction with some satisfaction, even a sense of vindication.

The sales of that album demonstrated that the public had not turned against him over his religious conversion and because of that there seemed no reason for him to hide the light he had seen under a bushel. In fact, he must have thought, there seemed no reason not to refuse to play his "ungodly" pre-conversion songs to people who had paid to hear him, and no reason to rant about the coming Armageddon and the sordid behaviour of homosexuals from the stage – all of which he proceeded to do. Naturally this sort of behaviour attracted the derisive attention of the press, particularly the music press, whose predominately liberal and secular writers were appalled and astonished by this metamorphosis. Meanwhile, at his gigs, Dylan's behaviour infuriated his fans. The last time sections of his audiences booed him, of course, was back in 1966. It is not known whether anyone shouted "Judas!" this time, but it would have been perfectly ironic if they had. In short, he was suddenly not coming across as a man who had found religion – something a lot of his fans could live with, if reluctantly – but as a nutcase. When his next album came out, a tidal wave of tuts erupted across his fanbase and interested bystanders: even taking into account the Christian tradition of rejoicing in being taken under the wing of the Lord, the title *Saved* seemed presumptuous, arrogant and self-regarding. Even worse was Tony Wright's cover painting of a celestial hand reaching down to dispense salvation by touching fingertips with a selected one of a clamouring mob. It repulsed many. It has subsequently been changed to a painting of Dylan on stage, although the spotlight beam falling on him therein seems to be conveying the same message, and in any case it hasn't been changed in all territories. Many Dylan fans were so disgusted by all of this that it marked the first time they refused to buy a Dylan album. Those ever-loyal British fans sent it to No.3 (though even their patience was about to wear thin), but it stalled at No.24 Stateside, before its sales graph followed Dylan's reputation in a southward trajectory.

All of this was richly ironic, for *Saved* is a fine album.

Recorded in the first half of February 1980 at Muscle Shoals, this LP saw Wexler and Beckett once again sharing production. Tim Drummond was retained from the previous album's musicians. Famous drummer Jim Keltner came on board, although his drums are given that slightly unappealing hollow, compressed sound that became a production fetish of the Eighties.

In the sleevenotes, Dylan includes a biblical passage, Jeremiah chapter 31, verse 31: "Behold, the days come, saith the Lord, that I will make a new covenant with the house of Israel, and with the house of Judah." Even most of those who bought the album probably never bothered begging, stealing or borrowing a Bible to check it out, but the chosen passage seems very significant, for it is concerned with an abandonment of not just the tablets of Moses' commandments and other such written examples of God's law for a more direct communication with humanity ("I will put My law within them and on their heart I will write it") but more importantly forgiveness: "I will forgive their iniquity and their sin I will remember no more." By no coincidence, *Saved* is a far less judgemental album than its predecessor. As a consequence, it is far more likeable.

The opener is 'A Satisfied Mind', by Red Hayes and Jack Rhodes, Dylan's first cover version since *Self Portrait* (discounting the *Dylan* album). This Christian song was also done by The Byrds on *Sweetheart of the Rodeo*, though such is Dylan's vast knowledge of the blues and spirituals, he had doubtlessly heard it years before then. Though from an outside source, it basically sets in motion the salvation message Dylan proffers throughout the rest of the album. The rendition is low-key and Dylan's singing is soulful.

'Saved' – a Dylan co-write with Tim Drummond – is the album's anthem. It has a superb opening-verse image – "Born already ruined/Stone-cold dead/As I stepped out of the womb" – that is almost enough to inspire solidarity in an unbeliever. It also rocks more than all of *Slow Train Coming* put together. Better still, though Dylan talks of what he has been saved from as "the pit/Full of emptiness and wrath/And the fire that burns in it", he is not admonishing people who have not chosen to be saved but instead expressing his thanks to the Lord.

'Covenant Woman' fulfils the same function as 'Precious Angel' did on *Slow Train Coming*, and in fact is probably about the same person. No stuff here, though, about there being no middle ground between belief and unbelief but instead more thankfulness. It's pleasant not just in tone but in its sedate prettiness. Spooner Oldham provides a great warbling organ solo. 'What Can I Do for You?' sees Dylan asking the man who "laid down Your life for me" how he can reciprocate. In the middle and at the close of another attractively humble and pleasantly played if lyrically unimaginative song, Dylan gives us his first studio harmonica work since *Desire*, and very fine it is too.

'Solid Rock' is an uptempo number with, courtesy of Fred Tackett, the type of electric-guitar solo rare on a Dylan record. It's muscular and powerful and has some impressive wailing backing vocals. Dylan briefly touches upon the fundamentalism of *Slow Train Coming* with the lines, "Nations are angry, cursed are some/People are expecting a false peace to come", but broadly the track is in line with the non-judgemental devotion of the rest of the album.

Original side two opener 'Pressing On' is a ballad that explores similar territory to the last album's martyr's anthem 'I Believe in You', but it does so with far greater musical and lyrical dexterity, to such an extent that it is genuinely moving. Dylan's emotional delivery, a female chorus redolent of the euphoria of black church congregations and a lovely melody all mean that though we may never be in the position that Dylan is articulating in the lines, "Many try to stop me, shake me up in my mind/Say, 'Prove to me that He is Lord, show me a sign'," we can – crucially – finally sympathise with his sense of frustration. During 'In the Garden', Dylan wonders aloud about the motivations of the people who betrayed Christ at Gethsemane and the reaction of the witnesses to the miracles. A slowly building and smouldering backing is let down slightly by a suspicion of being out of tune.

Though 'Saving Grace' is excellent, it also illustrates the irreconcilable problems involved in the obsessive, insular nature of Dylan's religiosity. It is the musically richest cut on the record and, heard in isolation, its combination of humility, honesty about doubt ("It gets discouraging at times, but I know I'll make it"), soulfulness, sound tune and fine instrumentation would probably make it seem a classic. By this point, though, we're conscious that it is yet another permutation of the same limited theme.

'Are You Ready' disappointingly ends the album on a note of the judgementalness Dylan had been eschewing almost throughout ("Have you decided whether you want to be in heaven or in hell?"), but it's mild stuff compared to *Slow Train Coming*'s nastiness, and we are prepared to forgive much, for this is a truly cookin' track, with a sinewy texture, a mellifluous organ solo and some steely harmonica work. Dylan even leavens things again with some more uncertainty ("Hope I'm ready").

Saved has a relatively miserly playing time for a Dylan album of forty-three minutes but feels substantial. It also provokes a variation of the Gleason "We've got Dylan back again" line. Although it is still befuddling that an intellect like his believes this God-fearing stuff, unlike with *Slow Train Coming* we are not being asked by virtue of enjoying this music to additionally buy into hateful invective, something that moves the artist a smidgeon back in the direction of those songs suffused with humanity that caused us to like him in the first place.

SHOT OF LOVE

By Sean Egan

US release: 12 August 1981
Produced by: Bumps Blackwell/Bob Dylan and Chuck Plotkin
CHARTS: US#33; UK#6

SIDE ONE
Shot of Love
Heart of Mine
Property of Jesus
Lenny Bruce
Watered-Down Love

SIDE TWO
The Groom's Still Waiting at the Altar [added in 1985]
Dead Man, Dead Man
In the Summertime
Trouble
Every Grain of Sand

As with his previous two Born Again albums, Bob Dylan is not to be seen on the front cover of *Shot of Love* (sin of idolatry?). Instead, we have truly appalling cover artwork by Pearl Beach in the style of pop-artist Roy Lichtenstein spelling out the album title like it's a sound effect in a comic book panel, with impact-implying lines shooting out in all directions. The artwork of *Saved* may not have been to everybody's taste, but at least it conveyed what the album contained. This cover conveyed nothing but the suggestion that Dylan had lost any sense of discernment. The contents the album, in fact, actually suggested he was reacquiring such.

Shot of Love had a troubled genesis, taking in three different producers (including Dylan himself), three different studios (including Dylan's own Rundown) and oodles of outtakes. The first *Shot of Love* session took place in March 1981 and recording continued desultorily into late May. There are various permutations of musicians. Keltner, Drummond and Tackett were retained from the last album but augmented by people ranging from nobodies to luminaries Ron Wood and Ringo Starr. The title track's production is credited to Bumps Blackwell, while Dylan and Chuck Plotkin share production credit on everything else. No doubt this was to Plotkin's fury: stories abound of Dylan vetoing and changing his mixes. The result is cold, echoing, crimped and slightly lumpen. The production is the album's undoing. Though not exactly a return to form, and not exactly imaginative musically, it is generally a decent collection of songs that doesn't sound half as impressive as it could.

However, the production might not even have mattered were it not for Dylan's bewildering choice of contents. 'Ain't Gonna Go to Hell (For Anybody)', 'Angelina', 'Caribbean Wind', 'Let's Keep It Between Us' and 'Yonder Comes Sin' were all high-quality songs of this period that could have been included, while 'The Groom's Still Waiting at the Altar' was dropped from the album at a late stage and issued only as a B-side. With the latter, even the notoriously wasteful Dylan seemed to realise he had made a mistake and in 1985 it was added to the start of the second side of the album, making it now officially a component of *Shot of Love* – though not before the reviews, whose main theme was the paucity of good songs, had been published. Still, there was one blessed relief surrounding the album. Dylan had reinstated secular material/his old hits in live shows in November 1980 (reputedly at the insistence of concert promoter Bill Graham), and they remained there. *Shot of Love* is an album that similarly eases back on the religiosity.

Though the brawny opening title track is an example of scattershot rage, the lyric displays infinitely more imagination than we have heard from Dylan since 1978, especially a vitriolic verse that seems to be aimed at journalists. 'Heart of Mine' is sweet and vulnerable, Dylan telling himself not to betray his emotions to the object of his affection. Though the title track complains about people mocking his God, it's only three tracks in that we get the kind of pious anthem that exclusively comprised the previous two Dylan albums. The lyric of 'Property of Jesus' is in the second person, but it's obvious to whom the artist is referring in this new sibling of 'I Believe in You' and 'Pressing On': "Laugh at him behind his back just like the others do/Remind him of what he used to be when he comes walkin' through."

'Lenny Bruce' is a curious little tribute to the Sixties cutting-edge comic whose combination of liberalism and scatology led to a hounding by the authorities that helped cause his premature death. Curious not just because of its timing (fifteen years after Bruce's fatal drugs overdose), but because of its banality. Lines like "Maybe he had some problems, maybe some things that he couldn't work out/But he sure was funny and he sure told the truth and he knew what he was talkin' about" are simply embarrassing. A further curious layer is provided by the occasional second-person pronoun: the seasoned Dylanologist may appreciate that, for instance, Dylan's comment that Bruce was "more of an outlaw than you ever were" is almost certainly Dylan talking to himself, but the casual listener will just think it's reasonless confrontationalism with the listener and/or lazy writing. The track is dominated by Dylan's piano, which along with the maudlin melody gives the song a patina of pathos, albeit undeserved.

'Watered-Down Love' has a sunny melody that belies its message that the person addressed (Dylan again probably) has unrealistic expectations of romance. Though like everything else, it's undermined by that slightly boring production, it's quite winning, and when Dylan sings the ad-libbed refrain "Yes you do, you know you do", he sounds disarmingly like a teenager shimmering with the excitement of his first gig. Dylan's omission of 'The Groom's Still Waiting at the Altar' from the original tracklisting gave it an aura of martyr/orphan, with the consequence that people started speaking of it more highly than it really deserved. However, it rings with both energy (veritably snarling along) and poetry ("Try to be pure at heart, they arrest you for robbery/Mistake your shyness for aloofness, your silence for snobbery") largely absent from the rest of the album. On 'Dead Man, Dead Man', Dylan expresses disgust at the ungodly. It feels however less objectionable than any of his previous such rants, partly because of the fine reggae backing, partly because

he is flexing his lyrical muscles once more ("What are you tryin'
to overpower me with, the doctrine or the gun?/My back is
already to the wall, where can I run?") Excellent harmonica
work – in Dylan's current metallic style – underpins 'In the
Summertime'. So does his faith, but nobody would know it from
a casual listen, for here Dylan dresses up his tribute to the
Almighty like it's a love song, the bright tune part of the quasi-
subterfuge. A close listen yields up phrases like, "Then came the
warning that was before the flood" and references to things like
"the glory that is to be" that leave no doubt that this dialogue is
not with a lady love whom he met on a sunny day but with somebody profoundly more important in his affections.

Hard-rock-oriented, faintly anthemic and vaguely possessing
a social conscience, it's almost as though 'Trouble' is Dylan's
cack-handed attempt to produce a track in the style of The
Clash, who had been making waves in America that year.
Unfortunately, he comes up with a din with stupid words.
Example: "Trouble in the water, trouble in the air/Go all the way
to the other side of the world, you'll find trouble there." From
the ridiculous to the sublime: after the deafening mediocrity of
'Trouble', the album closes with 'Every Grain of Sand'. It's
unapologetically religious but appealing in a way that not even
the best of his Born Again songs have thus far been. Dylan
combines his faith with his lyrical craft in such a way that he
makes suddenly clearer to us how he came to be converted: "In
the fury of the moment I can see the Master's hand/In every leaf
that trembles, in every grain of sand." He also candidly speaks of
the voices of temptation calling out his name, and confesses
touchingly to further glimmers of doubt in the wonderful
couplet, "I hear the ancient footsteps like the motion of the sea/
Sometimes I turn, there's someone there, other times it's only
me." His melodic and instrumental craft are also in fine fettle,
particularly in two exquisite lengthy harmonica passages. So
lovely is this creation, for the first time on the album we even
forget about the substandard production.

What is perceived as Dylan's born-again period ended with
this LP. Some have cynically assumed that he jettisoned his faith
when it threatened his career, but Dylan has never formally
renounced religion, nor has a strain of religiosity (specifically

one revolving around disagreeably superior judgement-day concerns) ever completely disappeared from his songs. However, he certainly downplayed his beliefs from hereon.

Had *Shot of Love*'s mixture of secular material and unpreachy gospel been the way Dylan had first presented his new faith to the world, it would have been profoundly more palatable to the public. By now, though, the damage was done. People already sick of Dylan were turned off by the poor reviews. The album made an apparently respectable No.6 in the UK, but at a juncture where the compilation of charts was changed in such a way that it was easy for records to make a high chart placing upon release that did not accurately reflect long-term sales performance. Meanwhile, in the States, the album didn't even make the Top 30. A mark of how far and fast Dylan's star had fallen was the fact that this period marked the point at which second-hand record shops found themselves flooded with the albums of a man who had enraptured 200,000 at Blackbushe only three years previously.

The late John Bauldie and Alan 'A. J.' Weberman are the yin and yang of Bob Dylan fans. Bauldie was a polite Englishman who loved Dylan's music so much that he set up the magazine The Telegraph *(whose title came from the line in 'John Wesley Harding':* "All across the telegraph, his name it did resound"*), a publication that attracted many admirers, including – there is strong evidence to suggest – Dylan himself. Weberman – a man brash even by New York standards – was also a Dylan fan, but of the type that reminds one that "fan" is an abbreviation of "fanatic". His hounding of Dylan was the sort of thing Bauldie would never dream of, even though he respected Weberman's superior knowledge about their mutual object of admiration. In the summer of 1982, the two men met. Bauldie was intrigued at the prospect of seeing Weberman's Dylan archive and his semi-legendary work-in-progress analysis of Dylan's lyrics. What he found was so depressing that it led to, he explained, "a lot of soul-searching and breast-beating" amongst the editors and readers of* The Telegraph *about whether they were "all involved in a pursuit that was essentially unworthy". The upshot was that* The Telegraph *continued but its editors were careful to maintain a healthy self-knowledge and self-deprecation about its activities. Bauldie was responsible for five books on Dylan as author, co-author or editor. Weberman, too, has published works on Dylan – subsequent, it may surprise some to learn, to the encounter detailed below, including* Dylan to English Dictionary *and* RightWing Bob: What the Liberal Media Doesn't Want You to Know About Bob Dylan.

Margaret Garner, owner of John Bauldie's literary estate, requested that it be pointed out that this article shows Bauldie in an uncharacteristically light-hearted mood. She also asked it to be mentioned that she waived a fee for the reproduction of this article in favour of a donation to the charity British Heart Foundation (www. bhf.org.uk).

A MEETING WITH A. J. WEBERMAN, SUMMER OF '82

By John Bauldie

First published in *The Telegraph*, October 1982

I think I'll call it America, I said as we touched down.

It took two phone calls to persuade A. J. Weberman that he'd like to see me. I used to write to A.J. sixteen years ago. I sent him money; he sent me tapes the like of which the world had never heard – concerts from 1963! Studio cuts that hadn't been released! Not just that: A.J. had this key to a secret code . . . Now it's common knowledge but it wasn't then. Not too many of us knew A.J. then.

Shelly did though. Shelly used to be in A.J.'s class. He was on the field-trip down MacDougal Street when Dylan confronted Weberman and his students; he was at The Bob Dylan 30th Birthday Street Party (organized by the Dylan Liberation Front and staged outside Dylan's Greenwich Village house on Sunday 23 May 1971); he was in the Dylan Archive when A.J. was neck-deep in his researches, pounding out the Book which would finally tell the truth – the concordance-based work on symbolism in Dylan's writing.

I stayed with Shelly in New York. (Saw more Ribakoves in his drawer than I've seen in any one place.) So I told A.J. on the phone that the two of us would like to see him.

I wanted to see his Dylan Archive too. The Dylan Archive! It used to be written on A.J.'s notepaper: *Dylan Archive – Al Weberman, Dylanologist*.

"Don't come here!" the A.J.-like voice at the other end of the telephone wire yelled. "I'll meet you on the corner of Mercer and Houston at 11.30. I'll be with the dogs." He hung up.

The following morning we were there early. A fine rain fell for a few minutes.

"Think he'll show?" I asked doubtfully. Shelly didn't see A.J. as a punctual appointment-keeper, and street-corner rendez-vous in strange and potentially hostile territory isn't really my scene, man.

As the second hand on my Seiko watch hit the top of the dial at 11.30, there he was! A.J. Weberman, Dylanologist, champion of causes, liberator of garbage. But wait. Was that really A.J.? He'd cut his hair, cut off all of his hair – real short. He walked two Dobermans – Helga and Morgecai – on iron chains.

"John. Shelly." A.J.'s handshake was firm and cool. It was a hot day. He took us into the local dog-walking pound: through two chained gates, behind railings, a concrete oasis at the bottom edge of Greenwich Village, bordering on the Bowery. He let the dogs run free. We sat down on a bench. I tried to talk to him for about twenty minutes. He wasn't too responsive.

Shelly had written to him months back, and sent some cash for a copy of the ill-fated Weberman book-manuscript. "Hey, Shelly, I couldn't find the book. I'll give you your money back." The money wasn't important. Shelly had wanted the book.

Weberman stood up and walked into the shade. Shelly and sat sweating in the sunshine.

Weberman talked to some neighbours, kicked one of his dogs and came back: "We'll go see if we can find the book."

Shelly hadn't heard. "Come on Shelly, we're going back to A.J.'s!"

We walked down Elizabeth Street.

A.J. suddenly turned. "This is where Dylan jumped me!" A strange light glowed in his eyes. "'Laughter down on Elizabeth Street'! Can't you see these buildings, how they close in? This is 'the valley of stone'." There was certainly a stream of pure heat. "'It felt out of place, my foot in his face'! Just here, man, near this trashcan. 'The book that nobody can write'. That's my book!"

We got to Bleecker. The Yippies were just getting onto their bus. We stopped at A.J.'s door.

"Still got the same place?" Shelly asked.

"I got the whole building," said A.J.

The whole building? He pushed a big key into the steel door and swung it open. It clanged, locked behind us. It was as if we were in an airlock. Another solid steel door faced us. Up to the right a TV camera peered at us. To our left were tear-gas canisters, ready to be triggered by remote control.

The second door opened. We went up some stairs. "This is the dog's floor." We went up some more stairs. The office. No Archive.

"Do you still listen to Dylan?" I asked, as A.J. changed into camouflage shorts to match his shirt.

"I listen to the records, man, I don't have much to do with anything else."

"What about the symbolism, A.J.?"

"Still there, man, still exactly the same."

"Do you still write, A.J.? The last thing I read was your review of *Renaldo & Clara*."

"That was the last thing I did."

"You should write it down," I said, "some of us still want to hear it."

"I guess so," he said. "Nobody knows more than I do about Dylan's poetry." He turned to the cupboard and pulled out a loaded shotgun.

"See this? Nobody will get me in here." He glanced at the TV monitors which focused on the steel doors and the tear-gas bombs. "Let's get the boxes." We went briefly upstairs. "This was A.J.'s flat," said Shelly. No Dylan pictures. No records. No tapes. No Archive.

"Do you still do the garbology, A.J.?"

"Naw, not much."

The garbology murals were still there – perhaps the garbage too. Down in the stairwell were three hefty cardboard boxes. "Bring those up here," A.J. directed. The boxes were brought and opened.

Dylan. Piles of articles, cuttings glued to sheets, sellotaped to sheets; yellow, musty, stuck together. Piles and piles. Photographs. Dylan 1965, Columbus, Ohio; November 1966, Seattle; New Year's Eve with The Band. Galley roughs for the original *Freewheelin'* sleeve, discarded covers for *Tarantula*. A *Tarantula* badge! Dylan in magazines: colour photo in 1966 *McCalls; Movie World, Intellectual Digest*. A treasure-chest and a terrible mess. And in the second box, more and more. And in the third box, Weberman's book.

More than 400 pages, and this is just volume one: up to *Blonde on Blonde*.

"Here, Shelly, you can have the book." Shelly didn't know what to say.

A.J. looked at both of us: looked very carefully.

"You want this stuff?" he asked, casually pointing to the boxes.

"You're kidding," I said.

"Take it," he said, "I'm all through with it."

Shelly went to get the car. While he was gone, A.J. began to talk about Dylan again, but he seemed very confused and I felt sorry for him – for something that had been lost.

"What do you do with your time?" I asked him, although I already knew.

"I manage."

"What about money?"

"I have more money than I ever had. I get more in a day than I got in a lifetime. I don't need money."

Then Shelly appeared on the grey monitor screen.

We loaded the boxes into the VW, and left A. J. Weberman, the world's first and greatest Dylanologist, staring at a steel door on a flickering TV screen in an empty building at the bottom of Bleecker Street. New York New York.

And yes, Weberman did scare me; but then again I'm easily scared, and anyway those are my best days, when I shake with fear.

INFIDELS

By Sean Egan

US release: 1 November 1983
Produced by: Bob Dylan and Mark Knopfler
CHARTS: US#20; UK#9

SIDE ONE
Jokerman
Sweetheart Like You
Neighborhood Bully
License to Kill

SIDE TWO
Man of Peace
Union Sundown
I and I
Don't Fall Apart on Me Tonight

There was quite a sense of anticipation surrounding the release of *Infidels*.

Dylan's prolonged inactivity leading up to it was very unusual for him at the time. Though he had been away for long periods before, he played no live dates in the three years after November 1981 and released no album for two years and three months after *Shot of Love*. In contrast, between 1974 and 1981, he had issued seven studio albums and three live albums and had toured quite extensively. He had also released a movie. Leaving aside the fact that a duets album Dylan recorded with girlfriend Clydie King in the early Eighties was rejected by Columbia, the sudden invisibility and silence seemed to suggest hesitancy and an anxiety to please. His Born Again trilogy had caused much of his audience to perceive him suddenly not as a man of wisdom and mystique but as somebody just as susceptible – more so, even

– to psychological weakness and pettiness as any other human being. That Dylan was somewhat shaken by his commercial and critical fall from grace is indicated by the fact that whereas in 1970 he had furiously tried to shake off fans who considered him the font of human wisdom by releasing sub-standard product, with *Infidels* he seemed to be trying to persuade his fanbase that he was worthy of their respect again. He asked Columbia (with whom he had recently re-signed) for an extended production period on his next LP. At one point, he attempted to enlist Frank Zappa, turning up unannounced at the great rock eccentric's home, although in the end nothing came of this intriguing potential pair-up. Ditto for Dylan's next interesting choice of producer, Elvis Costello (the latter was committed to a tour). He finally enlisted Mark Knopfler for the role. Dylan recruited a stellar line-up of musicians: Sly and Robbie (then considered the best rhythm section in the world), ex-Rolling Stone Mick Taylor and Knopfler and keyboardist Alan Clark of Dire Straits. Moreover, Dylan booked an unprecedented entire month in a recording studio, attending New York's Power Station in April/ May 1983. When the relevant album – *Infidels* – came out, he even embraced videos, the new term for promotional films which had long been around but which had lately acquired motion-picture-like budgets and storylines.

After all of that effort and care, though, Dylan screwed it up. With groan-inducing predictability, he left off tracks which would have profoundly enhanced this album. The most famous example is the epic, tortured 'Blind Willie McTell', one of his greatest songs since *Blood on the Tracks*, but there were several other discarded tracks better than much of what did end up on the record. By now the bootleg industry and the less commerce-oriented tape-trading amongst fans was so developed that the public were aware of these omissions as soon as the album came out, rather than belatedly learning about them via fanzine articles and suchlike as had always happened before, and this occasioned no little contemporaneous disgust. This disgust was partly down to the inescapable suspicion that there was something wrong with Dylan's head: such behaviour seemed to go well beyond simply being a bad judge of his own material and entered the realms of self-sabotage and self-loathing. One part anger at being expected to pay for sub-standard product and one part pity for the man intermingled in fans' minds.

As for what was included on *Infidels*, rarely have such talented musicians been so wasted. Anyone expecting cooking percussion from Sly Dunbar and Robbie Shakespeare, coruscating guitar breaks from Mick Taylor, slick fretwork from Knopfler or sleek organ runs from Clark was going to be severely disappointed: Dylan used these great sidemen like they were an anonymous pick-up band, requiring them only to chug featurelessly along behind him.

Meanwhile, though the glossy production is preferable to the cavernous din of *Shot of Love*, it too has its deficiencies. Like so many veteran artists at that period in time, Dylan embraced the production modes of the day and ended up with an album that soon sounded dated due to its quintessentially Eighties echoey chilliness and thinness. Knopfler, incidentally, claimed that these weren't his mixes, which were scrapped by a Dylan either impatient or contractually unable to wait for him to return from a Dire Straits tour. Some sources state that entirely new lyrics were overdubbed on some songs in Knopfler's absence. Perhaps it was inevitable though: the common factor with almost all of Dylan's classic records is spontaneity and brief recording spans.

There was an additional profound problem with the album, at least for all the old lefties who had grown up with Dylan. Though the album was, from their point of view, mercifully almost completely devoid of religious content, there was no disguising the fact that Dylan could in no way be posited as having returned to them and their values. 'Union Sundown' is partly anti-trade union. 'Neighborhood Bully' is unapologetically Zionist. The line "A woman like you should be at home, that's where you belong" from 'Sweetheart Like You' shows a man uninterested in being in tune with feminist thinking. Dylan was no longer anything resembling a man of the Left. And while his newfound dislike of space travel touched upon several times in the album might have arcane religious rather than political origins, it did seem a rather peculiar and irrational concern even to those who thought the budget of the space programme would be better spent on feeding the starving. Some of those Dylanites who had been disappointed by the apolitical nature of his early Seventies work were no doubt left half-wishing for a return to those days, for at least back then there was still a way to pretend to themselves that Dylan was situated on the same side of the fence as them.

Though the weedy intro of 'Jokerman' hardly makes for a great curtain-raiser, the opening track is actually a good one. Dylan, in that second-person mode that he uses either to disguise his target or create a psychological distance that frees him to be candid with himself, engages in torturous self-analysis for over six minutes. Nobody holds the key to the metaphor-draped poetry but him, but it's quite obvious from the language of departure and lines like "Shedding off one more layer of skin" that he is no longer a true believer, at least in the strain of religion for which he has been proselytising the last few years. It's also painfully apparent that this is not the source of great rejoicing for him that it is for his fans, what with comments like, "Keeping one step ahead of the persecutor within" and "Freedom just around the corner for you/But with truth so far off, what good will it do?" There are even *ouch* moments: the apparently self-lacerating line about having to execute his U-turn, "Fools rush in where angels fear to tread", and the implication of self-hatred in the very title.

Though 'Jokerman' is a good song, it really means nothing to anyone not intimately knowledgeable about Dylan's life and career. Furthermore, despite the prettiness of the imagery, and Dylan's thankful return to imaginative lyrics, one is uncomfortably conscious that there is a glimmer of truth in the dismissive review of it by the *NME*'s Tony Parsons that coincided with its release as a single in the UK. Parsons said its allusiveness was like someone playing knock-down ginger (what Americans call ding-dong ditch) with nobody willing to answer the door anymore. In the no-nonsense world of punk and post-punk, Dylan's old-man status was compounded by the fact that he seemed blissfully oblivious of the fact that people no longer hung on his words.

'Sweetheart Like You' has the trappings of a love song but the line "got to play the harp until your lips bleed" indicates that this is a continuation of the self-analysis of the previous track. It's quite attractive and emotionally sung, but its message is not even partly decipherable. Meanwhile, that Eighties echoey production works against the tenderness. 'Neighborhood Bully' is the sarcastic title and refrain of a song which protests that Israel is not the aggressor that many allege but a country fighting for its very life against the enemies that encircle it. Though we can raise the objection that a more considered précis of such geo-political complexities is not beyond the powers of such a genius – Dylan's perspective takes no account of the massacres of Palestine non-combatants, nor the fact that Israel came into existence as a result of fatal bombings and other activities that could be said to undermine its right to preach about terrorism – somewhat more pertinent is the music: this uptempo affair could be sonically powerful but is reduced to tiresome by that prominent Eighties placement of the drum track in the mix. Only four-and-a-half minutes long, one wants it to end before it does.

'License to Kill' is the second track on the album requiring an American spelling to remain true to its title. It's also a very unexpected song. Though Dylan bangs on about the evils of space travel, there is something far more agreeable to his usual fanbase in the lyric. Talking of the false values taught "man" (and here the word is not being used to mean the human race), he laments, "Now, there's a woman on my block/She just sit there as the night grows still/She say who gonna take away his license to kill?" The man who had lately been accused of sexism, even misogyny, is suddenly revealing that he has more in common with feminists than anyone would ever have imagined. The thoughtfulness, however, is undermined sonically, by the burying of a nice piano part deep in the mix and those in-your-face reverberating drums.

'Man of Peace', the opener of the original side two, is the only full-on religious track, with Dylan depicting an Armageddon scenario against a mid-tempo blues-reggae hybrid. The Satan-wears-many-disguises message is a banality dressed up as a profound statement – not just in Dylan's "You'll never guess" patronising delivery but also its unwarranted six-and-a-half-minute length, the latter particularly unfortunate considering the hackneyed tune. 'Union Sundown' is actually not as right-wing as the climate of the times – when Thatcher and Reagan were rolling back trade-union rights, albeit with some considerable support from UK and US citizens – made it seem. Though Dylan accuses labour activists of driving business away with high wage demands ("The unions are big business, friend/ And they're goin' out like a dinosaur"), he reserves most of his ire for the American public for buying foreign goods whose cheapness is a reflection of the slave-labour conditions in their countries of manufacture. (Apparently, he practises what he preaches and tries not to use goods not made in the States.) The line "You know, capitalism is above the law" is not meant to signify approval. In many ways, it's a far more nuanced and honest song than his protest material. Unfortunately the production lets it down again: interesting backing vocals from Clydie King are buried and Mick Taylor fights a losing battle for audibility with the drum work.

How significant it is that the one time we can clearly hear Clark's lovely piano playing, the result is a high-quality track. 'I and I' is as rich and mysterious as *Street-Legal*'s 'Senor'. Dylan is gazing upon a beautiful sleeping woman in his bed and reflecting on the time he "took an untrodden path once, where the swift don't win the race". What relevance the Rastafarian phrase for the oneness of God "I and I" has to this is not quite clear, and Dylan's punning reference to an "eye for an eye" is clumsy, but in its vulnerability and aural loveliness, this is by far the most substantial thing here.

'Don't Fall Apart on Me Tonight' feels like Dylan's version of that quintessentially Eighties beast the power ballad, right down to that voguish title phrase and the chart-friendly chorus couplet, "Yesterday's just a memory/Tomorrow's never what it's supposed to be." And of course those bloody drums. It's an interesting and surprising exercise, but you'll never willingly seek it out.

What sums up as much as anything the failed objectives and the sense of self-sabotage surrounding *Infidels* is the photography. On the original inner sleeve was a beautiful colour picture of a crouching Dylan against the backdrop of the city of Jerusalem. The symbolism of the picture may or may not be Dylan turning his back on Jerusalem and finding stony ground. However, the fact that such a lovely piece of photography is hidden inside while the cover boasts a sub-standard out-of-focus facial close-up is, like the album's a crying and unnecessary shame.

The reception to the album was lukewarm, with mixed reviews and a US chart placing that was only a moderate improvement on *Shot of Love* and a UK chart placing that was actually lower than that predecessor. The point could be made that *Infidels* was an infinitely more thoughtful and solid album than contemporaries like Paul McCartney, The Rolling Stones and The Who released around this point, but the very fact of having to compare *Infidels* to the likes of *Pipes of Peace, Undercover* and *It's Hard* in order to stake a claim for it possessing any kind of substantiality says it all.

The idea that it was impossible for Dylan to recover fairly quickly from the reduced cultural and commercial standing engendered by the Born Again trilogy is not necessarily true at all. Witness Neil Young. In the 1980s, he was a Reaganite who embarrassed even some fellow Reaganites. Now, however, it is as though his comments of that period such as "You go to a supermarket and you see a faggot behind the fuckin' cash register, you don't want him to handle your potatoes" were never uttered. There persists an adverse overhang from Dylan's intolerant religious phase that there does not when it comes to Young's intolerant Reaganite period. The reason few mention Young's right-wing chapter in their fawning profiles of him is because of the continuing relatively high quality of his output. Dylan could have effected this same rehabilitation, starting with *Infidels*. He blew it.

REAL LIVE/EMPIRE BURLESQUE

By Sean Egan

REAL LIVE
US release: 3 December 1984
Produced by: –
CHARTS: US#115; UK#54

SIDE ONE
Highway 61 Revisited
Maggie's Farm
I and I
License to Kill
It Ain't Me, Babe

SIDE TWO
Tangled Up in Blue
Masters of War
Ballad of a Thin Man
Girl from the North Country
Tombstone Blues

That the opportunity to fully rescue Dylan's critical stock had been wasted was made excruciatingly obvious by the commercial performance of his next piece of product, the in-concert collection *Real Live*, a "celebration" of Dylan's return to live work in May '84 after thirty months away. It was Dylan's first album since his debut to fail to make the US Top 100, and (discounting *Dylan*) his first ever not to crack the Top 50 of the British charts. You could almost smell it coming: when Dylan was unable – even after stupendous, unprecedented effort – to come up with a worthwhile studio album, who on earth would want to pay to hear him cranking through his old material, in the case of some songs here for the third time on a Dylan live album?

Amazingly, it had only been a decade since Dylan's first live album sailed to No.3 in the American charts.

Dylan's live band at the time was an impressive one, with keyboardist Ian McLagan (Small Faces/The Faces) and Mick Taylor among the musicians. Dylan even included a performance of 'Tombstone Blues' on which the celebrated guitarist Carlos Santana guested, and hired a big name – Glyn Johns – to produce (even if he only tops the "special thanks" list). The result of all this, however, was rock ordinaire, with much meaningless and inappropriate wailing of guitar. Not to mention the wailing of Dylan's voice, now so stylised that the artist sounds embarrassingly like he is doing an impersonation of someone mocking his worst vocal tics.

'Highway 61 Revisited' and 'Tombstone Blues' are interesting choices, considering that many a Christian would surely consider their content sacrilegious, but that's the only way their performances are in any way remarkable. However, said tracks come off better than 'I and I', which ham-fisted rendition lacks all the mystery and sensuality of the original. 'Tangled Up in Blue' is completely rewritten to no apparent purpose. The six-and-a-half-minute band version of 'Masters of War' achieves less than the quiet, seething, solo original of half that duration, although is mildly admirable for its unapologetic rock roar. The only thing approaching a truly bright spot is a solo 'It Ain't Me, Babe', which not only has harmonica work that is impressive for how long it's sustained, if not exactly for technique, but features some sweet, affectionate audience participation that is the kind of thing that validates a live album.

The cover shot of Dylan at the microphone with acoustic guitar, light glowing around the outline of his head and torso, is the most attractive thing about this shoddy release.

EMPIRE BURLESQUE
US release: 8 June 1985
Produced by: –
CHARTS: US#33; UK#11

SIDE ONE
Tight Connection to My Heart (Has Anybody Seen My Love)
Seeing the Real You at Last

I'll Remember You
Clean Cut Kid
Never Gonna Be the Same Again

SIDE TWO
Trust Yourself
Emotionally Yours
When the Night Comes Falling from the Sky
Something's Burning, Baby
Dark Eyes

Empire Burlesque is Dylan's sell-out album.

Dylan approached Arthur Baker, the hottest producer of the age, and reportedly told him he wanted to shift the quantities of records that Prince and Madonna were then managing to do. To achieve this, Dylan was – as the aural evidence attests – prepared to allow Baker to subject his music to his leaden-fisted trademark style.

The album cover gave away the nature of the enterprise. Framed by the sort of day-glo and computerised abstract eyesore graphics of the day, Dylan is pictured coyly posed in one of those Eighties satiny, panelled jackets that nobody would be seen dead in one minute into 1990. This was a man who wasn't even disputing that he was prostituting himself.

Just as with *Infidels*, Dylan took an inordinately long time to deliver the album – and then threw all the hard work away. This doesn't just apply to retaining Baker to mix the results of Dylan-produced sessions that ranged across the middle of 1984 to March 1985, but to the same process of bad song selection and poor use of good musicians that marred the album's predecessor. Dylan's hankering to match the sales figures of the above-mentioned artists (and no doubt those of one-time Dylan manqué turned original voice and superstar Bruce Springsteen, about whom he has made many tartly dismissive comments down the years) was no mere delusion: only the following year Paul Simon (also once a Dylan manqué) obtained himself a whole new audience and the sort of stratospheric sales figures he thought he'd left behind with *Bridge Over Troubled Water* via *Graceland*. However, that album contained great new songs and sparkling (and novel) musicianship. It also had good and generally traditional production techniques.

Baker being the hottest producer of the age in 1985 means nothing other than an indictment of surely the worst decade for recorded music in history, as evinced by coldly echoing vocals just when warmth and intimacy are required, simultaneously puny and bombastically huge drums and horn sections (some or all artificially created by synth) cluelessly low in the mix. As for the songs, as usual there were a number of outtakes that were actually superior to much of what made it on to the album, and those who think the previous claims in this text of self-sabotage and self-loathing are over-the-top are directed to this comment by guitarist Ira Ingber, who said of the failure to include the song 'New Danville Girl', "It's like he was doing it to spite people who were all liking it, and he just held on to it." As well as Ingber, Dylan employed more than two dozen musicians on sessions in New York and Los Angeles. Alan Clark, Sly Dunbar, Jim Keltner, Al Kooper, Robbie Shakespeare, Mick Taylor and Ronnie Wood were just some of the players whose great talent earned them the gig but whose talent is nowhere particularly in evidence. Not that they had much with which to work. Dylan's songs (or the ones that were released) are both completely lacking inspiration and mostly seem to whine at some unspecified female about an inchoate set of grievances. His lyrics are reduced to self-parodic pseudo-profundity ("Oh the French girl, she's in paradise/And a drunken man is at the wheel").

Though the opener is hardly a classic, for the five or so minutes of 'Tight Connection to My Heart (Has Anybody Seen My Love)', we can believe that this whole experiment can actually work. Gospel singers sing the title refrain rather attractively and Mick Taylor contributes spiky but mellifluous guitar. But by 'Seeing the Real You at Last', the drums are already tiresome and a good brass line is reduced to a shadow. Ballad 'I'll Remember You' is a nice song with a good melody, if you can ignore the banality of lines like "You to me were true/You to me were the best." Any warmth, though, is drained by the cacophonous drum sound and the echo plastered on Dylan's voice.

'Clean Cut Kid' is atrocious. Intended as a pastiche of Andrews Sisters-type wartime pop, period authenticity is destroyed by an oblivious Baker with his space-age techniques. The well-intentioned lyric is about a Vietnam vet who goes murderously insane, but is comprised of stock images ("When he was ten years old he had a watermelon stand"), one suspects not so much through a desire by Dylan to juxtapose the subject's blissful all-American childhood with his awful fate but because these are the kind of clichés that now fill his head.

'Never Gonna Be the Same Again' features the kind of glistening, garish, synth-dominated instrumentation that people thought sounded like the future in the Eighties but which now seems about as prescient as 1950s magazine illustrations portraying everybody in the year 2000 possessing their own jetpacks. Dylan sings tunelessly alongside female vocalists. Ironically for such an empty song, it contains about the one lyrical highlight on an album almost bereft of great lines: "Don't worry, baby, I don't mind leaving/I'd just like it to be my idea."

The first couple of verses of original side-two opener 'Trust Yourself' see Baker finally lay off most of the cold-as-ice, thin-as-a-wafer techniques and a good groove is worked up, especially by keyboardist Benmont Tench. But just as we have got our hopes up, Baker throws in a beatbox and things descend robotically from there. 'Emotionally Yours' sees Dylan explore power-ballad territory again, only more formulaically than in 'Don't Fall Apart on Me Tonight', right down to the sort of trite title and banal lyric that were once completely beneath him. It's shockingly undignified. 'When the Night Comes Falling from the Sky' could have been a substantial song on another album, but any sense of atmosphere on this seven-and-a-half-minute would-be epic with a foreboding mood and dark melody is destroyed by the random squeals of synth and the relentlessly thudding drumming. 'Something's Burning, Baby' seems to be about the end days ("Something is burning baby, something's in flames/There's a man going round calling out names"), in which case never has an apocalyptic scenario been so unworrying. Also, why is he now addressing all these sermons to women? 'Dark Eyes' is a solo Dylan number, so Baker can't screw this one up. Dylan does that himself, mumbling incoherently over a sub-nursery rhyme melody.

The result of an album that was indeed as vacuous and unlistenable as most of everything else then shifting platinum was not the stratospheric sales of Prince and Madonna, but a failure to crack either the US Top 30 or UK Top 10.

Remarkably, *Empire Burlesque* was not the worst way Dylan made a fool of himself this year. In January he participated in the 'We Are the World' single for starving Ethiopians by stepping up to the mic to do his bad-Dylan-impersonator impersonation for a verse. His heart was in the right place, though, as it was toward the end of the year when he participated in the Arthur Baker-produced Artists United Against Apartheid single 'Sun City'. Sandwiched between those records that July, however, was Live Aid, where Dylan's heart was in the right place but his brain seemed to be located in a part of his anatomy south of there. Despite being flanked by Keith Richards and Ronnie Wood of The Rolling Stones, Dylan turned in an unspeakably bad set at the event organised by Bob Geldof to further help the stricken Ethiopians whose plight had led him to co-write and organise the recording of 'Do They Know It's Christmas', the UK precursor to 'We Are the World'. Dylan's two fellow superstars were thrown when he changed the songs at the last second, although monitor problems and a broken guitar string also contributed to the wince-making nature of their renditions of 'Ballad of Hollis Brown', 'When the Ship Comes In' and 'Blowin' in the Wind'. However, the goodwill generated by the fact that he had turned up at all would have made this a negligible sin. What makes the set live on in infamy is that Dylan then proceeded to bracket the plight of the starving with debt-troubled farmers in America, suggesting from the stage that "one or two million, maybe" of the money raised that day could be diverted to the latter, thus at a stroke seeming to validate the cliché of Americans as a people who think their country is the centre of the planet. Geldof was not alone in thinking it "crass, stupid, and nationalistic". Having said that, there was a valid point buried amongst the inappropriateness and lack of proportionality and without Dylan's comment Willie Nelson, John Mellencamp and Neil Young would not have set up Farm Aid later that year. Dylan naturally appeared at this concert to help US family farmers, and the event has subsequently become institutionalised. One somehow just wishes that it hadn't all been brought about by a comment that was worthy of the sort of parochial knucklehead Dylan had considered to be the enemy back in his protest days.

BIOGRAPH

By Sean Egan

US release: 28 October 1985
Produced by: Jeff Rosen
CHARTS: US#33; UK# –

DISC ONE
Lay Lady Lay
Baby, Let Me Follow You Down
If Not for You
I'll Be Your Baby Tonight
I'll Keep It with Mine
The Times They Are A-Changin'
Blowin' in the Wind
Masters of War
The Lonesome Death of Hattie Carroll
Percy's Song
Mixed-Up Confusion
Tombstone Blues
The Groom's Still Waiting at the Altar
Most Likely You Go Your Way (And I'll Go Mine)
Like a Rolling Stone
Lay Down Your Weary Tune
Subterranean Homesick Blues
I Don't Believe You (She Acts Like We Never Have Met)

DISC TWO
Visions of Johanna
Every Grain of Sand
Quinn the Eskimo
Mr. Tambourine Man
Dear Landlord
It Ain't Me, Babe

You Angel You
Million Dollar Bash
To Ramona
You're a Big Girl Now
Abandoned Love
Tangled Up in Blue
It's All Over Now, Baby Blue
Can You Please Crawl Out Your Window?
Positively 4th Street
Isis
Jet Pilot

DISC THREE
Caribbean Wind
Up to Me
Baby, I'm in the Mood for You
I Wanna Be Your Lover
I Want You
Heart of Mine
On a Night Like This
Just Like a Woman
Romance in Durango
Señor (Tales of Yankee Power)
Gotta Serve Somebody
I Believe in You
Time Passes Slowly
I Shall Be Released
Knockin' on Heaven's Door
All Along the Watchtower
Solid Rock
Forever Young

He can't possibly have planned it that way (such were the elongated schedules of record companies then), but that terrible year of 1985 saw Dylan manage to both salvage some credibility and give cause to his increasingly dismayed fans to remain loyal. The reason on both counts was *Biograph*, which was for the mainstream purchaser a good summary of why he had achieved his status of legend and to his more fanatical followers, in part, a veritable wet dream.

The awkward title may be a reference to the archive blues and jazz label Biograph founded in 1967. The cover – a head shot of the mid-Sixties Dylan against a computer-generated abstract background almost as garish as that of *Empire Burlesque* – is also not too clever. However, the set contained for the knowledgeable Dylan fan astonishing treasures about which they had previously only read in fanzines or heard on often bad-quality bootlegs.

At the time, *Biograph* was a curious release because it was an unusual cross between a best-of and a collection of previously unreleased songs from the archives. Dylan had done this before of course with *Greatest Hits Vol. II*, but this was on a grand scale. It's not so curious now: that description applies to the standard career-spanning multi-disc collection. Dylan had invented the box-set. Said box-sets were soon to explode in number as the new medium of the compact disc enabled the assembling of compilations that were not prohibitively cumbersome or difficult for shops to display, and in fact 1985 marked roughly the breakthrough for the CD in terms of market penetration. For that reason, though *Biograph* was also released as a five-LP set, it is the way that the tracklisting was divided on its three-CD configuration that is printed above, and detailing of the division of vinyl sides is henceforth dispensed with in this text.

Not only did the collection round up rarities like 'Can You Please Crawl Out Your Window?' and 'The Groom's Still Waiting at the Altar' (only added to *Shot of Love* that year, so many who had the original album didn't yet possess it), just over a third of it consisted of previously unreleased material either in the form of live or alternate studio versions of officially issued songs or else songs that had never previously been released by Dylan in any form. In truth, once stripped of the mystique conferred by unobtainability, most of these unreleased tracks weren't all that exciting, and there was a curious dearth of the unreleased Basement Tape material. Meanwhile, the morality of forcing fans to shell out again for the other two-thirds of the collection in order to acquire such material was dubious, especially in light of how expensive the package was. Then again, the opening of the archives added to the aura of importance about Dylan that *Biograph*'s release was effectively asserting, and at this point in history Dylan fans would grab any opportunity to continue to believe in the idea that Dylan still deserved his iconic status.

The two magazines included in the package contained unusually candid and lengthy comments from Dylan on his career and songs. One would assume that this implied a hands-on approach from Dylan and that therefore the selections must be his. Additionally, not only is it illogical that even a contrarian like him would allow another hand to compile a definitive summation of his career up to *Shot of Love*, but as with *Greatest Hits Vol. II*, the sequencing is non-chronological and if it conforms to any logic, it is one only the artist would understand. In fact, Dylan was dismissive about the collection in interview, suggesting another hand was indeed responsible for decisions about inclusion – which thereby turn from idiosyncratic to often unfathomable. There is always argument about compilation tracklistings, but why include 'Most Likely You Go Your Way (And I'll Go Mine)' and 'All Along the Watchtower' in their inferior *Before the Flood* incarnations? And does the compiler really think that 'You Angel You' and 'On a Night Like This' are the two most worthy songs from *Planet Waves*? And why go to the effort of representing for the first time ever on a UK/US album the song that was the A-side of his first single, 'Mixed-Up Confusion', but not include the version that was originally released but instead a new mix of the alternate take first issued on *Masterpieces*? And what is intended by starting the whole shebang with 'Lay Lady Lay', which though a fine song is unrepresentative?

'Baby, I'm in the Mood for You' is a *Freewheelin'* outtake and like so much of that album is young, exuberant and horny. 'Mixed-Up Confusion' is like a lot of side one of *Bringing It All Back Home*: the band behind Dylan is a featureless blur, compounding the demerits of a slight song. 'Percy's Song' and 'Lay Down Your Weary Tune' are typical Dylan songs from 1963, their archaically worded, circular, stately refrains betraying them as adaptations of aeons-old songs, even though the former tackles the very modern issue of imprisonment for causing death by careless driving. The repeat of the 'Percy's Song' refrain – "Turn, turn again" – every second line would probably make it tedious even were it not over seven-and-a-half minutes long, while there is the smack of faux protest in its depiction of a judge dismissive of the narrator's insistence on a miscarriage of justice. 'Lay Down Your Weary Tune' (recorded by The Byrds in 1965) remarks on the symphony provided by nature to only moderately pleasing effect.

Though 'I'll Keep It with Mine' is not as good as many Dylan fanatics claim, this ballad of knowing deception (How many times have people heard "Come on, give it to me, I'll keep it with mine" just before getting ripped off?) would have been a welcome inclusion on *Bringing It All Back Home*, of which it is an outtake. The only backing is harpsichord-like piano and subtle drum work. It first became known through a 1967 version by chanteuse Nico.

'Jet Pilot' and 'I Wanna Be Your Lover' are post-*Highway 61 Revisited* 1965 outtakes. The chugging 'Jet Pilot' is intriguing-sounding but unfortunately is just a snippet of less than a minute. Rocker 'I Wanna Be Your Lover' is not as amusing as it thinks, tiresome in the way it poses and preens as it goes nowhere.

There are three live tracks from the remarkable boo-shrouded UK tour of 1966. 'I Don't Believe You (She Acts Like We Never Have Met)', that lovely song from *Another Side of . . .*, is given a full electric treatment. It's to the song's detriment that Dylan is now coolly cynical, instead of newly cynical as on the original. 'Visions of Johanna' gets the opposite treatment, stripped back to acoustic guitar and harmonica. It's a remarkably slick and – considering how different it is by definition – faithful-sounding version. 'It's All Over Now, Baby Blue' is a solo acoustic version that adds nothing to the *Bringing It All Back Home* version except some extraordinarily brilliant harmonica work.

'Quinn the Eskimo (The Mighty Quinn)' is musty and mordant like so many of the Basement Tape recordings. It's surprisingly brief (2:17) and certainly different to that euphoric Manfred Mann hit, but it's good to finally hear the 1967 original.

'You're a Big Girl Now' is the original New York version that was shunted off *Blood on the Tracks* by the Minneapolis re-recording. Some Dylan scholars swear this more measured take is the superior one, but while it is certainly lovely and has a greater intimacy, the swelling organ and keening Hawaiian guitars over-egg the pudding, Dylan's cascading guitars from the re-recording are missed and Dylan's harmonica work is vastly less heart-breaking than what he executed in Minneapolis. 'Up to Me', meanwhile, didn't make it onto *Blood on the Tracks* in any form. A criminal shame, for this heartbroken beauty is among the ten greatest compositions for which Dylan has ever been responsible. Employing the same intimate Dylan-and-bassist format as on half of that album, it sees the narrator brood for more than six minutes over the end of a long but tortured relationship, but never maliciously so. As with 'Tangled Up in Blue', Dylan amazes us with the uncontrived ways he manages to keep finding a rhyme for the title phrase. The final verse in which he beseeches his long-gone lover that if they never meet again she should remember that he made sweet music for her on his guitar and harmonica is sweetly humble. Meanwhile, what pithier and more heart-tugging a summation of the post-relationship emotional wasteland could there be than, "In fourteen months/ I've only smiled once/And I didn't do it consciously"?

'Abandoned Love' is a high-quality outtake from *Desire* and absolutely of a piece with that album, Emmylou Harris, Scarlet Rivera, exotic timbre and all. The narrator is asking a woman for one more night of love before leaving behind the life of lies involved in such pursuits. There are two songs from the first leg of the Rolling Thunder Revue that was sadly unrepresented on *Hard Rain*. The slow piano that was the backbone of the studio 'Isis' is nowhere apparent on this stage version but is not really missed in a staccato, sinewy, almost snarling performance. That ratcheting up of the intensity of a *Desire* song is continued on 'Romance in Durango'. Though it's a minor song and therefore distinctions in quality are of little import, this is the better version.

'Caribbean Wind' shows not only what *Shot of Love* could have been (it's bog-standard rock but a higher bog-standard rock than much of what made the cut) but what Dylan's whole Born Again Christian period could have been (you have to listen hard to work out that there's religious content: the titular wind is "Bringing everything that's near to me nearer to the fire"). 'Heart of Mine' is a 1981 live version of the vulnerable *Shot of Love* track. It's immediately superior because it lacks the suffocatingly bad production that afflicted said album. Not only that, the instrumentation is less rigid and Dylan's singing better. That this is so well-recorded that nobody would know it was live were it not billed as such is the clincher for the conclusion that it would have been preferable if this rendition had been placed on *Shot of Love*.

The short version of 'Forever Young' here was recorded by Dylan in 1973 in order to register its copyright. The use of this musty demo of a song with a touching sentiment to close the collection just about works in its attempt to induce a sense of poignancy, even if we are more aware than we should be of being manipulated.

The mystique surrounding *Biograph*'s previously unreleased material may have been revealed as in many cases unwarranted and the selections may not have included every Dylan fan's favourite hidden gem, but that this material was being released at all was as much a fantasy come true for Dylanologists as the release of (some of) the Basement Tapes in 1975. Dylan had never indicated that he gave a damn about the wasted work and the crying artistic shame of top-quality tracks he had produced mouldering in the vaults. Now his public had to radically rethink that notion – especially in the coming years as, unbelievably, he proceeded to authorise a series of archive releases that not only became ever more frequent but made *Biograph* seem like small beer.

KNOCKED OUT LOADED

By Sean Egan

US release: 8 August 1986
Produced by: Sundog Productions/Bob Dylan and Tom Petty
CHARTS: US#54; UK#35

You Wanna Ramble
They Killed Him
Driftin' Too Far from Shore
Precious Memories
Maybe Someday
Brownsville Girl
Got My Mind Made Up
Under Your Spell

If people thought that the end of his evangelical phase meant that the period of being embarrassed to be a Dylan fan was now over, they were wrong.

As the Eighties progressed, Dylan got ever more weird. Considering his good looks, Dylan has always understandably been a vain man, refusing to wear spectacles despite his chronic short-sightedness, preferring to sport prescription shades. However, those 1968 Elliott Landy Woodstock photographs had seemed to indicate a man who had put such narcissism behind him. The flamboyance of his Rolling Thunder Revue get-ups could be dismissed as something dictated by the fact that he was also shooting a movie, but there was now no disguising the fact that Dylan was going through the kind of change that – of all people – Rod Stewart went through in the late Seventies when he morphed from unpretentious Everyman into preening embarrassment. The buccaneer boots Dylan wore on stage for a while actually suited him, and there's nothing particularly wrong in taking care of one's appearance, especially if you have the features to bring it off. But when Dylan began wearing studs in his ears and spandex trousers, a question of dignity arose. The man was in his mid-forties, for God's sake. Meanwhile, though he was no longer shoving the Bible down people's throats, his public utterances demonstrated that he was still a true believer, and furthermore a true believer in a somewhat weird branch of world religion. Dylan used the aftermath of the 1986 *Challenger* tragedy in which seven astronauts lost their lives to return to the subject of his extreme aversion to space travel, commenting, "They had no business being up there in the first place."

All of which would have been irrelevant to his dwindling number of fans if he was making even merely good music, let alone the type of epoch-marking classics that had once come so easily to him. In 1986, Dylan caused great excitement by touring with Tom Petty's Heartbreakers backing him, provoking the mouth-watering prospect of him recording with a cohesive unit hot off the road. Almost predictably, Dylan failed to do that. Petty has suggested he didn't have the songs, but surely he could have re-recorded unreleased stuff from the archives? Instead, Dylan unleashed *Knocked Out Loaded* on the world, a mixture of tracks recorded in April/May 1986 in Topanga Canyon and basic tracks from the *Empire Burlesque* sessions given new overdubs in May. It contained only two songs solely written by Dylan and – just as the CD age was making consumers expect more bang for their buck – boasted a playing time of just 35:34.

The cover of Little Junior Parker's 'You Wanna Ramble' that opens proceedings features esteemed names like Al Kooper and guitarist T. Bone Burnett. It might possibly have been engaging were it not for the fact that Dylan – the album's producer behind the Sundog Productions name – allows the engineers to utilise that pounding, unbearable Eighties drum technique. As with every other track, a female chorus is present. 'They Killed him' – Kris Kristofferson's equivalent of martyr's anthem 'Abraham, Martin and John' – is the utterly bizarre second cut. Kristofferson has written some great songs, and that line in 'Me and Bobby McGee' about the windscreen wipers slapping time to the characters' singing is worthy of Dylan himself. This one, though, is utterly mawkish. Dylan can't possibly be unaware of this fact – so why does he throw in a children's choir? A track you wouldn't believe unless you'd heard it.

'Driftin' Too Far from Shore' is the first Dylan song of the set, a dreary final kiss-off to an on-again, off-again partner that could be about Sara. Either way, Ron Wood's presence can't help a song engulfed in Eighties-alia. Nice solo though. A reggae arrangement is given to traditional song 'Precious Memories'. Compared to what surrounds it, it's mercifully understated – until such time as steel drums are introduced, and then it seems of a piece with the prevailing madness. The Dylan-written You'll-Be-Sorry anthem 'Maybe Someday' sounds like it might be addressed to the same person as 'Driftin' Too Far from Shore'. It's just as spiritually tiresome as that, though it might have amounted to something instrumentally if the backing didn't sound like it was covered by a film and wasn't obscured by those infuriating drums.

'Brownsville Girl' sprawls across eleven minutes of the album, i.e., about one third of it. This rewritten version of 'New Danville Girl', the song controversially not included on *Empire Burlesque*, is a collaboration with playwright Sam Shepard. The track is narrated by someone who views his life through the prism of a half-remembered Gregory Peck movie and who goes on a journey that gives rise to a picaresque lyric. It's got some poor lines ("It blows right through me like a ball and chain"), but some good ones too ("You always said people don't do what they believe in/They just do what's most convenient/Then they repent"). It also boasts some nice sax passages and intriguingly proactive female vocals. Unfortunately, what could have been a Dylan Hall of Fame entry is ruined by a ham-fisted muffled mix.

'Got My Mind Made Up' is co-written (and co-produced) with Tom Petty. It's a Gotta-Move-On song with a patronising tone. So was 'Don't Think Twice, It's All Right', but the drop in Dylan's technique and likeability since then is catastrophic. Those who point to the lines "Someone's watchin' over you/He won't do nothin' to you/Baby that I wouldn't do" as evidence of an intact genius are fooling themselves.

That the album ends with a previously unthinkable collaboration with Carole Bayer Sager – co-composer of lightweight fare like 'Nobody Does It Better', 'A Groovy Kind of Love' and 'Arthur's Theme' – is symptomatic. Sager later said that only her title survived intact from her input into 'Under Your Spell' but few would want to lay claim to this creation anyway. Interesting that even when co-writing with a woman, Dylan is still irredeemably patronising: he uses the word "baby" more times than one cares to count and tosses off charming sentiments like "You'll never get rid of me as long as you're alive". The song's crassness is exacerbated by a mix that all but makes the instrumentation sound like it's coming down a telephone line.

The significance of Charles Sappington's bandit movie-style album cover art is a mystery but it's about the only halfway impressive thing on an aesthetic disaster worse than *Self Portrait*, one made the more disturbing by the fact that – unlike that album – Dylan is clearly actually trying.

One of the few songs Dylan did record with the Heartbreakers was 'Band of the Hand'. Amazingly considering *Empire Burlesque* and other recent artistic failures, Dylan was commissioned to write the theme tune to the movie of the same title. Released in April 1986, it was about as good as might be expected, both artistically and in terms of chart performance.

On a happier note, June 1986 had seen Dylan marry his backing singer of recent years Carolyn Dennis, who had given birth to his daughter Desiree that January. The marriage remained unknown to his fans and the public at large until almost a decade after their 1992 divorce.

DOWN IN THE GROOVE

By Sean Egan

US release: 31 May 1988
Produced by: –
CHARTS: US#61; UK#32

Let's Stick Together
When Did You Leave Heaven?
Sally Sue Brown
Death is Not the End
Had a Dream about You, Baby
Ugliest Girl in the World
Silvio
Ninety Miles an Hour (Down a Dead End Street)
Shenandoah
Rank Strangers to Me

In July 1987, Dylan went on an American tour with the Grateful Dead. Naturally, this fascinating pair-up of two of the biggest counter-culture icons and recording artists of the Sixties did not result in a studio album. Nor did Dylan's European tour with the Heartbreakers in September and October. That would have been far too easy and far too likely to result in a good album worthy of Dylan's reputation. He preferred to besmirch that reputation by starring in the execrable movie *Hearts of Fire* with Rupert Everett, released in the UK on 9 October 1987, four days before the release of the soundtrack. He was reasonably effective in the film but the fact that he must have realized from the script how cheesy it was going to be begs the question of why on earth he signed up for it. Dylan played a rock star named Billy Parker who gave up his life of riches at the very top of the tree, but there the resemblance to the well-regarded 1970 Mick Jagger movie *Performance* ends. The two original songs Dylan contributed failed to convey why the character he played had become a superstar: it's rather difficult to write great songs to order even when you're not suffering from writer's block. It really is impossible to evaluate how Dylan's mind was working if he actually thought this movie was going to bolster his legend, the one he allowed to be celebrated by consenting to be inducted into the Rock and Roll Hall of Fame in January 1988. The *Hearts of Fire* soundtrack album featured three Dylan tracks in all, his originals 'Night After Night' and 'Had a Dream about You, Baby' plus 'The Usual', written by John Hiatt. Said soundtrack is exceedingly rare and sells for knocking on for £50 on the Internet, which only goes to show that rarity doesn't necessarily equate with high quality.

Dylan's next, "proper" album *Down in the Groove* wasn't actually much better than the *Hearts of Fire* soundtrack. As before, the dearth of new solo Dylan compositions screams out lack of inspiration: just two, with one of them having already appeared on the *Hearts of Fire* soundtrack in slightly different form. He is even co-writing less, collaborating on two songs (this time with the Grateful Dead's lyricist Robert Hunter) as opposed to three on *Knocked Out Loaded*. The remainder of the ten tracks are cover versions. Dylan is producer again (although doesn't seem prepared to take formal credit).

Wilbert Harrison's 'Let's Stick Together' has famously been covered by Canned Heat and re-imagined by Bryan Ferry. This version is stodgy but serviceable, though into what service one would wish to press it is difficult to imagine. The heart sinks at the introduction to 'When Did You Leave Heaven?', the type of dreary, cold synthesiser landscape that "graced" many a now forgotten Eighties recording. Despite that, it's a decidedly non-rock-era song, once a hit for Guy Lombardo. This ballad with archaic sentiments fades out not long past the two-minute mark, with no particular point having been made. 'Sally Sue Brown' was the first ever record by Arthur Alexander, the Sixties R&B star who was one of John Lennon's favourite artists. Dylan recruited The Sex Pistols' Steve Jones and The Clash's Paul Simonon to play on his version, although the female chorus indicates he wasn't looking for a punk ambience. There are Fifties-style rockabilly vocal "Uh-huh"s and a saxophone on the track, but buried deep in a maladroit mix in which pleasure-destroying drums are to the fore.

The tracks written or co-written by Dylan are all clumped together in the middle of the album. The presence of Sly & Robbie, Alan Clark and Mark Knopfler on 'Death is Not the End', the first Dylan song of the album, betrays it as an offcut from *Infidels*, raising questions about the vintage of some of the recordings. Though he engaged in half a dozen recording sessions across May and June 1987, in some cases Dylan was tarting up rejects dating as far back as six years. It's an indictment of Dylan's lack of inspiration at this time that a song previously considered second-rate by him is a highlight in this context. It's not a great track, and is unquestionably hardcore religious, with Dylan consoling himself that despite his loneliness and uncertainty, he has the prospect of a great reward, "When the cities are on fire with the burning flesh of men." However, it starts with some nice harmonica and possesses a quietude that comes as a blessed relief after the directionless cacophony of the first three tracks. The voguish hip-hop outfit Full Force were brought in for this revival of the track to give it a spurious contemporary relevance with some vocal overdubs. 'Had a Dream About You, Baby', the other cut Dylan wrote on his own, features Ron Wood and Eric Clapton. The spectacular results one might be tempted to expect from such a stellar line-up don't materialise and Dylan's attempt at a Fifties rock 'n' roll groove falls a bit short of authenticity, but in actual fact the track is quite agreeable, possessing energy and a catchy refrain. Dylan almost sounds relieved to be able to pen a lyric of jivin' mindlessness rather than poetic meaningfulness.

The gritty R&B track 'Ugliest Girl in the World' is the first of the Hunter collaborations. It's difficult for the track to surmount its mean-spiritedness – though Dylan says he loves the titular physically challenged lady, even the female backing vocalists chorus "Man, she's ugly!" – it does have a certain appeal on a cartoon level. The profoundly more sophisticated 'Silvio' is the other Hunter co-write, sequenced directly afterwards. A brisk and high-spirited rascal's anthem shot through with what sounds like more Armageddon rhetoric, it feels better thought-out than anything else here. It even has rich and worthwhile female backing vocals, as opposed to the weedy and pointless accompanying singing in other places.

It's back to the covers with 'Ninety Miles an Hour (Down a Dead End Street)', an old number by country artist Hank Snow. Like the two tracks that follow it, there are no drums. Dylan sings passionately against a piano-dominated backdrop, with Willie Green and Bobby King providing lugubrious supporting vocals. 'Shenandoah' is a Wild West song as old as the hills, or at least older than notions of copyright. Dylan's arrangement consists of his very good harmonica, bass and a four-woman backing chorus, the latter quartet's tones providing dulcet contrast to Dylan's grizzled old prospector voice. Pretty good. 'Rank Strangers to Me', a tale of a man returning to his hometown and finding himself the odd man out, is most well-known in a version by bluegrass outfit the Stanley Brothers. Dylan's intimate rendition – just him and a bassist – closes proceedings on a melancholy note.

The album, which has an unimaginative cover shot of Dylan shrouded in shadow with minuscule (and in the title's case vertical) lettering, is even shorter than its parsimonious predecessor. While not many can be imagined desiring more of this thin gruel, that it clocks in at thirty-two minutes is nigh-on insulting. Nonetheless, it's slightly more substantial than *Knocked Out Loaded* insofar as the new songs are better, some of the covers feel almost as if they were worth the effort of recording, the production is less insufferable and it doesn't at any point descend into insanity. Which is not the greatest review Dylan has ever received. Silence would probably have been a better option than releasing *Down in the Groove*. Amazingly, it didn't do disgracefully in the UK charts, although in America followed Dylan's reputation into freefall.

The month after the album's release, Dylan began what has come to be known as his Never Ending Tour. The nomenclature is misleading. Though he loves live work and said in 1984, "I only make records because people see me live", Dylan is by no means ceaselessly on the road. However, the hundred or so dates he has continued to play per year since 1988 is a quantity almost unknown for anybody other than artists trading in nostalgia, almost all of whom do not continue to record regularly. His schedule has become all the more astonishing as he ages. Some have suggested the schedule is additionally astonishing because of the fact that Dylan doesn't seem to enjoy gigging. He has offered that his lack of communicativeness is down to the fact that he thinks his songs say it all: "It breaks up my concentration to have to think of things to say or to respond to the crowd," he explained in 1989.

Dylan has made several comments down the years indicating a yearning for a group set-up, remarking almost with jealously that the Jagger-Richards and Lennon-McCartney songwriting axes of The Rolling Stones and The Beatles constituted the type of mutually supportive artistic environment to which he as a solo act had almost never had access. One day in 1988, fate conspired to give him – late in his career – just such a set-up: The Traveling Wilburys. Johnny Black provides the background to the group – and a reappraisal of a record that went down better with the public (Dylan had never previously sold records in such quantities) than the critics.

RECLAIMING *THE TRAVELING WILBURYS VOLUME ONE*

By Johnny Black

First published in *Q*, December 1999

As the millennium drew to a close, one *NME* reviewer found himself confronted by a Barenaked Ladies single. Trawling the depths of his thesaurus of odious comparisons, he elected to describe the offending item as sounding like "a Traveling Wilburys B-side". Similarly, a 1988 review of Ringo Starr's *Vertical Man* album lambasted it for its resemblance to the "Traveling Wilburys sound that Jeff Lynne concocted as a passionless, monochrome facsimile of What The Beatles Might Have Sounded Like".

Indeed, since its release to a veritable tsunami of critical apathy on 25 October 1988, *The Traveling Wilburys Volume One* has become a synonym for every ill that ever ailed the music business. It was the last fart of four old bores, and one slightly younger windbreaker, masquerading as a supergroup. It was self-indulgent. It was over-produced. It was irrelevant. And, possibly its worst crime of all, it caused punters to ignore the wit and wisdom of the world's critical elite, by actually going out and buying it. With no Top 20 single and no attendant tour, the album spent a slow-burning thirty-five weeks on the UK charts, peaking at No.16, and thirty-two weeks on the US chart, peaking at No.3. *Traveling Wilburys Volume One* went platinum within a year of release.

How could the public have got it so wrong?

The Traveling Wilburys came about almost entirely from the workings of serendipity. In the spring of 1988, the five participants were all, co-incidentally, in Los Angeles. Bob Dylan was readying himself for a summer tour. George Harrison, riding the success of his comeback album, *Cloud Nine*, was preparing a B-side for a single. Former ELO supremo Jeff Lynne, who had produced *Cloud Nine*, was in town handling production duties on Roy Orbison's comeback album, *Mystery Girl*. Tom Petty, his star not currently in the ascendant, was just around.

"Jeff Lynne and I were writing songs at Jeff's house and George came in," explained Roy Orbison when asked how it had all started. "We went out for dinner and George said he needed to write and record a third song for a European single and we all agreed to do it."

The song was planned as a B-side, but imminent release of the single tied Harrison to such a tight deadline that booking a major studio would prove difficult. Recalling that Dylan had a functioning home studio in Malibu, Harrison simply rang him up and secured an immediate agreement to pop over the next day and make use of the facility. Then, having recently left his guitar at Petty's house, Harrison popped round to collect it and invited Tom along to the impromptu recording session.

As Harrison subsequently pointed out, had he tried to organise such a superstar gathering through their managers and record companies, it would never have happened. Instead, necessity being the mother of invention, a bunch of guitar-strumming millionaire mates came together round the barbecue on Dylan's lawn and started knocking a song together. It was not even planned that Dylan should participate. In retrospect however it's obvious that, of them all, Dylan was the one famed for his spontaneous one-take approach to recording, the one who thrived in such situations.

Inevitably, when Harrison and Lynne found themselves stuck

for a lyric, they turned to Dylan. As Harrison tells it, "I was saying, 'Come on, give us some lyrics then.' And there was Bob saying, 'Well, what's it about? What's it called?' And I was looking round in Dylan's garage, and behind the garage door there was this big cardboard box that said 'Handle With Care'. I said, 'It's called "Handle With Care".' And he said, 'Oh, that's good. I like that.'"

Dylan's harmony vocal is unmistakeable in the bridge, his wheezy harmonica wails plaintively in the closing moments, but the whole song bears the stamp of his lyric, and the jangly guitars suggest what might have come about had Dylan ever been recorded in the pop context of The Byrds.

More than pleased with his hastily cobbled 'Handle With Care', Harrison took it to Warners, where it was immediately declared too good to throw away on a B-side. Harrison began to think seriously of recording a bunch more tracks and releasing an entire album with his buddies but Dylan's tour was scheduled to start in late May.

On the seventh of that month, with less than a fortnight to spare, the gang all came together at Eurythmic Dave Stewart's Los Angeles pad. Dylan was the first to wade in, with the idea of doing something that sounded like Prince. The resulting track, 'Dirty Mind', pieced together in Stewart's kitchen with lyrics found at random in the pages of glossy magazines, sounds nothing like Prince, but it does sound like Dylan having more fun than he'd had since the Sixties.

The most predictable clash of personalities, between the spontaneously improvising Dylan and the arch-perfectionist producer Lynne, never seems to have happened, presumably because Lynne knew he'd have time to work his post-production magic in the studio after Dylan had departed for his tour. But perfectionist or not, Lynne was more than sharp enough not to gloss over Dylan's rough edges because, throughout the album, while the others construct stylishly evocative Fifties pop pastiches, Dylan provides the grit that lifts it into another league. His righteous bitterness in the heavily ironic 'Congratulations', for example, is as incisive as anything from *Blood on the Tracks*, the ideal counterweight to Orbison's all-time-loser persona and Lynne's lightweight pop perfection.

Dylan comes into sharpest focus with 'Tweeter and the Monkey Man', a curiously straggling urban-nightmare tale fusing bluesy licks and Eagles-y backing vocals which he and Petty put together. "Jeff and I were there too," recalls Harrison, "but they were talking about all this stuff which didn't make sense to me – Americana kind of stuff. And then we got a tape cassette and put it on and transcribed everything they were saying and wrote it down. And then Bob sort of changed it anyway ... It was just fantastic watching him do it because he sang ... he had one take warming himself up and then he did it for real on take two, right through. It's just unbelievable seeing how he does it."

Having finished the album in record time, Harrison and Lynne concocted a fantasy press release based on an in-joke they'd evolved during the making of *Cloud Nine*, about an ailment known as the Trembling Wilburys which overcomes musicians as dawn approaches after a long night in the studio. Trembling became Traveling, and each band member took on a nom-de-clef, with Dylan becoming Lucky Wilbury, while Lynne, Harrison, Orbison, and Petty became, respectively, Otis, Nelson, Lefty and Charlie T Jr.

Given that the only 20–20 vision is hindsight, an objective listen to *Traveling Wilburys Volume One* now reveals five like-minded musicians having a good time together in the kitchen, and even hardened critics will acknowledge that Dylan's subsequent album, *Oh Mercy*, was easily his best work in two decades. As Harrison subsequently noted, "if that's all the Wilburys did, was help get Bob enthusiastic again, that's something".

DYLAN & THE DEAD/OH MERCY

By Sean Egan

DYLAN & THE DEAD
(Bob Dylan/Grateful Dead)
US release: 6 February 1989
Produced by: Jerry Garcia and John Cutler
CHARTS: US#37; UK#38

Slow Train
I Want You
Gotta Serve Somebody
Queen Jane Approximately
Joey
All Along the Watchtower
Knockin' on Heaven's Door

The cover of *Dylan & the Dead* features the sort of artwork you might expect in a fanzine: a coloured-in drawing depicting the Dead's "Stealie" skull logo opposite the head of Dylan circa 1966. The skull has a Dylan hallmark – a harmonica brace – and reflected in Dylan's shades is a streak of lightning, a hallmark of the Stealie skull. Even the album's title – succinctly descriptive though it is – feels like the phraseology of a fanboy's fantasy billing. The album's contents are hardly more professional. The Dead were a band very familiar with Dylan's oeuvre (*Postcards of the Hanging*, a collection of Grateful Dead live performances of Dylan songs down the decades, appeared in 2002.) A bit of a pity then that the album that was the commercially released aural representation of the Dylan/Grateful Dead tour reduces the excitement of these two titans together on a stage to a collection of oldies more poorly performed than you might expect of the average bar band.

The album provides selections from four concerts. It starts

off fairly well, the version of 'Slow Train' presenting an intriguingly different angle on the song via a chugging, slightly funky arrangement and neat Grateful Dead harmonies. Additionally, the low-key 'I Want You' is sweet. However those nice harmonies and the occasionally decent Jerry Garcia solo can't salvage songs subjected to clattering, metallic arrangements and Dylan lead vocals that are fuzzy either through sloppiness or fatigue. Both the Dead and Dylan are atrocious on 'Joey', and remain so for the nine-minutes-plus duration. Moreover, the Dead seem to be playing the same backing as they do on 'Queen Jane Approximately'. By the time we are treated to some blissful piano and guitar work on 'Knockin' on Heaven's Door' (which in any case don't gel with the song), patience and goodwill are gone. Due to, presumably, the two sets of fanbases, the album did quite well, but there was no disguising that this was pure product and in no way artistic statement.

OH MERCY
US release: 22 September 1989
Produced by: Daniel Lanois
CHARTS: US#30; UK#6

Political World
Where Teardrops Fall
Everything is Broken
Ring Them Bells
Man in the Long Black Coat
Most of the Time
What Good Am I?
Disease of Conceit
What Was It You Wanted
Shooting Star

Shortly before he began to write the songs that made up *Oh Mercy*, Dylan had contemplated giving up music.

A combination of a bad hand injury that prevented him playing guitar, a conviction that he was no longer cutting it live and a disinclination to write new songs caused him to think about entering the "real world" and becoming a businessman.

However, canvassing the advice of someone versed in that real world profoundly depressed him, specifically when he contemplated what business he might pick to run. When the song 'Political World' poured out of him one day, he found the appetite for writing coming back. Seeing his new lyrics (there were no melodies), Bono put him in touch with Daniel Lanois. Like Baker before him, he was a name producer with a recognizable sound. Unlike Baker's, though, Lanois' sound was warm and classic, not the result of momentarily fashionable gimmicks. Moreover, via his involvement with Peter Gabriel's *So* and U2's *The Joshua Tree*, he had helmed two of the major albums of the recently inaugurated CD age. Dylan had the opportunity to work with a producer associated with success, therefore, whose participation would not constitute something beneath his dignity. Dylan agreed to record in New Orleans with a group of musicians assembled by Lanois. The often bad-tempered recording process is documented by Dylan at length in *Chronicles Volume One*, including Lanois refusing to accept both Dylan's occasional laziness and his one-take modus operandi (basic tracks were recorded in March 1989 but Dylan went back in April to overdub vocals). The result was a very listenable album – even if there are several clinkers, nothing on it is classic and the whole enterprise sounds suspiciously like a self-conscious attempt to come up with something that might be perceived as a blessed return to form.

Ironically, the song that kicked all this off, and which kicks off the album, is empty. 'Political World' shows as much insight into geopolitical conflict and the crises afflicting mankind as *Shot of Love*'s risible 'Trouble' ("Wisdom is thrown into jail/It rots in a cell, is misguided as hell"). 'Where Teardrops Fall' gets things going properly. Floating on a bed of keening guitar and finished with a dreamy saxophone flourish, it sees Dylan showing unusually unequivocal sentiment, even if one suspects that some of the imagery is half-baked ("We could hold up a toast if we meet/To the cuttin' of fences/To sharpen the senses/That linger in the fireball heat"). 'Everything is Broken' sounds like it was written to sum up, albeit impressionistically, Dylan's recent period of depression. It's an exercise in laziness that sees Dylan opting for a melody that is more a rhythm and for rhymes easy to the point of meaninglessness like, "Hound dog howling, bullfrog croaking/ Everything is broken". 'Ring Them Bells' is one of those songs which belch fire and brimstone in as veiled a way as possible which Dylan had taken to including on recent albums. This attractive piano ballad contains lines like "Ring them bells for the chosen few/Who will judge the many when the game is through."

On album highlight 'Man in the Long Black Coat', pinging guitars, droplets of piano and lonesome harmonica are treated with echo and mixed cleverly to create an atmosphere perfect for a song infused with the voodoo menace of New Orleans. For once, Dylan's increasingly croaky voice matches the material. 'Most of the Time' sees Dylan reflecting on the ghost of a love affair in a song sweetly honest about his ambivalence ("I don't even care if I ever see her again/Most of the time"). The fragility continues on 'What Good Am I?', a litany in which Dylan against a lovely aural backdrop questions his worth in his moments of neglecting to do the right thing, usually in domestic scenarios. 'Disease of Conceit' is in the same vein as the previous track in its implicit humility, even if we are uncomfortably aware that the intact sense of having been saved from on high Dylan has demonstrated in 'Ring Them Bells' would seem to contradict the message. It also doesn't offer any insight but instead, like much here, sees Dylan expending his energies solely on finding rhymes ("Then they bury you from your head to your feet/From the disease of conceit").

The shimmering soundscapes created by Lanois make the five minutes of 'What Was It You Wanted' a perfectly pleasant way to pass the time but – again like much here – Dylan makes his point across several more verses than his message (a vague statement of uncertainty of where he is in a relationship) merits. Willie Green's pulsing work, incidentally, reminds us that this is the first Dylan album in a long time whose drums don't assault our senses. 'Shooting Star' would be a touching closer were it not for the fact that Dylan spoils the meekness of the verses ("Did I miss the mark or overstep the line?") with a bridge that shows him still on his high horse of piety ("All good people are praying/It's the last temptation, the last account").

Oh Mercy – which has sleeve art by a graffiti merchant called Trotsky – is a series of slow, sensual soundscapes that shows that

Dylan still has something to offer but that he is also quite a way short of his former abilities. Several times we are reminded by self-consciously Dylanesque lines that this is a man feeling his way back into his talent. We are also as uncomfortably aware as Dylan must have been that Lanois – whose production work on more than one track makes all the difference between interesting and negligible – needs Dylan less than Dylan needs him.

UNDER THE RED SKY

By Sean Egan

US release: 11 September 1990
Produced by: Don Was and David Was and Jack Frost
CHARTS: US#38; UK#13

Wiggle Wiggle
Under the Red Sky
Unbelievable
Born in Time
T.V. Talkin' Song
10,000 Men
2 X 2
God Knows
Handy Dandy
Cat's in the Well

"Dedicated to Lefty Wilbury" read the liner notes to *Traveling Wilburys Vol. 3*, the mischievously titled follow-up to the Traveling Wilburys' debut released on 23 October 1990. It was an acknowledgement of the fact that Roy Orbison had sadly not lived to see the mega success of that release, having passed away less than two months later. Without Orbison, or the novelty factor of that first star-studded occasion, the second Wilburys release shifted two-thirds fewer units, though did respectably enough.

Bob Dylan later complained that recording the second Traveling Wilburys album in March/April 1990 more or less simultaneously with his follow-up to *Oh Mercy* resulted in his *Under the Red Sky* being sub-standard. In fact, Dylan seems to have written an entire album of shallow, playful tracks that would have been better suited to the Wilburys – and better played by them even though this album was packed to the gunnels with famous musicians, David Crosby, George Harrison, Bruce Hornsby, Elton John, Al Kooper, Slash and Stevie Ray Vaughan among them. Said musicians were employed more in a cameo capacity than as an integral part of a recording process that mainly took place in the second half of March 1990, with vocal overdubs (and apparently lyric re-writing) going into the next month.

The cover depicted Dylan crouching thoughtfully on a barren landscape, the picture black and white but his name and the album title spelled out in crimson. Dylan co-produced (using the *nom de guerre* Jack Frost). His collaborators in the control booth were the Was brothers, the most prominent component of which was Don Was, yet another fashionable producer. Though Was had given a new lease of life to veterans like Bonnie Raitt, The B52's, Iggy Pop and Michael McDonald, resorting to him was a bewildering backward step by Dylan after having availed himself of the exquisite subtly of Lanois' approach. Was is, quite simply, one of the most overrated producers of all time and it remains astonishing that people who should know better like Dylan and The Rolling Stones rather than point out that the emperor has no clothes instead ask Was to be their tailor. It is embarrassing that Dylan, who once dismissed producers ruthlessly if he felt they weren't up to snuff, now seemed overawed by any knob-twiddler with an aura of fashionability.

The first bad sign is that the album clocks in at a paltry thirty-five and a half minutes. The second bad sign follows quickly thereafter in the shape of opener 'Wiggle Wiggle', which slice of nonsense has oxymoronic thudding drum work. Slash doesn't bring any of Guns N' Roses' sonic power with him to a track that is never as charming in its silliness as it thinks it is.

Someone's having a laugh on the title track, which has keyboard runs very similar to some of 'Like a Rolling Stone' and 'Positively 4th Street' – and, what do you know, Al Kooper is one of the personnel. Another of the personnel, George Harrison, contributes lovely slide guitar on an enjoyable and well-crafted rock 'n' roll nursery rhyme. 'Unbelievable' is a bulldozing uptempo number whose second verse seems to be taking a pop at yuppies that is not only belated but somewhat undermined by a crass liner comment that "a limited edition of notes by the artist to the songs that appear on the album" has been "secured" by Entertainment Connections, who invite anyone interested in "receiving this collector's item" to write to a provided address to find out how to place their order. One wonders what said notes have to say about the lazy-bordering-on-trite rhyming in 'Unbelievable', the kind we have unfortunately come to expect of Dylan's lyrics in recent years. 'Born in Time' is also what we have latterly come to expect: a song seemingly written for a partner with whom he has a long, long history, not necessarily unbroken and of mixed degrees of contentment. It's difficult not to see it as another ode to Sara, but one doesn't need detailed knowledge of Dylan's private life to find it affecting. It's full of creamy guitars and would merit the adjective gossamer were it not for the inappropriately loud drums.

'T.V. Talkin' Song' is a story song. The narrator sees a man at London's Hyde Park Corner preaching about the evils of television. The narrator's concentration wanders but the speech is enough to provoke unrest in the crowd, which furore gets filmed by visiting television cameras. The narrator watches this furore on his television screen later that evening. This tale of irony-flecked mundanity could work: after all, Dylan made more out of even less with 'Clothes Line Saga'. But that song talked about nothing in a highly amusing way to understated accompaniment. This track has vaguely irritating monotonous mid-tempo instrumentation and a lyric that provides no memorable lines or interesting viewpoints other than that banal twist in the tail.

The reference to men dressed in Oxford blue in the bluesy '10,000 Men' makes us momentarily think it's a Civil War parable or narrative, but by the time we get to the couplet "Ten thousand men digging for silver and gold/All clean shaven, all coming in from the cold", that certainty is dissipating, and evaporates altogether with "Ten thousand women all sweepin' my room/Spilling my buttermilk, sweeping it up with a broom", as does any conviction that this number amounts to anything whatsoever aesthetically. The slow, incantation-like '2 X 2' is aurally pleasant but lyrically meaningless, seeming at points to be about entry to heaven or to the Ark, but then receding from meaning with lines like "Six by six/They were playing with tricks". 'God Knows' is the now obligatory You'll-Be-Sorry track ("God knows there's gonna be no more water/But fire next time"), but there's no denying the enjoyability of this sprightly, bare R&B, with Dylan's raw guitar to the fore. 'Handy Dandy' is a curious number, and not just because – typical of his ham-fistedness – Was makes the piano less audible than the drums. Dylan sings of the titular semi-mythical character to a not-half-bad melody and against something approaching a nice groove. There are the odd pleasing lines like "Handy Dandy, if every bone in his body was broken he would never admit it/He got an all-girl orchestra and when he says 'Strike up the band,' they hit it". Unfortunately, though, like so much current Dylan fare, it doesn't go anywhere, departing the stage with the audience puzzled as to what point has been made. 'Cat's in the Well' is R&B crossed with fable. Though it is confused and certainly not possessed of menace, if that was the object, it could have been a good track had Was given prominence to some nice brass instead of obscuring it in the shadows.

And that's it. All the hopes that had been raised by *Oh Mercy* that we were just about to be in the position once more where we'd Got Dylan Back Again had been dashed. The sense of deflation and disgust for those Dylan fans who hadn't already walked away from his music was bottomless. It seemed to be a feeling shared by Dylan. *Traveling Wilburys Vol. 3* followed the month afterwards and contained a clutch of good new songs written by or with significant input from Boo Wilbury, as Dylan was now billed, but *Under the Red Sky* was the last collection of new songs from Dylan for seven years. Though he continued to play the live shows he loved, he had apparently given up the impossible task of finding within him the genius he had once possessed and resigned himself to being yesterday's man, unable to do anything but crank out his old classics on the world's stages and purvey new versions of traditional songs in the recording studios.

He'd had his fallow periods before, but this now did indeed seem to be – to use a phrase that had cropped up more than once in his songs – the final end.

THE BOOTLEG SERIES VOLUMES 1–3: (RARE & UNRELEASED) 1961–1991

By Sean Egan

US release: 26 March 1991
Produced by: Jeff Rosen
CHARTS: US#49; UK#32

DISC ONE
Hard Times in New York Town
He Was a Friend of Mine
Man on the Street
No More Auction Block
House Carpenter
Talkin' Bear Mountain Picnic Massacre Blues
Let Me Die in My Footsteps
Rambling, Gambling Willie
Talkin' Hava Negeilah Blues
Quit Your Low Down Ways
Worried Blues
Kingsport Town
Walkin' Down the Line
Walls of Red Wing
Paths of Victory
Talkin' John Birch Paranoid Blues
Who Killed Davey Moore?
Only a Hobo
Moonshiner
When the Ship Comes In
The Times They Are A-Changin'
Last Thoughts on Woody Guthrie

DISC TWO
Seven Curses
Eternal Circle
Suze (The Cough Song)
Mama, You Been on My Mind
Farewell, Angelina
Subterranean Homesick Blues
If You Gotta Go, Go Now (Or Else You Got to Stay All Night)
Sitting on a Barbed Wire Fence
Like a Rolling Stone
It Takes a Lot to Laugh, It Takes a Train to Cry
I'll Keep It with Mine
She's Your Lover Now
I Shall Be Released
Santa-Fe
If Not for You
Wallflower
Nobody 'Cept You
Tangled Up in Blue
Call Letter Blues
Idiot Wind

DISC THREE
If You See Her, Say Hello
Golden Loom
Catfish
Seven Days
Ye Shall Be Changed
Every Grain of Sand
You Changed My Life
Need a Woman
Angelina
Someone's Got a Hold of My Heart
Tell Me
Lord Protect My Child
Foot of Pride
Blind Willie McTell
When the Night Comes Falling from the Sky
Series of Dreams

On 20 February 1991, Dylan accepted a Lifetime Achievement Grammy award.

His acceptance speech was disturbing. Though rock stars are somewhat less gushing and pseudo-sincere than are Hollywood celebrities when accepting baubles, they at least give the impression of being happy to be a recipient – and exhibit a modicum of pleasure at the fact of being alive. Dylan instead recalled the words of his father, who he said told him, "It's possible to become so defiled in this world that your own mother and father will abandon you, and if that happens, God will always believe in your own ability to mend your own ways." Perhaps a similar despair and self-loathing was what motivated the release the following month of *The Bootleg Series 1–3*.

The chronology and comments by friends suggest Dylan had refused to countenance the release of *The Basement Tapes* until he'd proven to the world that his talent hadn't been left behind in the Sixties. The issuing of the treasure trove of archive material that was this release when he was at a low critical and commercial ebb seemed, in contrast, to signify that Dylan was resigned to having lost whatever original talent he'd once had and that he was surrendering to the perception of him as a man only interesting for his past. Even the cover – a black-and-white shot of a mid-Sixties Dylan standing before an archaic-looking overhead mic – underlined this.

The Bootleg Series 1–3 was for the hardcore fans, the people who, as its wry title alludes, love Dylan so much they buy some of the many illicit releases comprised of his album offcuts and live performances. Significantly, Dylan's office commissioned Dylan fandom's John Bauldie to write the annotations in the lavish interior book. The compilation covers the entirety of Dylan's career up to *Oh Mercy* and consists of all manner of recordings: polished, finished studio tracks left off albums nestling alongside demos, fragments and live performances. The quality is variable but the historical interest consistently high.

The album starts with a private recording made just after Dylan had recorded his debut album. 'Hard Times in New York Town' was one of more than two dozen songs captured by Dylan's university chum Tony Glover in Minneapolis. The tape fell into the hands of bootleggers and became well-known amongst collectors. This was the first time any part of it had seen official release. The track is of surprisingly high fidelity and quality. As previously mentioned, this droll song of a Minnesota kid getting used to the ways of the Big Apple is far better than the debut album's similarly themed 'Talkin' New York'. There are three outtakes from that eponymous debut.

The traditional 'He Was a Friend of Mine' is lovely, featuring some fine harmonica work, while Dylan's singing sensitively teases out the pathos of the story of losing a pal. It would have made a far better inclusion than some of the preposterously world-weary material that did make the cut. As would have Dylan's composition 'Man on the Street', the tale of a vagrant whose dead body is prodded by a less-than-sympathetic police-man with his club, even if it ends too abruptly and casually to reach the heights of 'Only a Hobo', to which it is a precursor. Dylan's rapid-fire guitar work on 'House Carpenter' is impres-sive but like so many public-domain numbers, the song is full of flowery, courtly phraseology that one wonders about the rele-vance of. 'No More Auction Block', recorded at the Gaslight Café in Greenwich Village in the month before the sessions for that debut, is not an outstanding performance but is historically interesting because this anti-slavery traditional is the melodic bedrock upon which Dylan shortly built 'Blowin' in the Wind'.

There are a staggering eight outtakes from *The Freewheelin' Bob Dylan*, thus making for almost an alternative version of an album that ran to thirteen tracks. 'Talkin' Bear Mountain Picnic Massacre Blues' takes as its subject a true-life boat frenzy (though no fatalities occurred in reality) and was written over-night after Dylan had been shown a newspaper clipping. It's funny, although in truth a little too similar in structure and deliv-ery to 'Talkin' World War III Blues', the topicality of which was always going to make it the winner in a fight for a place on *Freewheelin'*. In the quite good 'Let Me Die in My Footsteps' Dylan cocks a snook at the Cold Warriors by announcing that he would rather be incinerated than entomb himself in the type of nuclear fallout shelters that were then doing a roaring trade off the back of the assumption that it might be worth living through a nuclear winter. Bad boy anthem 'Rambling, Gambling Willie' is essentially uninteresting, dealing in the kind of pat scenarios and language that might have gone down well in the coffee-houses but which were really beneath Dylan's gifts. 'Talkin' Hava Negeilah Blues' is forty-nine seconds long. Its bog-standard harmonica riff and unfunnily nonsensical lyric indicates a full version wouldn't have amounted to much. On the rural blues 'Quit Your Low Down Ways', Dylan puts on a growling, yodel-ling and syllable-stretching vocal performance as he inhabits the chiding persona of the narrator who somehow we imagine to be a Negro woman. It's an extraordinary and startling track. The melancholy traditional 'Worried Blues' is nondescript, while 'Kingsport Town' – also a traditional – is simply boring. 'Walls of Red Wing' has been suggested as Dylan's way of expressing his anger at a rumoured despatch by his parents to a strict Pennsylvanian boarding school called Deveraux when he was around eighteen. Unfortunately, any fury at his treatment at the hands of this pedagogical regime is neutered by the song's archaic, bland language and by the flatness of the melody of whatever traditional he had commandeered for his purpose.

The most famous outtake from *Freewheelin'*, of course, is 'Talkin' John Birch Paranoid Blues' and although that pulled track isn't included here, we do get a live version recorded at Carnegie Hall. The infamy of the Ed Sullivan ban sees the audi-ence greet its announcement with gusto. In a song that tickles the funny bone, Dylan mocks the anti-red paranoia that marked the era, the narrator vainly trying to catch commies he imagines disappearing down the toilet bowl and getting punched out by the mailman when he accuses him of being a pinko. Another performance included from the same Carnegie Hall gig is 'Who Killed Davey Moore?', in which the artist explores the culpabil-ity for the recent death in the ring of the real-life boxer of the title, although it has to be said that Dylan's musing on whether the blame lies with the likes of the cigar-puffing manager or the baying audience while declining to acknowledge Moore's own free will is more than disingenuous. But then not having some-body to blame was not what protest music was about.

There are a whopping six outtakes from the album *The Times They Are A-Changin'*. 'Paths of Victory' is a poor man's version of that LP's title track ("There's a clearer road a-waitin'"), even if Dylan's enthusiastic piano self-accompaniment has an attraction. 'Only a Hobo' does what isn't often done: marks a vagrant's passing: "He was only a hobo, but one more is gone" Dylan notes in a compassionate composition. Traditional distiller's anthem 'Moonshiner' is the recipient of some unusually haunting singing by Dylan and some superbly dramatic harmonica work. The fact that gallows song 'Seven Curses' has to reach back into the past to discuss the abuse of power makes it another song that constitutes faux protest. 'Eternal Circle' – a troubadour's tale of failing to hook up with a girl because the gig needed to be fulfilled – is in the same olde worlde vein but can't even boast a tale of judicial injustice to give it some grit. This boring number boasts the rather unfortunate line in the circumstances, "The song it was long and it had to get done". 'Suze (The Cough Song)' is an instrumental with a pretty, winding guitar pattern and competent harmonica work, no doubt titled in tribute to Miss Rotolo. It would have made a good inclusion on the album, complete with Dylan's humorous comment "That was the end", in reference to the point before he is overcome by a cough.

There is a trio of demos recorded for the Witmark Music Publishing Company. Tracks laid down to enable copyright registration rather than intended for wide consumption are hardly a recipe for great art but at least two are fine stuff. The spirited 'Walkin' Down the Line' – nominally a Dylan song but like so many of his originals at that point owing a huge debt to anonymous predecessors – is far more infused with the rock 'n' roll spirit that he was responsible for bringing to the folk scene and therefore far more zestful and enjoyable than the likes of 'Kingsport Town'. The piano-based, almost jaunty 'When the Ship Comes In' is strangely compelling, and indeed preferable to the solemn album master. The demo of 'The Times They Are A-Changin' ' is also just Dylan and piano and unexpectedly works in this arrangement, even if it will never be preferable to the fire-breathing performance of the familiar rendition.

'Last Thoughts on Woody Guthrie' is a poem without music that Dylan recited from the stage at New York City's Town Hall in April 1963. On the page, the tribute to his hero reads well, but Dylan's verbal delivery here is simply too fast, nervous and un-nuanced to have an impact.

'Mama, You Been on My Mind' is the sole *Another Side of Bob Dylan* outtake. The "mama" of the title is of course a lover, a term of endearment Dylan (like the bluesmen in whose music he was steeped) once used more frequently than the likes of "baby" but which began to sound ever more peculiar in a culture increasingly savvy with Freudian theory. Not that that detracts from the composition, which is lovely, especially the verse, "Even though my eyes are hazy and my thoughts they might be narrow/ Where you been don't bother me/Or bring me down with sorrow/I don't even mind who you'll be waking with tomorrow", a piece of writing light years beyond the dreary over-formal phraseology of stuff like 'Eternal Circle' – and indeed some of the less substantial songs on *Another Side*.

Bringing It All Back Home yields three outtakes. 'Farewell, Angelina' is stranded betwixt and between the old and new Dylans. Studded though it is with hipster language ("King Kong, little elves, on the rooftops they dance"), it is borne on one of those slightly tedious frilly melodies that were old when Henry VIII was a nipper, and the two never gel. 'If You Gotta Go, Go Now (Or Else You Got to Stay All Night)' is presented here not in the form that saw it released as a Benelux single but an alternate take. It actually possesses a pleasant groove and some impressive, busy keyboard work but it's not just dated by its ostentatious Sixties promiscuity but also by its slightly bullying tone.

'Subterranean Homesick Blues' here is take one – an acoustic version. What sounds like an exercise in pointlessness is in fact very interesting, for the song works surprisingly well without a band behind it, and Dylan's playful, split-second drop-out of guitar at one point shows somewhat greater sonic imagination than those musicians who backed him on the famous version did. Moving over to a full backing band was something Dylan had to do, but this track proves he needed no group to be rock 'n' roll. 'Sitting on a Barbed Wire Fence' is the first of a trio of tracks rejected for *Highway 61 Revisited*. Its combination of loping slow blues and drolly surreal tone makes it sound more like a *Blonde on Blonde* song, as does its slight insubstantiality – something tauntingly acknowledged by the writer when he intones, "Of course you're gonna think this song is a riff." 'Like a Rolling Stone' legendarily started out not as blazing rock but as a waltz, as proven by the fragment of an early run-through of Dylan's masterpiece heard here: gentle and piano-dominated, it sounds regretful rather than vengeful. It could have worked maybe, even without the lack of emphaticness in the enunciation of the title phrase, although would never have made history like the master take did. 'It Takes a Lot to Laugh, It Takes a Train to Cry' only became the slow, sensual song we know and love when Dylan rearranged it when the musicians were on a lunch break. This alternate (with different words in places) is of a similar pace and ambience to 'From a Buick 6'. It works on no level whatsoever. Interesting simply because it shows on what slender thread of happenstance quality can hang.

'I'll Keep It with Mine' is a sometimes faltering run-through of the song whose demo we heard on *Biograph*. From this, it sounds like it might have made a good selection for *Blonde on Blonde* had it been developed properly, Dylan finding new nocturnal richness in his melody two years on. Bob Johnston has often been dismissed as a cipher of a producer, but his encouragement to Dylan, "What you were doing" near the beginning of proceedings suggests he wasn't someone without opinions to offer. Another *Blonde on Blonde* outtake 'She's Your Lover Now' could also have slotted easily into that album. Which is not the compliment it might sound, this being one of these impeccably played but lyrically impenetrable tracks the type of which formed the uncomfortably substantial second tier of that overrated record.

'I Shall Be Released' and 'Santa-Fe' are two more selections from the Basement Tape recordings that Dylan has been doling out so grudgingly down the years. The former we know, of course, in several different versions, one by Dylan. This musty original is possibly not as good as the re-recording Dylan made with Happy Traum but is very nice, and Richard Manuel's harmony singing is ethereal. The slightly anthemic latter song seems to have an unfinished (or partially forgotten) lyric but is catchy. Never bootlegged either. Er, how do we know this is really from the Basement Tapes?

The alternate take of 'If Not for You' sounds "off" simply because we are so familiar with a different version, but there's no denying that this slower, bluesier rendition is devoid of the tinge of the soporific and the gormless that the master take possessed. 'Wallflower' was recorded at the 'George Jackson' sessions but given away to Doug Sahm and not released by its composer. Dylan's lonesome harmonica is excellent but apart from Jimi Hendrix's 'Manic Depression', great songs in waltz time are rare, especially when they feature lyrics of only moderate invention like this chat-up of a lonely girl. 'Nobody 'Cept You' is the track displaced on *Planet Waves* by 'Wedding Song'. It's suffused with that calm, well-fed, deep-seated affection that so many of the album's songs touchingly are, although the low mix of the vocals does a lovely song a disservice.

Three New York versions of *Blood on the Tracks* songs are featured, although, frustratingly, not cuts from the abandoned original version of the album. The solo version of 'Tangled Up in Blue', like the Big Apple-derived tracks that made it onto the LP, is luxuriant despite its bareness. The lyric is slightly different to the later version but that makes negligible difference. What does make a perhaps surprisingly big difference is the almost exclusive use of the third-person pronoun, making the song to its detriment feel much less immediate and the result of personal experience. 'If You See Her, Say Hello' sounds slightly anxious and hurried, compared to the stateliness – albeit agonised – of the Minneapolis full-band version. An 'Idiot Wind' that is low-key both words- and music-wise rather than seethingly delivered in front of a band sounds a contradiction in terms, although perhaps if we didn't know any better (or other) it might make sense. "I noticed at the ceremony your corrupt ways had finally made you blind" is here the limp-in-comparison "I noticed at the ceremony you left your bags behind". It has been said that part of the reason for Dylan re-recording half of *Blood on the Tracks* is that David Zimmerman felt what he had recorded in New York had too much of a uniformity of tone. With this track, he would seem to have been proven correct – although little brother was no doubt thinking more of a pick-up in tempo rather than the ladling-on of venom that transpired. Meanwhile, Dylan's complaint, excised from the original lyric, that "imitators steal me blind" would have been a valuable and relevant retention three years after Neil Young had hit No.1 in the USA with 'Heart of Gold', which perfectly aurally updated the sound of Dylan's acoustic days, and two years after Stealer's Wheel had had a transatlantic smash with 'Stuck in the Middle With You', an uncanny pastiche of Dylan's lyrical and vocal style circa *Blonde on Blonde*. (Dylan may have been unaware of 'Streets of London' by Ralph McTell, another Dylanesque hit of the period, because its success was restricted to the UK.)

'Call Letter Blues' is the only *Blood on the Tracks*-related song included here that unequivocally works, even though it features the same tune as 'Meet Me in the Morning'. Its lyric is harrowing where the other's is heart-wracked ("Your children cry for mother/I tell them mother took a trip"). Though one can understand Dylan's reluctance to place both tracks on the same album, this tough, brilliantly sung recording strikes one as so worthwhile and so much a complement to 'Meet Me in the Morning' that the solution occurs that the tracks might have topped and tailed the album and thereby created a pair of conceptual bookends.

A brace of *Desire* outtakes follow. 'Golden Loom' is dreamlike and, like all of *Desire*, sumptuously recorded. Its playfulness would have been a boon to that rather sombre album, but there's no denying an overall feeling of flimsiness. 'Catfish', a co-write with Jacques Levy, is a song about a real-life baseball player, which like so many of Dylan's unreleased recordings of all vintages found its way onto other people's records. Joe Cocker and Kinky Friedman also recorded this jazzy, woozy, meandering creation. 'Seven Days', a Dylan composition dating from circa early 1976, is represented in one of Dylan's few live performances before he abandoned it. That he did consign it to obscurity is a shame, for this is a fine song, both in its excited evocation of the week-hence arrival of "My beautiful comrade from the north" (who, going by the words, could even be Dylan's mother) and in its strong riffs on both bass and guitar.

The pace of 'Ye Shall Be Changed' would have made it the one uptempo cut on *Slow Train Coming* had it been included. It has a half-jaunty, half-wistful feel and some fine instrumentation. Good stuff. 'Every Grain of Sand' is the demo of the *Shot of Love* highlight that Dylan laid down for Special Rider Music, which publishing company's saucy title seems a bit inappropriate considering the song's subject matter. What is appropriate is the almost spectral quality the lo-fi nature lends this creation. The transcendent mood is somewhat spoiled by Dylan's dog barking in the background.

A trio of *Shot of Love* outtakes demonstrate how much better that album could have been. 'You Changed My Life' – a love song to a God who "Came along in a time of strife" – is not a great composition (especially when some good lines about Dylan's pre-conversion life "eating with the pigs off a fancy tray" are almost undone by a silly line that informs the almighty "You came in like the wind, like Errol Flynn"). It is, however, better than rubbish like 'Trouble'. 'Need a Woman' is very good (if over-long), its funkiness and slinkiness in no way precluding humility ("Searching for the truth the way God designed it/Well the real truth is that I may be afraid to find it"). The titular woman in 'Angelina' seems to be leading Dylan into temptation ("Your best friend and my worst enemy is one and the same") in another song in which Dylan turns his back on the one-dimensional evangelizing of *Slow Train Coming* to explore a more honest and troubled view of faith with which we can sympathize if not necessarily empathize.

A staggering five *Infidels* outtakes appear – songs whose partial or complete inclusion would have profoundly changed the composition and perception of that eight-track album. 'Someone's Got a Hold of My Heart' eventually morphed into 'Tight Connection to My Heart' on *Empire Burlesque*. The *Infidels*-era incarnation is preferable, an easy-rolling love song with no cacophonous Arthur Bakerisms, even if the pleasing vulnerability of Dylan's "You, you, you"s turns out disappointingly to be something once more intertwined with religious agonising. 'Tell Me' sees Dylan wondering at the unknown qualities of a prospective new paramour. The tinkling music would make it MOR were it not for the literate lyrics ("Ever gone broke in a big way/Ever done the opposite of what the experts say?"). 'Lord Protect My Child' is like 'Forever Young' but with added religiosity. Though it would be fatuous to suggest that Dylan compartmentalise his life, and though it's a different way of approaching his faith that is refreshing compared to the judge-mental stuff, one can't help but feel that it's a shame that where religion was only touched upon in the *Planet Waves* track with the line "May God bless and keep you always", Dylan here seems only able to express affection for his offspring through the prism of his faith, concerned for his/her welfare "In a world that's been raped and defiled". 'Foot of Pride' is a bewildering track that could be about Dylan's regret over his conversion ("Well, there ain't no goin' back/When your foot of pride come down") or conversely even about the unshakability of his faith, but quite frankly one becomes exhausted by the poetic and impenetrable metaphors quite early and uninterested in determining what it is he's blethering on about. 'Blind Willie McTell' is the song that all the Dylan experts agree should have been on *Infidels*. With crushing predictability, the version here is a stark guitar-and-piano rendition generally felt to be inferior to the full-band arrangement also committed to tape. It's no mere demo though, being a passionate performance. The narrator traverses a landscape pocked by "power and greed and corruptible seed" and caps every verse with the observation, "No one can sing the blues like Blind Willie McTell". The latter was a real-life recording artist who almost nobody had heard of until this song but whom music critics now talk sagely of as a seminal figure. It's difficult to understand in what manner Dylan is invoking his name – as a metaphor for himself or what he aspires to be, or perhaps merely as a man whose music provides a pleasure that brings him solace – but it's certainly haunting.

'When the Night Comes Falling from the Sky' is an alternate take of the *Empire Burlesque* track. Neither version is a classic but this one has a more impressive rock power, partly courtesy of the presence of Roy Bittan and Steve Van Zandt of the E Street Band. (What happened to Dylan's disdain for Springsteen?) 'Series of Dreams' (into which, for some reason, the previous track segues) is considered to be to *Oh Mercy* what 'Blind Willie McTell' is to *Infidels*. It's certainly better than some of the minor tracks on that album, but Dylan's droning recounting of his less-than-riveting nocturnal visions is discomfortingly reminiscent of being buttonholed by a bore in a post-office queue.

Though his rather vague public comments on it suggest that Dylan played little part in its compilation, *The Bootleg Series 1–3* was an almost unbelievable bounty for his fans. This was no halfway house like *Biograph*. A release featuring no previously issued material, it was nearly four hours of music never legally heard before. In some cases, such as 'Farewell, Angelina' and 'Santa-Fe', the tracks had even escaped the attention of those astonishingly resourceful bootleggers. As with the unreleased material on *Biograph*, once exposed to the open air, some of the contents proved rather perishable. Nonetheless, at least half of *The Bootleg Series 1–3* is an aesthetic joy and the discarded status of much of the material testament to the fecundity of this artist in the good times.

As Bob Dylan prepared to tour Britain in 1995, Andy Gill took the opportunity to coolly assess just what relevance a veteran artist in the depths of a protracted writer's block any longer possessed. Compounding Dylan's artistic nadir was an increasing tendency to mercenaryism and cosying up to the sort of public figures it has long been felt rockers best avoid, something else Gill examined. Since this article was published, both these tendencies have got more pronounced, grown with Dylan advertising cars on TV and entering into exclusive product deals with a women's underwear company and Starbucks, and in the latter performing for the Pope in 1996.

BOB DYLAN, A-CHANGIN'

By Andy Gill

First published in the *Independent*, 23 March 1995

"Forever Dylan Greatest Hits," claimed the sticker on the recent release of Bob Dylan's *Greatest Hits Volume 3*, somewhat bafflingly, before going on to list some of the tracks included. 'Knockin' on Heaven's Door', certainly; 'Tangled Up in Blue', understandably; 'Hurricane', historically; plus, the sticker continued, "a brand new Dylan classic: 'Dignity'". Well, maybe.

Like the Holy Roman Empire, this rather overstates the case for this relatively minor entry in the singer's canon of scolding prophesy, it being neither classic – in the sense that that term might be justly applied to other Dylan tracks – nor, as it happens, brand new, the track being a remixed version of a song originally recorded for his 1989 album *Oh Mercy*, and widely available as a bootleg outtake. The song's presence on this Greatest Hits compilation, in fact, serves to point up one of the concerns exercising long-haul Dylan-watchers as they prepare for his forthcoming series of concerts at oddly down-market venues like Brixton Academy: the widespread perception of this greatest of rock 'n' roll bards as suffering from a protracted writer's block dating back almost half a decade.

Fans have grown used to Dylan's often wayward reinterpretations of his own work in concert, which the singer explains, in a recent *Newsweek* interview to promote his new book of drawings, as an ongoing pursuit of perfection: "I've been working on some songs for 20 years, always moving toward some kind of perfection," he says, admitting, "I know it's never going to happen." But fine though this strategy may be for live performances, it's rather more worrying when it extends to his recorded output too.

Since *Oh Mercy*, there has been but one album of new Dylan material released, 1990's *Under the Red Sky*, an album widely criticised for the negligibility of its lyrical content, which found the songwriter reverting to repetitious kindergarten poesy and nonsense like 'Wiggle Wiggle'. Subsequently, Columbia have released a *30th Anniversary Concert Celebration* double-CD, consisting largely of other artists' versions of well-known Dylan songs; the excellent triple-CD box-set of unreleased songs and outtakes from the past three decades, *The Bootleg Series,Vols. 1–3*; and two volumes of solo acoustic performances of traditional folk and blues songs, *Good As I Been to You* and *World Gone Wrong*, which drew the proverbial mixed reception from critics. While some were impressed by Dylan's fingerpicking prowess – surely no great surprise after 30 years of calloused fingers – others found the recourse to chestnuts like 'Froggie Went A-Courtin'' small recompense for the heavyweight ponderances on which their interest was originally reared.

So there had already been a good seven albums' worth of stop-gap releases by the time Dylan fans – or Dylan customers, to use the correct service-industry parlance – were offered the one "brand new Dylan classic" on *Greatest Hits Volume 3*, and that had no sooner hit the racks than word came of yet another stop-gap release, the CD version of his *MTV Unplugged* show originally broadcast at Christmas, which – surprise! – consisted of yet more rehashed old material, this time done in a cosy country-rock style presumably intended to capitalise on the current popularity of New Country stars like Garth Brooks. Which makes nine CDs since a new Dylan song, and according to his record company, nothing on the horizon until 1996. What, some fans wonder, is going on?

"It's probably been his most fallow period ever," agrees John Bauldie, publisher of the authoritative Dylan fanzine *The Telegraph* and a Bob-watcher of international renown. "The only story I heard about that was that he was still writing songs, but not finishing them." Like many, Bauldie points to the detrimental effects of Dylan's endless touring schedule, which in recent years has winnowed his repertoire down to a core of greatest hits, performed mostly at outdoor festival venues in versions necessarily devoid of subtlety, whose effect can be glimpsed in the underwhelming *Unplugged* performance.

"I thought the MTV show was a total compromise, both in terms of the material he sang, and how it was presented," says the normally mild-mannered Bauldie. "It was completely unexciting, completely unadventurous, mid-paced, middle-of-the-road, unemotional schlock. Nothing like what he's capable of doing." The forthcoming tour, hopefully, will offer more substantial fare. Bauldie, who saw the opening show in Prague last weekend, reports that the new Dylan performance is unusual in that the singer hardly touches a guitar throughout. "He mainly just stood there with this hand-held microphone, like a cross between Leonard Cohen and Elvis Presley, throwing shapes – shadow-boxing, kung-fuing and the like." The mind boggles.

Rumblings of discontent in the Dylanological ranks were further exacerbated last year when, after decades of refusing to have anything to do with either politicians or advertising men, the singer broke both habits, performing at Bill Clinton's Inaugural Ball and allowing the use of 'The Times They Are A-Changin' ' in a TV advert. And not just any advert, either, but one for the accountants Coopers & Lybrand.

"Here's someone who has consistently condemned politicians, even boasting about it in his gospel shows, suddenly aligning himself with Clinton," says an obviously aggrieved Bauldie, "then afterwards coming up with this really mealy-mouthed excuse, along the lines of, 'He'd already been elected by then, so my presence didn't have any effect on the vote.' But these things may be deliberately contrived to cause unease in his long-term fans." If this is the case – and the decision to undertake an all-standing tour of small rock venues may suggest an attempt to garner a more youthful audience – he's some way to go before the strategy bears fruit, according to *NME* editor Steve Sutherland, who admits his readership may have lost interest in Dylan.

"At the moment, Neil Young is far more important to *NME* readers than Bob Dylan, because Neil Young: (a) sells records; (b) sounds like records that younger people make; and (c) seems to inhabit the same world as us. And I think if we asked some of the younger bands who're more aware of the past, they'd be listening to *Highway 61 Revisited* and all the records that we hold dear, and you'd have to go a very long way to find someone who thought that 'Wiggle Wiggle' was important in any way at all. It's weird, but Bob Dylan only exists, for many people, in the past."

The growing business hard-headedness suggested by the Coopers & Lybrand deal and the recent release of a Dylan CD-ROM package resulted last year in the ludicrous spectacle of Dylan getting engaged in litigation with the computer firm Apple over their use of the acronym DYLAN for their new Dynamic Language programming software. It's not the first time Apple have had run-ins with musicians – The Beatles settled out of court for between $20 million and $40 million in a dispute over the trademark "Apple" itself – but in this case, the suit seems all the cheekier given that Dylan himself first took his stage-name from the poet Dylan Thomas, who, being dead, was in no fit position to sue him.

"I just think he's got a team of lawyers whose remit it is to sue people," believes John Bauldie. "The most absurd one was suing the San Francisco Transit Authority for putting out a revised timetable with the billing The Times They Are A-Changing!"

What most saddens Dylan fans is the general perception that he's fallen amongst lawyers bent on capitalising upon him as a brand-name. If there were one artist you might have expected would resist the creeping corporatisation of rock 'n' roll iconography, it's Dylan; yet while, for instance, Tom Waits successfully sues his old publisher for allowing his songs to be used to sell denim jeans and potato chips, here's the pre-eminent social commentator of his generation apparently selling out, on as many fronts as possible.

"It may well be the classic case of someone whose canon of work means so much more to us than it does to him," suggests

Steve Sutherland. "His performances on stage are the way most of us lead our lives: weeks of miserable non-events when he just can't be arsed, like the way most of us go into work, then there'll be that one spectacular day when he'll get a result and something good will come of it. It's like he lives his life on stage, and that's it. Maybe he's constantly out there, on the road, because when he stops he effectively ceases to exist – he doesn't know who he is. Certainly, the word 'enigmatic' could have been coined for him."

GOOD AS I BEEN TO YOU/
THE 30TH ANNIVERSARY CONCERT CELEBRATION/
WORLD GONE WRONG/MTV UNPLUGGED

By Sean Egan

Bob Dylan is fond of quoting movie dialogue (*Empire Burlesque* for instance is littered with Humphrey Bogart lines). It seems apposite, then, to quote a movie line (in this case, from *Goodfellas*) to summarise the period of Dylan's career between *The Bootleg Series 1–3* and 1997's *Time Out of Mind*: "This is the bad times."

Dylan didn't even seem able, or inclined, to work his way through his writer's block by knocking off ten or so examples of pop songs undemanding of his psyche or craft like 'Mozambique' or 'The Man in Me'. It was during this writer's block period that Jakob Dylan began to really acquire success. Dylan's youngest child, Jakob, was born in 1969 and looks eerily like Bob Dylan circa 1968. Some sources cite him, rather than his brother Jesse, as the subject of 'Forever Young'. As a professional musician, he was hardly going to have his father's cultural impact when no one else ever had. However, he secured a different sort of validation: *Bringing Down the Horse*, the second album by his band The Wallflowers, released in 1996, ultimately sold over six million copies – more copies, in other words than any Bob Dylan album ever. Whenever he has been asked about this fact, Dylan Sr. has had a stock answer: that he feels pleased for Jakob and how else would he feel about it? While this is no doubt genuine, that his flesh and blood was doing so conspicuously well while he himself was in a professional pit can't have done much for his psychological equilibrium.

That the most barren period of Dylan's career saw a series of retrospectives celebrating and/or summarising his past may have done further damage to his equilibrium – or perhaps offered him some form of consolation for the knowledge of his current grim state.

THE 30TH ANNIVERSARY CONCERT CELEBRATION

US release: 24 August 1993
Produced by: Jeff Rosen and Don DeVito
CHARTS: US#40; UK# –

DISC ONE

Like a Rolling Stone (John Cougar Mellencamp)
Leopard-Skin Pill-Box Hat (John Cougar Mellencamp)
Introduction by Kris Kristofferson
Blowin' in the Wind (Stevie Wonder)
Foot of Pride (Lou Reed)
Masters of War (Eddie Vedder and Mike McCready)
The Times They Are A-Changin' (Tracy Chapman)
It Ain't Me, Babe (June Carter Cash and Johnny Cash)
What Was It You Wanted (Willie Nelson)
I'll Be Your Baby Tonight (Kris Kristofferson)
Highway 61 Revisited (Johnny Winter)
Seven Days (Ronnie Wood)
Just Like a Woman (Richie Havens)
When the Ship Comes In (The Clancy Brothers and Robbie O'Connell with special guest Tommy Makem)
You Ain't Goin' Nowhere (Mary Chapin Carpenter, Rosanne Cash and Shawn Colvin)

DISC TWO

Just Like Tom Thumb's Blues (Neil Young)
All Along the Watchtower (Neil Young)
I Shall Be Released (Chrissie Hynde)
Don't Think Twice, It's All Right (Eric Clapton)
Emotionally Yours (The O'Jays)
When I Paint My Masterpiece (The Band)
Absolutely Sweet Marie (George Harrison)
License to Kill (Tom Petty & The Heartbreakers)
Rainy Day Women #12 & 35 (Tom Petty & The Heartbreakers)
Mr. Tambourine Man (Roger McGuinn)
It's Alright, Ma (I'm Only Bleeding) (Bob Dylan)
My Back Pages (Bob Dylan, Roger McGuinn, Tom Petty, Neil Young, Eric Clapton, George Harrison)

Knockin' on Heaven's Door (Everyone)
Girl from the North Country (Bob Dylan)

The 30th Anniversary Concert Celebration – or Columbia
Records Celebrates the Music of Bob Dylan, to give it its formal
title – was something that surprised many and began a process
that in recent years has confirmed their impression of a man
who has sold out.

It was a gargantuan concert at Madison Square Garden on 18
October 1992 commemorating Dylan's three decades as a
recording artist at which the biggest names in music, past and
present, took turns extolling his influence on the world and singing one of his compositions. A double CD of the occasion was
released, although not until ten months later, plus a video set.
The event was the type of ego-massage and backslapping corporate function that we had always assumed Dylan despises. While
nobody should be held to the views they possessed (let alone
what they were merely presumed to possess) when they were
twenty-five, it did seem a little depressing that Dylan should
succumb to such blandishment. On the other hand, we don't
know what his motivations were, and if his viewpoint was that, a
very large pay day aside (it was a pay-per-view TV event), this
occasion provided a means by which to force himself into the
collective consciousness of music consumers who literally
weren't born when he made his first album, it's something with
which we should sympathise: a generation who think that R.E.M.
are the epitome of good music could do with some educating.

Of course, the nature of the event meant that Columbia
conveniently forgot that it once promoted Dylan with the strap-
line "Nobody sings Dylan like Dylan", but there's no denying
how impressive it was that this man's allure could bring together
on the same stage superstars old and young and of all shades of
the musical rainbow. The billings only tell half the story: legendary Stax house band Booker T and the MGs comprised most of
the backing group for much of the evening. Not that this meant
that undiluted brilliance was witnessed. The performances range
from very good (Willie Nelson's 'What Was It You Wanted', an
unexpected choice of song but done atmospherically, with fine
harmonica work from Mickey Raphael) to competent but dull

(Eric Clapton turns 'Don't Think Twice, It's All Right' into one of his exercises in blues taxidermy) to stupid (John Cougar Mellencamp was always on a hiding to nothing by tackling the perfection of 'Like a Rolling Stone', so why does he have to let Sue Medley wail random lines hysterically?) (Excluded from the album, incidentally, is the night's performance by Sinead O'Connor, who abandoned her planned rendition of 'I Believe in You' and sang a much modified version of Bob Marley's 'War' after her entrée inspired booing that seemed to be related to a controversial television appearance a fortnight previously in which she had torn up a picture of the Pope. Some felt her actions to be in the rebellious spirit of Dylan's Sixties persona, others that she was hijacking a night that was supposed to be Dylan's.) Despite the variable treatments, the songs do generally get across the man's genius to those not au fait with it. This applies particularly to the performances collectively: one is struck by the fact that few are responsible for a body of work of such variety and richness. Additionally, the nature of the tribute is quite moving.

Dylan himself chooses to perform solo – competently rather than well – 'It's Alright, Ma (I'm Only Bleeding)' and 'Girl from the North Country'. The latter was presumably chosen for sentimental reasons attached to the formative years in which his relationship with his first big love was a large feature. If he is telling us with the former choice that he thinks this phantasmagorical creation is his greatest ever song, it's not that big a shock or outrageous a choice.

The cover of the album is a suitably handsome affair, with some of the night's performers pictured in montage within lettering spelling out Dylan's name.

GOOD AS I BEEN TO YOU
US release: 3 November 1992
Produced by: –
CHARTS: US#51; UK#18

Frankie & Albert
Jim Jones
Blackjack Davey

Canadee-i-o
Sittin' on Top of the World
Little Maggie
Hard Times
Step It Up and Go
Tomorrow Night
Arthur McBride
You're Gonna Quit Me
Diamond Joe
Froggie Went A-Courtin'

After all the hullabaloo of the thirtieth anniversary concert, it must have been something of an embarrassment to Columbia that the next Dylan album they had the responsibility of releasing into the world was so completely lacking in the brilliance they had orchestrated the celebration of. Fully two years had passed since *Under the Red Sky* but this gap was no harbinger of a noble failure like the long gestation period of *Infidels* had been. Instead, the artist could only come up with an album consisting of old folk and blues numbers, a regressive step that took him even further back than his debut album, which could at least boast a brace of his own efforts. No wonder he looked pensive on the cover shot in which he gazed off camera against an unimaginative blue backdrop.

The album began life as a full-band affair, recording for which began in June 1992 in Chicago, supervised by David Bromberg. However, it changed nature dramatically when Dylan began laying down some traditional songs acoustically in July/August in his Malibu garage studio. Ultimately, he decided to jettison the electric tracks and put out his first album of solo acoustic recordings since 1964's *Another Side of Bob Dylan*. His friend Debbie Gold got a "Production supervised by" credit, although her production work seems to have not consisted of much more than pressing the "On" button and being slapped down when she suggested that 'You Belong to Me' be included. (The latter ended up, as have so many recent extraneous Dylan recordings, covers and originals, in a movie, in this case *Natural Born Killers*.) As with his previous recordings of traditional material, Dylan claimed the publishing credits on the grounds that the arrangements were his. Knowledgeable folk-publications were outraged by this, pointing out that some of the arrangements were unmistakably those of certain other artists, with one saying "Somebody should sue." There have subsequently been adjustments to the information between the parentheses. It should be pointed out that there was probably no sinister intent on Dylan's part: the folk tradition involves so much appropriation and adaptation of source material usually in existence before the adapter was born that concepts of ownership are hugely debatable – even risible – in this context. Additionally, people were much more relaxed about such things when Dylan first started out. Though him assuming that 'Tomorrow Night' was public domain when it was written only in 1939 was careless, people instead should have been far more concerned by just how bad this album – a needlessly generous fifty-five and a half minutes – is.

Dylan's guitar picking across songs associated with as broad a range of artists as Mississippi John Hurt, Stephen Foster, Paul Brady and the Original Bushwhackers is consistently impressive, especially on 'Blackjack Davey', but his slurred and/or mumbled singing throughout is simply embarrassing: the difference between his honking but clear enunciation the last time he made a folk record is painful. On tracks like 'Sittin' on Top of the World', the combination of Dylan's ultra-authentic blues picking and wailing harmonica and his time-ravaged vocal technique make it sound uncannily as though we are hearing a shellac 78, but the novelty of that hardly sustains the collection as a listening experience. The only two tracks approaching worthwhile are the blues 'Step It Up and Go', which has an almost rockabilly-like vitality, and 'Tomorrow Night', which boasts not only lovely harp but some mercifully clear diction, though its Tin Pan Alley craftsmanship means it sits oddly with the grit of the rest of the material. Even with those songs, we end up wondering why we would be expected to want to hear them from Dylan when the originals are out there and probably done better. The album ends with 'Froggie Went A-Courtin'', which may not have started as a children's song but which modern sensibilities can't accept as anything else. It might have been appropriate for a private performance for the artist's young daughter but is an excruciating listen for anyone else, particularly considering Dylan's incongruously grizzled tones.

Good As I Been to You could plausibly have been viewed as Dylan's celebration of his roots – sort of *Self Portrait* done sincerely – and in fact, it was in some quarters. However, this self-deception could no longer be maintained when Dylan's next album – *World Gone Wrong* – turned out to be more of the same, i.e., not just old songs but old songs done badly. This was an artist who hadn't a clue what to do on any level.

The mediocre sales figures of the album indicated that any partial recovery started by *Oh Mercy* had been squandered. While The Rolling Stones and the ex-Beatles – the closest figures to him in terms of influence on popular music – continued (most of the time) to achieve chart placings commensurate with their legend despite the fact that their music was no better than his had been lately, it was now thirteen years since any Dylan album had climbed higher than No.20 in his home country, hardly the sales levels of a major artist.

WORLD GONE WRONG
US release: 26 October 1993
Produced by: Micajah Ryan
CHARTS: US#70; UK#35

World Gone Wrong
Love Henry
Ragged & Dirty
Blood in My Eyes
Broke Down Engine
Delia
Stack A Lee
Two Soldiers
Jack-A-Roe
Lone Pilgrim

The best thing about *World Gone Wrong* is its cover. In a colour picture dominated by a wall painted an aqua green, Dylan is seated at a café table wearing a top hat, looking for all the world like that impudent genius of the 1960s. That he is far from that becomes clear dismayingly quickly.

Debbie Gold was apparently involved in the production again, though it's Micajah Ryan who gets a "Recorded and mixed by" credit. Dylan tackles the liner notes himself for the first time since *Planet Waves* (unless you count his brief jottings on the jackets of *Desire* and *Saved*). In a rambling discourse (which at least wasn't impenetrably surreal like so many of his previous notes), he explains what these songs mean to him (which is assuredly not what they will mean to you), as well as – apropos of nothing – informs us he disagrees with the nomenclature of "Never Ending Tour". The folk element is much smaller than on *Good As I Been to You*: the majority of the recordings herein – laid down in May 1993 at his home in Malibu – are blues songs.

'World Gone Wrong' – a song Dylan learned through Blind Willie McTell – gets things off on a half-respectable footing. Though Dylan's voice is now gravelley beyond belief, the fact that we can hear the words shows there's nothing wrong with his enunciation when he makes the effort. However, it's essentially just a blues. In some cases, like 'Ragged & Dirty', Dylan comes up with such stunningly authentic rural blues performances that if you didn't know better you'd swear they were recorded by Alan Lomax in 1938. But then again, so what? Dylan is a genius poet, and – contrary to those critics who insist that the blues is a large component of Dylan's allure – down-home inarticulacy has got nothing to do with why we admire him. 'Blood in My Eyes' is a smoother variant, well sung and, within the melodically restrictive parameters of the blues, attractive. However, those restrictive parameters eventually overwhelm the listener. One of these tracks might have made a charming interlude on a normal Dylan album – in much the same way as 'Prodigal Son' is a delight within the context of The Rolling Stones' *Beggars Banquet* – but a whole album is heavy going indeed, particularly considering Dylan's ravaged voice. The only mercy is that it clocks in at a relatively modest forty-four minutes.

After this, a third instalment of Dylan's greatest hits was, of course, just what the public was not clamouring for. Sure enough, November 1994 saw *Volume 3*, which continued neither the abbreviated form of "volume" nor the Roman numbering of its 1971 predecessor. The selection is OK, though, if not exactly representative of where Dylan's greatness had been most concentrated in the two decades the album covered (there's just one track apiece from *Planet Waves, Blood on the Tracks* and *Desire*). At over seventy-seven minutes, it would have taken a double set to accommodate this release in the days of vinyl. Though anyone coming to Dylan new was not hearing anything pre-*Planet Waves*, they were hearing amazingly literate and sophisticated songs the like of which they would find nowhere else in popular music. People not coming to Dylan new and who already had this stuff were "enticed" by an *Oh Mercy* outtake, one given a remix and new overdubs by Brendan O'Brien as though Dylan was even hoping to draw in the fanatics who had it on bootleg. How ironic that it should be titled 'Dignity', such avaricious cynicism evincing anything but. The track would have been amongst the beefiest and most uptempo on that album, although the pseudo-profundity that characterizes much of Dylan's *Oh Mercy* writing is in evidence in a lyric in which the narrator searches high and low for dignity and comes out with meaningful-sounding drivel like "Drinkin' man listens to the voice he hears/In a crowded room full of covered-up mirrors". There is one priceless couplet, though: "Met Prince Philip at the home of the blues/Said he'd give me information if his name wasn't used." Though there was no fanfare attached to it, 'Silvio' had also been subjected to a remix.

MTV UNPLUGGED
US release: 30 June 1995 (UK: 25 April 1995)
Produced by: –
CHARTS: US#23; UK#10

Tombstone Blues
Shooting Star
All Along the Watchtower
The Times They Are A-Changin'
John Brown
Desolation Row
Rainy Day Women #12 & 35
Love Minus Zero/No Limit [Note: Europe only]
Dignity

Knockin' on Heaven's Door
Like a Rolling Stone
With God on Our Side

February 1995 saw the release of *Highway 61 Interactive*. That Dylan should have been one of the first artists to allow himself to become a subject of the new-fangled technology of the CD-ROM surprised many: this apparent luddite suffers concert video screens so reluctantly that he refuses to allow close-ups to be shown on them. Even more surprising was how intriguing the release was: to this day, many who shelled out the then-high $60 price tag have not discovered every hidden screen and feature of this joyride of Dylanalia. Among the treasures revealed by clicking on the right areas are all the recorded takes of 'Like a Rolling Stone', the Tom Wilson-overdubbed 'House of the Risin' Sun' and footage from Newport 1965. Though this sort of release was quickly dated by the Internet – which can offer similar experiences and more – it was at the time a rare example of Dylan being relevant. Pretty soon, though, it was back to the same old feeling of redundancy.

Since its late-Eighties inception, MTV's *Unplugged* series had become an institution. Its invitation to artists to play acoustically or in much-stripped-down style was an interesting and then novel idea (if almost certainly lifted from the "in the round" Elvis Presley performances in his 1968 TV special). The notion that it enabled established artists to prove their authenticity might have been overplayed, or possibly spurious, but there certainly seemed to be a transference of vitality to some artists who participated, not least Eric Clapton, whose 1992 set, when shortly released on album, gave him accolades, sales and a profile he hadn't had for years. As with any success turned institution, it began to pall, probably with the farcical Bruce Springsteen appearance in 1993 when after starting with a mesmerising acoustic performance of 'Red Headed Woman', he proceeded to make a mockery of the concept by bringing out a full band to complete the rest of the gig. (Not the E Street band either, but his current clod-hopping, tone-deaf, clichéd-shape-throwing mob.) Dylan's *MTV Unplugged* concert and album rivals Springsteen's for meaninglessness and low quality. The album omits some of the songs he performed but still runs to over an hour.

To some extent, Dylan seems to have been mocking the whole occasion. Rumours abound of him wanting to do a set comprised of traditional numbers but eventually being persuaded to go the usual best-of route. Perhaps this is why he turned up for the occasions (the album was recorded across two nights in November 1994) looking like himself circa *Highway 61 Revisited*: his hair was the length and vague style it had been in 1965, he wore the sort of wraparound shades he had in that era, he had shaved the facial hair he had mostly sported since 1967 and his polka-dot shirt would have been very familiar to anyone who had seen photographs of him rehearsing for his Newport 1965 appearance. All very droll, but the joke was on Dylan.

Instead of doing the reverse of his 1966 tour – accoustic arrangements of formerly electric numbers – Dylan opted to play with a full-blown band (including Brendan O'Brien on Hammond organ). (The fact that he didn't have an electric guitarist presumably made the set fit the programme's requirements.) What we get therefore is not much different from the usual mediocre live album – only it's even more of a letdown, because, as with Clapton, Dylan had an opportunity to reinvigorate his art.

A country-esque 'Tombstone Blues' starts off the album on the boring footing on which, with only a couple of exceptions, it continues. 'Shooting Star' works reasonably well, but that may be partly due to the fact that its recent vintage means its original arrangement hasn't become fixed in our collective consciousness as inviolable. 'John Brown', meanwhile, is a very surprising choice. A Dylan original dating from 1962, it had never been released by him, not even picked up in the rarity trawl of *The Bootleg Series 1–3*. It's an anti-war song, powerfully performed, although the reference to flying cannonballs not only betrays it as another old song that Dylan adapted for protest purposes but robs it of true relevance. (Conversely, the sorrowful seven-minute version of 'With God on Our Side' with which Dylan closes the set has had out-dated Cold War references expunged.)

'All Along the Watchtower' is a semi-acoustic version after decades of the composer doffing his cap to Hendrix's electric re-imagining. Unfortunately, we already have an acoustic version with which to compare it – the original one on *John Wesley Harding*, of which it is a pale shadow. That drummer Winston Watson is ham-fisted where Kenny Buttrey was nimble doesn't help either. 'Desolation Row' of course was already unplugged, so this version would make no sense even without its added percussion. The way Dylan caresses the melody and occasionally slips into melodramatic country-style crooning is the kind of thing that some view as a delightfully playful approach to his material, but even they would probably not care if they never heard it again. Across the nine-minute version of 'Like a Rolling Stone', Dylan manages to drain one of the greatest songs ever written of any import.

Typical of Dylan's contrariness/unpredictability/self-loathing, he had recorded and then scrapped four unplugged sets (full-band but acoustic instruments) at the Supper Club in November 1993 (filmed at his own expense) which eyewitnesses swear were of mesmerising power. A bootleg of the event inevitably circulated, and just as inevitably its excellence caused Dylan fans' blood pressure to rise dangerously (the original Dylan admirers were now of that age). Yet again, it was time to give up on Dylan.

TIME OUT OF MIND

By Sean Egan

US release: 30 September 1997
Produced by: Daniel Lanois in association with Jack Frost
Productions
CHARTS: US#10; UK#10

Love Sick
Dirt Road Blues
Standing in the Doorway
Million Miles
Tryin' to Get to Heaven
'Til I Fell in Love with You
Not Dark Yet
Cold Irons Bound
Make You Feel My Love
Can't Wait
Highlands

Time Out of Mind was recorded in Miami in January 1997. Daniel
Lanois was hired to helm what was Dylan's first set of original
songs since 1990, although Dylan co-produced under his Jack
Frost pseudonym. Musicians were a mixture of choices by Dylan
and Lanois, and at times came close to the chaotic big band
Dylan assembled in the first stages of *Desire,* with instruments
doubled- or even trebled-up. The monochrome and out-of-focus
cover shot is of Dylan sitting, guitar in hand, at a studio console.
Some swear they can make out the ghostly image of Allen
Ginsberg – Dylan's recently deceased long-term friend – behind
the artist. The CD artwork harked back to the days when records
would boast of being made through an "electrical process".
Dylan's invoking of times past was not restricted to the artwork
– he had also clearly found his mojo again. The fact that the

album ran to seventy minutes – which would have required a double LP (it not a particularly long one) in the days of vinyl – indicated that Dylan had more than regained his appetite for songwriting. The compositions themselves – sometimes almost chillingly – indicated that he hadn't exactly retained an appetite for life.

Though a dozen musicians are credited in the album's liner notes, they are all utilised in the service of a uniformity of sound in which little is allowed to stand out. The setting is deliberately impressionistic: barely audible organ, subtle guitar flecks and unobtrusive drumming. Everything is self-consciously atmospheric, with Dylan gamely trying to inject the same drama in his voice that the musicians and producer pile on via their own methods (the mumbling of the previous two studio albums is significantly not in evidence). In that distinctive Lanois style, the mix is spare but also somehow rich. In several of the songs, Dylan is brooding bitterly over a defunct love affair (although it becomes clear not necessarily the same one in every case). The other theme of the album is death. Not only was Dylan approaching his sixtieth birthday, but in summer 1993 had had to cancel a show for health reasons (a recurrent back problem) for the first time ever. The fact of the winter of his life was increasingly moving from the realms of abstract notion to here and now reality, something that may be commensurately more painful to someone who operates in a medium associated with youth. Strangely, his conviction that there is an afterlife seems to offer Dylan no solace. 'Not Dark Yet' is the keynote song on that score. "It's not dark yet, but it's getting there" is its grim refrain. It's not just age that's on his mind either: "Sometimes my burden is more than I can bear" is one of the lines with which he makes that refrain rhyme. The track sums up the album's exhausted aura. Though the relentless self-pity can get a bit wearing and even contempt-making (he complains that he lives in "a world full of lies" when we know how much he has made truth a stranger), it's also somehow comforting – a warm blanket of misery. It's also terrain barely covered before in popular music.

Only on a couple of tracks like 'Tryin' to Get to Heaven' and 'Make You Feel My Love' does *Time Out of Mind*'s music jump out anything like forcefully as opposed to occupying the middle aural distance, although that's not to say those cuts are not still understated. Dylan's harmonica when audible is simply a ghostly presence or, in the case of 'Tryin' to Get to Heaven', distorted in the manner of the smudging of an oil painter. Sometimes this approach gets frustrating. The way that the occasional percolating keyboard part or interesting guitar arpeggio is obscured raises the question of when atmosphericness becomes featurelessness.

So much are the songs of a lyrical and production piece that it is pointless critiquing most of them: they mainly have the same tone and effect, although that is not the same as saying they all sound the same. However, some bear closer analysis. 'Make You Feel My Love' is a pop variant. Though possessed of the same minimalist and spirit-sagging qualities of everything else, it has a perky melody and is almost teenage in its emotions ("I would never do you wrong"). Late 2010 saw Adele's soulful, intimate 2008 version become a Top 5 UK hit after the song's exposure on TV talent show *The X Factor*. In 'Tryin' to Get to Heaven' we are conscious that in anybody else's hands the refrain "Trying to get to heaven before they close the door" would be poignant and moving but for those more familiar with Dylan's self-pity- and weakness-based religiosity, it doesn't quite wash. However, such contempt drains away with 'Highlands', which explores similar territory. At sixteen and a half minutes, this closing track would (unlike 'Sad Eyed Lady of the Lowlands') genuinely have merited an entire side of vinyl. Is the Highlands – in which Dylan says his heart is located but which he can only approach "one step at a time" – heaven? Certainly the line "That's where I'll be when I get called home" suggests so. It is essentially a grandiose mixture of fatalism ("I don't want nothing from anyone, ain't that much to take"), self-loathing ("If I had a conscience, well, I just might blow my top") and a fear of an ever-closer death ("All the young men with their young women looking so good/Well, I'd trade places with any of them in a minute, if I could"). A quite curious sequence of verses depicting a tetchy exchange with a waitress in which Dylan shows great disinclination to sketch her and when he does is told, to his irritation, that his vision is awry, seems to be addressing his recent writer's block. It's an extraordinary lyrical achievement, even if the almost monotonous accompaniment is not endlessly delightful like in that other Dylan epic 'Desolation Row'.

'Desolation Row', of course, had magnificent accompaniment from Charlie McCoy and superb singing by Dylan, aided by bright, clear production. The charcoal colouring of this instrumentation and mix affords no such acute pleasure, and though Dylan's cracked, weather-beaten voice of recent years finally finds its metier – it is superbly appropriate to this material and these soundscapes – it will never compare to his singing in his mid-twenties. There are other differences with previous Dylan milestones. Once a track is underway here, there are no surprises or highlights in store other than pleasing lines or couplets: musically, what has transpired in the first thirty seconds is what one is going to get for the duration. Additionally, *Time Out of Mind* is even more of an adults-only album than *Blood on the Tracks*: just as no teenager and few twenty-somethings could fully understand that album, so this recording only yields up true meaning to people who have been around the block several times. It doesn't even have *Blood on the Tracks*' cascading guitars and sublime melodies to cater to the young person's sweeter tooth. It's also not the type of album likely to convert the newcomer to the merits of Dylan's catalogue. For those Dylanites with considerable mileage on the clock, though, the album is the quintessential grower: almost a flat terrain on first listen, it reveals itself to be a landscape of hidden, intriguing gulleys and crevices each time one returns to it. 'Dirt Road Blues' – a twelve-bar with a tinge of jazz – is the only negligible song in an absorbing, thoughtful, subtle collection. Moreover, unlike with false-dawn comebacks like *New Morning, Planet Waves* and *Oh Mercy*, the feeling of substantiality does not evaporate after the first flush of infatuation.

It was a collection that returned Dylan to the status of heavyweight, obtaining him the Grammy for Album of the Year. (One would say it was amazing that this was his first ever in that category, were it not for the fact that the Grammy committee was still giving Frank Sinatra best album awards in the heyday of The Beatles.) The critical acclaim, the sales that saw him return to the UK and US Top 10 and the general perception of an artistic renaissance were to some extent unwarranted. This was

Dylan's best new album for almost a quarter century (i.e., since *Blood on the Tracks*), but this did not make it a classic. However, a willingness to believe in a comeback created by a respect for the artist's past achievements, by the overall self-conscious profundity of the album generally and by the epic quality of 'Highlands' specifically, as well as possibly the good wishes for Dylan generated by the heart infection by which he was stricken in the months before the album's release, all combined to create a mirage that everybody was happy to swear they were able to see. What also may have contributed to this impetus is a recognition that the depth of emotion and the warm (in fact rather scorched) instrumentation on this album were things almost completely lacking in a contemporary music scene in which the imperatives of the likes of (the now forgotten) Arthur Baker had triumphed: the popular music that Dylan had revolutionised in the 1960s was now a genre of cacophonous and/or soporific landscapes, its revolutionary questioning of the social order reduced to clichés of snotty adolescent rebellion. *Time Out of Mind* is a very good album but compared to most modern music, it's a masterpiece.

THE BOOTLEG SERIES VOL. 4: BOB DYLAN LIVE 1966 – THE "ROYAL ALBERT HALL" CONCERT

By Sean Egan

US release: 13 October 1998
Produced by: Jeff Rosen
CHARTS: US#31; UK#19

DISC ONE
She Belongs to Me
Fourth Time Around
Visions of Johanna
It's All Over Now, Baby Blue
Desolation Row
Just Like a Woman
Mr. Tambourine Man

DISC TWO
Tell Me, Momma
I Don't Believe You (She Acts Like We Never Have Met)
Baby, Let Me Follow You Down
Just Like Tom Thumb's Blues
Leopard-Skin Pill-Box Hat
One Too Many Mornings
Ballad of a Thin Man
Like a Rolling Stone

This is it. The Holy Grail, the one that made *The Basement Tapes* feel like it had been released five minutes after Dylan fans had begun baying for it.

Ever since bootleg copies of Bob Dylan's incendiary gig at Manchester Free Trade Hall on 17 May 1966 had started circulating as a bootleg in the early Seventies, it had been acquiring a legend. It had all the ingredients for one, starting with the fact that it captured the apex of the hostility Dylan drew from the folkies and radicals for his abandonment of acoustic music and protest, manifested in an audience member's shout of "Judas!" Such was its combination of muscular performance, crackling atmosphere and rarity status that in a 1978 poll conducted by a British DJ, esteemed critic Richard Williams even listed one of the bootlegs containing some of the concert's material as the second greatest rock album of all time.

Though a contemporaneous live LP was planned by Columbia – a mixture of two dates on the UK tour rather than just the Manchester concert – it was, like several Dylan live albums had already been, cancelled, although one suspects in this case more due to the deterioration in relations between Dylan and Grossman and the legal fallout therefrom than anything else. Long before 1998, many people had given up hope of ever seeing the Manchester tapes exhumed from the vaults. We don't know what changed Dylan's mind about issuing it legally. Some have suggested that just as *The Basement Tapes* was released notably soon after the Dylan renaissance marked by *Blood on the Tracks*, so the good reviews for *Time Out of Mind* made Dylan feel sufficiently secure of the fact of his intact talent to not think that the release of a cache of his recordings at his peak would draw unflattering comparisons. That theory omits to acknowledge the fact that *The Bootleg Series 1–3* was granted release when Dylan was in the artistic doldrums. Maybe Dylan's people simply apprehended how lucrative archive and back-cat releases had become since the early 1980s, the point when many of Dylan's original fans were entering prosperous middle age. Whatever the reasons, the presumably humorous title of *The Bootleg Series 1–3* was now pressed into service for the unexpected continuation of that concept. Volume four of what was now genuinely a series was sub-titled *The "Royal Albert Hall" Concert*, a reference to the fact that for many years it had been thought that the gig concerned had taken place at that plush London venue because that's how the early bootlegs had billed it, which in turn may have been down to some sloppy annotation on the tape canisters.

Fitting the sense of a fantasy come true for Dylan fans was sumptuous packaging, with the set boasting a card outer sleeve, a fifty-five-page booklet with notes from Dylan's life-long musician friend Tony Glover and lovingly researched photography.

The three-track master recordings were treated to a fresh mix. The album sleeve's boast of the content that the listener would "hear it as it's never been heard before" might have been accurate, therefore, but is that necessarily a recommendation? Surely the point of a live album is to present the music as it was heard by the audience on the night (leaving aside variables like location in the venue)? However, few were going to make such an argument for purity at a time like this.

There are claims that the acoustic element of this concert – the first half, to which disc one is devoted – is irrelevant. The argument has long been that well before 1966 Dylan was bored with one-man-and-a-guitar scenarios and that his grudging inclusion of such sets to appease his long-term fans is reflected in his performances. Perhaps this is true, but it is also true that in the acoustic half, Dylan – as he has done so many times – exploits the opportunity of a concert environment to offer harmonica work that is far and away above his mouth harp solos and colourings on the original studio versions.

That those who objected to his band were wrong-headed should have been brought home to them by opener 'She Belongs to Me', which *Bringing It All Back Home* electric track, shorn of its instrumentation, is much reduced – with the exception of eye-wateringly sustained harmonica. The concert took place one day after the notional release date of *Blonde on Blonde*, but as discussed before it is unlikely that any consumer had that record in their hands yet. Just like all the *Blonde on Blonde* selections, then, 'Fourth Time Around' (as it is called here) was new to the audience, although Dylan doesn't introduce any of the songs to them. No doubt they took it for the piss-take of The Beatles many have always assumed it to be – and for much of this audience, The Beatles genuinely were deserving of derision. Again, the harmonica is the sole truly noteworthy part of a performance that just sounds like a nude version of the one with which we are familiar. Much the same can be said of 'Visions of Johanna', although it's a very smooth recital and must have sounded like eight minutes of phantasmagoria to the rapt crowd.

'It's All Over Now, Baby Blue' is the one previously included on *Biograph*. 'Desolation Row' is a little limp without the focused, sharp singing of the album version and a little one-dimensional without the second guitar from same, although yet again Dylan's mouth harp is stunning. The tender guitar work and splendiferous harmonica of 'Just Like a Woman' make for a looser, mellower alternate to the tight pop of the studio track. 'Mr. Tambourine Man' is extended by three-and-a-half minutes to just under nine minutes. One would say that this is too much, but without this epic approach maybe we would not have got Dylan's harmonica work, which by now almost defies superlatives.

On disc two, the electric band whose appearance for the concert's second half aroused no little consternation in some quarters of the audience, is made up of Mickey Jones, the stand-in drummer recruited when Levon Helm proved unwilling to endure the boos, plus names that would within a few years be world-famous as members of The Band: Rick Danko (bass), Garth Hudson (organ), Richard Manuel (piano) and Robbie Robertson (electric guitar). Meanwhile, by this point of the evening Dylan was wielding a Fender Telecaster. Though this was the first time British audiences had witnessed his electric music in concert, it is inconceivable that they hadn't heard *Bringing It All Back Home* and *Highway 61 Revisited*, so it can't have come as much of a shock. In any case, it's more likely that they were offended not by amplification but by his self-absorption. One of the hecklers later told author C. P. Lee, "there he was marching with Martin Luther King, and suddenly he was singing this stuff about himself. We made him and he betrayed the cause." Dylan's garish checked suit and frothy hair – the accoutrements of somebody who looked like he hankered to be a pop star rather than a serious artist – wouldn't have helped.

'Tell Me, Momma' opens the proceedings. A song for which Dylan clearly had some regard if never enough to record a studio version, it's the usual scathing Dylan concoction of the period and has the clever, catchy refrain, "I know/That you know/That I know/That you show/Something is tearing up your mind." It should be noted that applause and no audible boos greeted this number. "It used to be like that and now it goes like this," says Dylan at the beginning of 'I Don't Believe You (She Acts Like We Never Have Met)', the first of three songs in this set the audience had only ever heard from Dylan before in an acoustic arrangement. Well, the way it used to go on *Another Side of* was delightful and this can't match that, but the new arrangement involving roller-rink organ, a quick-marching tempo and Dylan stretching the melody lines to the point of transparency is fine too. It's before his electric revisit to the first album's 'Baby, Let Me Follow You Down' that unrest becomes audible, with hollers and slow-handclapping emerging. Inconveniently for the nay-sayers, the track is very good, with some nice bass playing, fine fretwork from Robertson, rolling organ passages and percolating piano. The band try gamely on 'Just Like Tom Thumb's Blues' but can't hope to match the elegance of the studio version.

The *Blonde on Blonde* preview 'Leopard-Skin Pill-Box Hat' must have seemed appallingly frivolous in subject matter to the people to be heard shouting abuse just prior to it. It's beefier and slightly more uptempo than the album version. The music is over by the 3:22 mark. The rest of the track's 4:47 duration is taken up by parts of the audience shouting and slow-handclapping, over which Dylan mumbles gibberish before ending in a sarcastic flourish, "If you only just wouldn't clap so *hard*", which sarcasm it should be noted is loudly applauded by those in the audience who have no problem with the man's new direction. The third electrification of an acoustic song is a plaintive 'One Too Many Mornings'. An excellent, expanded, eight-minute 'Ballad of a Thin Man' lives up to the doom of the original, with Robertson adding some guitar lines that were not a component before but are very welcome. The famous cry of "Judas!" precedes the eight-minute 'Like a Rolling Stone'. Dylan's almost equally famous bark of "I don't believe you! You're a liar!" may not have been, as is widely believed, a reaction to that but to a less audible threat from another stage-front presence to never listen to his music again. Dylan responds to the disdain with a staggeringly committed vocal performance on 'Like a Rolling Stone', virtually shouting the lyric, his voice catching with emotion. The musicians behind him are equally impassioned, creating an inferno of a track. Dylan is greeted by huge applause at the close – the booing and catcalling silenced – and his humble "Thank you" is the sound of a man who has been vindicated, albeit not without huge effort.

Live 1966, like other legendary Dylan material retrieved from storage, cannot possibly live up to its legend. Robbed of mystique or martyrdom status, faults become more apparent, and indeed, for the first time, relevant. Not only is it often slightly atonal and not only does Dylan's bewildered, syllable-stretching vocal style become tiresomely mannered in places, but in many cases the performances are on a hiding to nothing, attempting as they do to replicate the perfection of some of the greatest studio recordings ever laid down. It's also impossible to disentangle the quality of the music from its massive historical importance. It is, however, a gutsy performance in every sense.

"LOVE AND THEFT"

By Sean Egan

US release: 11 September 2001
Produced by: Jack Frost
CHARTS: US#5; UK#3

Tweedle Dee & Tweedle Dum
Mississippi
Summer Days
Bye and Bye
Lonesome Day Blues
Floater (Too Much to Ask)
High Water (For Charlie Patton)
Moonlight
Honest with Me
Po' Boy
Cry a While
Sugar Baby

October 2000 saw the release of *The Essential Bob Dylan*, a double CD compilation that provided a very good (and, unusually, chronologically sequenced) introduction to Dylan for the uninitiated. Part of the reason that it encompassed some of his more obscure classics as well as all of his famous songs is the massively expanded running lengths afforded by the medium of CD – at over 124 minutes, it would have taken a triple vinyl set to accommodate these contents without sacrificing sound quality. The closing track on the album was 'Things Have Changed', a song Dylan had written for the 2000 movie *Wonder Boys*. Though a serviceable track in his new scraggly, exhausted style ("I used to care, but things have changed"), the fact that it won both Academy and Golden Globe awards in the category of Best Original Song seemed more a mark of the self-conscious respect the world was lately paying Dylan than a prize based strictly on merit.

The album marked something of a saturation of the UK market, where *The Best of Bob Dylan Volume 2* appeared the following month. The first volume, issued in 1997, had featured an alternate version of 'Shelter from the Storm' first heard in the soundtrack of movie *Jerry Maguire* and came with a limited-edition bonus disc featuring live versions of 'Highlands' and 'Blowin' in the Wind', a marketing ploy that is the modern equivalent of that old tactic of including exclusive tracks to entice those who already own the entire catalogue, with the difference that the new material is almost always artistically negligible. No attempt is going to be made in this text to navigate such downmarket side avenues of the core Dylan canon.

The next instalment in that core cannon – *"Love and Theft"* – came with a cover in which Dylan is seen in a sombre black-and-white head-shot sporting a very old-fashioned showbizzy pencil moustache, which may or may not have had something to do with the fact that the title of this album appears to be lifted from a book by Eric Lott subtitled *Blackface Minstrelsy and the American Working Class*. The assumption is that Dylan's quotation marks around his album title are an acknowledgment of the debt to Lott. There are also a whole load of other debts Dylan scholars have had hours of fun discovering, such as examples of the artist paraphrasing or lifting passages from Junichi Saga's *Confessions of a Yakuza*.

The music (chiefly provided by Dylan's Never Ending Tour band – a first) is R&B and jazz, much of which shares the Basement Tapes' quality of sounding like it is untouched by the modern world. "Jack Frost" is now the producer. Although the Dylan-dictated mixes possess greater delineation of individual instruments than did Lanois', there is still a sense of the mono-chrome about the soundscapes, as well as the unfortunate feeling of some instrumental passages not being as prominent as they deserve to be.

'Tweedle Dee & Tweedle Dum' is lyrically chilling, sounding like it's Dylan talking about a duality in himself ("Tweedle-dee Dee is a lowdown, sorry old man/Tweedle-dee Dum, he'll stab you where you stand"). Little bits and pieces give credence to this idea (the streetcar named Desire to which he refers may not be a Tennessee Williams reference but an allusion to his own *Desire* album; Dylan also seems to refer to his Born Again phase and to his song 'Is Your Love in Vain?') Even if all these suppositions are correct rather than wild flights of fancy, it hardly makes a difference to the quality of the cut, which is a rather meandering and dreary curtain-raiser. However, with an album just under an hour long there's plenty else on offer of higher quality. 'Mississippi' is far better, although its world-weary, end-is-nigh tone – recently very familiar in Dylan's songs – emphasises the fact that this artist's work is now old man's music. Lines like "Your days are numbered, so are mine" and "Time is pilin' up, we struggle and we scrape" are hardly going to speak to the soul of anybody under fifty.

'Summer Days' is breakneck old-time R&B and expertly done, if at nearly five minutes it unwisely spurns the traditional brevity of music of that vintage. 'Bye and Bye' is upbeat jazz with drummer David Kemper utilising brushes. The tune is sufficiently pretty that you actually long for someone to sing it whose vocal cords are not as shot as this artist's. There's no getting round it: Dylan's voice is now wrecked beyond repair. 'Lonesome Day Blues' is a swaggering mid-tempo twelve-bar. Again, it outstays its welcome, although its six-minute length would have been far more bearable had Kemper's excellent drum work been brought forward. 'Floater (Too Much to Ask)' is a delightfully authentic slice of summery Thirties-style pop but boasts a lyric well beyond the banalities of that era (or any other, in fact): "Honey bees are buzzin'/Leaves begin to stir/I'm in love with my second cousin/I tell myself I could be happy forever with her." Towards the end of the song, the narrator threatens somebody's life, something of a contrasting note to Larry Campbell's dulcet violin. 'Moonlight' covers similar Bing-Crosby-gone-bad territory.

'High Water (For Charley Patton)' sounds like an outlaw ballad, partly through some fine banjo picking by Larry Campbell, but a closer inspection reveals it as another Armageddon scenario. 'Honest with Me' is the only thing on the album resembling something even approaching contemporary rock. Courtesy of a repetitive guitar lick and the failure to make the most of a far better descending riff that marches in time with some sizzling hi-hat work at the end of every verse, it has already become slightly tedious within a couple of minutes of its nigh-six minute playing time.

The shuffling jazz 'Po' Boy' is probably the album's best song. Its smack of autobiography is clearly illusionary, yet it has an absolute verisimilitude, courtesy of brilliant writing like, "My mother was a daughter of a wealthy farmer/My father was a travelling salesman, I never met him/When my mother died, my uncle took me in – he ran a funeral parlour/He did a lot of nice things for me and I won't forget him". A different kind of authenticity informs the snarling, bruising blues 'Cry a While'. A finely detailed tableau of what sounds like the old Deep South, it carries the genuine menace ("Well, I cried for you, now it's your turn to cry awhile") of the rougher end of vintage blues recordings, some of whose artists were not unfamiliar with the local penitentiary.

'Sugar Baby' is a closer that has a sweet tune but is spiritually sinewy. As with so many of the album's songs, Dylan's approach is novelistic. Though the narrative cannot be drawn from his own experience, there's no mistaking the fact that this track seems shot through with his own psychological malaise ("Every moment of existence seems like some dirty trick/Happiness can come suddenly and leave just as quick").

"Love and Theft" confirms that modern Bob Dylan is very much an acquired taste. Concentration on the lyrics provides reward but many listeners – especially the younger ones – will find it hard to get past the lack of joyousness, the trainwreck of a voice, the minimalist instrumentation, the unvarnished production and the overall sense of antiquatedness. Though there is a variety of style, the tone is largely uniform, leading to an erroneous if understandable assumption of sameyness. The lyrics are glittering, but even they can become a bit wearying in both their elaborate artifice and general grimness. You long for Dylan just once to dispense with the metaphor and the finely detailed stories and to address the listener directly with naked emotion. You also long for some music that is significantly more than functional. This dearth of virtuosity is not helped by Dylan's abandonment of the harmonica for the duration.

Nonetheless, this album was a landmark. The build-up to the release of "*Love and Theft*" was rather tense for long-term Dylan fans, who were all too familiar with the way that the promise of artistic renewal suggested by a good Dylan album had so often been squandered by a mediocre successor. For once, Dylan turned in a worthy follow-up.

In this offbeat but also revealing article dating from 2002, Gary Pig Gold is as enigmatic about identity as Bob Dylan often is in his songs.

N.Y. DRIVEN WOMEN #12 & 35

By Gary Pig Gold

First published in *Encounters with Bob Dylan: If you See Him, Say Hello* (Humble Press)

Bob Dylan's ex-wife sits on the bleachers in a smoky little Hoboken nightclub watching her latest son-in-law belting out his latest demo tape to an appreciative but slim audience of friends and scene-schemers. Bob Dylan's ex-wife's looks certainly belie her too many years of lawsuits and sleepless months: she's still slim, dark, and her eyes still sparkle mischievously with the magics of eras gone by.

"I'm here tonight, really, to support *him*," she tells me as she glances supportively at the figure anxiously replacing a string in mid-verse. "Of course, I know only too well how much it takes to step out on that stage with only a song between You and," as her hand sweeps over the dance floor, "*them*. It's a rough game. No, wait a minute: it isn't a game . . . It's a way of *life*, isn't it? It *is* life for them, isn't it? All these singers; all these kids. All their songs. But what can it really all add up to? In the end, I mean?"

Strange to hear Bob Dylan's ex-wife unloading baggage onto a stranger like me – and in *Hoboken*. But then, one doesn't get to be Bob Dylan's ex by keeping one's thoughts to oneself, I should imagine.

"You'll excuse me now, won't you?" she smiles as a final chord fades from the speakers under-foot. "I must get Peter out of his wet shirt and into a dry cab." Bob Dylan's ex-wife pops to her feet and, with a somehow sincere "Take care!" flung at me over a shoulder, rushes around the nearest corner out of view.

*   *   *

Bob Dylan's girlfriend called me at 11:30 one night. She wondered if I could possibly make it over later to help her arrange some songs. "I have a show Monday, and I'm absolutely *frantic*," she bleats. "It'll only take an hour or so. I *promise*."

Ten minutes later I'm deposited outside her building on one of the Upper East Side's most uppity blocks. I look up to see her already waving crazily through her Pella windows. A second later, she's dashed downstairs to haul me in.

"I'm sorry, I'm *really* sorry, but the intercom's on the blink and we're between doormen. And during *this* of all weeks! I'm really terribly sorry, but you know what they say about if it's not one thing it's another . . ." I'm scrambling to keep apace as she whisks me through the lobby and up the stairs to her majestic double oak doors.

Bob Dylan's girlfriend's apartment is huge and sumptuous in the extreme, despite the fact its lone contents at the moment are a futon, a piano, and a fireplace full of orchids. "I'm sorry there's nowhere to sit yet – there's hardly anything to *eat* yet – but I've only just moved in three nights ago and my furniture's still somewhere between here and the coast. At least I *hope* it is! With the kind of week I've been having, I'll bet the trucks have broken down somewhere in the wilds of Minnesota and I'll be living on Ritz Bits for the rest of my life!"

As I glance overhead at the ornate chandelier and, higher still, clumps of Renaissance angels painstakingly painted over the ceilings, I can't help but realize a goodly percentage of Grand Central Station's homeless could most comfortably spend their remaining days in Bob Dylan's girlfriend's *closet*.

"Okay, okay. I have half an hour, maybe forty-five minutes, to do on Monday night, and between the fittings and the pre-shoot – what *am* I going to do about this hair! – I have to whittle down the absolute best set of songs I can before I can hire all the back-up people. Now, I think it's important above all else to showcase the *width*, the *depth* of my repertoire: after all, we're no spring chickens here! I mean, I've been working that Village since I was *fourteen!* I met Bob in '65, you know. What a little twerp he was then. You know, sometimes I *still* call him my little twerp! Anyways, I met him in one of those awful dessert places on Bleecker and Bobby was, how shall I put this . . . SHIT-FACED.

He was *drunk*, okay? And he was *hitting* on me for God's sake. Hitting on me! And I just kept saying to him, 'Get *away* from me you little twerp' – that's what I used to call him – but he could *not* leave me alone! *All night* he's going 'You're beautiful. What's your name?' Hitting on me, right? And I was so young and so scared I just wanted to get OUT OF THERE. But Bobby said – and I'll never forget this – Bobby said 'That's okay. That's okay. We're gonna meet together again someday. Out on the coast.' And dammit, nine years later – and just about as many husbands! – I'm out in L.A. searching *everywhere* for the man, and would you believe it? We *got* together. We meet again. Just like he *said* we would! He even let me sit on the couch for that After the Flood [sic] tour. Would you *believe* it? And you know what? He's just as big a little twerp today as he ever was!"

By 4 a.m. I was getting hungry and even a little bit tired. Not that I don't mind listening to Dylanspeak upon Dylanspeak direct from the girlfriend's mouth as it were . . .

"I'm awfully sorry, but I don't want to keep you here *all* night, but would you believe I don't even have a *clock* here? With my luck, I've left it out on the coast . . . not that you ever need to know the time out there! But thank you so *very* much for coming by so late. And at such small notice too! You *know* I appreciate it much. But I'm sorry, but I've got these damn fittings and that damn cheek thing of mine all *day* tomorrow, and God, will I *ever* get everything banged together by Monday night?"

Bob Dylan's girlfriend saw me into another cab and, you know, we never did get to work on any songs.

THE BOOTLEG SERIES VOL. 5: BOB DYLAN LIVE 1975 – THE ROLLING THUNDER REVUE

By Sean Egan

US release: 26 November 2002
Produced by: Jeff Rosen and Steve Berkowitz
CHARTS: US#56; UK#69

DISC ONE
Tonight I'll Be Staying Here with You
It Ain't Me, Babe
A Hard Rain's A-Gonna Fall
The Lonesome Death of Hattie Carroll
Romance in Durango
Isis
Mr. Tambourine Man
Simple Twist of Fate
Blowin' in the Wind
Mama, You Been on My Mind
I Shall Be Released

DISC TWO
It's All Over Now, Baby Blue
Love Minus Zero/No Limit
Tangled Up in Blue
The Water is Wide
It Takes a Lot to Laugh, It Takes a Train to Cry
Oh, Sister
Hurricane
One More Cup of Coffee (Valley Below)
Sara
Just Like a Woman
Knockin' on Heaven's Door

In recent years, Dylan seems to have abandoned new live albums in favour of the archive in-concert recordings of the *Bootleg Series*. Some will consider that a blessed relief considering the quality of the post-*At Budokan* live releases. Even so, many Dylan fans were furious when in 2001 the Japanese market was treated to *Live 1961–2000: Thirty-Nine Years of Great Concert Performances*, a compendium of extracts from Dylan gigs across the span of his career the vast majority of which were either very rare or previously unreleased.

'I Don't Believe You' is from *Live 1966*, 'Knockin' on Heaven's Door' from *Before the Flood*, 'Shelter from the Storm' from *Hard Rain*, 'Slow Train' from *Dylan & the Dead* and 'Dignity' from *MTV Unplugged*. For the Dylanite to already possess the rest of the previously released material, however, would require the ownership of the long out-of-print *A Tribute to Woody Guthrie Part One*, a *Renaldo & Clara* promotional EP, cassette and foreign singles and the special edition of the DVD *Dont Look Back* ('To Ramona'). The remainder of the material includes a 1961 Minneapolis home recording ('Wade in the Water') and a 1962 recording from the New York café The Gaslight ('Handsome Molly'). The three other tracks are from a 2000 English Portsmouth concert.

The album – which features an evocative, ecstatic Dylan stage shot on the cover – was clearly compiled by somebody who knew his onions. The selection was also breathtaking for the fact of the hitherto unknown treasures it suggested existed in Columbia's vaults. This time there was to be no Western release as a consequence of irate protests from the Dylanologists, although in the age of readily available imports and the Internet/ Amazon, this didn't matter as much as it had back in what now seems prehistoric 1978.

Meanwhile, back in official release land ... After the Free Trade Hall gig, a representative selection of Dylan performances from the first leg of the Rolling Thunder tour would have been the next thing on the wish-list of the average Dylan fanatic, at least when it came to live recordings. Lo and behold, in 2002 came this hundred-minute, double-CD fifth volume of the *Bootleg Series*. It was only four years since the last *Bootleg Series* release, as opposed to the gap before that of seven years. It was almost as though Dylan – seen on the cover in a B&W head-shot in full Rolling Thunder hat-and-scarf gypsy mode – was rewarding his fans for their patience with him during the bad times.

With many tracks here, its impossible to tell what the song is until the lyric kicks in. This is not a criticism: in almost all cases although the melody (and sometimes lyric) is new, the song doesn't feel debased or our memories robbed of meaning. The most startling examples are 'A Hard Rain's A-Gonna Fall' and 'The Lonesome Death of Hattie Carroll'. The former is given a quick marching tempo similar to that of the title track of the *Highway 61 Revisited* album and an insanely jolly – considering the subject matter – ambience that includes gleefully repeated cymbal splashes during the chorus. The latter, never previously heard on an official Dylan release in an alternative arrangement, is provided a staccato vocal delivery by Dylan that gives it the urgency of 'Hurricane'.

A quartet of duets with Joan Baez reminds us, presumably deliberately, of when they were the king and queen of the folk revival. Because of his obligations to his vocal partner, Dylan for once is obliged to follow the original melody lines on their pleasing joint performances, 'Blowin' in the Wind', 'Mama, You Been on My Mind' (given a countrified electric arrangement which slightly works against the brooding melancholy of the unadorned version, even if it's, like all of the arrangements of the first leg of the Rolling Thunder tour, thoughtfully done), 'I Shall Be Released' and probably best of all (partly because we have no other version with which to compare it) the traditional 'The Water is Wide', which as well as fine singing boasts lovely keening guitar work.

Boston Music Hall (which sounds tiny) yields many of the best performances. It even amazingly sees Dylan responding to a shouted request. "We'll try it," he says of an appeal for 'Just Like a Woman'. They do more than try it, but even better is a sensual 'Oh, Sister' and a version of 'One More Cup of Coffee (Valley Below)' from that venue with some incredible violin work from Scarlet Rivera. The closing 'Knockin' on Heaven's Door' from Harvard Square Theatre, Cambridge, Massachusetts sees Dylan team-up with Roger McGuinn for a rewritten, powerful version of that song. The only time the cranked-up intensity level that characterized even the acoustic stuff on Rolling Thunder doesn't work is 'Romance in Durango'. Always an irritating song, it is here caterwauling.

In July 2003, Masked and Anonymous, *Dylan's latest cinematic venture, was put on general release. Dylan starred in the film as Jack Tate, who is released from prison into future dystopia. As it was funded by the BBC, not much money was on offer to the cast and crew, but it is still studded with celebrity cameos. The script touches on many of the same deep philosophical questions that* Ronaldo & Clara *did, so was never destined to have the wide appeal of the average Saturday night popcorn experience. However, like* Ronaldo & Clara, *it has a fine soundtrack and its philosophizing is far more accessible than that in its first film, partly because of populist trappings, partly because it's not nearly so long. Dylan's performance was, as to be expected, gnomic. Dylan scholar Michael Gray here examines the latest instalment in Dylan's unique movie oeuvre.*

MASKED AND ANONYMOUS

By Michael Gray

First published in *The Bob Dylan Encyclopedia* (Continuum)

This large-scale film marked Dylan's first ambitious movie project since the badly received four-hour *Renaldo & Clara*, released in 1978. This time the acolytes surrounding Dylan are Hollywood rather than rock and poetry stars: Jeff Bridges, Penelope Cruz, John Goodman and Jessica Lange instead of Allen Ginsberg, Joan Baez, Ronnie Hawkins and Scarlet Rivera. The production companies behind the making of *Masked and Anonymous*, however, are comparable not to those of *Renaldo & Clara* but of *No Direction Home* (2005).

Dylan's chief factotum Jeff Rosen, plus film man Nigel Sinclair, co-produced both. When the forthcoming project of *Masked and Anonymous* first made the papers, in February 2002, it was said to be based on a short story called 'Los Vientos del Destino' ('The Winds of Destiny'); in April this was said to be by an Enrique Morales and there was speculation that perhaps this was a Dylan pseudonym; on July 2 Morales was said to be "an obscure Argentinean writer"; ten days later Morales, who was indeed both a real person and an Argentinean writer, and living in Paris, denied all knowledge of any such short story. By this point it was strongly suspected that the movie's credited writers, Sergei Petrov and Rene Fontaine, were Bob Dylan and the director, Larry Charles.

The pseudonym Sergei Petrov was taken from the name of an actor from the silent-movie era, who had appeared as a soldier in the weird 1928 Russian film *Arsenal* and had survived to take a final role in 1960 in the much-admired *Roman i Francheska*, directed by Vladimir Denisenko. (Another Sergei Petrov is a contemporary photographer working out of Arlington, Virginia; another is a distinguished Russian architect.) At any rate, this pseudonym sounded a better name than that of the character Dylan was to play in the film: Jack Fate. That did sound bad.

Filming took place in Los Angeles from June 17 to July 21, 2002, in the period between that year's Never Ending Tour spring leg, which ended with two exceptionally good concerts at London's Docklands Arena on May 11 and 12, and the start of the next leg, in August in the USA.

Those who like the result use terms like "an imaginative allegory" that "overturns expectations" with "a barrage of wit", "energy and spirit" and "creative vision". Salon.com declared it "an exhilarating jumble" and a "brilliant must-see film". Well, First, it's only two hours long but like *Renaldo & Clara* it is partly a film about Bob Dylan's mystique, which dooms us to watching much forelock-tugging to the maestro while little more is required of him than that he stand there looking unimpressed.

The finest moment in the entire two hours of *Masked and Anonymous* occurs in the caravan of tiresome scuzzy-manager character Uncle Sweetheart, as Bob Dylan sits sideways and drapes his contrastingly bony, bony legs over one arm of the chair (naturally, he is placing himself obliquely). The enormous John Goodman protests that he is only human, and Bob responds: "I know. It ain't easy bein' human." Dylan delivers the line disarmingly, sounding, for almost the only time in the film, well, human, yet contriving to look, while saying it, uncannily like a monkey.

What seems welcome in this perplexing, vexing, lavishly tatterdemalion movie is its preparedness to say things like that. To hold out lines that are not from Hollywood; to offer a script that plays by a different set of rules. This is not "realistic" dialogue. Everyone is constantly discussing the meaning of life. If they are speaking at all. It is all as stylised as can be, and its cadences are familiar to anyone who has ever heard Dylan's songs or even read his album sleevenotes or interview answers.

To hear Goodman cascading on about Alexander the Great and crankcase oil is to remember the mutterings about soldiers in the mud in Dylan's notes to the *World Gone Wrong* album. To listen to Jessica Lange holding forth about Muslims, Buddhists, Hindus and war is to recall the long harangues on the inner sleeves of *Biograph*. But sometimes to listen is to squirm, and to watch this film tensed against those moments when the script is so Dylanesque it's just dismal. There are less stressful (and funnier) moments, when these pronouncements veer towards the Donald Rumsfeld cliff-edge of cleverness, as when the Jack Fate character (Dylan) intones that "Sometimes it's not enough to know the meaning of things: sometimes we have to know what things don't mean as well."

As recurrent as the lengthy preacher-like pronouncements is the opposite stylistic tic, the dialogue built of extra-compressed monosyllables. Often the two forms meet: the Jeff Bridges character, or the Val Kilmer madman, rap on at wizened, silent Bob for minutes on end, only to elicit a grunt in response. Bob's facial expressions are so enigmatic they're often motionless. Sometimes he's so gnomic he's garden-gnomic. But constant discussion of the meaning of life makes a pleasant change from soap-opera atavism and piety, and it's by no means always portentous.

When the two idle members of the road crew are talking their earnestness is nicely comic. The always-compelling Bruce Dern, though here distressingly shrunken and almost as simian as Bob in that chair, has a nice line: "What am I drinking? I'm drinking my life away."

The postmodern discussions of the meaning of Dylan's songs are comic too – at one point Penelope Cruz discusses their open-endedness with the Pope and Gandhi – except that this is a running joke that rests on knowingness, which is never as attractive as sincerity. Throw-ins like the wall of song titles that includes 'I Hate You' as well as 'I Want You' – these are the jokes that wear thinnest quickest.

Best is when the dialogue brings an unexpected moment of human warmth into the verbal play as when Jeff Bridges, the loathsome journalist (and in Bobland there is no other sort) is grinding out his weary cynical take at Penelope Cruz, belabouring her with the standard orator's trick of three-point argument, that "It's an overcrowded world. It's hard to get to the top. There's a long line at the elevator," and she undercuts him with humane simplicity, saying: "It doesn't matter. We'll take the stairs."

This is Bobland in other ways too. Here is the same world he sings of in 'Angelina' (whose melody, uncredited, plays at the film's final end) and 'Groom's Still Waiting at the Altar': the world of interminable war and corruption, greed and meaninglessness, the America that is not merely North America but teems with the poor and the enslaved, the third world, the world that speaks in Spanish and knows that everything is broken. But unlike the songs, the film works so hard and so clumsily to say so. And though, as he wanders through his fallen world, there's a sense of Dylan the Sam Spade fan behind it, terse one-liners are not enough, and Bob looks more David Niven than Humphrey Bogart.

The big downside of characters who are archetypes instead of individuals is that they're doomed to be cardboard, managing therefore to be both flimsy and stiff. (Blame Dylan's lifelong fondness for Francois Truffaut's film *Shoot the Piano Player*.)

It's no triumph of form that you never for a moment watch a single scene and forget that it isn't real. You watch Bob on the bus and he's keeping up a ponderous rocking from side to side that is clearly false in itself and shown to be the more so by the fact that none of the other passengers moves remotely like this. And there's an awful lot of watching Bob riding in vehicles to be got through, just as there's a great deal of watching him walk a hat around the place.

Worse, several key ingredients found only in truly bad films that are conventional Hollywood are here too. One: war backdrop or not, the whole plot rests upon people saying "Hey! Let's put on a concert!" Two: we're asked to take at face value, solemnly, that the main character and a suitably subservient buddy (Bob and Luke Wilson) are Firm Friends who'll do anything for each other. Three: there's a random moment when, for no reason (there's not even a lame attempt to convey one) our main character walks out on things, and has to be begged to remain – and this is imagined to be a moment of drama. Four: there's a gruellingly pathetic fight scene, in which our hero is pushed reluctantly into Man of Action.

Scenes like these force you to concede with shame and sadness that for all its strenuous efforts to be art, and all its good intentions, at bottom Dylan's *Masked and Anonymous* is just an Elvis movie. The music's better though.

Other artists on the soundtrack album include Swedish vocalist Sophie Zelman muttering 'Most of the Time' (in English) and Turkish pop star Sertab Erener singing 'One More Cup of Coffee'. (Sertab, born in Istanbul in 1964, had made her début album in 1992, and the same year as she appeared on the *Masked and Anonymous* soundtrack she won the Eurovision Song Contest for Turkey.) The more interestingly "foreign" soundtrack items were Japanese duo the Magokoro Brothers with a cover of 'My Back Pages' sung in Japanese, taken from their 1995 album *King of Rock* (their début single had been in 1989; they'd disbanded by the time the Dylan film came out) and two contrasting Italian items: Francesco de Gregori (born in Rome in 1950, whose début album had been made in 1970) singing a translation of 'If You See Her, Say Hello' titled 'Non Dine Che Non E' Cosi', and the "spaghetti funk" rap duo Articolo 31 with their splendid rapping-in-Italian 'Like a Rolling Stone', 'Come Una Pietra Scalciata', which incorporated fragments of Dylan's original studio version. This comes from their 1998 album *Nessuno*, recorded in New York City. (The duo, J. Ax, a.k.a. Alessandro Aleotti, and DJ Jad, a.k.a. Luca Perrini, named their act after the article of the Italian Constitution that guarantees the freedom of the press, and made their début album in 1993.)

Dylan's own Jack Fate "concert sequence" was filmed at Canoga Park, California, on July 18, 2002 and comprised eleven numbers, nine of which are featured in the film, with a tenth ('Standing in the Doorway') shown as a "deleted scene" in the "extras" on the commercially issued DVD. The nine are 'Down in the Flood', 'Amazing Grace', 'Diamond Joe' (not the same song as on the solo acoustic album of 1992, *Good As I Been to You*), 'Dixie', 'I'll Remember You', 'Drifter's Escape', 'Watching the River Flow', 'Cold Irons Bound' and 'Dirt Road Blues'. The eleven number, recorded but unreleased, was 'If You See Her, Say Hello'. On the soundtrack album the four "concert sequence" tracks included are 'Down in the Flood', 'Diamond Joe', 'Dixie' and 'Cold Irons Bound'. Again, opinions vary from how thrilling this music is and how great to see Dylan and his excellent band playing at such close range, through to how embarrassingly bad Dylan's vocal is on this version of 'Dixie', how tediously raucous 'Down in the Flood' and 'Cold Irons Bound' are, and how aesthetically displeasing it is to see Dylan in his overly tight, urine-yellow suit.

Dylan's band at the time, and therefore in the film, comprised guitarists Larry Campbell and Charlie Sexton, bass player Tony Garnier and drummer George Receli. In late July Dylan and Buff Dawes mixed the "concert sequence" recordings in Studio City, California.

The film was premiered on January 22, 2003 at the Sundance Film Festival in Park City, Utah; various editing changes (shortenings) were then made; it was released in movie theatres that July 24. The DVD was issued on February 17, 2004.

[*Masked and Anonymous*, dir. Larry Charles, written by Bob Dylan & Larry Charles as Sergei Petrov & Rene Fontaine, prod. BBC Films / Destiny Productions / Grey Water Park Productions / Intermedia Films / Marching Band Productions / Spitfire Pictures, US, 2003. The DVD release (Columbia TriStar Home Entertainment, US, 2003) also includes the 16-minute "making-of" feature *"Masked and Anonymous" Exposed*, dir. & written (it says here) by Alexander Yves Brunner & Matt Radecki, Spitfire Pictures, US, 2003, with movie main participants interviewed by co-producer Jeff Rosen. *Shoot the Piano Player*, dir. Francois Truffaut, Les Films de la Pléiade, France, 1960.]

THE BOOTLEG SERIES VOL. 6: BOB DYLAN LIVE 1964 – CONCERT AT PHILHARMONIC HALL

By Sean Egan

US release: 30 March 2004
Produced by: Jeff Rosen and Steve Berkowitz
CHARTS: US#28; UK#33

DISC ONE
The Times They Are A-Changin'
Spanish Harlem Incident
Talkin' John Birch Paranoid Blues
To Ramona
Who Killed Davey Moore?
Gates of Eden
If You Gotta Go, Go Now (Or Else You Got to Stay All Night)
It's Alright, Ma (I'm Only Bleeding)
I Don't Believe You (She Acts Like We Never Have Met)
Mr. Tambourine Man
A Hard Rain's A-Gonna Fall

DISC TWO
Talkin' World War III Blues
Don't Think Twice, It's All Right
The Lonesome Death of Hattie Carroll
Mama, You Been on My Mind
Silver Dagger
With God on Our Side
It Ain't Me, Babe
All I Really Want to Do

August 2003 saw the releases of fifteen of Dylan's albums in SACD (a format in which *Blonde on Blonde* had already been made available). SACD was a hi-fi craze only fleetingly fashionable (and the 5.1 surround-sound format that five of the albums were additionally presented in has yet to take off). Meanwhile, pre-release hype that talked of the releases being as they were meant to be heard was a nonsense in light of the fact that none of the 1962–7 albums were in their original, Dylan-approved mono mixes. However, they were at least better than the first-generation vinyl-to-CD Dylan transfers that were unusual in not having had an upgrade. Then came the next instalment in the mouth-watering *Bootleg Series*, only fourteen months after the last one.

Volume 6 was another live performance, this one recorded on 31 October 1964, a Halloween date at New York's Philharmonic Hall that captured Dylan between *Another Side of . . .* and *Bringing It All Back Home*. Once again, it was a hundred-minute affair. The unsymmetrical slicing of the two discs accurately reflected the one-hour point of the show's interval. As usual with this series, everything is impeccably researched, with a moody Dylan head-shot from the relevant period gazing out from the card cover and eyewitness liner notes. There is the now expected feel of a luxury item to the whole package.

That Dylan is still a solo, acoustic artist makes this gig an ostensibly illogical choice for release: there's not going to be much scope for variation on the original versions. On the other hand, we don't have to put up with any unsubtle backing musicians (especially clod-hopping drummers) and the intensity of Dylan's performances – for instance on 'The Times They Are A-Changin' ' – keeps one listening even though the knowledge sits at the back of one's mind that the original is the better rendition. On a precious few occasions, he tops the original. This is all despite the fact that he is "relaxed and high-spirited" as the booklet notes put it. Some have suggested that Dylan was stoned at this gig, and his comments before (and haphazard harmonica work on) 'To Ramona' certainly suggest this. Which doesn't mean to say it's not a well-performed version of his sensitive minor masterpiece. Similarly, though he is giggly and incapable just before 'I Don't Believe You (She Acts Like We Never Have Met)', even having to ask the audience for the opening line, his rendition is more than competent.

Dylan previews three songs from *Bringing It All Back Home*,

'Gates of Eden', 'It's Alright, Ma (I'm Only Bleeding)' – introduced as 'It's Alright, Ma (It's Life and Life Only)' and extended to nine minutes by a slower pace – and 'Mr. Tambourine Man'. All must have sounded mind-blowing on the night, although the applause for the announcement of the last song indicates it was already both familiar to and highly regarded by some of the audience from previous gigs. He stumbles at one point over the lyric of 'It's Alright, Ma (I'm Only Bleeding)', but given that it is an amazing feat in the best of circumstances to remember its complex and very long lyrics so well, this is forgivable. 'Mr. Tambourine Man' – of course allegedly a paean to the joys of what he seems to be on this night – is also well-performed.

It's noteworthy that, judging by their reception, some of the songs Dylan plays – 'Talkin' John Birch Paranoid Blues', 'Who Killed Davey Moore?', 'Mama, You Been on My Mind' and 'If You Gotta Go, Go Now (Or Else You Got to Stay All Night)' – have become signature numbers despite him never having formally issued them. The last is the one big surprise, its pop strains sitting oddly with the rest of the material. It's also the one out-and-out failure, not because of the way it is played but because of its outmodedness: the delight the audience takes in Dylan mocking a girl who is worried what people will think of her if she stays the night is now embarrassing. 'Spanish Harlem Incident', meanwhile, is amazingly Dylan's only ever concert performance of this fun number. His singing here is excellent, as it is on 'A Hard Rain's A-Gonna Fall' – in which he displays hair-raising sustain – and 'All I Really Want to Do', on which he holds the last word of the title phrase in the manner of a hyena. This praise for his vocal prowess is not withstanding his buffoonish, shouted rendition of 'Don't Think Twice, It's All Right' and the fact that throughout he is cawing even by his standards.

'Don't Think Twice' is one of the exceptions on the second disc, on which he is more *compos mentis*, suggesting that the doobie has worn off now. Though on the traditional 'Silver Dagger' – one of four duets with Joan Baez in the second half – he, to her apparent surprise, leaves his partner to handle all the singing (she does so beautifully), Dylan produces some fine harp work. He appropriately dispenses with all buffoonery on 'The Lonesome Death of Hattie Carroll'. He also puts heart and soul into an excellent 'Talkin' World War III Blues', on which he plays around with the lyric and illustrates its great resonance for the audience at a time when nuclear incineration seemed so much a daily possibility that in 1961 New Yorkers were fined if they did not duck into subways when nuclear attack drills took place. The song comes alive with the to-and-fro between him and the crowd, an addition of dimension that truly is what in-concert recordings are all about. The Baez quartet is enjoyable, especially 'With God on Our Side', which becomes profoundly more attractive by the fact of her voice serving as the cream in his coffee.

In a way, this concert is almost the obverse of the Manchester Free Trade Hall gig, capturing Dylan at the zenith of his status of hero of the left/folkies. His fans' amused indulgence of his condition (which obvious intoxication probably felt to them like a rebellious act in its own right) underlies a touching connection Dylan has with his audience – even if we now know he was, unbeknownst to them, drawing away from them.

Bob Dylan's memoir Chronicles Volume One *appeared in October 2004. This reader found it amateurishly self-conscious (Dylan is so intent on impressing us with his facility with language that he often ends up drowning in meaningless similes), slightly exhausting (do we really need so much detail about the layout and contents of friend Ray Gooch's apartment?) and inadvertently myth-busting (who'd have known that the poet of his age doesn't know the difference between "incredible" and "incredulous"?) However, this reader was in a minority. Mark Ellen's enthralled appraisal sums up the general acclaim to which the book was released.*

DYLAN CHRONICLES

By Mark Ellen

First published in *The Word*, October 2004

It's 1957 and, propelled by Ginsberg's line about searching for "the hydrogen jukebox world", the teenage Dylan is firing on all cylinders. Everything in his Midwest town has the brightness control turned all the way up. "Summers were filled with mosquitoes that could bite through your boots, winters with blizzards that could freeze a man dead."

Folk music has launched him into overdrive. The guitar in his hands, he feels, is like a crystal magic wand that he can use to change the world around him. Alongside the obvious influences already shaping his perspective – Little Richard, Blind Blake, Charley Patton, Woody Guthrie, extinct song folios, sea shanties, Civil War songs, cowboy songs, Church house songs and biographies of Robert E. Lee – there's an unlikely regiment of showmen he's identified either as magnetic live performers or groundbreaking salesmen with mass-market appeal.

There's Gorgeous George the wrestler, who rolls through Minnesota with fellow grapplers Goliath, The Vampire, The Strangler and The Bone Crusher. George himself sports a majestic fur-lined gold cape and long blond curls and "seemed like forty men". There's visiting four-piece softball giants The King And His Court – "a pitcher, catcher, first base and roving shortstop . . . the most thrilling event of the summer". There's the last of the blackface minstrel shows that bowls past Hibbing in a county carnival. There's 'Kubla Khan' by Coleridge and blues recordings by Robert Johnson – "sparkling allegories and big-ass truths wrapped in a hard shell of nonsensical abstraction". There's Harry Belafonte whose magic appeal plays to steel workers, symphony patrons, bobbysoxers, even children – "everything about him was gigantic". And there's life itself, a strange new world of Cold War paranoia where the quaking Zimmerman and classmates were trained to hide under their desks when they heard the sirens as, likely as not, heavily armed Russians would be parachuting into their town at any moment (though years later, faced with the threat of offshore nuclear testing, his big fear is that "my guitar will go out of tune").

We've subscribed for so long to the idea of Dylan as a jaded pessimist confined – and thus embittered – by his own success, that I'm not sure which is the more extraordinary about those images of his early life. That you can never imagine him feeling that enthusiastic any more? That he still remembers that he ever did? Or – just possibly – that the distracted individual we've seen touring for the last twenty years, bashing though perfunctory sets while apparently locked in a private universe, could *still* feel as energised by the world around him today – though for the answer to that part we'll have to wait 'til the next instalment.

Dylan's last literary work was *Tarantula*, written in '66 and officially published five years later, a collection of head-scratching fiction and beat poetry apparently scrawled on the napkins of Manhattan grill bars, so the overriding emotion on opening *Chronicles Volume One* is simply one of relief. I immediately rang someone involved who assured me that every immaculately crafted word of this sparkling work was hand-chiselled by the author himself and not agonisingly tacked together by some seasoned hack from hours of transcribed interviews. Almost every page of my copy is covered in pencil marks under lines I never want to forget.

It breaks every rule in the game. Where the average rock

memoir begins "It's a boy, gasped Mrs Wyman, that fateful night
in 1936 ...", Dylan's hits the ground running – in a taxi, to be
precise, in '61, with a cigar-chewing music executive, careering
towards the West 70th Street studio where Bill Haley recorded
'Rock Around the Clock', and thence to dine at Dempsey's where
the booths have red leather upholstery. He juggles the time-
frames. None of it's in chronological order. We leap from the early
folk clubs to life in Hibbing in the Second World War – his uncles
returning home with their mementoes, German dust goggles,
Japanese straw cigarette cases, and never saying a word about it –
to a star-studded party in Greenwich Village, to the Woodstock
period, to the *Oh Mercy* sessions of March '89, and finally back to
Manhattan for the significant midwinter of '61. Sections of his life
either get the full beam of his attention or are excised completely.

The detail is absolutely mesmerising, some of it recalled with
pin-sharp precision and some presumably shaded in from his
vivid mental snapshots of the time. It's the nearest you could
possibly come to seeing the world through Dylan's eyes, with the
ability to process the view and edit out all but the indelible
images. At the height of beatnik bohemia he wakes up in an
apartment off Canal Street – this is forty-three years ago – and
tells you there was a small desk of violet wood veneer with flip-
down drawers, a padded car-seat with spring upholstery used as
a couch and the room "smelled of gin and tonic, wood alcohol
and flowers". Hibbing in June, he remembers, had the fragrance
of "true summer – glints of lights dancing off the lakes and
yellow butterflies on the black tarred roads". Joan Baez had a
voice that drove out bad spirits and when she sang she made
your teeth drop – "I couldn't stop looking at her. I didn't want to
blink. She was wicked-looking – shiny black hair that hung down
over the curve of her slender hips, drooping lashes, partly raised,
no Raggedy-Ann doll. The sight of her made me high."

But the monumental pivot in his life-story to date is the change in
its subject before and after success. Prior to the Woodstock episode
the book is all about Dylan looking at the outside world. From then
on it's about the outside world looking at Dylan. The New York
sections feature an overloading twenty-year-old intoxicated by
everything around him. David Van Ronk's voice sounds like rusted

shrapnel. Ricky Nelson sings "like it didn't matter, like he was in the middle of a storm, men hurling past him". Long-playing records are the bold way forward – "next to them, 45s were flimsy and uncrystallised". He's already consumed the present and constructed a plan for the future. Now he begins devouring the past, inhaling every molecule of American social history he can capture. At the start of the '60s "what was swinging, topical and up to date for me was stuff like *The Titanic* sinking, the Galveston flood, John Henry driving steel and John Hardy shooting a man on the West Virginia line." Crucially for his artistic output, there's no concept of yesterday, just of a wider present, and this vast learnt lexicon of folklore still surfaces on his records today (just listen to 'Tryin' to Get to Heaven' on *Time Out of Mind*).

But most astonishing of all are his observations of people. At any juncture he can cast an eye across a crowded room and sieve out six characters that sound like an outtake from *Blood on the Tracks*. At the Kettle of Fish pub one night he notes "a pistol-packing rabbi and a snaggle-toothed girl with a crucifix between her breasts". At Camilla's get-together in the Village the crowd looked "more like tug-boat captains or baggy pantsed outfielders or roustabouts". A glance through his downtown window in '62 reveals a guy scooping frost off the windshield of a snow-packed black Mercury Montclair and a scurrying priest in a purple cloak. Some of this is clearly fantasised but it doesn't half paint a picture. You or I might have pondered the wisdom of renting a flat right by the urban railroad, but in Dylan's fevered imaginings "I fell asleep to the sounds of the night train rumbling through Jersey, the iron horse with steam for blood". It's the heightened multi-coloured vision of someone on the way up, exploding with excitement and believing everything is possible.

So the contrast with the Woodstock period couldn't be more marked. We're plunged into misery and isolation. He's besieged by gatecrashers, spooks, trespassers, demagogues, gargoyle-looking girls, scarecrows and strangers looking to party and raid the pantry. Touchingly affectionate about the wife who'd later feel the full force of 'Idiot Wind', he tries desperately to be the hands-on father-of-four when the goons routinely breaking into their mountain retreat want him to be the New Messiah. "I was more a cowpuncher than a Pied Piper," he points out. "It seems like the world has always needed a scapegoat, someone to lead the charge against the Roman Empire. But America wasn't the Roman Empire and someone else would have to step up and volunteer. I really was never any more than what I was – a folk musician who gazed into the gray mist with tear-blinded eyes and made-up songs that floated in a luminous haze."

He is appalled when Ronnie Gilbert of The Weavers ushers him onstage at the Newport Festival with the words "take him, you know him, he's yours!" He's even more destabilised when Robbie Robertson asks him where he's "gonna take the whole music scene". Dylan recoils in horror: "Everything was wrong, the world was absurd. I felt like I might as well have been living in another part of the solar system. I rolled [the car window] down the rest of the way, felt a gust of wind into my face and waited for what he said to die away." He's imprisoned and, either way, he just can't win. When he accepts an honorary degree from Princeton and is introduced as someone who prefers isolation from the world, "it was like he told them I preferred being in an iron tomb with my food shoved in on a tray".

This sense of estrangement hits rock bottom in the late '80s. We've already had some insights into the pragmatic realities of the record-making business – "Dostoyevsky wrote stories to ward off his creditors, just like in the early '70s I wrote albums to ward off mine" – and Dylan's now leaving new songs on the studio floor "like shot rabbits". He thinks maybe he should pour lighter fluid over them. At one unimaginable low-point – the kind of thinking you suspect might only derive from some sort of depression – he approaches a venture capitalist with a view to getting out of the business altogether and investing elsewhere. Their mercifully unappetising options include a flower plantation, a fish farm and – oh yes – a wooden leg factory in North Carolina.

While rehearsing a tour with the Grateful Dead, the man you fondly imagined was above such crises of confidence walks out intending never to return (and, to be fair, a lot of the audience felt the same way). He's on cruise control and his back catalogue is "like carrying a package of heavy rotting meat". A night draining a case of Guinness with Bono persuades him to place himself in the extravagantly creative care of producer Daniel Lanois – "scuff-proof," Dylan observes, "*noir* all the way, a black prince from the black hills" – and the result, recounted in the most agonising detail, is the record that reversed his decline and launched him on the trajectory he's maintained ever since, *Oh Mercy*.

Even those who consider themselves up-to-speed with Dylan will learn more about him than they ever thought possible. He's connected in ways you never imagined – at one point he wishes he'd recruited Mick Jones "the quintessential guitarist from The Clash"; at another he wants to bid for Elton John's pinball machine at the auction of his furniture and costumes. He's not above trying to buy a bumper sticker that reads WORLD'S GREATEST GRANDPA. One entire album, he reveals, is based on Chekhov short stories but the critics thought it was autobiographical – presumably *Blood on the Tracks*. He acquires an unnamed second wife in the late '80s (who we now know to be his then-backing singer Carolyn Dennis), though the only information on offer is that she's reading a John Le Carré novel. There's much red-blooded evidence of his passion for women – Carolyn Hester is "eye-catching, down home, double-barrel beautiful", Suze Rotolo is "the most erotic thing I ever saw, fair-haired and golden-skinned. The air was suddenly filled with banana leaves". And he operates almost entirely without ego: in the first half he's fuelled by ambition; in the second he scatters generous credits in the direction of those – particularly Bono and Lanois – who gave him the courage to carry on. It's interesting, too, that only once in his life did anyone feel inclined – or dare – to pass comment on his guitar playing. It took Sonny Boy Williamson in John Lee Hooker's hotel room – imagine it! – to suggest "Boy, you play *too fast*" , and Dylan for one certainly wasn't going to contest it. And the book is very, very funny, shot through with a kind of rumpled shrugging humour – "There's a lot of places I like but I like New Orleans better."

Chronicles Volume One is the best autobiography I've ever read in my life. It will be the benchmark against which all others will now have to be measured. And it's not even over. There are sequels to follow. If its author was to apply the same piercing spotlight, and the same honesty, humility and humour, to some of the other chapters of his supernatural story – the Isle of Wight Festival, Rolling Thunder, the "Albert Hall", *Dont Look Back*, his unspecified quantity of children, 'Love Sick' being used in a lingerie commercial, Live Aid – then I for one will expire content.

THE BOOTLEG SERIES VOL. 7/LIVE AT THE GASLIGHT 1962/LIVE AT CARNEGIE HALL 1963

By Sean Egan

THE BOOTLEG SERIES VOL. 7: NO DIRECTION HOME – THE SOUNDTRACK

US release: 30 August 2005
Produced by: Jeff Rosen, Steve Berkowitz, Bruce Dickinson and Martin Scorsese
CHARTS: US#16; UK#21

DISC ONE
When I Got Troubles
Rambler, Gambler
This Land is Your Land
Song to Woody
Dink's Song
I Was Young When I Left Home
Sally Gal
Don't Think Twice, It's All Right
Man of Constant Sorrow
Blowin' in the Wind
Masters of War
A Hard Rain's A-Gonna Fall
When the Ship Comes In
Mr. Tambourine Man
Chimes of Freedom
It's All Over Now, Baby Blue

DISC TWO
She Belongs to Me
Maggie's Farm
It Takes a Lot to Laugh, It Takes a Train to Cry
Tombstone Blues

Just Like Tom Thumb's Blues
Desolation Row
Highway 61 Revisited
Leopard-Skin Pill-Box Hat
Stuck Inside of Mobile with the Memphis Blues Again
Visions of Johanna
Ballad of a Thin Man
Like a Rolling Stone

The 2005 TV documentary *No Direction Home* felt like Bob Dylan's answer to The Beatles' *Anthology*. A massive three-and-a-half-hour summary of Dylan's career up to 1966, it intertwined new interviews with Dylan and his friends and associates (not all of them with complimentary things to say) with archive footage. Much of the latter was impossibly rare – including barely aired material from *Eat the Document* and the never-before-seen (as opposed to heard) Manchester Free Trade Hall "Judas!" moment. Dylan's office had the inspired idea of recruiting famed director Martin Scorsese to mould the material they had painstakingly shot and gathered, thus acquiring a higher profile for the end product. Scorsese had previously directed *The Last Waltz*, the film of The Band's final concert and would go on to direct The Rolling Stones' cinema release *Shine a Light*, but despite his rock credentials a large part of the editing was actually done by his colleague David Tedeschi. Broadcast across two nights on PBS in America and BBC2 in Britain, the film was both fascinating for long-term fans and an eye-opener for a generation who had no immediate knowledge of how brilliant rock can be.

Another similarity with *Anthology* is that it was accompanied by a loosely related CD release. Also as with *Anthology*, the CD version was not a soundtrack to the television programme of the same name. Though there are some recordings common to both projects, the soundtrack album is, as the CD booklet notes, actually more of a "companion" to the film. As with *Anthology* again, it constitutes almost an alternative history of the career (or part thereof) it traces via musty home recordings, demos, live performances and alternate takes, in this case almost two-and-a-half hours' worth. The front cover depicts Dylan during the

1966 British tour, a frizzy-haired alien presence in Gloucestershire waiting for a ferry to take him to Wales.

The set opens with the eighteen-year-old Dylan singing an early original composition, 'When I Got Troubles'. No doubt this blues owes much to antecedents – what blues doesn't? – but in any case at a minute-and-a-half it's too fleeting to form much of an opinion about its worth. From the following year comes Dylan performing in similarly informal conditions a competent version of the traditional 'Rambler, Gambler'.

Dylan's debt to Woody Guthrie is carefully acknowledged on *No Direction Home*. 'Song to Woody' from his debut LP is the only track from his studio catalogue included on the set. It sits beside a live version of Guthrie's signature song 'This Land is Your Land', recorded at Carnegie Chapter Hall four months before the release of that debut which is done too reverentially and could almost be anyone. There is a brace of songs from the Tony Glover Minnesota tape made after the recording, but before the release, of Dylan's first album. Neither the traditional 'Dink's Song' (given a Bo Diddley beat) nor Dylan's 'I Was Young When I Left Home' are interesting as anything other than stepping stones to the rounded artist he would become.

'Sally Gal' is yet another outtake from *The Freewheelin' Bob Dylan*. A high-spirited quasi-instrumental, it sees Dylan impressively pulling off the remarkable musician's scratch-your-head-while-rubbing-your-belly trick, executing simultaneous rapid-fire guitar and harmonica. 'Don't Think Twice, It's All Right' is presented in the form of the demo Dylan recorded for the Witmark publishing company. Though it's not quite as good as the familiar version, the extended instrumental intro shows that, though Bruce Langhorne may have played the guitar on the *Freewheelin'* take, Dylan is a pretty fine picker himself. In March 1963, Dylan appeared on the TV show *Folk Songs and More Folk Songs*, and the version of 'Man of Constant Sorrow' here – interesting mainly for the harmonica work – derives from that broadcast.

'Blowin' in the Wind' and 'Masters of War' are from Dylan's gig at New York Town Hall in April 1963 and would be impressive performances to people who have never heard the great studio recordings. By October of the same year, Dylan had graduated to Carnegie Hall, from where the performances of 'A Hard Rain's A-Gonna Fall' and 'When the Ship Comes In' derive. The former is powerful, besting the (admittedly over-rated) studio cut due to the amazing sustain in Dylan's voice. 'When the Ship Comes In' is a passable version of a slight song.

An alternate version of 'Mr. Tambourine Man' is where it feels as though the album really starts. What was the first complete take of the song features fellow folkie Ramblin' Jack Elliott singing the choruses with the composer – at Dylan's touching voluble insistence, heard at the beginning. Dylan states there "ain't" no place he's going to; it had become the grammatically correct "is" by the time of the master take, an update of which The Byrds had evidently not been informed. Dylan's hesitancy over his words (which are slightly different in other ways too) mean it would never have made a master, but it does provide an intriguing insight into the way the track developed.

A performance of 'Chimes of Freedom' at the 1964 Newport Folk Festival is again respectable but never preferable to the album version. The same is not true of an alternate take of 'It's All Over Now, Baby Blue', which is less intense and self-consciously dramatic and possibly superior to the master take. Also possibly superior is the alternate 'She Belongs to Me' that opens disc two. The backing instrumentation on *Bringing It All Back Home* was rather perfunctory, so it shouldn't come as a huge surprise that this two-man rendition is attractive, an always pretty tune and affecting sentiment complemented perfectly by the subtle but sparkling work of Bruce Langhorne.

'Maggie's Farm' is the opening number from the infamous set at the 1965 Newport Folk Festival. In light of all that's been said about the bad acoustics and the disquiet they allegedly created in the crowd, it's seriously doubtful whether the clarity evident on this cut is what the audience experienced on the day. Had it been, it would most likely have gone down reasonably well, being not only well-played, if slower than we are used to, but of a muscular blues that Newport attendees had no problem with, while the bellyaching of the lyric would probably have been accepted by the audience as in the rebellious spirit of this artist's protest songs.

We are presented with no fewer than five outtakes from

Highway 61. 'It Takes a Lot to Laugh, It Takes a Train to Cry' is present in an uptempo version virtually indistinguishable from the outtake of the song heard on *The Bootleg Series 1–3*. That it follows straight on from the rhythmically similar 'Maggie's Farm' makes it seem even more one-dimensional, which in turn makes Kooper's organ runs – clueless and desperate compared to the poised piano work by either Frank Owens or Paul Griffin on the familiar master – even more irritating. The breakdown of 'Tombstone Blues' heard here (Dylan's laughter brings the take to a halt) is lyrically toned-down, the shocking sacrilege replaced by tame references not to John the Baptist but to "John the blacksmith", thus making the reference to the "commander-in-chief" anodyne. However, the contributions of the backing band to the chorus vocals (even if mixed too low) suggest that the unreleased version with the soul vocal group the Chambers Brothers harmonising might have been a preferable inclusion. 'Just Like Tom Thumb's Blues' has piano work noticeably different to, but just as elegant as, that on the famous version, and Dylan tackles the opening line – which he negotiated awkwardly on the album master – adroitly. Dylan tweaks the melody line slightly in a very pleasant track. Take one of 'Desolation Row' is an electric version, minus drums, with Dylan accompanied by Harvey Goldstein (a.k.a. Brooks) on bass and Al Kooper, who is not playing organ but guitar, and peels off atmospheric, flaring lines. There are many minor differences in the lyric, all of which seem inferior – or is that an illusion generated by familiarity? Dylan's vocal performance doesn't have the edge it does on the album. On the master, the way he onomatopoeically enunciates "blow it up" illustrates his absolute immersion in what he is singing. Again, it might be partly illusion, but a song we know to be a twenty-four-carat classic just seems dreary in this format. 'Highway 61 Revisited' is represented in a take recorded prior to the one that featured the penny-whistle sound. Apart from that, the differences are negligible.

'Leopard-Skin Pill-Box Hat' is the first of a trio of alternate takes from *Blonde on Blonde*. This version is slower and richer, lacking the unattractively brittle tone of the master. It also has an additional pair of verses. Even so, six-and-a-half minutes is too long for any blues, even one as funny as this. 'Stuck Inside of

Mobile with the Memphis Blues Again' is rhythmically and melodically different to the master take. It lacks that elegant, leisurely feel of the album version, as well as that wonderful cymbal tapping at the close of verses, and Dylan takes the song to its conclusion even despite stumbling over the lyric more than once. 'Visions of Johanna' is from the abortive pre-Nashville sessions with The Band. The marching beat of the song makes it feel like a declaration rather than a rumination, to its detriment.

Two recordings from the boo-drowned 1966 UK tour follow. The Free Trade Hall version of 'Like a Rolling Stone' which closes the set we know and love from volume four of the *Bootleg Series*. (They could hardly leave it out considering the lyric gives the project its title and its performance provides its most dramatic moment.) 'Ballad of a Thin Man' derives from the ABC Theatre in Edinburgh three days later. It's almost eight minutes long but never drags courtesy mostly of the almost berserk commitment Dylan had to his material on that tour.

LIVE AT THE GASLIGHT 1962
US release: 30 August 2005
Produced by: Jeff Rosen and Steve Berkowitz
CHARTS: US# – ; UK# –

A Hard Rain's A-Gonna Fall
Rocks and Gravel
Don't Think Twice, It's All Right
The Cuckoo (Is a Pretty Bird)
Moonshiner
Handsome Molly
Cocaine
John Brown
Barbara Allen
West Texas

LIVE AT CARNEGIE HALL 1963
US release: 15 November 2005
Produced by: –
CHARTS: US# – ; UK# –

The Times They Are A-Changin'
Ballad of Hollis Brown
Boots of Spanish Leather
Lay Down Your Weary Tune
North Country Blues
With God on Our Side

Around the same time as the release of *The Bootleg Series Vol. 7*, Dylan allowed an irritating limited issue of other treasures from the vaults. *Live at the Gaslight 1962* was an intimate in-concert recording made between his first and second LPs that was very well known to collectors. A pensive Dylan is seen strumming in a workshirt on the black-and-white front. The album is comprised mostly of covers (including a version of 'Cocaine' he would never have dared try to get on an album at the time), but it also includes the rare originals 'John Brown' and 'Rocks and Gravel'. That not all the songs known to derive from this performance (which could possibly have been two gigs) were included was irritating enough, but that people who wanted it were obliged to visit Starbucks, who had exclusive retail rights for eighteen months, infuriated many. The left's disdain for that coffee chain may seem as manufactured and inchoate as was their contempt for Dylan going electric back in the day, but the no-doubt lucrative deal he struck with Starbucks did seem the thin end of a nasty corporate wedge that was cheapening his work. It also caused needless upset at a time when traditional music retail outlets felt under more pressure than ever before due to the Internet, with some record stores pulling his back catalogue from their shelves in protest. Far more irritating for the wider public is the fact that not long after it gained a mainstream release, the album was deleted.

Three months after the Gaslight album's Starbucks release came *Live at Carnegie Hall 1963*, a recording of a slightly later vintage, the cover depicting a lonely-looking Dylan sitting on a stool on the stage of a vastly bigger and more prestigious venue. This product has been described in some quarters as an EP, but Dylan has released albums shorter than this half-hour affair. However, again those collectors who had illicit copies knew it omitted several songs, even if in this case ones that had already become part of the official canon. It was a release that was again quickly, and for no good reason, deleted (although at least remains legally available as a download). Both albums of course would have made perfect *Bootleg Series* releases, if not separately then together.

The news that he was going to host his own radio show would have been jaw-dropping had it not come in a decade in which Bob Dylan had repeatedly surprised his fans – and by no means always in a good way. Fortunately, Theme Time Radio Hour *– which began broadcasting on the satellite subscription-only XM Channel 40 in May 2006 – was not one of Dylan's unpleasant surprises. Each sixty-minute show saw Dylan select songs with a common subject (mothers, baseball, divorce and coffee amongst them), displaying a deep knowledge of pop history in the process. While his between-song chat necessarily robbed him of much of his mystique – it was astonishing to hear his lengthy rambling (however fascinating) when we had mostly been only used to gnomic silence or elliptical interview answers from him – no one disputed that he did his job brilliantly.*

Gavin Martin's booklet notes for a 2008 Ace Records compilation that rounded up some of the tracks Dylan played in the first of his three series so far gives a flavour of Dylan's singular approach to his new sideline.

THEME TIME RADIO HOUR: DYLAN AS DJ

By Gavin Martin

First published as the booklet notes to *Theme Time Radio Hour with Your Host Bob Dylan*

Bob Dylan's *Theme Time Radio Hour* is an essential strand in a process of renewal and revelation that has hallmarked the man's seventh decade.

Dylan's emergence as a funny, fastidious and impeccably informed DJ is perfectly in keeping with his role as the award-winning autobiographer of *Chronicles*, the wily big screenwriter of *Masked and Anonymous* and the ink and watercolour art Bob presented recently in the Drawn Blank Series at the Kunstsammlungen Chemnitz museum in Germany. And, of course, Bob the DJ is an essential counterpart to Bob the indefatigable live performer who regularly breathes fresh, unexpected life into old and new songs – his own and others – on his hundred-plus gigs a year. It is small wonder that he should put so much care, attention and detail into his broadcasts. As a child growing up in the Minnesota rust belt, it was through the magic of the radio that Dylan first heard the myriad performers who would inspire his future career.

His expansive choice of music provides a treasure trove of joy and wonder. Each song tells a story, revealing another element in his kaleidoscopic vision of America – and the universe at large. Deeply respectful of his forebears, Dylan proffers between-song commentaries which consistently supply apposite details of the performers' lives and often – movingly – their deaths, too. The relish with which he quotes song lyrics – or complements the music with lines of wisdom from the likes of Shakespeare or Rilke – provides further layers of edification.

The combined wealth and warmth of words and music is a perfect expression of Dylan's capacity to, in the words of one of his many heroes Walt Whitman, "contain multitudes".

This is a DJ who believes passionately in the power of music and, even more specifically, in the magical power of song. Dylan is naturally obsessed with the science of song, forever weighing up what qualities and insight make a tune tick or become an essential aid to living.

Dylan at the decks follows a simple but too often forgotten rule of radio DJing – he tells you the name of song and the artist before and after each play. Thereafter, his free-flowing conversation touches on subject matter sparked off by the songs – which is to say everything from stay-at-home dads to nuclear war, from the racial iniquity of Deep South justice in the 1950s to life, death, taxes and the history of men's haircuts as catalogued on decades of George Jones album sleeves.

Enjoyable enough in themselves, the between-song discursions are the embodiment of *Theme Time Radio Hour*'s underlying belief that songs can engage with life at every level – from the mundane to the frivolous, from the deeply philosophical to the socially aware and deathlessly spiritual. Or, as Dylan puts it, "I never understood no border patrol when it comes to music."

Bob Dylan, the character Robert Zimmerman created out of

a swirl of musical, cinematic and literary influences, has always thrived by communicating his passions and opening up new, undiscovered worlds for the listener. It's easy to hear how the *TTRH* choices do the same thing for him – Patsy Raye & The Beatniks' 'Beatnik's Wish', for instance, suggests the dark dangerous excitement of the exotic women who stalk the pages of *Chronicles*. Another *TTRH* selection, Jack Teagarden's 'Stars Fell on Alabama', is directly referenced on Dylan's own ' 'Cross the Green Mountain', a contender for his greatest masterpiece of the twenty-first century.

Such insights are all part and parcel of the generous spirit that has informed his career; since the Damascus-like experience he has described as having taken place on a Swiss stage in the 1980s. That quasi-religious sense of duty is about charting the road map which has brought him and his audience to their current destination. And, in the age of digital mass communication, who better than Bob Dylan to do justice to all those great good and sometimes too easily forgotten warriors who have made that journey possible?

The voice Dylan uses to present *TTRH* is that of a wry, rasping and waggish rock 'n' roll general, one who has explored the furthest edges of his art and culture and remembers his comrades with a combination of love and awe. The show is an oasis and jewel in the expansive treasury that has been his gift to the world. Seldom has one of the greats devoted such a wealth of love and learning to such an expansive legacy.

Accompanied by his abundant output on *TTRH* – which, each week, uncovers new jokes, insights and musical discoveries – is also the most direct and enjoyable way of uncovering the many facets of Dylan's musical life. By hosting this show in his inimitable style Bob Dylan ensures that, for listeners young and old, his own work has never been so vividly explained or appreciated – as autobiographical in its own way as *Chronicles*.

MODERN TIMES

By Sean Egan

US release: 29 August 2006
Produced by: Jack Frost
CHARTS: US#1; UK#3

Thunder on the Mountain
Spirit on the Water
Rollin' and Tumblin'
When the Deal Goes Down
Someday Baby
Workingman's Blues #2
Beyond the Horizon
Nettie Moore
The Levee's Gonna Break
Ain't Talkin'

November 2005 saw the US-only release of *The Best of Bob Dylan*, yet another compilation of, naturally, mainly the same material previously included on such releases. No doubt the brilliance of much of what it contained converted anyone beneath whose radar his previous best-ofs had flown. Three months before that had come a new album that – like his two previous efforts – one would have imagined would win no new converts to Dylan's music. On the contrary. Though people with memories long enough to recall when entering charts at No.1 was rare are unimpressed by the marketing cunning that saw *Modern Times* debut at the summit of the *Billboard* chart, not so easy to dismiss is the fact that Dylan's first No.1 US album since *Desire* has subsequently gone platinum and picked up two Grammies. Not bad for a man who would qualify for a state pension in Britain. Just a pity that the album is so dreary.

The hour's worth of music on *Modern Times* was recorded at

a Manhattan studio in February 2006, Dylan's current touring
band once again the musicians. It had been five years since
Dylan's last studio album, and though the hunger pangs of his
fans had been sated by some wonderful archive Dylan product
in the interim, even without the *Bootleg Series* releases it probably would not have seemed an inordinately long gap. The record
industry had changed fundamentally since the days when Dylan
released two LPs a year. By the Seventies the industry standard
had settled down to one album release per year, but the gaps
grew ever longer from the late-Eighties onwards as artists realized they could "tour" an album for two years or more. Dylan of
course didn't quite fit this marketing approach, but fell into line
with the way things were now done release-wise – as befitting
someone who had pioneered long absences from the release
schedules.

Modern Times is a most curious record. Its music takes Dylan
further down the road of cultivated antiquity, from its 1947
front-cover photograph of a New York cab to its retro sound to
its quite blatant appropriation of snatches of lyrics and melodies
from songs not all of which are even old enough to be public
domain. Though it features a full (if minimal) band, it is in all
other respects a throwback to the days when his albums featured
traditional tunes co-opted by him for his singular lyrical vision.
In an interview a couple of years before, Dylan had disclaimed
the idea that he was a "melodist", insisting, "My songs are either
based on old Protestant hymns or Carter Family songs or variations of the blues form." This is nonsense, of course, and no
doubt another manifestation of that old familiar self-loathing
and terror of failure, deliberately doing himself down so that
criticism somehow means less. Dylan provided his own refuta-
tion: he made this comment one month after he had pointed out
in *Chronicles Volume One* that Duane Eddy wouldn't have
recorded an instrumental album of mainly his songs if he was
only good at words. However, on this album those melodic gifts
are conspicuously not in evidence, and one can only assume that
the explanation is that the artist decided deliberately to recreate
the spirit of the years 1962–64. The canons of a couple of historical poets – Ovid and Henry Timrod – also get raided for the
odd line or phrase.

'Thunder on the Mountain', a piece of old-time rock 'n' roll, opens proceedings. Yet another Armageddon scenario with some more very traditionalist domestic prerequisites ("I want some real good woman to do just what I say") is provided a novelty factor by the way Dylan works in a verse about modern-day chanteuse Alicia Keys. Dylan's piano is frustratingly buried here, "Jack Frost" in his second successive solo production surely to blame.

'Spirit on the Water' is another audacious attempt at crooner's music by a man who can only rasp. Vocal aside, it's quite authentic, although it's difficult to think of a Thirties pop song that went over seven-and-a-half minutes, nor one containing a line as delightful as "I can't go back to paradise no more, I killed a man back there." One of the few high points. Yes, 'Rollin' and Tumblin' ' is *that* 'Rollin' and Tumblin' ', the blues standard most associated with Muddy Waters that was beloved of a thousand R&B bands in the Sixties. Dylan uses the first verse as a jumping off point for his new lyric, but the retooling doesn't prevent it from being amazingly boring.

Bing Crosby's 'Where the Blue of the Night (Meets the Gold of the Day)' provides the tune for 'When the Deal Goes Down'. As usual, Dylan uses crooner pop for the most incongruous lyric, this one looking forward to the unravelling of the mystery of life offered by death ("We live and we die, we know not why/ But I'll be with you when the deal goes down"). 'Someday Baby' is another blues rewrite, in this instance 'Worried Life Blues', to which the riff of John Lee Hooker's 'Dimples' is bolted. It's awful. That the album won a Grammy for Best Contemporary Folk/Americana Album isn't too outlandish – how many releases fit that description? – but that Dylan picked up the Best Solo Rock Vocal Performance award at the same ceremony for the way he croaks though 'Someday Baby' is – considering the number of competent performances there must have been in front of a mic that year – a joke.

The clear, sparkling piano that opens 'Workingman's Blues #2' briefly reminds us that there is more to music than the primordial audio and spiritual murk through which we have been wading since *Time Out of Mind*. The poverty tableau of the lyric is grim, though, and not alleviated at all by the thought that it may be a metaphor for Dylan's spiritual state. The lyric, as with so many on this album, remains frustratingly outside the borders of meaning ("They will lay you low/ They'll break your horns and slash you with steel, I say it so it must be so").

'Beyond the Horizon' is similar territory to 'When the Deal Goes Down' in that a Thirties pop framework is utilised to address heavy religious issues ("Beyond the horizon, in the Springtime or Fall/Love waits forever for one and for all"). The melody Dylan is singing here is that previously belonging to old-time pop number 'Red Sails in the Sunset'. 'Nettie Moore' is not (largely) the nineteenth-century composition 'Gentle Nettie Moore'. There is some mercifully clean delineation of instrumentation but the song sums up how tired the type of lyric Dylan has taken to writing lately is becoming, with its American mythology and colloquial poetry ("I'm the oldest son of a crazy man/I'm in a cowboy band") and understated but overly recurrent religiosity ("Got a pile of sins to pay for and I ain't got time to hide"). 'The Levee's Gonna Break' is most famous to rock fans as 'When the Levee Breaks', the closer of Led Zeppelin's untitled fourth album. If only this rewrite approached the cosmic foreboding of that variant of the blues standard recorded by, amongst others, Memphis Minnie, an artist beloved of Dylan. Unfortunately, this is just another of the dreary twelve-bars that have proliferate in too much of Dylan's recent music.

'Ain't Talkin'' ends proceedings on a relative high note. At nearly nine minutes, this woozy, dream-like concoction is the album's epic. However, lines like, "I practice a faith that's been long abandoned/Ain't no altars on this long and lonesome road" would be far more impressive if we hadn't just sat through a whole album of this (increasingly scattershot) kind of despair. And two albums before that.

More and more, it feels like the desolation that was attractive and moving on *Time Out of Mind* is a pose that is getting tiresome, or if it's not a pose is a state of mind that is producing diminishing artistic returns. Ditto for the American-myth lyrics, old-world music and production murk. A newer habit – juxtaposing blues and Thirties pop – is already wearing thin. Additionally, one can't even take some sort of solace from liking the artist, for it's difficult to get away from the fact that Dylan's narrators come across as wheezing, sinister figures with no warmth or capacity for love.

Simultaneous with the release of *"Love and Theft"* came the iTunes release *The Collection*. Though it is a good thing that Dylan/his management are open to new means of disseminating his music, and though *The Collection* (his entire album oeuvre to date) was a bargain (763 tracks plus a hundred-page PDF booklet for a total of $199.99), that needs to be counterbalanced by several demerits: that digital downloads involve a significant diminution of sound quality, that the collection included six compilations (meaning multiple duplication even within the compilations let alone the whole collection) and that there were a couple of cynical enticements. The presence of the 1973 *Dylan* album meant that it could only be obtained here, leaving latecomers to the Dylan canon having to duplicate previous album purchases if they wanted to get hold of it. Moreover, the throwing in of an otherwise unavailable set called *Rare Tracks from the Vaults* was reminiscent of placing unheard tracks on *Greatest Hits Vol.II* and *Biograph* – but on a gargantuan scale. It wasn't even an accurate title: all the material – obscure recordings, live performances, soundtrack entries, remixes, alternate versions, B-sides – had been previously commercially released, even if some of it was mouth-wateringly scarce. In order to posses it all, one would have needed to already own the bonus disc from a limited edition *"Love and Theft"*, a CD given away with a Swedish magazine, *Live at the Gaslight 1962*, the iTunes exclusive bonus tracks for *The Bootleg Series Volume 7, Live at Carnegie Hall 1963* (included in its entirety here), the DVD of *Dont Look Back*, the 'I Want You' single, *A Tribute to Woody Guthrie*, the 'Went to See the Gypsy' 2004 iTunes single, the 'George Jackson' single, the *Renaldo & Clara* promo EP, the 1976 single 'Stuck Inside of Mobile with the Memphis Blues Again', the single 'Everything is Broken', the reggae Dylan covers-album *Is it Rolling Bob?*, the soundtracks of *Hearts of Fire, Folkways: A Vision Shared – Tribute to Woody Guthrie & Leadbelly, The Sopranos, Divine Secrets of the Ya-Ya Sisterhood, Gods and Generals, Masked and Anonymous* and *North Country*, various European 'Love Sick' singles or alternatively the limited-edition Australian version of *Time Out of Mind*, the Japanese album *Bob Dylan Live 1961–2000: Thirty-Nine Years of Great Concert Performances*, the album *Postcards of the Hanging: The Grateful Dead Perform the Songs of Bob Dylan*, the various-artists album *Gotta Serve Somebody: The Gospel Songs of Bob Dylan* and – in a crescendo of implausibility – the album *Victoria's Secret Exclusive: Lovesick* that compiled some of his songs and a remix in association with the lingerie company. As can be seen from the bewilderingly disparate sources of rarities, such a release was a highly useful (if not thorough) mopping-up exercise for those who wish to have absolutely everything Dylan has produced, but in this context was also an insult to them. It provided an almost perfect moral argument for a generation whose concept of intellectual property has been rendered almost non-existent by the ready availability of music on the Internet for refusing to pay for such material and instead downloading it illegally. Some might suggest that the "almost" part of that "almost perfect" argument was itself blown away by iTunes dropping the collection from its catalogue at the end of 2009.

Up until November 2007, there had never been a Bob Dylan biopic. Perhaps inevitably, when Dylan did give his permission for such a project, it was one that was in his own tradition of eccentricity and fractured reality. In this blend of two previously published articles, Stephen Dalton tells the story of a movie that took its title from one of the rarer Basement Tape recordings, 'I'm Not There,' (1956) which became legally accessible to the public for the first time in the movie's soundtrack.

I'M NOT THERE

By Stephen Dalton

Originally published in *The Times*, 15 September 2007 and *Venue*, 14 December 2007

Todd Haynes talks a good fight. When we meet in a wintry Vienna, the forty-six-year-old director is in the final stages of his festival-hopping world tour to promote *I'm Not There*, the unorthodox Bob Dylan "biodrama" that is rapidly turning into the most anticipated and debated film of 2007. Reaction so far has been broadly positive, but Haynes has always made the kind of experimental dramas that divide critics and audiences. He is ready for trouble.

Featuring six different actors (including Heath Ledger and Christian Bale) as fictionalised fragments of Dylan's personality, *I'm Not There* is part compilation album, part PhD thesis. Some of it is stunning, especially a dragged-up Cate Blanchett's uncanny evocation of the singer in his mid-1960s prime as an arrogant, antagonistic, androgynous proto-punk superstar. Other sections are slow and pretentious, obscuring rather than illuminating the weight of mythology around Dylan. And yet Haynes insists all these fantastical fabrications add up to a deeper truth.

"I just wanted to make a film about Dylan in a way that used the cinematic medium to get close to something that I think is really true about him," he argues. "Which is that he refuses to stay in one category, doing the same kind of music, fulfilling the same expectations."

Haynes scored a major coup by securing the rights to Dylan's music and image for *I'm Not There*. When he attempted a similarly fanciful re-working of various 1970s glam-rock stars in his flawed but fascinating 1998 film *Velvet Goldmine*, David Bowie denied him access to all but one song. Way back in 2000, Haynes won Dylan's approval with a one-page summary of his plans. The reclusive rocker's manager Jeff Rosen came back with a green light. But even now, with the project complete, Haynes has never met or spoken to Dylan directly.

"I never got feedback at any time from Dylan," Haynes laughs. "All I got is a message from Jeff that he looked at the proposal and said, 'You like this guy? Let's give him the rights.' That's all I ever heard quoted from Bob Dylan about the project. Otherwise Jeff became our present, active, personable, incredibly generous link to Dylan. Or just link to the things we needed to make the film, because I didn't really need Dylan at all, after he gave me . . . everything."

Considering this largely experimental director has only one previous commercial success to his name, this deal was clearly a matter of trust. But it may be significant that the words "Bob" or "Dylan" do not appear even once in the film. Haynes took a gamble that a more orthodox factual biopic, along the lines of *Ray* or *Walk the Line*, would have been knocked back. "It became quite clear he would not have given approval to something that was putting him in the same-sized box," Haynes nods. "I think he's had many offers over the years for films to be made about his life that I assume would have followed a more conventional pattern, which he said no to."

Born in LA in 1961, Haynes studied art at Brown, an exclusive Ivy League university in Rhode Island. There he met Christine Vachon, who remains his producer to this day. Their debut collaboration was *Poison* in 1991, which drew criticism from right-wing Congressmen furious with Haynes for using public arts money to make a sexually explicit gay melodrama. A longtime AIDS activist and founding member of the short-lived New Queer Cinema movement of the early 1990s, Haynes includes gay themes and characters in almost all his films. Some have suggested *I'm Not There* breaks with this convention, although the scene in which Blanchett angrily sings Dylan's 'Ballad of a Thin Man' to Bruce Greenwood's media inquisitor is charged with gender-bending sexual menace. "It's an incredibly sadomasochistic, homoerotic song," Haynes argues, "with all of these images of high heels, going down on his knees, Freudian slippages for fellatio and all that stuff. Which is curious if you are starting with this idea of Dylan as a male, white, heterosexual master of the popular song. This song arguably shows another side of Dylan's imagination."

Haynes says he chose to cast a woman in this section in order to recreate the shock value of Dylan's mid-1960s rebirth as an alien, androgynous, proto-punk rocker. "I can't think of an artist, particularly of Dylan's stature, who first was met with such antagonism by a disappointed fanbase when he plugged in electric and just fucking went for it," grins Haynes. "He used that energy to fuel him further, crank up the music louder and basically invite violent dissent! That is punk rock! In 1966, before anybody did that. Dylan is so canonised, so worshipped, so approved nowadays that you forget his genuine weirdness. When you worship someone too much, you lose the grit and sweat and the risks he took."

I'm Not There coincided with a series of life changes for Haynes. He conceived the film in a burst of revitalised creativity after leaving New York at the dawn of this decade. Fifteen years in the city had left him jaded with hipster scenes and high rents. He settled in Portland, Oregon, close to his sister Wendy and his film-making friend Gus Van Sant. With the Dylan project still in gestation, Haynes wrote and directed his sumptuous 1950s retro-drama *Far from Heaven*, earning four Oscar nominations and his only significant commercial success to date. As *I'm Not There* neared completion, he also lost his former partner and longtime editor, Jim Lyons, to AIDS. The film is dedicated to Lyons.

An audacious act of cinematic collage, *I'm Not There* is drawn almost entirely from Dylan's dense hinterland of musical, literary and cultural references. Some scenes quote directly from lyrics and interviews. Others distort and rewrite real events into dreamlike digressions. It is a technical marvel, but arguably something of an arid intellectual exercise, with no emotional heart. "There better be, or it shouldn't be a movie," Haynes bristles. "I don't think any movie works that way, and I don't think that's how Dylan's music works – even though that too is full of references, allusions, jokes, and inside information. You don't have to understand every reference because music is an intensely emotional, primarily visceral medium, and I think film is too. John Lennon said about Dylan, you don't have to understand a single word he says to know what he's talking about."

Ultimately, it is not too surprising that Dylan approved *I'm Not There*. Haynes has essentially composed a gallery of opaque half-portraits that mirror the singer's own restless, shape-shifting, myth-making nature. "These so-called connoisseurs of Bob Dylan music, I don't feel they know a thing or have any inkling of who I am or what I'm about," Dylan himself complained in a rare 2001 interview. "It's ludicrous, humorous and sad that such people have spent so much of their time thinking about me. Get a life please . . . you're wasting your own." Haynes agrees, conceding *I'm Not There* is not a film for fundamentalist fans. "The fanaticism around Dylan fans is one more symptom of the desire he ends up creating by never staying put," the director says. "When you want something and you can't ever completely attain it, that's the definition of desire. That's what's so funny about the fans, how much they want to keep him in place and define him and fetishise all traces of him. We are all fetishists in one way or another, but there is a humourlessness to it that I think Dylan finds particularly annoying."

As well as heavily lacing the script with direct quotes from Dylan interviews, song lyrics and biographies, Haynes layers cinematic allusions to the singer's film appearances, from the classic 1960s rockumentaries like *Dont Look Back* and *Eat the Document* to Sam Peckinpah's lyrical anti-western, *Pat Garrett and Billy the Kid*. A further welter of references reflect Dylan's musical, literary and cultural influences: Arthur Rimbaud, Woody Guthrie, Allen Ginsberg, Joan Baez, The Beatles, dust-bowl blues, born-again Christianity and more. It's a rich, overwhelming, occasionally confusing mix. But Haynes has the perfect response to aggrieved fans who may feel like shouting "Judas!" from the gallery.

"Everything in the film came from Dylan," he shrugs. "From his work, his interests, his biography, the music. Almost every line is from Dylan. Mostly it's just a mass of research and a process of distillation and reorganisation of a very dense creative output, an incredibly dense historical backdrop and a rich and varied series of influences. We got through the Beat poets, the Symbolist poets, the Old Testament, the pop songs of the 1960s. I felt it was my duty to almost follow in his steps and explore all of those elements."

I'm Not There is as much a post-modern essay on the history of cinema, twentieth-century America and the distorting mirror of fame as it is about one artist and his music. In this sense, the film's subject is arguably Haynes himself as much as Dylan. But the director boldly claims his fragmented, prismatic, highly subjective approach comes closer to capturing the reality of Dylan than any straight biopic ever could. "I always feel that's truer to what the artist is about," Haynes nods. "Because even if you try to be absolutely objective and invisible as a storyteller, you're making choices, you're fictionalising. There are a million biases, a million opinions, a million projections and acts of distortion that you are imposing. There's no such thing as objective construction of anything, your blood and guts are all over it, so why keep resorting to this idea of an invisible medium? It doesn't exist."

The film's final section, a surrealistic pastoral western featuring Richard Gere, has attracted the most criticism. Drawing elliptical parallels between Dylan's late 1960s retreat to rural upstate New York and the autumn years of retired outlaw Billy the Kid, it feels ponderous and stilted after Blanchett's wired energy. "The Richard Gere story is a very ambitious part of the film," Haynes says. "It tries to include a whole lot of Dylan's work, so it leaves a lot of people scratching their head. But it seemed like a necessary element in this otherwise very urban film. Dylan maintains this fantasy about the rustic past and roots of American folklore, and originally concocted himself out of some of those myths. So I felt it important to end the film in the same place, to have it come full circle."

If *I'm Not There* leaves you feeling confused, you will not be alone. Movie mogul Harvey Weinstein, whose company bought the distribution rights for Britain and America, also had serious doubts after seeing an early cut back in May. He even pushed Haynes to delete the Gere chapter entirely, but the director had final cut and fought his corner. "Harvey was actually very honest," Haynes recalls. "He said 'I don't know if I'm the right person to distribute this movie, I don't understand it . . .' But his heart's in the right place. In the end I have to be thankful Harvey came in at all. He was the only US distributor to step up."

A riddle wrapped in a mystery inside an enigma, *I'm Not There* is essentially a homage from one fiercely single-minded artist to another. Whatever its flaws, it is a bold, beautiful and commendably ambitious work. Haynes fought for years to make it, and he's ready to fight for it still.

"I was prepared for defending the movie," he says, "or maybe people never liking the movie. But at a certain point I was able to see it for what it was and think: that was the film I wanted to make. I can't believe we pulled it off, and I'm very proud of it. That's all I needed to know. The rest I can handle."

THE BOOTLEG SERIES VOL. 8: TELL TALE SIGNS – RARE AND UNRELEASED 1989–2006

By Sean Egan

US release: 7 October 2008
Produced by: Jeff Rosen
CHARTS: US#6; UK#9

DISC ONE
Mississippi
Most of the Time
Dignity
Someday Baby
Red River Shore
Tell Ol' Bill
Born in Time
Can't Wait
Everything is Broken
Dreamin' of You
Huck's Tune
Marchin' to the City
High Water (For Charley Patton)

DISC TWO
Mississippi
32–20 Blues
Series of Dreams
God Knows
Can't Escape from You
Dignity
Ring Them Bells
Cocaine Blues
Ain't Talkin'
The Girl on the Greenbriar Shore

Lonesome Day Blues
Miss the Mississippi
The Lonesome River
'Cross the Green Mountain

DISC THREE
Duncan & Brady
Cold Irons Bound
Mississippi
Most of the Time
Ring Them Bells
Things Have Changed
Red River Shore
Born in Time
Tryin' to Get to Heaven
Marchin' to the City
Can't Wait
Mary and the Soldier

Though 2007 did not see either a new Dylan album or another
Bootleg Series release, there was a lot of Dylan on the release
schedules, albeit all compilation-related.

In June came a useful rounding-up of the Wilburys material
(unavailable for years, partly because of the 2001 death of
George Harrison, on whose label it had been issued) in the form
of *Traveling Wilburys Collection*, featuring volumes 1 and 3, plus
bonus tracks and a DVD. It did staggeringly good business. The
first week of October saw yet another best-of for the man who
had been Lucky and Boo Wilbury, although the fact that it was
titled *Dylan* indicated this was the one that was intended to be
definitive. (The title of course was slightly confusing even if the
wretched outtakes-of-crap 1973 album of that name was now
deleted as a standalone product.) It was issued in two versions,
a single disc (which went Top 40 in the USA and Top 10 in the
UK) and a triple set running to a mind-boggling 3.6 hours. Both
editions featured just the word "Dylan" on their minimalist
covers, in raggedy black lettering against a painted red backdrop. That *Self Portrait* and *Dylan* (1973) were two of only three
of his studio albums not represented on the triple set was

understandable, but not so comprehensible was the fact of *Saved* being ignored: even Dylan seems to undervalue this album. As a publicity stunt to coincide with the new compilation's release, fashionable young British producer Mark Ronson (chiefly known for his work with edgy UK chanteuses Amy Winehouse and Lily Allen) was commissioned to remix *Blonde on Blonde*'s 'Most Likely You Go Your Way (And I'll Go Mine)' for a download-only single (a single not actually included on the album it was effectively promoting). A 2004 reggae mix of 'I and I' was Dylan's only previous such authorisation of tampering with his product.

If Dylan fans and music critics raised an eyebrow at the *Rare Tracks from the Vaults* collection as a continuation of the grubby marketing ploys to which Dylan has always been surprisingly open, the stunt that he allowed to be pulled to sell volume 8 of the *Bootleg Series* – a collection with a close-up head shot of Dylan with pencil moustache on the cover entitled *Tell Tale Signs* – left them positively fuming. There was a two-disc version retailing at $18.99, the version for which chart statistics are given on the previous page. There was also an "expanded deluxe" version, a three-CD affair which would set the consumer back $129.99. Some fans might have been able to swallow shelling out more than a hundred dollars extra for twelve songs, a hardback version of the CD booklet and an additional hardback 172-page book reproducing Dylan singles covers from down the years if, say, that money was going to crippled children. (He once made a substantial unsolicited donation to the costs of building a disabled kids' playground after seeing an item about it on television.) In the absence of any such declaration of noble destination, they assumed that greed motivated the disproportionate differential and reacted with outrage – and in many cases, one imagines, by seeking out the extra disc or even whole set on one of the bittorrent or rapid-sharing websites that partly thrive on such disgruntlement.

The collection is comprised of songs from movie soundtracks, miscellaneous live recordings, alternate and demo versions of previously released material, rarities and album outtakes. Though the deluxe version of the collection consisted of the same number of discs as *The Bootleg Series Volumes 1–3*, that inaugural instalment in the brand covered not only a span of twenty-eight years but took in Dylan's peak period. It seemed a little surprising, even presumptuous, that a timespan shorter by eleven years, part of which saw Dylan in the worst artistic doldrums of his career, should take up an equivalent amount of audio space. Unsurprisingly, the overall quality doesn't approach that of *Biograph*.

Considering both the length of *Time Out of Mind* and its quality, the number of tracks rejected for it is astounding. Several are featured here, some of which outtakes share lines with songs that did make the album's cut. 'Mississippi' of course ended up on *"Love and Theft"*. There are no fewer than three versions of it recorded at the *Time Out of Mind* sessions present, and – genuine bootleg style – that does not make it unique on this release. The first, which opens the whole collection, is sparse and although most of the instrumentation is in soft focus in the style of *Time Out of Mind*, Dylan's voice and the main guitar are clearly delineated. The third version is inappropriately light-hearted. Version two – crisp and matter-of-fact – is the most impressive. Though 'Red River Shore' conforms to *Time Out of Mind*'s almost parodic determined glumness (it even features the line "I'm wearing a cloak of misery"), it would probably have been a good replacement for one of that album's weaker tracks, not least because its celebration of the virtues of a girl from the place of the title would have made a thankful contrast to the otherwise accusatory tone employed with females therein. The second version has more of a Cajun flavour. Like most of the other *Time Out of Mind*- and *Oh Mercy*-vintage selections here, it hasn't yet been put through Lanois's muffling production technique. 'Can't Wait' is an alternate version of the *Time Out of Mind* track and shows in its rejection of impressionistic murk for crystal-sharp instrumentation what that album could have been, even if the drums are a bit too invasive. Alternate version #2 is even better, striking the right balance between the lack of aural fog and overinsistent backing. Outtake 'Dreamin' of You' is well-crafted lyrically and musically but by now this slow-burning misery is becoming nondescript. 'Marchin' to the City', a prototype ' 'Till I Fell in Love with You', is presented in two versions. All you need to know about the first is that it's a 6:36 slow blues. In contrast, the second version is quite a peppy, strident thing. Neither is worth investigating again, though.

The pros and cons of Lanois's production techniques are demonstrated by two versions of the *Oh Mercy* track 'Most of the Time'. A guitar-and-harmonica rendition lacks the atmospheric ness a band and Lanois's shimmering methods confer, while a full-band alternate version features a more conventional production – instruments, especially lovely bass work, pleasingly prominent rather than kept behind an atmospheric film á la Lanois's usual methods. A piano demo of 'Dignity' is mildly impressive for the way Dylan invests everything in the vocal as though a formal recording. A proper alternate take is a curious affair, ramshackle and shambling compared to the slick version on *Greatest Hits Volume 3*. 'Born in Time' is an *Oh Mercy* outtake. The first version here strangely almost has an MOR feel while fitting right into that album's charcoal texture. It should have made the cut. A second version, though, takes that middle-of-the-road and slightly anthemic feel to such an extreme than it is uncomfortably reminiscent melodically of Tina Turner's Eighties work and makes one think it could have fitted on the execrable *Empire Burlesque*. With the alternate version of the *Oh Mercy* track 'Everything is Broken', what was always a slight song – as bad as *Shot of Love*'s 'Trouble' in its empty profundity – is at least given a modicum of beef by an arrangement and production that doesn't seek to give it an inappropriately mystical air. 'Series of Dreams' is an alternate take of that you'll-never-guess *Oh Mercy* song that ended up on *The Bootleg Series 1–3*. It's probably slightly better while at the same time not really worth its second airing here. 'God Knows' is a wonderful rockin' *Oh Mercy* reject that was later rewritten to make a mediocre *Under the Red Sky* track. This less preachy version would have done much to bolster the spotty *Oh Mercy*, although one does get the depressing feeling that after Lanois had finished with it, its brawny timbre and nicely untidy burps of instrumentation would have been obscured by his homogenous fog. The forced re-exposure to 'Ring Them Bells' via an alternate of the *Oh Mercy* track convinces us it does have a memorable tune and impressive melancholy but reminds us too that it is at bottom a song of distasteful judgementalness. There is also a live version from Dylan's acoustic shows at the Supper Club in November 1993 – the ones that could have made a far better acoustic album than *MTV Unplugged* – which is sympathetically and sensitively handled.

'Someday Baby' is an alternate version of the *Modern Times* track that won Dylan an inexplicable Grammy. It lacks the 'Dimples' guitar lick and is still a boring song. The alternate version of 'Ain't Talkin' ' is not as pleasantly dreamlike as the *Modern Times* master but enjoyable nonetheless. '32–20 Blues' is a *World Gone Wrong* outtake written by one of Dylan's musical heroes, Robert Johnson. The composition sees the narrator explaining in quite explicit detail the violence he is planning to do to his woman. It's well performed and better than much of what appeared on that album, although one could never say one liked a song so chillingly nasty. The traditional 'Mary and the Soldier' – another *World Gone Wrong* outtake and the set's closer, at least on the deluxe version – doesn't even have that unpleasant frisson.

Dylan has in recent years been strangely in demand for soundtrack work, of which there are a few examples here. 'Tell Ol' Bill' is an alternate version of a song included on the soundtrack to the 2005 movie *North Country*. The line "I lay awake at night with troubled dreams" should be enough to tell you about the timbre of a song that is respectable enough but is one of countless variants of the same type from this period. 'Huck's Tune', from the *Lucky You* soundtrack, is a superior example of this style of grizzled, weary worldview set to a traditional melody. ''Cross the Green Mountain' is from the movie *Gods and Generals*. It's quite surprising that Dylan is prepared to "waste" this well-written and played 8:15 epic on a movie score. Having said that, it's the same-old, same-old God's-gonna-get-ya stuff and the lack of relevance of lines like "I look into the eyes of my merciful friend/And then I ask myself, 'Is this the end?'" to a movie about the American Civil War seems to have been dismissed by the movie-makers in their excitement over the cachet of having Dylan's name in their closing credits.

A live version of 'High Water (For Charley Patton)' from Canada in 2003 is quite funky, with Dylan snarling out a powerful vocal and one of the three guitarists present contributing some fine work. Superior to the studio original. 'Cocaine Blues' derives from a Vienna gig in August 1997. Dylan performs a minimalist and spiky version of this old blues standard. 'Cold Irons Bound' is represented by a grimy, tired-sounding Bonnaroo version from 2004. 'The Girl on the Greenbriar Shore' is a 1992 solo performance in France of the traditional folk song that gave Dylan the tune for 'Red River Shore'. Dylan's retooling was a lot better than this courtly, stately, boring folk song, which is greeted with embarrassing sycophantic applause. 'Lonesome Day Blues' originates in Florida in 2002. It's a rather scruffy version. 'Things Have Changed' is respectable in its June 2000, Portland incarnation but at the same time nothing to get excited about. As for 'Tryin' to Get to Heaven', it's passable but you probably had to be in London on 5 October 2000 to fully appreciate it.

'Can't Escape from You' is a 2005 song commissioned for a movie that ultimately wasn't filmed. Another example of gnarly old-man's music that can just as easily be either absorbing or depressingly devoid of zip. 'Miss the Mississippi' and 'Duncan & Brady' are a pair of tracks from the album Dylan began in 1992 of full-band versions of the sort of material he covered solo on *Good As I Been to You* and *World Gone Wrong*. The first was written by Jimmie Rodgers, the second is too old to have an acknowledged composer. Both are competent, but not enough in any way to make one wish for the instalment in the *Bootleg Series* dedicated to these sessions that Larry "Ratso" Sloman proposes in the booklet notes. 'The Lonesome River' is a duet with Ralph Stanley from the latter's album *Clinch Mountain Country*. It's mildly interesting, though a version of a country standard captures nothing of the quintessence of Dylan.

Though a generally agreeable, if almost never exceptional, listening experience, *Tell Tale Signs* is also rather dispiriting. The fact that it is disproportionately comprised of songs deriving from the sessions of Dylan's two most depressive studio albums, *Oh Mercy* and *Time Out of Mind*, gives rise to some rather uncharitable thoughts about him. After being immersed in his glum psyche for three hours, thoughts turn to those people who have characterized Dylan variously as "not a very nice man at all, but a sociopath who, in his songs, became ten times the man he was in real life" (Victor Maymudes, Dylan associate-cum-employee from 1964 to 1996) and the "most convoluted personality" he'd ever met (Sam Peckinpah). Once upon a time, his first marriage seemed to offer Dylan salvation from those aspects about himself. His art since that marriage broke down has traced the downwards progression of a personality that has attempted to pin the blame for his discontent on everybody but himself, the most excruciating manifestation of which self-deception was the born-again period. Dylan strikes one as a man perpetually running from himself, possessed of enough intelligence to know on some level that it's him, not the world, that is the reason for his wretched inner feelings, but is stricken with too much insecurity to ever fully admit it to himself. This may sound a little melodramatic – he's not a murderer or a maniac, and acts of personal and financial generosity are not at all unknown in his life – but he is now so completely engulfed in his sepia-toned, bring-on-death mindset that one finds it no wonder he talks in 'Mississippi' of "the corner that I painted myself in".

TOGETHER THROUGH LIFE

By Sean Egan

US release: 28 April 2009
Produced by: Jack Frost
CHARTS: US#1; UK#1

Beyond Here Lies Nothin'
Life is Hard
My Wife's Home Town
If You Ever Go to Houston
Forgetful Heart
Jolene
This Dream of You
Shake Shake Mama
I Feel a Change Comin' On
It's All Good

If we are to accept Dylan's (contentious) latter-day argument that he is no melodist and therefore it is natural for him to raid public-domain numbers to find vehicles for the lyrics that are his artistic *raisons d'être*, what on earth are we to make of *Together Through Life*, an album whose lyrics are supplied by Robert Hunter on all but one track?

Dylan and the Grateful Dead lyricist had of course previously collaborated on 'Ugliest Girl in the World' and 'Silvio' on 1988's *Down in the Groove*, but that was at a point when Dylan could not muster enough inspiration to fill an album with his own compositions. While melodic inspiration might have been short on *Modern Times*, Dylan's lyrical abilities had been operational, even if within very narrow parameters. This confusion was only added to by Hunter when he told *Uncut* magazine, "He often makes it clear exactly what sort of song he wants, and I have no problem writing to his specifications. He generally adds what enhances the lyric from his point of view, sometimes doing large-scale rewrites, sometimes just a touch or two." Leaving aside the obscurity of Dylan's motives, the team-up means we are back in that awkward and inconvenient territory that *Desire* occupies, with the listener unsure as to whom to credit or admire for what pleasures him about what he hears, or whom to blame about what displeases him.

As with *Modern Times*, the album came with an impressionistic cover, this one of a couple canoodling in a car on a motorway. There were two deluxe editions, but these did not create the controversy that the deluxe version of *Tell Tale Signs* did, firstly because there was no exorbitant pricing structure and secondly because the bonuses – a DVD featuring an interview with Dylan's first manager that was an outtake from the *No Direction Home* documentary and a CD containing an edition of one of Dylan's *Theme Time Radio Hour* broadcasts – were nice to possess for the Dylan fanatic but not essential for those who are merely interested in the canon. The standard album comes in at a lately shortish 45:31.

The album was recorded at the end of 2008. Once again, backing is supplied by Dylan's current touring band and the tone is spartan. The deficiencies of Dylan's recent records – glumness, his shot voice, understatement verging on somnambulance and nobody at Jack Frost's shoulder to tell him that things aren't mixed to their optimum state – are present and incorrect. The main tonal difference on this recording is the predominant accordion work of David Hildago.

One suspects that Dylan had some input into the title of opener 'Beyond Here Lies Nothin' ', it being a quote from Ovid in best Dylan magpie tradition. However, the rest of it seems hardly the kind of message with which Dylan would agree, urging an exultation in here-and-now romance because life is not a rehearsal. Some interesting guitar work by Mike Campbell, naturally, sits slightly too low in the mix to be properly appreciated. 'Life is Hard' sounds like the usual and by now tiresome latter-day Dylan subject matter but in fact the title phrase leads to the line "without you near me", making it the closest thing to a conventional love song Dylan seems capable of (co-)writing these days. A delicate musical arrangement features mandolin and brush drumming.

Although *Together Through Life* sees Dylan recover the abilities as a "melodist" he had recently denied possessing, there is one recognizable (and duly credited) lift from another song, namely Willie Dixon's 'I Just Want to Make Love to You', which provides the tune for 'My Wife's Home Town', a song about a man's hatred of both his spouse and her background. As with most Dixon songs, the melody is a cut above most twelve-bars and Hildago lifts things further by proving what nobody suspected: that the accordion can sound devilish.

On 'If You Ever Go to Houston' Hildago's accordion is, by contrast, obtrusive, an insistent presence that detracts from more interesting organ and guitar work. That the song trundles on inconsequentially and incomprehensively for nearly six minutes only worsens the monotony and irritation. The swirling 'Forgetful Heart' is quite enjoyable, if its brooding over a lost love profoundly over-familiar in Dylan's recent work. 'Jolene' is a strutting blues with a keening guitar riff that would be devastating if it were fully audible.

'This Dream of You' is the only solo Dylan composition. It has an almost jolly French café ambience but its subject matter is very serious indeed, if hardly unknown territory for Dylan. When he sings, "All I have and all I know/Is this dream of you/Which keeps me living on", he's not talking about a departed lover. Horribly for him, however, he's not 100 per cent sure that the God he is addressing exists: "There's a moment when all old things/Become new again/But that moment might have come and gone." Rarely can a man have publicly paraded his despair over such an extended period as has Dylan in the first part of the twenty-first century.

'Shake Shake Mama' addresses some of the earthly pleasures that offer some sort of comfort in this vale of tears. It's a horny blues, absolutely authentic in the way of recent Dylan twelve-bars, and rather enjoyable. 'I Feel a Change Comin' On' has the brightest, peppiest melody of anything here, although that doesn't stop it meandering, while uncertainty about any insight it offers into Dylan's psyche makes one unwilling to delve too deeply into its lyrical waters. On the closer 'It's All Good', it's not clear whether Dylan and Hunter are mocking that ghastly, flabby-minded Nineties catchphrase from which the song takes its title. The persistence of the accordion is by now annoying. In the lyric, Dylan sings that everywhere one looks, there's more misery. To which one feels like retorting, "Only on your albums, Bob." Having said that, this album is considerably less depressive than the three studio works that preceded it. Perhaps it was for the best that Dylan turned to another lyricist: how many more albums could he have turned out exploring the limited interior life of the husk of the man he is (or wants us to believe he is)? However, following up an album of mostly second-hand tunes with an album whose lyrics are largely written by someone else is disturbingly suggestive of an artist in creative crisis again. Meanwhile, the sonic palette that he seems to have decided not to move beyond is ultimately dispiriting and boring. That this album was Dylan's second successive US No.1 album and his first UK chart topper since *New Morning* (a gap of forty years) is a worrying fact: in the face of such apparent public approval, what incentive is there now for Dylan to change a musical modus operandi that is pretty close to a state of ossification?

But then, we've been here before, and Dylan has proven over and over that he can never be counted out.

CHRISTMAS IN THE HEART/FOLKSINGER'S CHOICE

By Sean Egan

CHRISTMAS IN THE HEART
US release: 13 October 2009
Produced by: Jack Frost
CHARTS: US#23; UK#40

Here Comes Santa Claus
Do You Hear What I Hear?
Winter Wonderland
Hark the Herald Angels Sing
I'll Be Home for Christmas
Little Drummer Boy
The Christmas Blues
O' Come All Ye Faithful (Adeste Fideles)
Have Yourself a Merry Little Christmas
Must Be Santa
Silver Bells
The First Noel
Christmas Island
The Christmas Song
O' Little Town of Bethlehem

When it was announced, out of the blue, that late 2009 would see the release of a Dylan album called *Christmas in the Heart*, it almost seemed like a practical joke.

The greetings-card-like cover artwork – two people making their way through the snow on a horse-driven sleigh on the front, silhouettes of the three wise men following the Star of the East on the back – did nothing to dispel that idea. The saucy shot of Betty Page inside with the cheesecake legend in a revealing Christmassy outfit was more in Dylan's irreverent style, as was the photograph of his band (three of whom had appeared on *Together Through Life*) looking humiliated in Santa Claus outfits. But the contents still seemed impossible. For 42:20, Dylan truly was croaking his way through the likes of 'Winter Wonderland', 'Little Drummer Boy', 'O' Come All Ye Faithful' and all the other well-known Yuletide favourites that drip with a sentimentality and an exultation in unthinking tradition that we have always assumed that even the post-born again Bob finds risible. Perhaps our reaction represents the fact that we are always projecting a high-mindedness on Dylan that he possibly doesn't possess (especially in the last decade or so, when he has shown a pronounced venality), perhaps we are failing to take into account the fact that seeing Christmas through the uncynical eyes of one's offspring changes one's perception of it irrevocably and perhaps the fact that Dylan donates all the artist royalties from *Christmas in the Heart* to homelessness charities renders the laughable scenario the album represents irrelevant. However, if one were to nominate the type of album most comedically incongruous in light of Bob Dylan's latter-day musical persona – religious certainly, but also battered, weary, nicotine-voiced, even slightly menacing – then it would have to be an album like this.

Jack Frost is credited as producer again, but the fact that this work has a far brighter sonic picture than Dylan's last four studio albums leads one to assume that David Bianco has had a bigger influence than his "recorded and mixed by" credit suggests. It is presumably Dylan, though, who is responsible for a palette the richness of which hasn't been heard in his music for well over a decade, as exemplified by the sleigh bells that kick off the opener, and the celeste and choir that augment a version of Gene Autrey's 'Here Comes Santa Claus'.

Although a delightful breakneck version of 'Must Be Santa' comes close to comedy, throughout Dylan gives no hint of being ironic, which is actually a good thing: once the decision to make a Christmas album had been made, it would have been a sour act indeed to mock the festival or the music that celebrates it. Despite Dylan's wrecked vocal cords, he often genuinely does capture the season's sad-happy flavour – that impossibly good spirit so unsustainable that it spills over into melancholy – whether it be in a secular, holiday gathering way ('Winter Wonderland') or by a worshipful approach ('Hark the Herald Angels Sing').

Some will have been confirmed in their impression of Dylan

as a bit of a joke by this album, but it's not only the charitable impetus for it that ultimately makes one conclude, "Well, why not?" It's a decent listen – even if, by definition, of relevance to just a small portion of the year – and if a man like Bing Crosby could become indelibly associated with a time of the year whose joyousness was absolutely inimical to his glacial and severe nature, there is no reason why a self-loathing man with a voice like rocks and gravel shouldn't commit to posterity his celebration of Yuletide. Additionally, the worldview of *Christmas in the Heart*, though it might be somewhat cartoonish, is certainly something of a relief from the grimness of recent Dylan fare.

FOLKSINGER'S CHOICE
US release: 16 August 2010
Produced by: –
CHARTS: US# – ; UK# –

(I Heard That) Lonesome Whistle
Fixin' to Die
Smokestack Lightning
Hard Travelin'
The Death of Emmett Till
Standing on the Highway
Roll On John
Stealin', Stealin'
Makes a Long Time Man Feel Bad
Baby Please Don't Go
Hard Times in New York Town

The music on *Folksinger's Choice* has long been familiar to bootleg collectors but is distributed widely for the first time via this release from Left Field Media which seems to fall into a legally grey area created by different countries' rules on when broadcast material becomes public domain. (At the time of writing, it can be found on the UK Amazon site but not its American counterpart.) With Dylan having now been a recording artist for nigh on a half-century, releases like this will presumably become commonplace. It certainly doesn't feel substandard, being well-packaged and featuring lengthy and knowledgeable booklet notes by one Deryck Gordon. The cover features a full-length shot of a very young Dylan standing, guitar at the ready, before a studio microphone.

Cynthia Gooding was a folk recording-artist who also presented shows for New York's WBAI radio station, one of which was *Folksinger's Choice*. The latter show clearly had its finger on the pulse, for Dylan was booked to make a substantive live appearance on it in early 1962, even if Gooding had a heads-up through knowing Dylan in his Minneapolis college days. The cover claims that the recording dates from 11 March that year, although some have disputed this, suggesting that that is a repeat transmission date, and that it more likely derives from a day in February. Either way, it was before the release of Dylan's debut album and catches him on the cusp of only becoming moder-ately well-known, let alone famous.

Much of the almost hour-long recording and hence this release is given over to interview. It's hardly penetrating stuff and both Gooding and Dylan are rather gauche (Dylan is as anxious to know at the end of each number if the host likes what she has heard as she is to gushingly confirm that she does). Dylan is also in that phase when he is building a myth around himself which took many years and assiduous work by several journalists and biographers to dispel. He tells Gooding that he once worked on a carnival that boasted an Elephant Lady as one of its attractions. Gooding, incidentally, is mightily impressed by what she calls his necklace, which reminds us that the harmonica rack was a little-known tool until Dylan popularised it.

From today's perspective, it seems a bit quaint that so much airspace, time and analysis should be dedicated to a twenty-year-old primarily singing versions of other people's songs, and furthermore rendering them solo, a method that leaves little room for reinterpretation. Having said that, this collection of songs – even recordings, because audio fidelity is pristine – would have been preferable to Dylan's debut. Versions of Hank Williams's '(I Heard That) Lonesome Whistle' and Woody Guthrie's 'Hard Travelin'' might have grim subject matter but are easy on the ears in a way that so much of the morbid material on *Bob Dylan* is not. Meanwhile, it is inexplicable that the three Dylan originals here – 'The Death of Emmett Till', 'Standing on the Highway' and 'Hard Times in New York Town' – were not included on his first or second albums.

Dylan's preternatural facility with words has caused critics to dub him such things as Poet Laureate of Rock 'n' Roll. That is, rock critics. Critics from other fields have sometimes been less laudatory, hence the "Keats is better than Dylan" debate kicked off by playwright David Hare in the early Nineties. Hare's argument was, of course, fatuous: Dylan and Keats worked in separate fields. That song composition requires a different discipline to printed poetry – and that the exigencies of melody and vocal performance often create a tension with those things in a song lyric that might be deemed to be poetic – is a subject explored in depth by John Herdman below, in a piece of writing in which he also, it so happens, discusses those occasions on which Dylan has engaged (via programme notes and album sleevenotes) in printed poetry.

SOME OTHER KINDS OF POEMS

By John Herdman

First published in *Voice Without Restraint: Bob Dylan's Lyrics and Their Background* (Paul Harris Publishing)

One of the favourite classifications used by journalists in their attempts to categorise Dylan has been that of the "poet". An article called 'The genius who went underground', printed in the *Chicago Tribune* in 1967, is a typical case in point. The writer tells how "Dylan is looked upon as a practising member of the craft" by "bearded guru poet Allen Ginsberg", Kenneth Rexroth, Robert Creeley and others. The tone attributed to these luminaries is embarrassingly patronising: Ginsberg, for instance, informs us that "He writes better poetry than I did at his age", while Michael McClure ("author of the controversial play, *The Beard*") is said to have called 'Gates of Eden' "the key to his completing a set of poems". It is perhaps fair to point out that the poets concerned were probably less responsible for this tone than the journalist quoting them. The whole piece has the true journalistic stench, with Dylan being offered to the man-in-the street for approval as endorsed by the mystic authority of "poets" (in the same way that "doctors say that . . ." and "scientists believe that . . ."), even though most of these poets couldn't hold a candle to him. The nadir of this "poet" preoccupation is probably reached in Johnny Cash's well-meaning but excruciating tribute on the jacket of *Nashville Skyline*:

> Here-in is a hell of a poet.
> And lots of other things
> And lots of other things.

Dylan has given his view of this classification of himself in an interview, and typically he went straight to the point which the *Chicago Tribune*'s poets missed. In response to the question, "Do you consider yourself primarily a poet?" he replied: "No. We have our ideas about poets . . . I don't call myself a poet because I don't like the word. I'm a trapeze artist." Ellen Willis is useful here with a comment which can serve as a gloss on Dylan's own: "When critics call Dylan a poet they really mean a visionary. Because the poet is the paradigmatic seer it is conventional to talk about the film poet, the jazz poet. Dylan is verbal, which makes the label even more tempting. But it evades an important truth – the new visionaries are not poets."

This does not, all the same, exhaust the argument. In another context Dylan acknowledges what people mean by the attribution when, on the cover notes to *Bringing It All Back Home*, he writes, "A poem is a naked person . . . some people say that I am a poet." Then again, he has written poems, and published them. Not only that, he has published his lyrics up to 1970 in a volume without the music, and included as illustrations in the hardback edition of *Writings and Drawings* some examples of his rough drafts, which show his methods of lyric composition to be not strikingly different from those of many poets. There are aspects of Dylan's song writing which will yield to critical analysis almost as if we were dealing with poems: Michael Gray's work on his language and imagery makes that clear. Dylan's lyrics are composed in writing, after all; in that sense he is not an oral artist. His art is a hybrid thing, influenced by poetry and other literary forms as well as by a profusion of musical traditions; and sometimes there are internal conflicts between its different aspects. This chapter will attempt to do two things: first, take some notice of Dylan's early poems, whose virtues seem to have been largely overlooked, and then consider certain aspects of the construction of his song lyrics which show a variable tension between the demands of the music and the look and feel of the words on the page. That Dylan is first and foremost a song writer is obvious; but there *are* some senses in which he is also a poet, and in which, I suspect, he thinks of his writing as being analogous to the writing of poems.

We have seen again and again that Dylan conceives his art as being a matter of giving embodiment to feelings in such a way that they can be experienced as real by his audience, felt anew by others. Ezra Pound said once that "The poet's job is to define and yet again define", and we can say that for Dylan making a song or a poem is a process of defining a feeling in as immediate and concrete a form as he is able to give it. The method of reaching this goal which he chooses in the poems that he was writing contemporaneously with his very early albums is that of accretion, the building-up of a sense of life from an accumulation of small particulars. That he was already able to convey a feeling in song lyrics with great economy is clear from such numbers as 'Girl from the North Country' and 'One Too Many Mornings', but his approach in the poems is utterly different. Here he uses the line-break entirely as a device for separating discrete impressions, attributes or experiences – there is almost never a run-on of sense from line to line:

> Hibbing's got the biggest open pit ore mine in the world
> Hibbing's got schools, churches, grocery stores an' a jail
> It's got high school football games an' a movie house
> Hibbing's got souped-up cars runnin' full blast on a
>   Friday night
> Hibbing's got corner bars with polka bands . . .

'My Life in a Stolen Moment' goes on to build up a picture of Dylan's experience in the same way that it builds an impression of his home town, by adding detail to detail in a succession of "atmospheric" images. The principle of one idea to a line is strictly adhered to, and when the idea is physically too big for a line of print the unit is nonetheless maintained in the way the words are set out:

> I looked up a long time friend in Sioux Falls an' was let down,
>> worried blind, and hit hard by seein' how little we had to say
> I rolled back to Kansas, Iowa, Minnesota, lookin' up
>> ol' time pals an' first-run gals an' I was beginnin'
>> to find out that my road an' their road
>> is two different kinds a roads . . .

The method is saved from monotony by switches of focus – from places to people to experiences to influences and back to places again. It is a device seen in its most extreme form in 'Last Thoughts on Woody Guthrie', where it is underlined by the use of rhyme (mainly couplets, though with some variation) and by the habit of beginning line after line with the same word – "And" or "When", for instance – in successive series of accretions from an initial thought or image. The poem centres on two lines near the middle, consisting of an almost meaningless phrase which is repeated in such a way that the first half of the poem leads up to it and the second expands away from it again:

> And you need something special
> Yeah, you need something special all right . . .

The first part tells us how you feel when you need it (that second "need" is in fact the poem's first main verb), and the second what it is that you need (it turns out to be God or Woody Guthrie, take your pick, and the poem ends with the rather trite thought that both may be found "in the Grand Canyon/At sundown"). This naïve construction is the excuse for assembling an impressive array of vivid images which in accumulation really do succeed in giving substance to a number of feelings that would otherwise remain vague and diffuse.

★   ★   ★

And there's somethin' on yer mind that you wanna be
  saying
That somebody someplace oughta be hearin'
But it's trapped in yer tongue and sealed in yer head
And it bothers you badly when you're layin' in bed
And no matter how hard you try you just can't say it
And yer scared to yer soul you just might forget it
And yer eyes get swimmy from the tears in yer head
And yer pillows of feathers turn to blankets of lead . . .

In this poem the apparent point – the needing of "something special" – is little more than a hook for yoking together a scatter of disparate impressions: the much more successful *Joan Baez in Concert Part 2* notes, by contrast, have a real and strong idea at their core, and the poem is genuinely exploratory. It takes as a starting-point a striking picture, that of Dylan as a boy kneeling beside the railroad line near his aunt's house as he waits for the "iron ore cars" to roll by, yanking the grass out of the ground and ripping "savagely at its roots". When the train has passed he looks at his green-stained hands and sees that he has "taken an' not given in return". This image provides him with a grip on what he wants to say about the way he was then and is now:

> An' I walked my road like a frightened fox
> An' I sung my song like a demon child
> With a kick an' a curse
> From inside my mother's womb –.

As he grows up he learns to intellectualise his instincts and impulses; he finds symbols to represent what he wants to fight and idols "T" be my voice an' tell my tale". His first idol is Hank Williams because he sang about the railroad lines, which symbolized reality to the boy. He comes to see beauty only in what is ugly, for only the ugly is real to him, and to reject everything that is conventionally beautiful. (Years later he was to tell an interviewer that "I see beauty where other people don't.")

Dylan describes how as he develops the symbol "beauty" continues to represent for him something to be resisted, how he shouts:

> The voice t' speak for me an' mine
> Is the hard filthy gutter sound
> For it's only this that I can touch
> An' the only beauty I can feel . . .

Then he meets Joan Baez and hears her sing, and for the first time is confronted by the need to ask himself whether there can be a value in the kinds of beauty which hitherto he has rejected. Asked about this poem by his *Playboy* interviewer in 1978, Dylan commented: "I was very hung up on Joan at the time. [Pause] I think I was just trying to tell myself I wasn't hung up on her." That is no doubt true, and it is honest of Dylan to say so; but the poem itself gives form to a very much more intricate kind of honesty, a slow and painstaking analysis of the acquiring of a certain self-knowledge. It is something that could not have been done in a song, and indicates what sort of function the writing of these poems must have had for him at that stage in his career. It gave him the opportunity to stand back from himself and look coolly at his past and at his present situation, providing a different kind of outlet from the inspired immediacy that characterizes his songs. Dylan is thinking here not instinctively but contemplatively, trying to get certain things clear through detachment rather than through the swift stab of insight. The effect is slower, more careful than that of the songs, and just because of that contrast the exercise is especially valuable, telling us much about the inner drives that forged Dylan's achievements in his major mode. It shows, too, that his success is not due to instinct alone, though instinct comes first. He has also thought about himself, criticised himself and modified his understanding as a result. The poem ends by returning to the image of the torn grass:

> I'll bend down an' count the strands a grass
> But one thing that's bound t' be
> Is that, instead a pullin' at the earth
> I'll jus' pet it as a friend . . .

What the poem does is to show, concretely, how realities give rise to feelings, which in their turn engender ideas; how these ideas can ossify and become rigid when divorced from their origins; and how eventually fresh experience, with the new feelings and emotions which stem from it, mounts an assault on the old ideas, and finally modifies or dissolves them. Dylan is always on the hunt of reality, trying to pin it down, but at the same time allow it its livingness, its dynamic. In this poem he does his work with patience and honesty, and with the help of much effective – and sometimes ambiguous – imagery:

> For the breeze I heard in a young girl's breath
> Proved true as sex an' womanhood
> An' deep as the lowest depths a death
> An' as strong as the weakest winds that blow . . .

The '11 Outlined Epitaphs' have a more "literary" feel to them. They have shorter lines, are more impressionistic and less direct in their approach than the earlier poems, and a few of them are obscure in places. They also show a number of definite literary influences: numbers three and four, for example, contain references to, or echoes of, Villon, Rimbaud and Eliot. The title indicates a certain provisional quality which sometimes shows through. The best of them however have again the purpose of commenting on Dylan's development and present situation, clarifying certain experiences for him in ways which were not available to him through the medium of song. In the second, for instance, he returns once more to his roots in an eloquent evocation of Hibbing which is at once a leavetaking of his early youth and a coming to terms with it. The fourth epitaph similarly looks back at his education and the decisive point at which he turned away from it, "not carin' no more/what people knew about things/but rather how they felt about things"; the sixth bids farewell to his "last idol", Woody Guthrie, who "just carried a book of Man/an' gave it t' me t' read awhile." All have, as might be expected, a certain valedictory quality: Dylan faces a nagging, troublesome idea and by giving it concrete and exact form is able to dismiss it and put it behind him.

Many of these ideas are thrust upon him from without; they represent the accusations and misunderstandings suffered by an artist in the public eye who is the eternal victim of comment and interrogation ("I am on the side a them hurt feelings/plunged on by unsensitive hammers"). The resulting apologias are the reverse of apologetic. The eighth epitaph, evidently an answer to accusations of plagiarism, magnificently overturns the false idea of artistic "originality", with a sharp and convincing analysis of the way an artist makes use of old material:

> t' make new sounds out of old sounds
> an' new words out of old words
> an' not t' worry about new rules
> for they ain't been made yet
> an' t' shout my singin' mind
> knowin' that it is me an' my kind
> that will make those rules . . .

In fifty-odd lines he says all that needs to be said on the subject and is able to bury it. The following epitaph performs a similar office for the magazine interview, for the journalists who complain when he fails to co-operate with them in presenting a picture of himself that will satisfy people "who want t' see/the boy nex' door":

> I don't like t' be stuck in print
> Starin' out at cavity minds . . .

A few lines of dialogue deftly present the kind of implied threat, the submerged blackmail which is used in an attempt to pressurise him into conforming. The exposure of those who seek to "expose" Dylan (which, he points out, he does himself "every time I step out/on the stage") is complete and unanswerable.

The last set of poems which Dylan allowed to be published in *Writings and Drawings* were those called 'Some Other Kinds of Songs'. They are, indeed, closer to his songs than the earlier poems, and closer too to the material and approach of his novel *Tarantula*. Some of them read like sketches for what he does more tightly and succinctly in the songs; and the beginning of the first could almost be from a discarded draft of 'Subterranean Homesick Blues':

baby black's
been had
ain't bad
smokestacked
chicken shacked
dressed in black
silver monkey
on her back . . .

These poems are less linear than those which went before, contemplative passages being interspersed with impressionistic anecdotes and little thumbnail sketches. Sometimes they are loosely linked by a recurring motif such as that of the man threatening to jump off Brooklyn Bridge; in general the ideas are less sharply focused than in the 'Epitaphs' or the Joan Baez concert notes. But they can be included with those poems in adding up to a picture of what Wordsworth, in his sub-title to *The Prelude*, called 'The Growth of a Poet's Mind'. We may presume that Dylan stopped writing these poems, or at least publishing them, when he felt sufficiently confident in his primary activity of song writing no longer to need to explain himself to himself or to others.

2

Before turning once more to the songs it is as well to remind ourselves that the distinction between song and poetry would not be readily understood by the people of many, if not most, cultures, including that of medieval Europe. Song form was the only form for lyric poetry throughout most of the artistic history of mankind. Poetry was designed to be sung and listened to, and visual elements simply did not enter in to the making of a poem. It was only after the advent of printing that the visually orientated forms of poetry to which we are mainly accustomed in modern Western culture became dominant. Dylan's aural orientation is scarcely something new within a wider frame of reference. The complexity of the music to which many of his songs are set, however, *is* innovatory, and this often results in a reduced conduciveness to visual appreciation when the words are seen on the page. There are many things which the words (as written) do not have to do because the voice and the music are doing them. In printed poetry, because meaning is abstracted from the sound of the spoken word, total sense must be contained within what is written, whereas in Dylan's work much of the sense may be contributed by aspects of the music. Even such a quintessentially emotive phrase as "How does it feel? How does it feel?" can look cool, detached and unemotional in print. If it does not, or to the extent to which it does not, it is because we carry into our reading a knowledge of how it sounds when sung, perhaps in a variety of tones and moods. (Unless such a know-ledge of how Dylan sounds could be assumed in the readers of this book, the writing of it would clearly be a fruitless exercise.) On the page the words may lose much of their emotional tonal-ity, their dynamic properties, and become relatively inert. But (and this is the main theme of this chapter) this does not always happen, or not always to the same degree. Because Dylan's art is a mixed form, influenced by the traditions of Western poetry as well as by oral and aural determinants, it often has qualities which are closer to visual poetry than its primarily aural charac-ter might suggest.

Dylan will often use half-rhyme and assonance in ways which make them sound more or less like a full rhyme when sung: the structural patterns are intended for the ear and not for the eye. In 'When the Ship Comes In', for example, "laugh" rhymes with "path", "spoken" with "ocean", "roll" with "gold", "tribe" with "tide", "numbered" with "conquered". Similarly in 'Boots of Spanish Leather' we have "morning" corresponding to "land-ing", "ownin'" to "ocean" (twice), "golden" to "Barcelona". In 'Mr. Tambourine Man' "wanderin'" rhymes with "under it". Dylan is expert at bending sounds with his voice to turn them into rhymes. One of his favourite eccentric rhymes is that of "mirror" with words ending "-eer" or "-ear". It probably sounds much less strange to American ears than to British ones, but it must still look odd on the page:

> Louise, she's all right, she's just near
> She's delicate and seems like the mirror
> But she just makes it all to concise and too clear
> That Johanna's not here . . .

Dylan's pronunciation is roughly "meer'r", one and a half syllables. He uses the same rhyme internally in 'No Time to Think': "You glance through the mirror and there's eyes staring clear/At the back of your head as you drink"; and in 'Went to See the Gypsy' rhymes the word with "rear", "fear" and "here".

In these cases the aural principle enhances or fills out dubious rhymes; Dylan imposes heavy duty upon procedures which in written poetry would be reserved for subtler effects. But the opposite can happen too. More frequently, effects which would be too strong for the printed page are toned down, made into subtler instruments, by their musical context. The piled-up internal rhymes of 'All I Really Want to Do' provide a good example (though the phrase "internal rhyme" itself betrays a visual prejudice: it is often hard to say whether a Dylan rhyme is or is not internal, because the rhyming units correspond to musical phrases rather than printed lines):

> I don't want to straight-face you,
> Race or chase you, track or trace you,
> Or disgrace you or displace you,
> Or define you or confine you.

The swift rattle of rhyme and alliteration only makes its point fully within the musical scheme which carries it, where it retains no trace of the crudity which it may look to have in print. Similarly, this from 'Only a Pawn in Their Game' cannot be properly appreciated until heard:

> From the poverty shacks, he looks from the cracks
>   to the tracks,
> And the hoof beats pound in his brain.

The hurried, cramped delivery of the first line gives substance to a feeling of confinement, limitation and monotony; then the slow, drawn-out passion of the second gives us in contrast the sense of thrilling, intoxicated liberation. The incisive opening lines of 'Like a Rolling Stone', again, are too "heavy" for print:

> Once upon a time you dressed so fine
> You threw the bums a dime in your prime, didn't you?
> People'd call, say, "Beware doll, you're bound to fall"
> You thought they were all kiddin' you . . .

The machine-bug effects are here thrown into relief by the phrases "didn't you" and "kiddin' you", the emphasis on which is determined much more by the musical than by the verbal patterning.

There are whole songs whose rhythms differ essentially from those of a poem, and where the imagery is lusher, the effects brasher, the meaning thinner than would be acceptable in a poem that was not also a song; 'Chimes of Freedom' is a good example of such a work. 'Mr. Tambourine Man' is more finely honed, the verbal patterning more careful, but the lyrics stand essentially as a "correspondence" to the music; they evoke through imagery a feeling which is evoked musically by the melody, but which has little intellectual content; in that sense this is musical poetry:

> Then take me disappearin' through the smoke rings of
>   my mind,
> Down the foggy ruins of time, far past the frozen leaves,
> The haunted, frightened trees, out to the windy beach,
> Far from the twisted reach of crazy sorrow.
> Yes, to dance beneath the diamond sky with one hand
>   waving free,
> Silhouetted by the sea, circled by the circus sands,
> With all memory and fate driven deep beneath the waves,
> Let me forget about today until tomorrow.

Though the imagery is visual in character it is impressed upon us, forced upon our attention primarily through the sound effects, the very strong rhyming, assonance and alliteration, and the patterns which these form relate to the structure of the music and not to any design based upon a visual principle. We respond to this poetry for its evocative qualities, as they fall musically upon our ear, and the eye is not on the scene to rest upon a phrase like "circus sands", ask just what it pictures, and conclude that it is there mainly to provide an assonance with the preceding "circled".

When setting his songs out on the page Dylan does nevertheless pay attention to the needs of the eye in making sense of the words. Sometimes he will transfer a phrase from its true position in the aural pattern so as to make a sense unit of a line. This happens several times in 'It's Alright, Ma', as for example in the second verse:

> Pointed threats, they bluff with scorn
> Suicide remarks are torn
> From the fool's gold mouthpiece
> The hollow horn plays wasted words . . .

As sung, "The hollow horn" forms a rhythmic continuum with the preceding line, which tends to break up the meaning; printed like this, it is both easier to follow the sense and to savour the image of "the fool's gold mouthpiece" which otherwise tends to be submerged in the general flood of words. (The end rhyme of "horn" with "torn" is naturally lost to the eye, but it is strong enough anyway for this not to matter.)

It does sometimes happen like this, that the music and words interact in such a way as to make it difficult to follow the sense. This does not often matter much in the earlier Dylan, where a great deal of the excitement of the lyrics lies in the sudden stab of reality, often of psychological recognition, out of the prolixity and obscurity of the images – such moments are usually carefully constructed so as to allow the maximum impact. In the later work, however, where the poetry is more conscious and defined, such "clashes of interest" can operate, as we shall see, to the disadvantage of the latter. There are some songs which are almost poems set to music, in which the language is dense and complex enough to make listening by itself insufficient for full appreciation; we need to supplement our aural acquaintance by familiarity with the text, and thus armed return to the music. In some of the narrative songs, too, notably 'Black Diamond Bay', the action is almost too swift and involved to be followed by the ear.

One of the most exacting tasks in the reconciling of the demands of the reading eye with aural patterning, when transferring the lyrics to the printed page, must have been presented by 'Visions of Johanna', and it is very effectively surmounted in the *Writings and Drawings* text. This great song reads very well as a poem, yet its concertina-like structure, based on expandable musical units, appears at first glance to militate against the possibility. The underlying rhyme scheme is shown straightforwardly by the first verse: AAA BBBB CC. This scheme is in fact strictly adhered to throughout (except that the final stanza expands to allow for three extra B lines), but it is concealed in all the later verses by expansion *within* the basic lines, achieved through miracles of inspired phrasing. In setting out the lines for the page Dylan has worked on a principle of making each line a sense unit, so that there may or may not be extra lines which accommodate expansions of the musical phrases; the basic lines may be telescoped together if the sense calls for it, or broken up even where there is no expansion. All these processes can be seen in the third stanza: it has the same number of printed lines as the paradigmatic first, but they are quite differently arranged, even though the underlying rhyme scheme is maintained for the ear:

> Now little boy lost, he takes himself so seriously
> He brags of his misery, he likes to live dangerously
> And when bringing her name up
> He speaks of a farewell kiss to me
> He's sure got a lotta gall to be so useless and all
> Muttering small talk at the wall while I'm in the hall
> How can I explain?
> Oh, it's so hard to get on
> And these visions of Johanna, they kept me up past the
>   dawn.

What has happened here is that the third A line has expanded to provide lines three and four, the four B lines have been contracted to two (with extra internal rhyming in the second), and the first C line has been split into lines seven and eight of the printed verse. This arrangement answers to the sense of the words as apprehended by the eye, without any disturbance of the aural pattern, that being strong enough to take care of itself.

Dylan's most prodigious feat of phrasing and breath control is however reserved for the final verse, whose three basic A lines are set out like this:

> The peddler now speaks to the countess who's pretending
>   to care for him
> Sayin', "Name me someone who's not a parasite and I'll
>   go out and say a prayer for him."
> But like Louise always says,
> "Ya can't look at much, can ya man?"
> As she, herself, prepares for him . . .

It can be seen that the sense unit principle operates again here, so that the first two rhyming lines are not split up in spite of their great length, while the phenomenally long third divides into three. And while on the subject of phrasing, it is worth just looking, with a memory of how it is sung, at an amazing pair of lines from another *Blonde on Blonde* song, 'Absolutely Sweet Marie':

> Well, anybody can be like me, obviously,
> But then, now again, not too many can be like you,
>   fortunately.

This aspect of Dylan's artistry probably reaches its peak on *Blonde on Blonde*.

The experience of writing *John Wesley Harding* in a more conscious, less spontaneous and overflowing way than the albums which came before it probably had a permanent effect on Dylan's approach to composing his songs. In the records which immediately follow it the structure of the lyrics is simple in the main; they cannot be looked at as if they were in any sense poems. When Dylan emerges from his country period with *Planet Waves*, into renewed complexity of theme and richness of language, the lyrics are tauter, more "defined" in his own phrase, controlled by a more disciplined simplicity. Often, the stress seems when we are listening to be mainly on the music: the words do not draw attention to themselves, tending to sound like an underlining of the musical message, a "punctuation" of the sound, to borrow Dylan's terminology once again. Paradoxically, though, they sometimes stand on their own feet on the page much better than many earlier songs whose lyrics are imposed on our attention more successfully. This is true, I think, of 'Tough Mama':

> Dark Beauty
> Won't you move it on over and make some room
> It's my duty
> To bring you down to the field where the flowers bloom
> Ashes in the furnace
> Dust on the rise
> You came through it all the way
> Flyin' through the skies
> Dark Beauty
> With that long night's journey in your eyes

This number, which I take to be a hymn to Dylan's returning Muse, is marked by a sharply realised field of imagery and a more continuous thread of sense than can easily be picked up by the half-attentive ear. In 'Never Say Goodbye', also, we are so aware of the sound-poem which is the music that concentration tends to focus on a number of separate phrases and pictures and we fail to take in the connected lyric sense which is actually there.

Blood on the Tracks and *Desire*, on the other hand, achieve a very satisfactory integration of the musical and verbal components and there are few instances of one working against the other, though as noticed earlier the events of the more complicated narratives can be hard to follow at early hearings. Some versions of 'Shelter from the Storm' do however yield an example of how lazy phrasing can break up sense:

> In a world of steel-eyed death and men
> Who are fighting to be warm/born . . .

In the recorded concert treatments (less so in the original) Dylan makes little effort to connect "and men" with the following clause with which it belongs, so that it sounds as if "steel-eyed" qualifies "men" as well as "death". It is hard to imagine the Dylan of *Blonde on Blonde* failing to find a solution to this problem; and in fact he carries off beautifully a comparable moment in 'Simple Twist of Fate':

> He felt the heat of the night
> Hit him like a freight train
> Moving with a simple twist of fate.

"Train" is here trapped, as it were, between two lines, "freight" really providing an end-rhyme with "fate", but Dylan experiences no difficulty in coping with it. The structure of 'Hurricane' makes good use of phrases similarly caught in the middle: in most verses the penultimate line contains two rhymes, one of which refers backwards to the preceding line and the other forwards to the following. In verse seven an extra internal rhyme is thrown in for good measure:

> . . . We want to put his ass in stir
> We want to pin this triple murder on him
> He ain't no Gentleman Jim.

The two syllables of "murder" each command a stress equal to that on "him".

It is on *Street-Legal* that tensions between music and poetry are most in evidence, and these tensions inflict some damage upon our appreciation of certain of the songs as integrated wholes. This is noticeable because the lyrics are of a very high quality, and though the music too is remarkable it does not always display the words to the best advantage. In two of the most impressive songs on the album, 'Señor' and 'Where Are You Tonight?', the balance succeeds, with striking poetry and magnificent music working together and defining each other; but in two others, 'Changing of the Guards' and 'No Time to Think', they sometimes seem to act at cross-purposes. The latter is a fine song, reminiscent of some of the classics of 1965–6 in its interspersing of arresting and exotic, if sometimes obscure imagery with swift flashes of insight, and like them too it is notable for the intensity of its portrayal of the disaffected individual at war with society and self. Unfortunately Dylan's performance is uncharacteristically sloppy, marred by poor diction and careless phrasing, and the unsatisfactory sound of the record – at once harsh and muffled, especially on side one – adds to the resultant confusion. He has admitted that the record was made in a hurry, and it shows. Some of the problems however spring not essentially from the performance but from the relation between verbal and musical structure. The first clear example occurs in verse three:

> I've seen all these decoys through a set of deep turquoise
> eyes
> And I feel so depressed.

The rhyme of "turquoise" with "decoys" ends a musical phrase; "eyes" belongs, in all ways except that of semantic meaning, with the line that follows. Dylan sings the words in accordance with the strict dictates of the melodic line, and indeed his scope for doing anything else is very limited. The result is to break "turquoise" and "eyes" completely apart, and the effect is not at all pleasing. On the other hand the way the lines are set out on the page is not satisfactory either, for the placing of "eyes" in the earlier line interferes with the integrated expectations of eye and ear: the rule of one idea to a line is observed at the expense of rhythm. Nor is this principle necessary here: the reader of poetry is perfectly accustomed to run-ons between lines. Exactly the same thing occurs in the eighth verse: "The bridge that you travel on goes to the Babylon girl/With the rose in her hair". The device works properly only in the splendid final verse:

> Bullets can harm you and death can disarm you,
> But no, you will not be deceived.
> Stripped of all virtue as you crawl through the dirt,
> You can give but you cannot receive.

The rhythmic movement here is not all disturbed by the split rhyme in lines three and four. Although "dirt" and "You" combine to rhyme with "virtue", "You" belongs with what follows it both semantically and in terms of its position in the melodic line. In this case, too, the *separation* of the two words on the page (again in accordance with meaning) avoids the kind of assault on the senses which Byron is liable to perpetrate in his more eccentric moments:

> The General Boone, backwoodsman of Kentucky,
> Was happiest among mortals anywhere!
> For killing nothing but a bear or buck, he
> Enjoyed the lonely, vigorous, harmless days
> Of his old age in wilds of deepest maze.

In 'No Time to Think' Dylan has experienced a certain diffi-culty in reconciling complicated lyrical and musical patterns, and this has resulted in a few localised clumsinesses. In 'Changing of the Guards' the problem is more general and harder to pinpoint. The song's imagery, in the first place, is exceedingly dense; it cannot really be taken in by the ear alone. The story (for there is one) is broken, dreamlike and elusive; the album's poor production, already referred to, makes individual words hard to identify. On top of all this, the musical pattern tends, in several verses, to be at odds with the lyric structure and to break it up. This can perhaps be seen most clearly in verse six. The words read so well that we may wonder whether the song was not conceived as a poem and then set to music, or at least whether each component did not have a separate evolution:

> The palace of mirrors
> Where dog soldiers are reflected;
> The endless road and the wailing of chimes;
> The empty rooms where her memory is protected
> Where the angels' voices whisper to the souls of previous
>   times.

The conflict between words and music can only be illustrated by setting the lyrics out in a different way, reflecting as closely as possible the phrasing with which they are sung. The repetitions in brackets represent the echoes contributed by the back-up singers, which form an integral part of the pattern:

The palace of mirrors (palace of mirrors)
Where dog soldiers are reflected; the endless road
    (endless road)
And the wailing of chimes; the empty rooms (empty
    rooms)
Where her memory is protected;
Where the angels' voices whisper
To the souls of previous times.

The insecurity of the relation between rhythm and sense is
easily observable here: words which belong with each other are
forced apart, and others which should have a distance between
them are yoked together by the dominance of the musical form.
The problem relates, it must be said, to the ambition of what is
being attempted. It is very hard to fit such dense, complex and
difficult poetry to a melody and make it work smoothly in a
succession of verses with widely differing grammatical struc-
tures. Rather than scrutinising the instances in which it is not
entirely brought off we should perhaps rather be wondering at
those in which the feat is successfully accomplished, as it notably
is in the last two verses of the song. The caesuras here fall in such
a way that meaning and music are in harmony throughout, and
the poetic form is enhanced by the musical design.

The main point to be made about these *Street-Legal* songs in
the present context, however, is how well some of them – and
especially, perhaps, 'Changing of the Guards' and 'Where Are
You Tonight?' – do stand up on the page. Unlike many earlier
pieces which certainly work better *as songs*, they do not have that
limp, flat look in print for which we have to compensate out of our
memory of the sound. This suggests strongly that if the time were
ever to come when Dylan was unable to sing, he could develop
into a poet of major stature in the traditional visually orientated
mode. There is no reason to suppose at the time of writing,
though, that such is the direction in which he is likely to move. On
Slow Train Coming he is very much writing songs again, rather
than musical poems, and showing no signs of any decline in his
talents in that form. It is a very strong record both musically and
lyrically, and in its boldness and conceptual clarity leaves behind
the dilemmas we have been discussing. This, in its turn, need not

indicate that he will not return to making songs out of a richer and more complicated poetry. The most constant feature of Dylan's development is that it has never been straightforwardly linear: a particular tendency may become dominant for a time and be traceable through a number of albums, but on each one he is attempting something different, something that belongs to it alone. Like Baudelaire, he has made it his consistent artistic endeavour "in the depths of the Unknown to find the *new!*"

THE BOOTLEG SERIES VOL. 9/
THE ORIGINAL MONO RECORDINGS

By Sean Egan

THE BOOTLEG SERIES VOL. 9: THE WITMARK DEMOS: 1962–1964
US release: 19 October 2010
Produced by: Jeff Rosen and Steve Berkowitz
CHARTS: US#12; UK#18

DISC ONE
Man on the Street (fragment)
Hard Times in New York Town
Poor Boy Blues
Ballad for a Friend
Rambling, Gambling Willie
Talkin' Bear Mountain Picnic Massacre Blues
Standing on the Highway
Man on the Street
Blowin' in the Wind
Long Ago, Far Away
A Hard Rain's A-Gonna Fall
Tomorrow is a Long Time
The Death of Emmett Till
Let Me Die in My Footsteps
Ballad of Hollis Brown
Quit Your Low Down Ways
Baby, I'm in the Mood for You
Bound to Lose, Bound to Win
All Over You
I'd Hate to Be You on That Dreadful Day
Long Time Gone
Talkin' John Birch Paranoid Blues
Masters of War

Oxford Town
Farewell

DISC TWO
Don't Think Twice, It's All Right
Walkin' Down the Line
I Shall Be Free
Bob Dylan's Blues
Bob Dylan's Dream
Boots of Spanish Leather
Girl from the North Country
Seven Curses
Hero Blues
Whatcha Gonna Do?
Gypsy Lou
Ain't Gonna Grieve
John Brown
Only a Hobo
When the Ship Comes in
The Times They Are A-Changin'
Paths of Victory
Guess I'm Doin' Fine
Baby, Let Me Follow You Down
Mama, You Been on My Mind
Mr. Tambourine Man
I'll Keep It with Mine

Dylan may not speak fondly of Al Grossman now, but it is his former manager's avaricious ambition for his client that is responsible for him becoming an artist whose songs others – lucratively – rushed to cover.

The first step in this process was to get Dylan a contract with M. Witmark & Sons. When this prestigious publishing company signed Dylan up in July 1962, it was highly unusual: besuited songsmiths were far more their line than scruffy folkies. However, Dylan repaid their faith several times over. Ironically, though Grossman was very successful in persuading other artists to record covers of the songs on the demonstration tapes recorded under Witmark's aegis, Dylan was no traditional Tin Pan Alley composer: he started the process of reducing the role of bespoke songwriter to a small part of the industry by being an artist who could write the songs he performed.

The Witmark Demos have been massively bootlegged – hence the definite article of the title. This release gives his fans the chance to hear the bulk of these semi-legendary recordings legally for the first time, as well as the (probably) single demo session done for Leeds Publishing prior to his Witmark contract that provide the first eight tracks of disc one. (Demo bootlegs have included 'He Was a Friend of Mine', a guitar version of 'Mama, You Been on My Mind' and 'Walls of Red Wing' – the last advertised as present here on Dylan's own site the weekend before release – but they have been omitted because they were in fact Columbia recordings provided to Leeds/Witmark by Dylan's label; they are the same recordings found on *The Bootleg Series 1–3*.)

The booklet notes cite the sake of completeness for the inclusion of the Leeds material, presumably the same motivation for including four other recordings released on previous *Bootleg Series* sets ('Don't Think Twice, It's All Right', 'Walkin' Down the Line', 'When the Ship Comes In' and 'The Times They Are A-Changin' ') as well as for the inclusion of some tracks that break down early. The eleven sessions that produced these songs spanned February 1962 to mid- to late-June 1964 – although this information is not provided in the package but rather was offered in the pre-release publicity.

Not only is Dylan's commitment in performance naturally less than it would be for material intended for public consumption, but he seems to have been stricken with a cough throughout this period (perhaps a smoker's hack?), as can be heard more than once – sometimes in the middle of songs. Meanwhile, 'Mama, You Been on My Mind' and 'I'll Keep It with Mine' are lo-fi even by demo standards. Nonetheless, the two-CD set of over two-and-a-half hours' duration throws up some unexpected delights, amongst both versions of songs already released by the artist and the fifteen songs never issued on any official Dylan product.

Songs released in different versions whose renditions here are nondescript-to-good are: 'Man on the Street' (two different versions, one a fragment), 'Hard Times in New York Town' (the song that for so many years was hidden in the vaults now available

in three different versions), 'Rambling, Gambling Willie', 'Talkin'
Bear Mountain Picnic Massacre Blues'. 'A Hard Rain's A-Gonna
Fall', 'Ballad of Hollis Brown', 'Quit Your Low Down Ways',
'Baby, I'm in the Mood For You', 'Talkin' John Birch Paranoid
Blues' (Al Grossman gets a namecheck), 'Oxford Town', 'I Shall
Be Free' (whose reference to a quickie divorce is not in the famil-
iar lyric), 'Bob Dylan's Blues', 'Bob Dylan's Dream', 'Boots of
Spanish Leather', 'Only a Hobo', 'Paths of Victory' and 'I'll Keep
It with Mine'. You will never want to hear any of these tracks in
preference to the famous/previously released takes, even though a
couple contain an impressive final guitar flourish.

Familiar songs at the poor end of the scale are an inappropriately forceful 'Girl from the North Country' and 'John Brown',
which doesn't match the version Dylan unexpectedly performed
decades after its composition on the *MTV Unplugged* dates.

'Masters of War' is unexpectedly just as intense as the
Freewheelin' version. Only the sound of a door being closed
shortly after the start prevents it being master-take quality. What
stops 'Blowin' in the Wind' being master-take quality is Dylan
coughing, and it's a crying shame that in a way demonstrates the
limitations of this collection, for the absence here of those peculiar "Yes'n'" vocal tics that pock the *Freewheelin'* version might
otherwise actually make this performance superior. 'Tomorrow
is a Long Time' is the first reading of the song released by Dylan
that might be termed a studio version. This performance – which
has differences in both lyric and melody to the *Greatest Hits Vol.
II* live cut – is sweet and affecting. The surprise of the power of
judicial abuse tale 'Seven Curses' is that it is not a great song to
begin with. Just as 'Let Me Die in My Footsteps' is becoming
enjoyable, Dylan breaks off, explaining that it's a "drag" because
"I've sung it so many times".

'Baby, Let Me Follow You Down' is a nice swinging rendition
of a song whose arrangement, despite Dylan's Sixties copyright
claim, is now officially credited to Eric Von Schmidt, Reverend
Gary Davis and Dave Van Ronk. 'Mama, You Been on My Mind'
is a musty piano demo, with more than a little distortion, but that
sort of adds to the atmosphere of this sombre, sweet take of a
great Dylan song. 'Mr. Tambourine Man' is another piano demo.
It sounds ponderous to our ears because we know the heights to

which both he and The Byrds subsequently took it, but it has a certain charm.

The meat of the set, of course, is the songs never officially issued by Dylan in any form (discounting stray releases as bonus tracks). To deal with the lesser newies first: "I'm just one of them rambling men" Dylan tells us in 'Bound to Lose, Bound to Win' – another of his myth-making hobo anthems – before petering out and promising to supply written verses to the engineer later because he can't remember them right now. 'Long Time Gone' is in the same myth-making vein. As is 'Standing on the Highway', whose pleasing percussiveness can't prevent it being numbingly repetitive. With 'Hero Blues' the world finally gets to legally hear a studio version of the obscurity with which Dylan weirdly opened some 1974 concerts. Unlike some other songs of his with the word "blues" in the title, it really is a twelve-bar. At 1:34 it can hardly be said to overstay its welcome and it boasts some nifty harmonica. 'Whatcha Gonna Do?' is passable if slightly hectoring. 'Gypsy Lou' is just another adapted formulaic folk song. The uptempo refusal to succumb 'Ain't Gonna Grieve' is pretty good, but ends abruptly. 'I'd Hate to Be You on That Dreadful Day' is ostensibly in the Our-Day-Will-Come vein of 'The Times They Are A-Changin'', but it is striking that its sentiment, phraseology and references (which include St. Peter) are rather similar to those of his born-again period.

As for the higher-quality newies: 'Guess I'm Doin' Fine' is a quasi-anthem for the happy-go-lucky that is sleepily melodic and quite pleasing. 'Poor Boy Blues' sees Dylan moanin' and groanin' like a knackered old cotton-picker instead of a nice Jewish middle-class boy. Unlike with his tiresomely mean-spirited if authentic latter-day explorations of the blues idiom, his youth makes this impressive feat of impersonation endearing. The same callowness informs his anxious explanation to the engineer during 'Ballad for a Friend' that he has changed the order of the verses. The song is a reminiscence about a North Country boyhood pal – to which somebody contributes what sounds like a padding foot – that culminates in the friend being run over. 'Long Ago, Far Away' is a composition that rather effectively argues that poverty and injustice are not things that have been consigned to history. A case in point being the terrible events detailed in 'The Death of Emmett Till'. This is the first official Dylan release of this great song, although it has previously turned up on – as well as *Folksinger's Choice* – *Broadside Ballads, Vol. 6: Broadside Reunion* (1972) credited to Blind Boy Grunt. This harrowing true tale of a fourteen-year-old black boy beaten to death for whistling at a white woman is one of the most powerful (and possibly the very first) of his protest songs and contains a truly chilling line in, "They tortured him and did some things too evil to repeat". The valedictory 'Farewell' is lovely, proving that adapting a patently olde-worlde ballad can reap dividends when the source is adroitly chosen and the updating beautifully sung. Best of the lot is 'All Over You', which Dylan tells the engineer he is putting down just "fer kicks". This gem has a great tune and wickedly filthy sentiments ("Well, if I had to do it all over again/Babe, I'd do it all over you") and should have been on one of the early albums.

As ever with the *Bootleg Series*, the packaging, research and design is beautiful, and the booklet notes (this time by Colin Escott) very informative. The cover shot depicts Dylan banging away on a typewriter (as he often did to write lyrics) in his home studio so is not strictly location-correct but is nonetheless evocative of his burning creativity at this juncture.

THE ORIGINAL MONO RECORDINGS
US release: 19 October 2010
Produced by: Steve Berkowitz
CHARTS: US# –; UK#157

Released simultaneously with like *The Witmark Demos*, the "Mono Box" was like the Witmark set for some reason released one day earlier in the UK. Ditto *The Best of the Original Mono Recordings*, whose release meant there was effectively yet another Dylan compilation on the market, although one at least preferable to the bizarre *Playlist: The Very Best of Bob Dylan '80s*, released a week previously.

With this CD box-set of his first eight albums, Dylan is clearly taking his cue from *The Beatles in Mono* (2009), which collected the Fab Four's oeuvre (apart from three albums that had never had mono mixes) for those who disdain the stereo versions.

Such people might seem eccentric, but in fact mono mixes were the definitive mixes up to and including 1968: stereo mixes were usually done quickly and without the artist's presence as a sop to the minority of wealthy people who possessed stereo record players. As Dylan's own site admits in bold type, these albums are presented here "as the artist intended them to be heard".

Unlike The Beatles' mono albums, which continued to be available on vinyl well into the Seventies, Dylan's mono albums were deleted surprisingly quickly, so many have never heard his Sixties albums "properly". This release therefore is welcome – although it would be remiss not to point out the dubious morality involved in (just as The Beatles did) making the mono mixes available as a set or not at all. That said, it's the type of beautiful artefact that may be the future of the record industry: nobody can find a way to fileshare a package containing miniature card facsimiles of the original album sleeves (the accuracy even extending to the inserts and to the warbled texture of the *Times They Are A-Changin'* front cover) and a glossy book with notes by Greil Marcus all housed in a handsome sleeve featuring yet another striking image of mid-Sixties Dylan by Daniel Kramer (the photographer who took the cover pictures of *Highway 61 Revisited* and *Bringing It All Back Home*).

The early albums certainly benefit from taking the sound-scapes back to original intent: having a guitar in one channel and a voice in the other was always idiotic. *Bringing It All Back Home*, meanwhile, is rounder, fuller and bolder, and the prominence given the bass in 'It's All Over Now, Baby Blue' draws attention to just how good is William E. Lee's playing. However, the fact that Dylan's stereo mixes were never as diluted as those of The Beatles is demonstrated by *Highway 61 Revisited*: the mono mix of 'Like a Rolling Stone' sounds antiseptic in comparison to the by-now far more familiar stereo version. Additionally, as was often the case, some of the mono mixes are significantly shorter: 'Queen Jane Approximately' and 'It Takes a Lot to Laugh' lose thirty and forty seconds respectively – not a good thing. While one is glad for reasons of historical accuracy that the mono mixes are at long last available again, the received wisdom that an artist's original intentions necessarily equate with a better product might have to be questioned.

"Useless and pointless knowledge" is a quote from Dylan's 'Tombstone Blues'. Some people will be able to identify the source of the line instantly – Dylan obsessives. Mark Ellen is one. One of many, in fact. Why else do you think this book has been published when there are already so many Dylan tomes on the market that Patrick Humphries and John Bauldie titled their 1990 work Oh No! Not Another Bob Dylan Book? *The publication in 2009 of Clinton Heylin's examination of the genesis of all Dylan songs written between 1957 and 1973,* Revolution in the Air, *gave Ellen cause – or perhaps an excuse – to talk about that obsession in public. Many Dylan fans will recognize his symptoms.*

USELESS AND POINTLESS KNOWLEDGE

By Mark Ellen

First published as 'Memory Almost Full' in *The Word*, April 2009

Has this ever happened to you? It's got to the nuts and sticky drinks stage and, through the candlelight, you can see some bloke at the far end quacking on about the Credit Crunch. Weak growth, apparently. Mortgage-backed security markets. Something about non-sub-prime lending. When he drops his bombshell about how three high-street banks – only last week – were on the verge of insolvency, there are gasps all round the table; looks of awe and envy from the men, admiration – possibly even lust – from the women. It's important stuff. It makes or breaks the world we live in.

But here's the big problem: you're not listening. You're nodding along looking suitably shocked and enthralled, but you're actually thinking about something else. In my case I'm thinking about Bob Dylan. On a road trip to the Mardi Gras in New Orleans. February 10, 1964. I can picture him now, lit up with weed and wine in a systematic "derangement of all senses" that the French symbolist Arthur Rimbaud had so eloquently encouraged one hundred years before. Dylan has fallen in love with Rimbaud, declaring "that's the kind of writing I'm gonna do!" No one is free, Rimbaud has taught him, "even the birds are chained to the sky". He's building up to compose a multi-coloured lyric that will beat the Frenchman at his own game. It will even echo Rimbaud's '*Le Bateau Ivre*' – described by its creator as "a little lost boat in swirling debris" which Dylan reconfigures as "a magic swirling ship" and . . .

Risk-management systems. Business defaults. *Yada yada yada*.

Anyway, out into the carnival he goes, the night a smear of sense impression, beside him Bruce Langhorne the multi-instrumentalist who'll play guitar on *Bringing It All Back Home* and who, on this occasion, is bashing a gigantic Turkish tambourine "as big as a wagon wheel". Dylan scrambles some verses together and is already performing the song when he returns to New York, but it's still in evolution. The words change every time he plays it – "the *hidden* frightened trees", "the *frozen* frightened trees", "the *haunted* frightened trees", and . . .

Loan-to-value ratios. Yes, yes, yes. We're all doomed etc . . .

But the delay pays off. A rejected outtake from *Another Side of Bob Dylan* finds its way to a manager trying to put together a band that's a West Coast hybrid of The Beatles and the New Lost City Ramblers and, when The Jet Set change their name to The Byrds and roll up for their first session for Columbia, they record a pop-confection called 'Mr. Tambourine Man' which gives its author his first No.1 on both sides of the Atlantic. Then . . .

You're still reading this so you must be vaguely beguiled, but I wouldn't dare try it on anyone around the table. Why? Because why on earth would they be interested unless they were as obsessed with Bob Dylan as I am? How do you convert a non-believer with waffle like this? You can't. In fact the more knowledge you acquire, the harder it is to remember the broad brush strokes that made him interesting in the first place. It's all lost in an ever-expanding ocean of detail.

That story about 'Mr. Tambourine Man' comes from a gripping new book by Dylan scholar Clinton Heylin which is so far in the deep end that it's borderline insane. Dylan's Sixties output is examined song by song (many of them unreleased) in the style of Ian MacDonald's *Revolution in the Head*, great screeds of peripheral intelligence that could only appeal to unsalvageable Dylan junkies like Heylin and myself. You're reminded that 'Bob Dylan's Dream' is based entirely on the old folk ballad 'Lady Franklin's Lament' and 'Masters of War' on 'Nottamun Town' – and that images in 'Tomorrow Is a Long Time' are lifted directly from a fifteenth-century folk song called 'Westron Wind' (news to me). And that the last reported words of the dying Baltimore waitress he immortalised in 'The Lonesome Death of Hattie Carroll' were "that man has upset me so, I feel deathly ill" – so custom-built for a murder ballad you can't believe Dylan didn't crowbar them into his lyric.

But will it really make my appreciation of the song any greater? Don't I have enough of this useless and pointless knowledge already? The more I know about him, the less the number of people I can pass it on to who won't back away nervously and, eventually, break into a run. And the fact that Dylan constantly brushed over his tracks to ramp up his own mythology – concealing, for example, his early rock and roll past – reminds you that he must surely despair of pedants like us who waste so much valuable time trying to unravel it.

The other four in the *Word* office are just as hopeless – Jon Sellers feels the same way about Sparks, Andrew Harrison with Morrissey, "Seventies" Mike Johnson with David Bowie and Kate Mossman about (for God's sake) Glen Campbell. Why do we do it? Are we just pouring petrol on the dying embers of a love affair? Is it purely the comfort of a story we already know but just seems to improve with length? Do we take more satisfaction in amassing this arcane information than the knowledge itself affords us? Why do we continually cram our heads with more of this gibberish when we could clearing the files for something useful?

And when does it end (and Dylan is far from my only fixation)? When is something too trivial to be worth remembering? What does the object of our affection have to do to finally break our interest in them? Some unforgivable release? Some indefensible remark? A duet with Duffy? Will I just wake up one morning and discover I'm over it or am I saddled with this obsession forever? Maybe all *Word* readers are the same and will end up mooching about in some attic somewhere lit by a bare light-bulb, eating hobnobs and drinking endless cups of tea in their underwear while hammering some bootleg they've heard a million times in a further bid for "clues". And that's just the *girls*.

One day, in the dim distance, another book like this will land on my desk and I'll smile knowingly, shake my head and fling it in the bin. But not now. This one has been devoured with a ravenous, insatiable appetite and I've even made notes in the margins.

SELECTED BIBLIOGRAPHY

Baez, Joan, *And a Voice to Sing With* (Century, 1988)

Bauldie, John (ed), *Wanted Man: In Search of Bob Dylan* (Black Spring, 1990)

Blake, Mark (ed), *Dylan: Visions, Portraits & Back Pages* (Dorling Kindersley, 2005)

Bob Dylan, *Writings and Drawings* (Grafton, 1974)

Cott, Jonathan (ed), *Dylan on Dylan* (Hodder, 2007)

Dylan, Bob, *Tarantula* (Panther, 1973)

Dylan, Bob, *Chronicles Volume One* (Simon & Schuster, 2004)

Gill, Andy; Odegard, Kevin, *A Simple Twist of Fate: Bob Dylan and the Making of "Blood on the Tracks"* (Da Capo, 2005)

Gray, Michael, *The Bob Dylan Encyclopedia, Revised* (Continuum, 2008)

Gray, Michael; Bauldie, John (ed), *All Across the Telegraph* (Sidgwick & Jackson, 1987)

Herdman, John, *Voice Without Restraint* (Paul Harris, 1982)

Heylin, Clinton, *Behind the Shades* (Penguin, 2001)

Heylin, Clinton, *Bob Dylan Day-by-Day 1941–1995* (Music Sales, 1996)

Heylin, Clinton, *Revolution in the Air* (Constable & Robinson, 2010)

Heylin, Clinton, *Still on the Road* (Constable & Robinson, 2010)

Humphries, Patrick, *Complete Guide to the Music of Bob Dylan* (Omnibus Press, 1995)

Irwin, Colin, *Legendary Sessions: Highway 61 Revisited* (Flame Tree, 2008)

Marcus, Greil, *Like a Rolling Stone* (Faber & Faber, 2005)

McGregor, Craig (ed), *Dylan: A Retrospective* (Angus & Robertson, 1980)

Polizzotti, Mark, *Bob Dylan's Highway 61 Revisited* (Continuum, 2006)

Rotolo, Suze, *A Freewheelin' Time: A Memoir of Greenwich Village in the Sixties* (Aurum, 2009)

Scaduto, Anthony, *Bob Dylan* (Abacus, 1973)

Shelton, Robert, *No Direction Home: The Life and Music of Bob Dylan* (Da Capo, 1997)

Sounes, Howard, *Down the Highway: The Life of Bob Dylan* (Doubleday, 2001)

Thompson, Toby, *Positively Main Street* (Coward-McCann, 1971)

Thomson, Elizabeth M (ed), *Conclusions on the Wall: New Essays on Bob Dylan* (Thin Man, 1980)

Trager, Oliver, *Keys to the Rain: The Definitive Bob Dylan Encyclopedia* (Billboard, 2004)

Williams, Chris, *Bob Dylan: In His Own Words* (Omnibus, 1993)

Williams, Paul, *Bob Dylan: Watching the River Flow* (Omnibus, 1996)

Williamson, Nigel, *The Rough Guide to Bob Dylan* (Rough Guides, 2006)

http://boblast.blogspot.com

http://en.wikipedia.org/wiki/Bob_Dylan_discography

http://expectingrain.com

www.bjorner.com/bob.htm

www.bobdylan.com

www.punkhart.com/dylan

www.searchingforagem.com

www.taxhelp.com/interviews.html

www.webhosting.interferenza.net/bcs

www.wsu.edu/~scales/dylan